The 103rd Ballot

Books by Robert K. Murray

THE 103RD BALLOT

THE POLITICS OF NORMALCY

THE HARDING ERA

RED SCARE

The 103rd Ballot

★ ★ ★ ★ ★ ★ ★ ★ ★ ★ ★ ★ ★ ★ ★

DEMOCRATS
AND THE DISASTER
IN MADISON SQUARE GARDEN

ROBERT K. MURRAY

HARPER & ROW, PUBLISHERS

NEW YORK, HAGERSTOWN, SAN FRANCISCO

LONDON

For

VICKI, BILL, and CONNIE

the products of quite a different

Garden

THE 103RD BALLOT: DEMOCRATS AND THE DISASTER IN MADISON SQUARE GARDEN.
Copyright © 1976 by Robert K. Murray. All rights reserved. Printed in the United
States of America. No part of this book may be used or reproduced in any manner
whatsoever without written permission except in the case of brief quotations embodied
in critical articles and reviews. For information address Harper & Row, Publishers,
Inc., 10 East 53rd Street, New York, N.Y. 10022. Published simultaneously in Canada
by Fitzhenry & Whiteside Limited, Toronto.

FIRST EDITION

Designed by Sidney Feinberg

Library of Congress Cataloging in Publication Data

Murray, Robert K
    The 103rd ballot.
    Bibliography: p.
    Includes index.
    1. Democratic Party. National Convention, New York,
1924. 2. United States—Politics and government—1923–
1929. I. Title.
JK2303 1924.M87 1976   329.3′0221   75–30340
ISBN 0–06–013124–1

76 77 78 79 10 9 8 7 6 5 4 3 2 1

C O N T E N T S

Photographs will be found following pp. 114 and 210

ACKNOWLEDGMENTS

If an author were to acknowledge fully the debt he owed to others in the research and writing of his book few pages would be left for the narrative. Each time I set out on this task I am amazed at the many individuals who in some way have contributed to the final product. Space requires that most of them remain nameless with only a brief "thank you" to them all. Yet I remember only too well how they looked up innumerable references for me, chased down manuscripts, dredged up little-used monographs, and answered my questions. In this regard the library staffs at the Pennsylvania State University, the University of Virginia, the University of Indiana, the University of Wyoming, Yale University, Columbia University Oral History Research Office, New York State Library at Albany, the Franklin Roosevelt Presidential Library at Hyde Park, and the Library of Congress were unfailingly helpful and patient.

For aid beyond all reasonable expectations a personal note of gratitude is directed to Judith A. Schiff of the Sterling Memorial Library at Yale, Peter R. Christoph and Juliet F. Wolohan of the New York State Library, and Joseph W. Marshall and Jerome V. Deyo of the Roosevelt Presidential Library. I am also deeply indebted to the McAdoo, Davis, and La Follette families, especially to Mrs. Charles (Julia Davis) Healy and Francis H. McAdoo, for allowing me access to critically important manuscript materials.

Several other persons deserve to be mentioned because of their unique help in bringing this project to completion. Professor Kent Forster already knows my appreciation for the Penn State History Department's research policy and his implementation of it. To Dean Thomas Magner and Professor Stanley Weintraub go my thanks for making travel and clerical monies available whenever I needed them. I am especially grateful to the Institute for the Arts and Humanistic Studies which elected me to membership while I was engaged in this study—a privilege which I took seriously and an honor which I hope to redeem. As usual, my wife,

Eve, was always my best and severest critic throughout the long hours spent in writing and revising the manuscript. How she managed to bear up under my repeated requests to "listen to this just one more time" escapes me.

Finally, to the three named on the dedication page goes a father's pride in having the best crew around, and a promise of at least a few long and uninterrupted voyages before the next writing project takes precedence.

R.K.M.

Eden West, Tortola, B.V.I.
August, 1975

P R O L O G U E

In June, 1924, three thousand Americans descended on the canyons of New York City. Some were Methodists, some were Baptists, others Catholics, and still others nothing. All had prejudices. There were Rotarians, Knights of Columbus, and members of the Ku Klux Klan. Some liked their liquor; others were dry. Some were whole votes, some were half votes, and some had no voting power at all. Together they represented democracy and Democracy, because all were delegates or alternates to the snarling and homicidal roughhouse known as the Madison Square Garden Convention.

This book is about that gathering, about the developments leading up to it, and about its significance to modern American history and to the Democratic party. William Gibbs McAdoo, one of the contestants in that convention, once said that he hoped someday to write a book about it. Although he never did, he indicated what was required. "It will have to be done," he exclaimed, "on a broad canvas; a picture vivid with fire and drama."

I am not certain that I have accomplished that. But, if I have failed, it is not because the event lacked color. Indeed, in the course of my quarter-century research on American life in the post–World War I era I have been the vicarious participant in some sensational and moving episodes— the bitter League of Nations fight, Woodrow Wilson's sudden illness and his last days in the White House, the hysterical outburst known as the Great Red Scare, the seamy Teapot Dome scandals, and the Greek-like tragedy of Warren Harding's demise. But no one of these was so charged with emotion or so much fun to write about as the Madison Square Garden Convention.

By their very nature political conventions are exciting and dramatic. James Farley once remarked, "A political convention blows in and out like a ninety-mile gale." "Why, if they ever took a sanity test at a political convention," said Will Rogers, "98 percent would be removed to an asy-

ix

lum." H. L. Mencken characterized a convention this way: "There is something about a national convention that makes it as fascinating as a revival or a hanging. . . . One sits through long sessions wishing heartily that all the delegates and alternates were dead and in hell—and then suddenly there comes a show so gaudy and hilarious, so melodramatic and obscene, so unimaginably exhilarating and preposterous that one lives a gorgeous year in an hour."

Mencken, Farley, and Rogers meant their comments to apply to all conventions, but political observers would undoubtedly agree that they apply most vividly to Democratic conventions. George Creel once said, "With the Republicans, politics is a business; with the Democrats, it is an emotional experience . . . a combination of Christmas and the Fourth of July." "Democrats only feel at peace with themselves when they are in an ecstatic boil," observed Walter Lippmann. Arthur Krock contended that "All Democrats would rather fight than eat." Indeed, Democratic conventions have often been turbulent affairs. "To a Republican," said Krock, "[peaceful] conventions are the light of his eyes and the breath of his nostrils. They mean victory, jobs, power, high tariff bills, White House receptions, Gridiron dinners, peace. To a Democrat they are ghastly because he cannot smell the warm odor of his party's life blood." William Allen White claimed that "A Democratic convention has to smell the blood of a death struggle before it can decide upon whom it will honor." Only then does it finally thrust its tattered standard "into the broken hands of some punch-drunk politician and he is pushed out into the lists where the unmaimed Republican candidate awaits him."

The Madison Square Garden Convention was all this and more. It was fitting that it was held in the Garden. John W. Davis, another of its participants, called it "a three ring circus with two stages and a few trapeze acts." Actually it was more like a war or, symbolically for the Garden, a sensational prize fight. There were preliminary matches, sweating and struggling handlers, brashly confident managers, and ambitious contenders. Finally there was the spectacular main event itself. The ultimate decision on this fight, however, was not really given until Franklin D. Roosevelt's election in 1932. Even that seemed anticlimactic by comparison.

As a historian my primary task is to recapture the flavor, the excitement, and the turmoil of that gathering for the reader, but before attempting to do so I must caution that this convention was but a part of the larger story of the development of the Democratic party in the post–

World War I years. Republican ascendancy in the 1920s has tended to minimize the significance of Democratic party history during this era. To most observers that party has appeared to be so ineffective and disorganized that it has received little more than passing attention. In their haste to explain the presidential administrations of Harding, Coolidge, and Hoover, historians have traditionally ignored their defeated Democratic opponents. Only Al Smith has elicited much interest, partly because he was so soundly beaten and partly because he was the alleged forerunner of the New Deal. In this process not only have Democratic leaders like James M. Cox and John W. Davis been overlooked but so have numerous other Democrats for whom the Republican party had no counterpart.

In the last several years this oversight has begun to be corrected. The most important work in this regard has been David Burner's *The Politics of Provincialism: The Democratic Party in Transition, 1918–1932*, published in 1968. Using careful research, offering elaborate citations, and employing some quantification techniques, Professor Burner traced the difficulties of the Democratic party from the breakup of the Wilson coalition during World War I to the emergence of Franklin Roosevelt in 1932. With even-handed coverage, he analyzed the divisive themes that split the party, the disastrous three-way election of 1924, the unsuccessful attempts at party reorganization, and Smith's ill-fated "Brown Derby" campaign of 1928.

Building on earlier suggestions made by such writers as William E. Leuchtenburg, Seymour M. Lipset, J. Joseph Huthmacher, and Samuel Lubell, Burner's general thesis was this: The Democratic party emerged from World War I shattered and confused. In the twenties it experienced further division because of certain moral and social issues and because of a developing struggle between rural and urban elements for political dominance. Through its own actions, and with a helpful assist from Republican prosperity, the party suffered horribly in the presidential elections of 1924 and 1928. Paradoxically, however, political trends at the state and local levels were running in its favor despite consistent Republican presidential victories. Finally, in 1932, Franklin Roosevelt came into office as the result of shifts in voting patterns which had been building for some time and which were only partially Depression-induced.

I accept this thesis; indeed, this present work tends to reinforce it. My path to this conclusion, however, was not premeditated and simply developed out of my attempt to tell an interesting story effectively. Moreover, I arrived at this conclusion by a different route from that followed by

Burner or the other scholars. Where some of them used scaling and quantification techniques to prove their points, I have relied almost entirely on the contemporary press, personal manuscripts, and autobiographies. Where most of these men handled their material analytically, I have tried to write an old-fashioned descriptive and literary narrative. Where Burner, in particular, gave careful attention to all aspects of the 1918–32 period, I have focused chiefly on the events surrounding only a single episode.

The net result, I trust, is complementary. I hope this present narrative will add to the work of the other scholars by illuminating more clearly the human side of the Democratic party's postwar internal turmoil—the resentment, the anger, the hatred, the doubts, the fears, the wrecked ambitions. Although I have chosen deliberately to emphasize these personal aspects, I know that as a historian I must remain sensitive to the general movements and societal trends of which they are a part. Consequently, I have endeavored to inject into the book, especially in the opening and concluding sections, material relating to those general developments which will impart meaning and balance. Even here, though, my thrust remains essentially biographical. Where other scholars see social, cultural, and demographic movements manipulating and controlling men, I still see men as the primary initiating agents. And I remain convinced that insofar as politics is concerned human reactions involving pride, vanity, lust for power, and revenge still dominate. When the precise moment of political combat arrives, symbols, myths, and shibboleths provide more understanding of the ensuing struggle than do social trends or party principles. At that moment human foibles, character defects, and heated verbal exchanges become more critical in their influence than the issues themselves. In the end I find that luck, or fate—whatever you wish to call it—frequently cancels out even the importance of general movements and emerges as the most powerful final political determinant.

For these various reasons the Madison Square Garden Convention became for me not only an interesting story but a logical focal point in the history of the Democratic party in the pre–New Deal period. Some scholars claim that the Smith campaign of 1928 was the most important episode during those years. A larger group believes that the Roosevelt election of 1932 was the watershed event. Perhaps all of us are a little wrong and a little right. As one recent study shows, there was probably no one year or episode that signaled the exact moment when the critical changes taking place in the Democratic party in the postwar period were most ideally expressed.

Yet the Madison Square Garden Convention was certainly the most acrimonious and bitterly fought event in the Democratic party's modern history. It involved more arguments, aroused more passion, left more wounds, and shed more political blood than any other single incident. During its sixteen days and 103 ballots the party virtually committed suicide. Daniel Roper, one of the convention participants, later said, "No man or woman who attended the Convention of 1924 in the old Madison Square Garden will ever forget it. This country has never seen its like and is not likely to see its like again." Thirty-two years later, Al Smith's daughter, Emily Smith Warner, wrote: "Even yet I cannot think of the convention of 1924 with any pleasure. Traits that I do not like to think of as American played too great a part that year at the old Madison Square Garden."

In his book, Professor Burner claimed that this fateful convention placed the Democratic party's difficulties in the post–World War I era "into definite form, assigning the participants and fixing the points of dispute." Indeed, the Madison Square Garden Convention acted much like the narrow waist in an hour glass. Before that convention, most issues and political attitudes prevalent in postwar America were perceived only as an undifferentiated mass. It was difficult to distinguish one from the other, just as with the grains of sand before they pass through the constriction. But at the convention, for a brief while, *each* issue, *each* reaction, *each* attitude became immediately identifiable. After it they tended once again to lose their separateness. For the moment, though, they had been clearly discernible, and they would never again be so anonymous. As Walter Lippmann claimed at the time, the nation learned through the Garden convention "more at first hand about the really dangerous problems of America . . . learned more of the actual motives which move the great masses of men, than anyone of this generation thought possible."

Lippmann's generation has passed but the historical record remains, along with the insights afforded by that suicidal gathering. Exhibiting many of the worst aspects of the American political tradition, this convention marked a crucial moment when normal democratic procedures resulted either in failure or were sorely tried. It sundered Democratic party loyalties and confused rather than clarified almost all the issues. It further

demonstrated that not all matters of vital concern to the national electorate are subject to or even capable of a reasonable political solution. Still,
the 1924 convention and its aftermath also provided eloquent testimony
to the tenacious belief of the American public in the efficacy of the
democratic process and to the Democratic party's persistent search for a
workable political consensus.

PART I

★

THE GENERAL ARENA

1

"It was a landslide, it was an earthquake," moaned Joseph P. Tumulty, President Wilson's private secretary. Franklin Roosevelt, the defeated Democratic candidate for Vice-President, wrote at the head of a letter to a friend: "Franklin D. Roosevelt, Ex V.P., Canned. (Erroneously reported dead)." Ohio's Governor James M. Cox, the primary victim of the avalanche, was too stunned to comment at all.

It was a fantastic victory. Although all indices had pointed to a Republican success in 1920, no one had dared predict such a staggering Democratic defeat. The vote as recorded by the *New York Times* was 16,181,289 for Warren G. Harding; 9,141,750 for Cox; and 941,827 for Eugene V. Debs (Socialist). Harding carried thirty-seven of the forty-eight states and received 404 electoral votes. His popular majority (60.3 percent) was the largest yet amassed in the nation's history. Because of the election, the Republican party now controlled the House 303 to 131, the widest margin in the party's annals. In the Senate the Republicans not only retained all their seats but captured ten from the Democrats, giving them a margin of twenty-four. Thus, the decade of the 1920s began with the Democratic party in full retreat and the Republicans preparing to establish their "return to normalcy."

The precise reasons for this change in the American political climate have been the subject of much debate. Some have said that support for American participation in the League of Nations marked the downfall of the Democrats. Some have claimed that the Democratic defeat was merely a product of "the times" and represented a reaction against the idealism of World War I. Others have laid the blame on a whole series of popular frustrations growing out of postwar socio-economic conditions collectively and derisively labeled "Wilsonism." Still others have contended that it was because of the personal magnetism of Harding along with the positive appeal of his normalcy proposals. Whatever the reasons, the overwhelming Republican victory in 1920 indicated that political alliances were in flux and that a sizable portion of the voting population was unfettered by party tradition. Significantly, on the very day that New York City gave Warren Harding a 400,000-vote plurality, it endowed incumbent Democratic Governor Alfred E. Smith with a margin of over 325,000.

Long before 1920 there had been a gradual loosening of political loyalties in both parties. For the Democrats this was accompanied by a creeping organizational paralysis. Beginning in 1916 a noticeable conservative trend had set in among Democratic congressional leaders as a crumbling of the old progressive New Freedom coalition became apparent. This development was accentuated by World War I. Some Democratic leaders, especially from the South and certain nonprogressive areas of the North, expressed increasing distress over President Wilson's handling of the war, particularly his expansion of executive power. With the advent of the Armistice, many of these Democrats joined with Republicans to speed up the dismantling of wartime boards and agencies, rivaling their Republican counterparts in calling for a quick return to prewar conditions. The ill-fated congressional campaign of 1918 and the ensuing struggle over the League of Nations added to the Democratic party's troubles and further sapped Democratic strength.

President Wilson's stroke in September, 1919, completed the Democratic disintegration. The impact of the President's helplessness was catastrophic, both on the proper functioning of the executive branch, and on the effectiveness of the Democrats in Congress. In the silence emanating from the White House sickroom, congressional leaders could discern no clues as to how they were to keep the party together or attack the nation's pressing postwar problems. By his earlier avoidance of postwar planning Wilson had left no guideposts for his congressional lieutenants. Resultant confusion over goals and a vacuum in executive leadership caused party unity to collapse. By 1920–21 the Democratic party had disintegrated into a confederation of sectional interest groups which argued angrily over such matters as railroad legislation, public power, taxation, farm relief, and the tariff.

The Republicans, meanwhile, enjoyed the Democratic discomfort. But, when they were presented the opportunity to assume the leadership role after the congressional elections of 1918, they could not capitalize on it because they too were divided on many of the issues. Both during the prewar and the wartime periods their opposition had been mainly negative; they had developed neither a program nor a blueprint for action.

Beyond demanding that all wartime regulatory controls cease, the Republican leadership had little to offer. Out of the White House for eight years and still infected by the animus arising from the 1912 Bull Moose schism, the party seemingly had no sense of purpose and no recognized leaders to look to for guidance.

Almost by default Warren Harding, a skillful compromiser and pacifier, stepped into the breach. From his front porch in Marion, Ohio, he articulated during the 1920 campaign those policies which most Republicans could embrace. Resting on Republican tradition, Harding promised tariff revision upward for the benefit of both farmers and businessmen. He advocated tighter immigration restriction, a big navy, and an expanded merchant marine. He championed the conclusion of peace treaties with all former enemy states but did not endorse American participation in the League. He favored an antilynching law and the appointment of more blacks to federal office. He supported the elimination of excess-profits taxes and the lowering of surtaxes on private incomes. He believed in remedial credit legislation for the farmer. And he was heartily in favor of economy in government and the creation of a budget system for monitoring federal expenditures. This last, he said, was especially necessary to effect a "return to normalcy."

The nation liked both what it saw and what it heard from the Marion front porch. Currently experiencing a sharp postwar depression, and suffering from the twin blights of an antiradical hysteria and widespread labor unrest, the electorate voted in droves for the handsome Ohio senator. Following his election the public applauded as Harding seemingly set a high tone for his administration by appointing to his official family such outstanding men as Charles Evans Hughes (Secretary of State), Andrew W. Mellon (Secretary of the Treasury), Henry C. Wallace (Secretary of Agriculture), and Herbert C. Hoover (Secretary of Commerce). Calling a special session of Congress to convene immediately after his inauguration, Harding presented it with a message that included all of the items he had mentioned on his front porch, together with the request that they be enacted into law without delay.

For the next two years the Republican-dominated 67th Congress struggled with Harding's normalcy program and ultimately passed most of it. As a result, by 1923 the administration's achievements were rather impressive. In foreign affairs it not only had normalized relations with former enemy countries (Germany, Austria, and Hungary) but had played host to a successful international disarmament conference (the

Washington Disarmament Conference of 1921–22). It encouraged a return of business confidence by eliminating wartime excess-profits taxes, lowering income-tax rates, and stimulating foreign trade. It rejected an expensive soldiers' bonus. It initiated a program of government savings and established a system of budgeting (Budget and Accounting Act of 1921). It attacked the rural postwar depression by supporting numerous farm relief measures as well as catering to rural demands for lower freight rates. It secured immigration restriction (Per Centum Law of 1921) and forced through a higher tariff (Fordney-McCumber Tariff of 1922). Only on the matter of an antilynching bill and the strengthening of the merchant marine did the administration fail to achieve its objectives.

2

The advent of an administration backed by a popular mandate and the subsequent enactment of its program into law should have reduced partisan friction and allayed much of the postwar political unrest. Instead, the opening years of the 1920s were stained by more inter- and intra-party strife than any period since Radical Reconstruction. As during the post–Civil War era, most of this strife was either a direct or an indirect outgrowth of war. In establishing the general parameters of American politics throughout the Roaring Decade, World War I had no peer. Where the war did not create new problems for the American political system, it exacerbated latent ones, especially as these latter became entwined with regional and class differences and with political partisanship. Some of these problems were traditional and remained the visible issues around which most political discussions swirled—taxes, the tariff, farm relief, government spending, and international cooperation. But equally important in agitating the political scene were other war-connected developments, for the most part noneconomic and nondiplomatic. Impervious to rational analysis and defying easy political categorization, these developments would prove to be the main transforming agents in the political arena and provide the basis upon which a reorganization of modern American politics would ultimately rest.

The first of these developments—nativism—was not new to the American experience, having assumed different forms at different times. World War I gave it tremendous impetus. Its postwar flowering was conditioned by the Red Scare hysteria of 1919–20 and the simultaneous arrival on American shores of waves of immigrants. More subtle, but supplying an additional basis for this nativist upsurge, were the racial and religious xenophobias of postwar American society, which were grounded in Biblical fundamentalism, anti-Catholicism, and anti-Semitism and which were reinforced by the quasi-scientific writings of such Nordic purists as Madison Grant (*The Passing of the Great Race,* 1916) and Lothrop Stoddard (*The Rising Tide of Color,* 1920). Moreover, the disillusionment of many former Wilson progressives, the stultifying effect of the postwar economic depression of 1920–21, and a fear that political power might come to rest in the hands of the "immigrant element" fed nativist attitudes.

The major political manifestation of this nativist feeling was the passage in 1921 of the Per Centum Law. Supported by the intellectual community, the southern and western farmer, organized labor, and the overwhelming majority of both parties, this law was adopted with little dissension. Besides continuing the traditional exclusion of Asiatics, the new act restricted immigration annually to 3 percent of a country's nationals residing in the United States in 1910. Designed specifically to discriminate against migrants from southern and southeastern Europe, the Per Centum Law reduced the number of entering aliens from 805,228 in 1920 to 309,556 in 1921–22.

Not content with this success, ardent restrictionists, such as Republican Representative Albert Johnson of the House Committee on Immigration, pushed for further action. In 1923 Johnson introduced a bill which dropped the allowable immigrant total to 2 percent and the base year to 1890. This bill received widespread support and was finally passed in 1924. Superseding the more lenient Per Centum Law, this act further reduced the number of entering immigrants from 357,803 in 1923–24 to 164,667 in 1924–25. The most drastic cuts were in the newer immigrant ranks. The numbers of British and Irish, for example, declined only 19 percent, but the Italians plunged over 90 percent.

The passage of the 1921 and 1924 laws, however, dealt only with the immigration problem as it related to future arrivals. Such laws did not change the residency status or the emerging importance of those millions of immigrants who were already in the country. Rabid anti-alien comments by many congressmen and by the media were inevitably double-edged. Though directed against those who were still overseas, such comments also betrayed an intense prejudice toward those immigrants who were already here. Underneath all this nativist rhetoric was an obvious concern about what their presence meant for the nation's future—socially, culturally, and politically. Worries about racial "mongrelization," social emasculation, and cultural degeneracy were heightened by the fear that these elements might one day gain political control. Naturally, the unflattering and prejudiced attitudes expressed by nativists during the postwar immigration restriction crusade reverberated through the resident immigrant community, causing resentment and forcing them to a reexamination of their political loyalties.

3

Nativism might have been of limited political importance if it had resulted only in immigration restriction. But interdependence among a variety of factors was a chief characteristic of the politics of the postwar period, and the ability of nativism to be co-opted bodily into other issues imparted to it a heightened significance. These issues, in turn, were deeply influenced by nativist attitudes.

Prohibition is a case in point. It had been a national issue for almost twenty years prior to the passage of the Eighteenth Amendment in 1919. Now wetness and foreignness were irrevocably joined in the person of the alien. For more than a generation the immigrant and the saloon had been judged inseparable evils from which Americans had to be protected. All immigrants, especially the "newer" immigrants, were assumed to be wet by habit and conviction. Such a belief was deeply held, particularly by rural Americans, and, after the passage of the Volstead Act, they persisted in assuming that all bootleggers were foreigners and that the wet areas of the nation were mainly populated by the foreign-born. It was also believed that booze and the immigrant went hand-in-hand with crime. By 1920 many newspapers, especially southern and western newspapers, were already lamenting a rising crime wave and pointing to its alleged alien origin. Billy Sunday found receptive ears when he loudly claimed in 1921 that any list of prohibition violators "reads like a page of directories from Italy and Greece."

Prohibition, of course, acquired a political significance and possessed a symbolism far surpassing the confines of nativism. Yet prohibition supplied a convenient mask for many of the darker nativist motives that lurked underneath. It allowed some prohibition partisans to talk about morality when in reality they were more worried about cultural dominance and political supremacy. In addition, prohibition played a special role because of its connection with religious belief. As one leading dry said, "Prohibition is part of our religion." Indeed, the primary organizations supporting prohibition were either churches or were staffed by clergymen. Prohibition revenues came mainly from the Baptist, Methodist, and Presbyterian denominations. The Anti-Saloon League, in particular, enjoyed wide church support, receiving money from over 700,000 contributors in the year 1922 alone. Such contributions ranged all the way from the proverbial "widow's mite" to thousands of dollars supplied by such Protestant stalwarts as S. S. Kresge and John D. Rockefeller.

Despite the belief of Prohibition Commissioner Roy A. Haynes at the beginning of 1922 that the "prohibition era of clean living and clear thinking" was off to a good start, it was quickly clear that the passage of the Eighteenth Amendment had had little decisive effect upon American drinking habits. Still, prohibition was staunchly defended and was an issue over which much emotion could always be aroused. Those who opposed it, such as the Association Against the Prohibition Amendment (founded with brewers' money), found it impossible to loosen the connection between Christian morality and alcoholic abstinence. By 1922–23 prohibition as an issue transcended the mere medical or social pros and cons of alcoholic consumption. For drys it had acquired the character of a religious crusade.

The political ramifications of this crusade were everywhere apparent. In many sections of the country, especially in the South and West, to be dry was essential to gain or hold public office. Simultaneously, strong pressure was kept on local, state, and federal officials to enforce all prohibition laws. Actually, the dry forces were somewhat unfortunate in having Harding as President, a man who not only drank but who was skeptical of the vigorous use of federal police power. But they overcame this drawback through the lavish expenditure of funds and through the watchdog activities of such ubiquitous snoopers as Wayne B. Wheeler, general counsel for the Anti-Saloon League. The Anti-Saloon League absolutely terrorized Republican officialdom and for a time in the early twenties held it hostage. Between 1920 and 1925 the average yearly expenditure of the League to support prohibition was almost $2 million, and no government appointment was too small and no bill too insignificant to be examined for its possible impact on the dry cause.

Even so, by 1923–24 prohibition was failing and controversy concerning its proper enforcement was increasing. Some eastern states like Maryland and New York were beginning to have second thoughts about the whole experiment. In these areas a marked rise in bootlegging, the appearance and growing popularity of the speakeasy, and an increase in local political corruption called into question the wisdom of having prohibition at all.

4

Like nativism and unlike prohibition, the phenomenon of fundamentalism was not a political issue in itself. But it drastically affected the postwar political scene and spawned developments that later turned political in character. Like prohibition, which it strongly endorsed, fundamentalism permitted the desire for the preservation of a particular life style to be clothed in appeals to morality and righteousness. Calling for the maintenance of a pure Biblical religion and opposing the twin dangers of modernism in theology and evolution in scientific theory, the fundamentalist crusade drew strength from those same sources that sustained both nativism and prohibition. In turn, it reinforced each of these movements in its own way.

Spearheading the fundamentalist drive in 1921 were the World's Christian Fundamentals Association, the Bible League of North America, and the Bible Crusaders of America. The single most influential fundamentalist spokesman was William Jennings Bryan, three-time nominee of the Democratic party for President. It had been Bryan's early ambition to be a Baptist minister, but it was claimed that his fear of water had led him away from the Baptists and into the Presbyterian fold. Raised by an extremely devout father, who read the scriptures constantly and prayed three times a day, Bryan never lost his fundamentalist faith. His political addresses were always studded with Biblical allusions, and Bryan found time to deliver religious lectures even at the height of his political career. His most famous talk, entitled "The Prince of Peace," was first given on the Chautauqua circuit in 1904. He once told a friend, "I would rather speak on religion than on politics . . . and I shall be in the church even after I am out of politics." Commenting in 1916 to another friend, he said, "The Bible has been more to me than any party platform."

Because of the notoriety of Bryan's anti-evolution stand and his sensational confrontation with Clarence Darrow in the 1925 "Monkey Trial," some of the more politically significant aspects of fundamentalism have been overlooked. In the South fundamentalism did involve mainly an attack on evolution, since anti-evolution sentiment was particularly strong in West Virginia, Kentucky, Tennessee, Oklahoma, Texas, Mississippi, Arkansas, and Louisiana; and in these areas Southern Baptists, Methodists, and Presbyterians, along with numerous small sect groups, forced through anti-evolution legislation and supplied the manpower for monitoring the teaching of science in the public schools.

But fundamentalism was also an assault on Catholicism. Bishop James Cannon, fundamentalist leader and head of the Southern Methodist Episcopal Church, claimed a careful reading of the Bible proved that the Catholic Church was un-Christian and the "Mother of ignorance, superstition, intolerance, and sin." Other fundamentalists openly stated that the Catholic Church had corrupted "the faith once delivered to the saints," and they deplored the liberalized gospel and the secularized culture which Catholicism condoned. Naturally, the fundamentalist insistence on "Biblical Christianity" sharpened the normal historic division between American Protestantism and Catholicism, and encouraged fundamentalists to equate American patriotism with Biblical purity and Catholicism with anti-Americanism.

Fundamentalism also involved an urban-rural cleavage. As some recent scholars have shown, not all modernists were in the city and not all fundamentalists were in Iowa or Tennessee; there were, for example, several large fundamentalist congregations in New York City. But the national pattern of fundamentalist development possessed a definite rural commonalty involving both geography and regional life styles. In the Northeast and in the Middle Atlantic states, only such rural areas as Maine and New Hampshire succumbed to any degree of fundamentalism. In the Middle West there was widespread fundamentalist activity, especially in Iowa, Kansas, and the Dakotas. On the West Coast the fundamentalists had their major support in southern California. It was in the rural South, however, that the movement's real strength lay. Not all southerners were fundamentalists by any means, but Wilbur Cash, who observed the phenomenon firsthand, remarked that fundamentalism in the South was an authentic folk movement which had the "active support and sympathy of the overwhelming majority of the Southern people." As for its anti-urban bias, one fundamentalist phrased it this way: "We are going to take this government out of the hands of city slickers and give it back to the people that still believe two plus two is four, God is in his Heaven, and the Bible is the Word."

One final dimension of fundamentalism, implicit in its anti-evolution position as well as in its literal acceptance of scripture, was its anti-intellectualism. To the fundamentalist the solution to national problems, political or otherwise, was not to be found in man's reason, but in the proper application of Biblical teachings. Intellectuals, especially those associated with the East and with the city, were constantly denounced, and the "expert," who had achieved considerable prominence during the Progressive era, was regarded with extreme suspicion.

In 1923, fundamentalism clearly was a force to be reckoned with in many parts of the country. The upsurge of nativism, the prohibition crusade, and the popularization of the scriptures by such famous spokesmen as Bryan had expanded its appeal. Still, by the early twenties the spread of science and "modernism" was outstripping fundamentalism, and many fundamentalists, who until now had practiced their brand of religion without much fanfare, suddenly felt threatened and decided to make a fight of it.

The battle first erupted within the Protestant denominations themselves, the greatest controversy occurring among northern Baptists, northern Presbyterians, and, to a lesser extent, northern Methodists. Modernists in these denominations were brought under heavy attack by minority fundamentalists, who, among other things, objected to the former's pro-evolution views. The showcase struggle occurred in the Presbyterian Church, where the fundamentalist cause was spearheaded by Bryan. Running for Moderator of the General Assembly at the church's convention in Indianapolis in 1923, Bryan attempted to swing northern Presbyterians into the fundamentalist camp. In a bitter contest he was defeated by the "liberal" candidate, Dr. Charles F. Wishart, president of Wooster College (Ohio) where evolution was taught not merely as a theory but as fact. Bryan also lost an attempt to expunge the teaching of evolution from all Presbyterian colleges and watched helplessly as his proposals were voted down one by one. He chafed more at this double defeat at the 1923 Presbyterian conference than at his three earlier failures to gain the U.S. presidency. Certainly these defeats caused him and fundamentalist followers to become all the more aggressive in their drive, not only to root out the liberal element in their own churches, but to protect all of American society from the ravages of secular godlessness.

5

United we stick
Divided we're stuck
The better we stick
The better we Klux!

That millions of Americans by 1923–24 could enthusiastically support this sentiment underscores the importance of the Ku Klux Klan as a formative factor in the political life of the early twenties.

Unlike fundamentalism or nativism, the Klan phenomenon was associated with a specific organization which, while drawing strength from a variety of sources, far surpassed all its contributors in effective coordinated activity. The general history of the modern Klan is well known. Founded in Atlanta in 1915, it remained only a small-time fraternal organization until a Dallas dentist, Hiram Evans, assumed control in late 1922. Naming himself the Imperial Wizard, he restructured the organization along business lines and for a $10 membership fee sold its services to the American public. According to estimates, Klan membership thereafter skyrocketed 3,500 per day, ultimately making Evans and his early associates rich and presenting the nation with what one observer called "the great bigotry merger."

The Ku Klux Klan indeed fed upon every type of distrust, suspicion, and fear that was prevalent in postwar American society. To be sure, fraternalism, good cheer, and camaraderie were also strong weapons in the Klan's arsenal, and its ritualistic mumbo-jumbo was virtually inexhaustible—robes, hoods, fiery crosses, Grand Goblins, Exalted Cyclopses, Hydras, and Genii. But its widespread appeal sprang as much from feelings of anxiety as from a desire for conviviality. Contrary to the Klan's critics, such anxiety did not represent a grotesque abnormality. The Klan was not a society of monsters gathered together to perpetuate a great evil, nor was it un-American in the technical sense. The Klan actually shared most of the basic aspirations of many postwar Americans. In a unique way it was all things to all men. Here it was a champion of prohibition; there it was a supporter of strict morality and fundamentalism; here it was an opponent of "entangling foreign alliances" and internationalism; there it was a promoter of nativism. Everywhere, however, it permitted a vicarious police lineup in which the nation's various "enemies" were labeled and identified. The Klan never called the *major* enemy by its right name—change. Yet, at base, the Klan was a counterrevolutionary movement which appealed mainly to those who believed their life styles were being threatened.

In any Klan listing of the primary dangers to the nation, the Negro, the Catholic, and the Jew occupied prominent places. Playing on existing nativist sensibilities, the Klan maintained that Negroes, Catholics, and Jews were undesirable elements "defying every fundamental requirement of assimilation." None of these, claimed the Klan, could ever "attain the Anglo-Saxon level." In the blood of the Negro was "the low mentality of savage ancestors"; the Jews were an "absolutely unblendable element"; and Catholics were incapable of a healthy patriotism because the state always had to be "subordinate to the priesthood at Rome."

To the modern Klan the black man appeared far less threatening politically or socially than either the Catholic or the Jew. The Klan, after all, wanted to perpetuate not merely a white supremacy, but an Anglo-Saxon white supremacy. Its membership, for example, was open only to native-born Protestant whites. Although the movement first gained strength in the South, it is significant that its most spectacular growth occurred in areas where there were few blacks. Still, opposition to the Negro was a cardinal Klan principle. Interestingly, this principle was rarely a matter in dispute between pro- and anti-Klan forces in the twenties, underscoring the fact that as of 1922–23 black discrimination was widely condoned by whites everywhere.

The Jew was a different matter. The Klan opposed Jews for their racial and religious cohesiveness and blamed their business leaders for unfair competition. The average Semite was considered to be a parasitic shopkeeper and not a nation builder. Also the Klan claimed that the Jew was inclined toward "internationalism." Political radicalism and the evils of international finance were further laid at his door. In the opening years of the 1920s Henry Ford helped popularize the latter through the pages of his Dearborn *Independent,* widely disseminating the spurious *Protocols of Zion* as proof of the insidious machinations of the rich international Jew. Inevitably, midwestern and southern small-town inhabitants and rural folk, who had earlier succumbed to the ethnic and racial biases of the Populists and of Bryan's silver crusade in the late nineteenth century, rallied again behind such assaults on international Jewry.

Of even greater concern to the modern Klan was the Catholic. To Klan minds, Protestantism and Americanism were synonymous. The Protestant way of faith and the American way of life were one. Catholicism smacked simultaneously of radicalism and authoritarianism. It was regarded as antidemocratic because of its monolithic tradition; yet it was also seen as encouraging radicalism because of the connection between the recent Catholic immigrant and the importation of foreign ideologies. The very name *Roman* Catholic Church suggested a dangerous alien influence. To many Americans, therefore, the emerging importance of Catholics in the life of the nation, especially in its political life, was ominous. As one Ohio Klan leader expressed it: "We want the country ruled by the sort of people who settled it. This is *our* country."

While many Protestant Americans, Klan and non-Klan alike, were bothered by the traditional Catholic stand on such matters as divorce and birth control, their primary concern centered on the Catholic belief in the infallibility of the Pope and the connection between church and state. At the philosophical level the Catholic–non-Catholic debate on these questions was not a matter of prejudice or bigotry. As Reinhold Niebuhr once said, every discussion of the role of the Catholic Church in America "is bound to begin with the issues of the relation of the Church to a 'free society.' " Catholicism did possess tendencies which perpetuated its separation from the mainstream of American life. Its position on religious education tended to keep some of its members in a cultural ghetto, while its Irish-dominated priesthood gave it a militancy and a lack of lay leadership which antagonized many Americans. If American Protestantism suffered from fundamentalism, American Catholicism had absorbed little of German and French intellectualism and had consistently fallen victim to its own brand of chauvinism and parochialism.

As a hate organization the Ku Klux Klan had no interest in debating these legitimate questions rationally, nor did it attempt to separate Catholic dogma from the way the church actually operated in the United States. Instead, it preyed on the unarticulated and latent fears of many in the Protestant community, distorting them and giving them substance. Fears of a Catholic conspiracy sprouted everywhere. In the hands of the Klan, latent anti-Catholicism became overt and virulent in some areas.

Only a form of lunacy could cause otherwise rational American citizens to see a rosary, a cross, and the head of the Virgin in the filigree of the dollar bill, allegedly put there by a wily Catholic engraver. The same applies to the widespread belief that a Catholic interior decorator during Wilson's administration had wangled the installation of "cardinal red" drapes in one of the White House reception rooms. When Harding died in 1923 some witless citizens were even willing to believe that he had expired from hypnotic waves generated by the minds of Jesuit telepaths.

The Klan not only spread such nonsense but twisted past and contemporary events to support their anti-Catholic assertions. It charged that all the existing leaders in the organized labor movement were Catholic and desired the demise of American capitalism, that all city slum dwellers were Catholics and breeding like rabbits, and that most city bosses were Catholic and were plotting a national political takeover. The Klan said that the nation had recently averted a tragedy under Wilson since his wife was a Catholic and so was his private secretary, Joseph Tumulty. As for the future, the Klan warned that unless vigilance was maintained the day would come when Catholics were a majority and would possess the legal power to destroy the American democratic system and erect a Catholic state. In that event, prophesied the Klan, freedom of speech, press, and religion would disappear and all non-Catholics would be reduced to second-class citizenship.

Such anti-Catholicism inevitably caused the Klan to draw support from Protestantism in general, but especially from fundamentalist elements. While not all fundamentalists were Klansmen almost all Klansmen were fundamentalists. Fundamentalism and the Klan were joined in their designation of the nation's chief enemies, in their emphasis on emotion rather than reason, and in their blend of faith and patriotic commitment. In some areas the Klan and fundamentalism shared the same leadership, and the Klan-oriented fundamentalist group known as the Supreme Kingdom supplemented the work of Bryan's Christian Fundamentals Association,

Not only did the Klan follow the fundamentalist approach to the Bible and to evolution, but it also developed prohibitionist leanings. Billy Sunday, for example, was aided in his assault on John Barleycorn by money from both the Anti-Saloon League and the Klan. Klan meetings, often held in churches, possessed a decided revivalist tinge. A heavy overlay of patriotism was blended with fundamentalist theology, abstinence pledges, and fervent promises to "fight sin." The Klan's symbol was the cross, its official hymn was "The Old Rugged Cross," and its code of conduct was the Ten Commandments. Local Klaverns opened and closed with prayer, and Christ was the Klansman's "criterion of character." The first action usually taken by an organizing Kleagle when he entered a new area was to waive the $10 initiation fee for local Protestant preachers. These preachers, disturbed by attacks on the "oldtime religion" and by their own declining community status, often became willing converts.

Although relying heavily on Protestantism, the Klan was not an instrument of Protestantism as the Inquisition was of the Medieval Church. The Klan drew on the Protestant churches' prestige and sometimes fought their battles, but the various Protestant churches did not endorse the Klan. Indeed, almost every governing body of a Protestant denomination denounced the organization. Moreover, the Federal Council of Churches and the leading Protestant journals—*The Christian Century, Christian Work, Christian Herald, Lutheran Christian,* and *The Presbyterian Advance*—were flatly against it. So were many southern church papers, such as the *Southern Churchman* and *Wesleyan Christian Advocate.* Only the Southern Baptist press gave it much support. Still, along with fundamentalism, prohibition, and nativism, Protestantism remained one of the Klan's major feeder sources.

In understanding the Klan's impact on politics in the 1920s, it is important to remember that the organization was neither predominantly southern nor primarily violent. It was mainly a rural, village, and small-town phenomenon—at least in a psychological sense if not always in a statistical one. Small-town mores, small-town life styles, and small-town thinking were always idealized by the Klan. The Klan especially reinforced small-town anti-city prejudices. New York City, for example, was "enemy country" for the small-town Klansman. That metropolis, with its thirty-seven languages and six million residents, was the most "un-American" place on the continent. The Klan also undoubtedly appealed to the small-town resident because of the essential isolation of small-town life. For some the Klan was indeed a means of escape from the dreariness of existence. Certainly the narrow angle of vision of the small town often meshed with that of the Klan, and the average small-town Klan member tended to be a mediocrity who suffered in various degrees from an inferiority complex in social, economic, and cultural matters.

Significantly, the Klan first found a seedbed for its growth in the villages and rural areas of the South and Southwest (Texas and Oklahoma). From the outset the Klan possessed a natural attraction for old native Scotch-Irish stock and for Baptists, who made up 40 percent of the South's church membership. But the Klan might have languished there had it not been for the Evans reorganization and the increasing notoriety given the organization by the press. Thereafter the Klan spread rapidly into the border states, along the Pacific slope (California and Oregon), and into the Midwest (Kansas, Indiana, Ohio, Illinois, Michigan, and Wisconsin). In 1922 the percentage of total membership in the Klan from the South and Southwest was 83.2. By 1924 that percentage had fallen to 41.7 while 40.2 percent were from the three midwestern states of Ohio, Indiana, and Illinois, alone.

If the Klan was no longer predominantly southern by the mid-twenties, its membership was also not exclusively rural or small-town either. By 1924 the Klan had chapters in Indianapolis, Chicago, Columbus, Pittsburgh, Dallas, Tulsa, Little Rock, Birmingham, Baltimore, and even Buffalo and Detroit. Such a development underscored the fact that intolerance in the 1920s was not always simply a matter of city versus country or urban East versus rural South and West. Intolerance appeared anywhere there was a cultural conflict between Protestant, Catholic, and Jew, and was sometimes most severe in the city, where the economic competition between poor white and Negro was keenest. Further, by 1923–24 much of the Klan's national leadership was city based. The Illinois Grand Dragon came from Chicago; the Texas leadership came from Houston, Dallas, and Fort Worth; Ohio's top Klan officials were recruited from Columbus; Colorado's came from Denver.

No matter where the Klan or its leadership existed, it was essentially a lower-middle-class movement. In the rural areas the Klan appealed to depressed small farmers and sharecroppers; in the small towns to shopkeepers, craftsmen, and day workers; in the city to rank-and-file blue-collar workers of business and industry. Few men of wealth, education, or distinction joined it. Hardly a single intellectual of note belonged. The Klan took pride in these facts, claiming that they proved its "mass" appeal and that it was a true "people's organization." There is no doubt that masses of the common people joined it. By 1924 its membership was variously estimated at between two and one-half and four million. Klan leaders spoke glowingly of eight million, but this was hyperbole.

With such a sizable and sprawling membership the Klan inevitably exercised an important social and cultural monitoring function on postwar American society. Sometimes resorting to violence but more often not, the Klan acted in many areas as a collective civic censor, forcing compliance with the "old" values and weeding out "immorality" and "corruption." However, as with prohibition, whose cause it ably served, the Ku Klux Klan was ultimately significant not so much because of the size and spread of its membership or its various coercive activities, but because of its impact on politics. According to the Klan, its original involvement in politics came about because of the Catholic Church. That church, claimed the Klan, was more than a religion—it was a powerful rival to American government and rested its influence on the secret confessional, papal edicts, and rigid membership control. Opposing Catholic candidates for public office quickly became a favorite Klan activity. Senator J. Thomas Heflin of Alabama once intoned: "God has raised up this great patriotic organization to unmask popery." One Klan leader phrased it more simply: "We do not intend to let the Catholic leaders run the country."

There were, of course, many other reasons for the Klan's entering politics. The complicated issues raised by the sudden economic downturn following World War I, the continuing grossly unequal distribution in wealth, the need for an extension of immigration restriction, the desire to enforce prohibition, and rural fears caused by rising urbanism prompted many Klan members to encourage the organization's involvement in politics. Symptomatic of the intricate alchemy between the Klan and the whole range of postwar problems was Gutzon Borglum, Mount Rushmore sculptor and former friend of Theodore Roosevelt, who joined the Klan in 1923 because he saw it representing a pro-farmer, pro-debtor, anti-tariff, Anglo-Saxon progressivism based on villagers and agrarians and standing against foreign ideologies and eastern, New York influence. Embracing such a grabbag of motives as this, the Klan's involvement in politics was not only natural but preordained. And, as that involvement grew, the Klan in many areas became more than a potent political force— it actually became the electorate.

By 1923 the Klan was already in the process of consolidating its political power. From Oregon, Texas, California, Georgia, Oklahoma, Kansas, and Indiana came indications that the Klan was becoming a serious statewide or regional political factor. By that time it had elected Klansman Earle B. Mayfield to the United States Senate from Texas and had helped elect governors in Georgia, Alabama, California, and Oregon. Perhaps as many as seventy-five members of the U.S. House of Representatives owed their elections to the Klan, and an undetermined number were actually Klan members.

In December, 1923, a pro-Klan reader wrote to *The New Republic:* "It is my opinion that within a short time it will be impossible for a man to be elected to any important office in the United States if he is opposed by the Klan." As the Klan's power grew many politicians did indeed fall into its net. It was cause and effect. The Klan could deliver votes, and by belonging to the organization or by securing its endorsement a candidate could gain access to those votes. In its political activities the Klan was peculiarly impartial, attaching itself to the dominant party in a given area. In the South and Southwest the Klan was Democratic. In Illinois and Ohio it was predominantly Republican. In Indiana it simply swallowed the GOP. Whether Republican or Democratic, the Klan's primary task was to see that the "right" persons were nominated and elected. The Klan consistently denied that it controlled votes but admitted that it flooded its membership with much political "information and advice."

6

Since disunity and confusion over social and cultural matters were characteristic of the American scene in the immediate postwar period, both major political parties were affected. American parties have traditionally been successful in resolving political, diplomatic, and economic problems; but in the face of serious social, moral, or cultural questions they have usually become impotent. By the mid-twenties the emerging critical issues confronting American society were primarily social, cultural, and moral. Rather than being able to provide solutions to these problems, the major parties quickly became their hostage. Both major parties were understandably fearful of such issues and sought to avoid them. It was much "safer" to concentrate on the tariff, taxes, and agricultural relief. But neither party could long afford to ignore these other issues because they increasingly related to votes and to internal party control.

Because of its historic development and the nature of its composition, the Democratic party was most immediately affected. Its first embarrassment was prohibition. The Democrats had already stubbed their toe on this issue in 1920. Prohibitionists in the party had gone to the San Francisco convention that year determined to nominate a dry presidential candidate and insert a strong enforcement plank in the platform. Among them was William Jennings Bryan, who, as a member of the committee on resolutions from Nebraska, sponsored a plank which pledged the party to strict enforcement of the Volstead law. Opposing him was Bourke Cockran, a Tammany spokesman from New York, who introduced a resolution favoring the use of light wines and beer. Both men debated the issue before the convention and both resolutions were voted down. Bryan's dry plank lost by the overwhelming margin of 929½ to 155½. In the end, the convention decided to say nothing at all about prohibition.

In the struggle over naming a candidate the prohibition issue again surfaced. Prohibitionists were convinced that James Cox's candidacy was a front for such wet urban politicians as George E. Brennan of Chicago and Charles F. Murphy of New York City. They also assumed that the presentation of Governor Al Smith's name as a presidential candidate was merely a camouflage for behind-the-scenes maneuvers for Cox. Horrified by the emergence of two such well-known wets as Smith and Cox, the prohibitionists rallied behind the candidacies of two equally well-known drys—A. Mitchell Palmer (Wilson's Attorney General) and William Gibbs McAdoo (Wilson's son-in-law and former Secretary of the Treasury). Bryan led the dry forces in their attempt to block the nomination of Cox and was strongly aided by Wayne Wheeler of the Anti-Saloon League, who told Bryan that Cox "must be defeated if there is any way possible to do it."

The successful nomination of Cox was regarded by militant Democratic drys as the beginning of a great offensive against prohibition by the party's big-city bosses, Tammany followers, and eastern liquor interests. Bryan was a sad and lonely figure when he left the San Francisco convention. Because of the Cox nomination, he told reporters, "my heart is in the grave." Still, he claimed that he felt "pretty well for a mangled corpse" and vowed to fight on. He warned of "no compromise" with the wet element and said that he would work to put the liquor interests out of business "so they never again will bother another Democratic convention."

After 1920 the Democrats had the bad luck of losing Bryan wholly to the prohibition crusade. For the first time he failed to do any stumping for the party's presidential candidate and devoted himself instead to fighting "the wet eastern element" as well as John Barleycorn. Firmly believing that America was destined to "lead the world in the great crusade which will drive intoxicating liquor from the globe," he began a feverish propaganda campaign on enforcement's behalf, and watched in anguish as various groups in his own party continued to forsake him. Many middle- and upper-middle-class urban Democrats refused to enlist in Bryan's battle, and the urban laboring element ignored it completely. Worse, in some areas, especially in New England, New York, Maryland, and New Jersey, Democratic leaders actually initiated an open assault on prohibition. In 1923, for example, the New York legislature repealed the state's enforcement act at Governor Smith's urging and thereby boldly challenged the federal prohibition laws.

Prohibition has frequently been called the straw man of American politics because it sometimes masked Protestant religious bigotry and hence appeared to be a "false" issue. But prohibition by the mid-twenties was definitely *not* a straw man. It was a factor that influenced more votes than any other contemporary issue, with the possible exception of prosperity. Protestants did not suddenly seize on prohibition as an issue in 1920, or 1922, or 1924. They had held this position consistently. As for the Democrats, Sam Blythe was correct in prophesying in the *Saturday Evening Post* in October, 1923, that the "likker problem" would become an increasing nightmare for them. They might demand reduced taxation for the poor, shed tears over the plight of the farmer, take various stands on the tariff, and nurse labor lovingly, "but sitting astride the neck of each and every one of them will be that horrendous liquor demon demanding incessantly, 'What are you going to do about me?' "

Democratic problems concerning prohibition were inevitably complicated by problems relating to the Klan. As early as 1922 Senator Thomas J. Walsh of Montana had warned Bryan and other Democratic leaders that the Klan was a rock upon which the party could founder. If the southern wing, in particular, did not reject "this harpy organization," said Walsh, "there will not be votes enough north of the Mason-Dixon line two years hence to justify obsequies over the Democratic Party." But by 1922–23 the Klan was already too important politically for many Democrats to oppose openly. Though Bryan, for example, did not support the Klan, he did not attack it either. After all, its racial views and its position on prohibition were not inimical to his. This was the crux of the Klan problem for many Democrats like Bryan. Many of the organization's basic tenets were compatible with their own, and except for its methods, its secrecy, and its repressive tendencies, they were not convinced that its presence was a bad thing. Besides, in those few instances when some Democratic leaders had attacked the Klan on its home ground, they had come to regret it. By 1923 anti-Klan Democratic candidates had virtually ceased to exist in large areas of the South and Southwest, and those few who were still around, like Senator Oscar W. Underwood of Alabama, were marked for early political oblivion.

Only in those areas where the Klan was weak could the Democratic leadership move without caution. Significantly, most of these regions were in the largest cities and in the North and East. The Klan issue therefore rapidly exacerbated the traditional geographic and regional divisions in the Democratic party. Catholic and ethnic areas of the North and East experienced a natural revulsion as the Klan's drive for 100 percent Anglo-Saxon Americanism gained momentum. Not surprisingly, a new unity began to emerge among the diverse and formerly antagonistic ethnic elements within the city. Poles, Italians, Greeks, Hungarians, and Jews all shared the common Klan designation as "inferior people" and commenced to pool their political efforts. Often inclined by habit and personal belief against prohibition, antagonized by Protestant fundamentalism, and being the primary victims of nativism, these objects of Klan scorn made heroes out of northern Democratic leaders like Al Smith and held the Bryans in contempt.

Of course, one of the basic factors underlying this turn of events was beyond the control of the Klan or anyone else—the physical growth and the rising political importance of the city. Because of this, an increase in national Democratic party disunity would have occurred in the 1920s without the emergence of the Klan or of fundamentalism, prohibition, and nativism as political factors. In the census of 1920, for the first time a majority of the people of the United States were classified as "urban." During the ensuing decade New York increased its population 23.3 percent, Chicago 25 percent, Detroit 57.4 percent, and Los Angeles 114.7 percent. More significant, by the middle of the decade (1925) almost 70 percent of the nation's population growth occurred in metropolitan districts. By that time the New York-Boston-Philadelphia metropolitan area showed a combined growth larger than that in twenty-nine states. Population in the Chicago area increased more than the combined growth of twenty-one states. Even more startling was the fact that the areas just outside the city were expanding even faster than the city itself. Indeed, the city's old well-defined boundaries were being blurred as suburbs began to multiply. Many former small towns were now absorbed into the city by bands of residential developments. Over this whole region "the city" still wielded dominant economic influence, but not necessarily a political or cultural influence.

Since the Democratic party historically was deeply involved with political developments in the city, it was dramatically affected by these demographic changes. Apprehensiveness descended on many Democratic city bosses as they sought to adjust to these new circumstances and yet retain their political control. Catering to the desires of the new urban voter, they concentrated less on issues of national importance (like the tariff and government economy) than on public welfare, sanitation, school bond drives, zoning laws, and so on. Moreover, they rapidly took positions on prohibition, religious freedom, and ethnic toleration which would obviously appeal to their various support groups. In such manner these Democratic leaders, especially in the East, not only added to Democratic power locally, but also enhanced their ability to influence national Democratic party decisions. Clearly, by 1923–24 the old sectional coalition of South and West that had dominated the Democratic party since Bryan's silver crusade in the 1890s was being challenged by the Democratic machines in the nation's major cities. By the mid-twenties the Democratic party was actually three parties: eastern and northern (urban and ethnic-dominated and opposed to prohibition); western (militantly farm-oriented and pro-prohibition); and southern (bone-dry, Klan-riddled, and fundamentalist-inclined). It was an impossible combination.

7

If the Democrats were divided and squabbling by 1923–24, so were the Republicans. From the outset, however, the Republican party managed to live with its divisions much more easily than did the Democrats. Partly this was possible because Republican differences never involved so much bitterness or emotion. Many of the Republican cleavages centered on economic matters which were more susceptible to compromise political solutions. But mainly this general absence of acrimony resulted from the soothing effect of returning prosperity and the relative homogeneity of the party's membership.

The major source of Republican disunity in the early twenties was the farm bloc. Composed of congressional representatives and senators, primarily Republican but also containing numerous southern and western

Democrats, this group had come together in the shared desire to wring concessions from the Republican administration which would benefit the farmer. But also implicit in the farm bloc's various activities was its worry about the rising cultural and political power of the city and the increasing dominance of industry in the nation's economic life.

The farmer had some reason to worry. Following World War I his economy had suffered a sharp decline from which it had not recovered. Business too had experienced a downturn, but it had succeeded in securing advantages from the federal government which had not been matched by aid to the farmer. The Harding regime, especially in the person of Secretary Mellon, seemed always to be more interested in relief for the businessman than in alleviating distress in the rural areas. Since farmers had represented one of the major ingredients in the Republican landslide victory of 1920, they felt betrayed and their representatives reacted angrily.

Pragmatic in its economic philosophy and extremely contentious in its actions, this congressional bloc was avowedly a class as well as a regional economic pressure group. Counting among its chief members such Republican leaders as Senators William E. Borah (Idaho), George W. Norris (Nebraska), and Robert M. La Follette (Wisconsin), the farm bloc forced through beneficial agricultural legislation while acting as a watchdog on pro-business administration activity. In the process the bloc naturally heightened the tension between the various competing economic interests in both parties, but especially in the Republican party. A growing antipathy between urban East and agrarian West, and between rural producer and metropolitan manufacturer, was a political fact that the bloc widely advertised. Simultaneously, most farm-bloc members revealed deep-seated cultural and status anxieties through a behavior pattern which usually included support for nativism and prohibition. Their western and southern backgrounds made this entirely understandable.

Farm-bloc maverickism, like the insurgent and Bull Moose schism of the preceding era, plagued Republican party politics throughout the twenties and from time to time threatened party chaos. Harding had to reckon with it; so did Coolidge and Hoover. The first two Presidents generally managed to contain its opposition by alternately compromising with the bloc and ignoring it. Republicans in the bloc frequently spoke of bolting the party, but in the end grumblingly accepted what they could reluctantly wrest from the administration. Republican bloc members soon discovered that they really had no place else to go despite their economic differences with other factions in their party. Certainly they could not shift to the Democrats in view of that party's difficulties with prohibition and with the Catholic-dominated urban and eastern element. Only La Follette would ultimately choose a third alternative—to go it alone.

The Republican party's success in surviving farm-bloc maverickism was unquestionably related to its stands on prohibition, on labor, and on the urban challenge in general. At no time in the 1920s did the national Republican party show much concern for the specific problems of the city. This was ironic since it was basically sympathetic to industry, which was interconnected with the growth of the city. Throughout the twenties the party managed to retain a hold on the smaller mill towns and on the emerging suburbs. But in the expanding city itself neither the Republican party's brand of economic "rugged individualism" nor its general social and cultural attitudes proved seductive. Squat, combative Fiorello La Guardia, elected originally as a Republican representative from the 20th New York City congressional district in 1922, illustrated the exception rather than the rule. Virtually everything he stood for or did demonstrated how far removed from "normal" Republican theory and practice he was. Attaching himself for a brief time to the farm bloc for lack of a better place to go, La Guardia finally declared himself an independent. Opposed to immigration restriction, Mellon's fiscal policies, the KKK, and prohibition, La Guardia was an early sponsor of state welfarism, free school lunches for children, slum clearance, the development of underground rapid transit, the creation of more city-owned public utilities, and the building of more parks, playgrounds, and art centers. Coming from a district composed of Italians, Jews, and Puerto Ricans, La Guardia symbolized the emerging political consciousness of the urban masses and the new ethnic political alliances which the Republicans generally ignored.

Prohibition, also a problem for the Republicans, was never the bugaboo that it was for the Democrats. Harding, Coolidge, and other Republican leaders consistently supported prohibition. To be sure, Republican administrations were constantly badgered by ardent drys for not being aggressive enough, but the matter in dispute was how to make prohibition more effective, not its existence. As a result, arguments in the Republican party over prohibition were relatively low key, never approaching the intense emotional outbursts heard among the Democrats. Further, the Republicans had no counterpart to Bryan. The Anti-Saloon League's militant Wayne Wheeler, although professing political neutrality, was actually a Republican and the spiritual leader of Republican drys, but Wheeler's position in the Republican party at no time could be compared with that of Bryan among the Democrats.

This is not to say that the Republicans harbored no anti-prohibition sentiment. There were indications by 1923 that the suburban non-ethnic middle class was being put off by prohibition and by the fumbling Republican attempts to enforce it. By that time, even as they continued to vote for prohibition, this element was avidly patronizing its own bootleggers and making jokes about the sanguine enforcement predictions of the Wheelers.

More serious for the Republicans was the growing defection of labor. The party's pro-business economic policies were primarily responsible, but its stand on prohibition was also contributory. Prohibition always possessed class side effects. The disgruntled urban middle and upper-middle classes could still get their booze through illegal outlets, but the working and lower classes, hampered by the high cost of bootleg liquor and inclined by custom anyway toward wines and beer, had no such easy way to quench their thirst. As early as 1922 the AF of L went on record as favoring modification of the Volstead law to exclude light wines and beer. Although there is no reliable quantitative evidence on the prohibition attitudes of workingmen, the declining vote given to Republicans in the cities in the congressional election of 1922 and labor's support of Al Smith in his anti-prohibition stand in New York in 1923 pointed to labor's increasing disenchantment with the Republicans over prohibition.

The Republicans' main problem with labor, of course, remained economic and not moral. Organized labor had supported the Republicans in large numbers in 1920. Fed up with "Wilsonism" and worried by declining employment and postwar inflation, labor saw in Harding's return to normalcy a promise of good times. After his election Harding attempted to retain labor's support by appointing James J. Davis, a former iron puddler and active union member, as Secretary of Labor. He also initiated a national unemployment conference in the fall of 1921 to consider ways to forestall unemployment, and he began a successful assault on the twelve-hour work day in the steel industry. But these positive efforts were canceled by the administration's general pro-business bias and by its action in the Railway Shopmen's strike of 1922. At the height of that struggle Harding's close friend and Attorney General, Harry M. Daugherty, sought and secured the famous Wilkerson injunction, which was one of the most sweeping injunctions in American labor history.

Despite general public support for this drastic action, it was a political mistake. Whatever chances the Harding administration possessed to build bridges of understanding between itself and organized labor, they quickly vanished. Thereafter labor became committed to the belief that Harding and his administration were unrelenting enemies of organized labor. After Coolidge took over in 1923 labor saw no reason to change its attitude. Such labor opposition might have been more damaging to the Republicans had it not been for the fact that labor itself was experiencing traumas. Intense public opposition to its strikes, declining union membership, the emergence of welfare capitalism, and the existence of severe cultural and ethnic differences within the working-class movement decreased labor's political effectiveness. Moreover, the return of business prosperity by 1923–24 markedly reduced labor's militancy.

While the Republican party was losing its position with labor, it was also missing an opportunity to strengthen ties with one of its traditional constituencies—the Negro. This was particularly short-sighted in view of the havoc the Klan was beginning to work on the Democrats. The Republicans possessed some decided advantages regarding both the Negro and the Klan. The party's general class structure and composition made it less susceptible to racism and to Klan infiltration, especially at the national level. Consequently the top Republican leadership never had to be as solicitous of the Klan as the Democrats. While some Republican state leaders were concerned about it and certain local Republican politicians had much reason to fear it, the party as a whole managed to stay clear of its grasp. Harding, while President, denounced the Klan, charging it with "misguided zeal and unreasoning malice" and claiming that it confused "secret fraternity" with "secret conspiracy." Harding's Attorney General even announced that the Justice Department, if asked by the states, would help investigate all infringements by the Klan on the First, Fourth, Fifth, Sixth, and Fourteenth amendments.

None of this, however, helped the Republicans with the Negro. In 1920 the black man had supported the Republican ticket, just as he had in all previous elections dating back to Radical Reconstruction. But a gradual, almost imperceptible, change in his political commitment was taking place. In prompting this change demographic developments were extremely important. In the decade between 1910 and 1920 over 400,000

Negroes moved from rural southern areas to southern cities. More important, an additional 600,000 Negroes crossed from the South into the North, most of them gravitating to northern cities. Nationwide, the rural black population declined 239,000 between 1910 and 1920, while the urban black population increased by 874,000.

Republican leaders were dimly aware of this development and attempted to hold blacks in line by a variety of promises. Harding's request for an antilynching bill and his desire to place more Negroes in federal positions obviously rested on more than an altruistic base. But the inability of the Republicans to deliver on such promises, coupled with a series of Harding-Coolidge moves to cement their gains in the South by backing a pro-white "southern strategy," angered the black community and generated increasing tension between it and the Republican leadership. The frequent willingness of the Republicans to exchange racial reforms for economic concessions from southern congressional Democrats seemed to blacks to be the grossest kind of betrayal.

Meanwhile, black consciousness, especially in the northern city, continued to grow. Such cultural developments as the Harlem Renaissance brought with them a new sense of black awareness. Simultaneously, the Marcus Garvey movement and its "black is beautiful" separatist theories sparked Negro pride and gained wide support, especially among the poverty-ridden, uneducated northern black masses. In a sense, black enthusiasm for the Garvey-sponsored "homeland in Africa" was the Negro's own chauvinistic answer to the Ku Klux Klan as well as a protest against the treatment of blacks under the American political system.

Not only the poor black, but even the better-educated black of the NAACP variety became disenchanted by the mid-twenties with Republican politics in particular and the American two-party system in general. Negro leaders such as W. E. B. Du Bois, who became a Socialist, expressed a diminishing hope in the ability of either major party to aid the black man—the Republicans because of their middle-class interests and pro-business biases, and the Democrats because of their white southern and xenophobic western elements. Hence, by 1923–24 the black man was politically disoriented and was tending to withdraw from political participation. If he did vote, he continued to cast his ballot nationally for the Republicans largely out of habit. But locally he was drifting toward the Democrats. There he was increasingly wooed by the urban Democratic machine.

8

The nation had already been treated to a concrete example of what all this confusion and divisiveness meant to post–World War I American politics. The second congressional election of the decade in 1922 revealed a pattern which with slight modification would remain for the rest of the era. Although the Republicans would retain consistent control of the presidency, their hold on Congress and on local politics would be far less secure. For that reason, national presidential politics and local-state politics (including Congress) have to be viewed separately if any understanding of the politics of the 1920s is to emerge. Local-state politics fed on the differences within the electorate; presidential politics tried to bridge these differences and coalesce divergent views. Local-state politics usually demonstrated the failure, and not the success, of presidential politics to relate significantly to local voter interests and signaled a breakdown in the traditional alliances within the two-party system.

The Republican party faced the congressional elections of 1922 with considerable concern. The national record on which that party had to run was by no means a failure. As has been mentioned, taxes had been lowered, a budget system had been created, a program of government savings had been effected, some farm-relief measures had been enacted, immigration had been restricted, and a new tariff had been passed. Still, intraparty friction over agriculture versus business, the acrimony of the farm bloc, and the growing disenchantment of labor were expected to cause voter apathy or outright antagonism at the regional and local level.

The result was apparent. Administration supporters in particular, and Republicans in general, lost heavily. In Indiana Republican Senator Albert J. Beveridge lost to former governor Samuel M. Ralston, a Democrat and favorite of the Klan. In New Jersey Senator Joseph S. Frelinghuysen, one of Harding's close friends, was defeated by former Democratic governor Edward I. Edwards, a wet. In Michigan Representative Joseph W. Fodney, a member of Congress since 1899 and one of those most responsible for the new tariff of 1922, lost his seat. In Wisconsin Senator La Follette, although bitterly opposed by the Anti-Saloon League, won a thumping majority. The same was true of Hiram Johnson in California. In Minnesota Senator Frank B. Kellogg, one of the more moderate leaders of the farm bloc, was beaten by an anti-business militant, Farmer-Laborite Henrik Shipstead. In Iowa Smith W. Brookhart, another rabid agrarian, won at the expense of a more moderate opponent. In all, the Republicans lost seven Senate seats while the Democrats picked up six, not including Farmer-Laborite Shipstead, thus cutting the Republican majority from twenty-four to ten. In the House, the Republicans lost seventy seats and the Democrats gained seventy-six, reducing the Republican House majority to twenty-six.

The reason for these results was the subject of much speculation. The apparent decline in Republican fortunes from 1920 to 1922, according to Secretary of Commerce Hoover, was caused by the machinations of the farm bloc. Other administration supporters claimed that congressional divisiveness was responsible. Some said that it was Harding's fault and pointed to the Wilkerson injunction. Most newspaper discussions centered on the tariff and the presidential veto of a soldiers' bonus.

Actually, there was no common factor in the outcome. While administration Republicans suffered most, some Democratic stalwarts were also turned out of office. Even some anti-administration Republicans went down to defeat. The 1922 election simply did not revolve around clearly definable issues. Much depended on local conditions and there was no unity among the opposition except a vague general discontent. Despite claims to the contrary, the election was not a repudiation of Harding's normalcy program. Instead, it signified a grassroots attempt to coalesce around new issues. The Klan, for example, was a more important matter in areas of the South or in Indiana in 1922 than the Wilkerson injunction. Similarly, the issue of prohibition was a more vital factor in Governor Smith's triumphant return to Albany than his stand on the Fordney-McCumber tariff.

The results, however, were misread not only by administration Republicans and their Democratic opponents, but by anti-administration Republicans and former Progressives as well. Kansas editor William Allen White, a former Teddy Roosevelt supporter, incorrectly saw in the election a sign that "the discontented farmer and the aspiring laborer have got together." Others claimed it showed a desire on the part of the country to return to the New Freedom days of Wilson. La Follette was positive that it signaled a rebirth of progressivism and called for renewed efforts on the part of "the true friends of the people" to "throw out plutocracy." Suddenly, liberal elements such as the Bull Moose–oriented Committee of Forty-Eight, cast adrift by the Harding inundation of 1920, revived and began to combine with intellectuals, single-taxers, and socialists in an attempt to form a third force in American politics in order to capitalize on this renewed spirit of liberalism among the electorate.

None of these groups sensed the increasingly emotional and xenophobic nature of American politics at the time or recognized the altered voting patterns that were emerging from the confusion. If 1922 held any encouragement, it was for the Democratic party in the cities, not for militant agrarians, old-line progressives, or laborite-socialists. The political change coming was foreshadowed by events in the most populated areas, not in trans-Mississippi Bryan country or in rural Ohio. Indeed, the year 1922 was a breakthrough for the Democratic party in the city. Here the electorate turned sharply Democratic. That party captured districts it had never had before and, more significantly, would not lose again. Boston, New York, Providence, Jersey City, Cleveland, Detroit, Chicago, and Cincinnati heralded the developing trend.

9

The Democrats, and others too, might have more easily divined the real meaning of the elections of 1922 if it had not been for Harding's untimely death in August, 1923, and the subsequent eruption of the Harding scandals. The necessity for the Republicans to find new leadership, the Democratic disdain for Coolidge, and the uncovering of Republican corruption led the Democrats into an optimistic frame of mind which rested more on fantasy than on reality. Attempting to pump up the scandals into an overriding political issue, eager Democrats, along with anti-administration Republicans, lambasted the administration as the most corrupt in the nation's history. Buoyed by the activities of Senator Thomas Walsh, the skillful Democratic prosecutor of the Teapot Dome investigation, and Democratic Senator Burton K. Wheeler, the bombastic investigator of the Justice Department, such elements looked enthusiastically toward the downfall of the Republicans in 1924. Exploiting every nuance of the corrupt practices of Veterans Bureau Director Charles R. Forbes, Alien Property Custodian Thomas W. Miller, and Secretary of Interior Albert B. Fall, these scandal mongers also tried to implicate Attorney General Daugherty, then other cabinet officials, and finally even the White House.

Except for Daugherty these latter attempts failed. Nevertheless, by early 1924 the Democrats had acquired enough ammunition to produce shellshock among almost all Republicans. In the process the Democrats succumbed to their own optimistic rhetoric concerning their party's future chances. It was inconceivable to them that Coolidge's corrupt inheritance from Harding would allow the Republican administration to long survive. A host of issues would be the Republicans' undoing. Bryan said it would come because of Mellon's tax policies and the tariff. William McAdoo claimed that it was inevitable because of the anger of the western farmer and the Republican surrender to eastern business. But all believed that the key issue was the scandals. Democratic newspapers and politicians alike agreed that the scandals had "altered the entire political map of the 1924 campaign" and had given the Democrats the "margin of victory." Ebullient Democratic Representative John Nance Garner of Texas wrote presidential aspirant McAdoo in late January, 1924, that "Cal" and the Republicans were thoroughly whipped because "Teapot Dome is giving us sufficient fuel to heat up the entire country." Said Bernard Baruch to Nevada Senator Key Pittman: "We have the next election in the hollow of our hand."

Lost in all this euphoria were warnings of trouble ahead and of Democratic disappointment if care was not exercised. As early as April, 1923, Cordell Hull, chairman of the Democratic National Committee and a man who kept his thumb on the nation's political pulse, cautioned against "overconfidence, dereliction, mismanagement, or mistakes on the part of Democratic leaders." Despite the added asset of the scandals, Hull was still repeating this admonition a year later in writing to one overzealous national committeeman: "Victory next fall is in the hands of the Democrats themselves. I trust we keep out of sinkholes in the meantime."

Many sinkholes were there—the Klan, prohibition, the rural-urban split—but even Cordell Hull could not foresee the violent struggle into which the Democratic party was about to be plunged. For the Democrats, the Harding scandals represented a welcome diversion. They acted as a shield which obscured the party's own divisive tendencies. Indeed, the scandals gave both the Republicans and the Democrats something "political" to worry about at a time when other less-traditional matters were acquiring political importance. The scandal development was especially timely for the Democrats because behind it a racial bigot like Alabama's Heflin, a militant prohibitionist like Nebraska's Bryan, and an urban Catholic like New York's Smith could temporarily join forces.

But not for long. The general political scene in 1924 was too filled with clashing moralities, antagonistic life styles, and shifting loyalties to be kept in the usual mold. Wet, dry, Catholic, Protestant, city, rural, fundamentalist, Klan, black, immigrant—these were the terms around which politics by the mid-twenties swirled. Largely immune to the customary procedures of political adjustment, these new matters rapidly relegated even government corruption to secondary importance. By the mid-1920s the voting public was no longer so much aroused by signs of economic or political skulduggery as by social, cultural, and moral "gut" issues.

Professor Samuel Lubell in *The Future of American Politics* states that the key to understanding politics in any particular period is to be found in the conflict among the competing elements in the majority party. This certainly was not true for the twenties, where the key to understanding lay in the struggles of the minority party. That party—the Democratic party—suffered those struggles not because it wanted to but because it had to. It had to because at the moment it was the only true *national* party despite its minority status. Only the Democrats contained all the various elements currently agitating the political scene in sufficient numbers to make themselves heard. Precisely because it was more nearly a microcosm of the entire nation, the Democratic party, not the ruling Republican party, represented the only arena in which the significant battles of the decade could take place. Yet, with no sense of impending doom, the Democratic party enthusiastically entered the presidential election year of 1924 to become the hapless victim of the emerging political realities of postwar America.

PART II
★
WITH THE TRAINING CAMPS

1

Rarely before had a political party been so leaderless yet contained so many potential standard-bearers as the Democratic party in early 1924. Actually, the party had begun to experience leadership difficulties as early as the 1918 congressional elections. Shortly thereafter, Wilson's debilitating illness caused a further decline in the quality of Democratic leadership. Wilson's personal dominance of the party now bore unwanted fruit. He had groomed no successor and no one in his official family came forward for fear of incurring his wrath. Democratic congressmen simultaneously found it impossible to coalesce around a new personality. Cox's nomination in 1920 was only a temporary solution to the problem as his futile campaign showed. However, as the congressional elections of 1922 proved, the Democratic party remained vibrantly alive in the local communities, and what effective leadership the party possessed was to be found there. From this local parochial milieu sprang all the potential candidates for 1924.

No sooner were the 1922 elections over than speculation began on a possible Democratic presidential nominee. The names most often mentioned were McAdoo, Smith, Cox, Senator Underwood of Alabama, Senator Ralston of Indiana, Senator Carter Glass of Virginia, former ambassador John W. Davis of West Virginia, and Henry Ford. By mid-1923 it was claimed that McAdoo and Ford were the strongest contenders, with Cox, Smith, and Underwood following behind. An early-summer *Literary Digest* poll of two thousand Democratic congressmen, mayors, and state officials showed that McAdoo was the first choice, with Henry Ford second, Underwood third, and Smith and Cox tied for fourth.

The fact that Henry Ford was considered a contender at all attests to the state of Democratic leadership in 1923–24. Though his political ignorance was monumental, he possessed a strong grassroots appeal. Many who would have perished at the thought of John D. Rockefeller for President accepted Ford even though he had as much money as Rocke-

37

feller and none of the latter's charitable instincts. Many plain people, especially in the South and the West, liked Ford because he hated Wall Street, rejected a rich palace at Newport, and lacked an "eastern" education. Tired of politicians of the intellectual type like Wilson, many citizens saw Ford as a "new breed." After all, he had given the farmer the Model T and the tractor and, if given the chance, might effect the same miracle in government that he had already worked in industry.

There were more subtle reasons for Ford's popularity. His barbershop sort of talk condemning Jews and Catholics as a bunch of bums struck a responsive chord in certain non-urban and rural sections of the country. His view that the nation needed to protect "the old values," along with his promise to supply farmers with cheap fertilizer through the purchase of Muscle Shoals, garnered him more support in the South than any northerner since the Civil War. Political pundit Mark Sullivan, although deploring Ford's prejudices, admitted that his xenophobic attitudes would help him more than hurt him and prophesied that the Ku Klux Klan would probably rally behind him. For all such reasons, the Jersey City *Journal* said, "Henry Ford would make a rattling good candidate."

If the possibility of Ford as President excited some people, it appalled others. Ford's erratic behavior, his historical and geographical stupidity, his ethnic and religious prejudices, and his messianic tendencies seemed to his critics to bar him from serious consideration. Writing for *The Nation* in May, 1923, Oswald G. Villard shuddered at the thought of Ford's controlling the nation's destiny. "It would be a triumph of the unfit," said Villard, and added, "Almost anything conceivable might happen to the Republic should he be elected." Certainly Ford's candidacy would have heightened tensions within the Democratic party and would have added immeasurably to its existing troubles. As it was, Ford removed a big question mark from the Democratic political scene on December 18, 1923, when he ringingly endorsed Calvin Coolidge's nomination by saying: "I would never for a moment think of running against Calvin Coolidge for President on any ticket whatever."

2

Eastern Democrats and liberals were not the only ones relieved by Ford's disclaimer. Significantly, the Ford boom had its locus precisely in that area where William McAdoo also hoped for major support. As Mark Sullivan put it, McAdoo spent considerable time in 1923 worrying about "being run down by a Ford." In the South and the West, Ford's removal left McAdoo as the man to beat.

William Gibbs McAdoo was born near Marietta, Georgia, on October 31, 1863, a small town twenty miles north of Atlanta and in the path of Sherman's famous march to the sea. McAdoo's earliest recollections were of victorious Yankee boys from such far-off places as Massachusetts and New York marching by in their closing drive to defeat southern secession. Being the son of a successful lawyer of Presbyterian stock, McAdoo received a good schooling despite the difficulties of Reconstruction and subsequently moved with his family to Knoxville, where his father accepted an appointment as adjunct professor of history at the University of Tennessee. In time, McAdoo prepared for the law and acquired his first taste of politics as a young law clerk in Chattanooga. Like most Tennesseans, he supported Grover Cleveland in the 1884 presidential campaign "because of the enemies he had made." McAdoo actually wangled an appointment to the Democratic Convention of 1884 as an alternate, and July found him in Chicago, not yet technically old enough to vote, booing anti-Cleveland Tammany speakers.

In 1892, after seven relatively unproductive years as a lawyer, McAdoo moved with a wife and two children to New York City. His subsequent attempt to establish a modest law practice was soon superseded by an interest in building a tunnel under the Hudson River. Meeting resistance from "the traction barons" and certain Wall Street financiers, McAdoo nevertheless persisted and ultimately pushed through construction of both uptown and downtown tunnels by 1908.

The success of the Hudson tunnels made McAdoo a "figure" in New York, but it did not unlock doors for him among the city's elite or bring him plaudits from Wall Street. McAdoo was still treated as an outsider. Nor did his tunnels' success, because of their excessive cost, bring him a fortune. This rankled. McAdoo desired both fame and fortune but his New York experience gave him neither. The tunnels did provide him one important thing—a contact with Woodrow Wilson. As president of the corporation owning the tunnels, McAdoo had a special interest in the politics of all surrounding areas and in 1910 supported Wilson for governor of New Jersey. In 1912 McAdoo was made a member of the New York delegation to the Baltimore convention and strongly supported Wilson for President, ultimately serving as one of his campaign lieutenants.

McAdoo's relationship with Wilson matured rapidly, leading him not only into government service in Wilson's cabinet but also into Wilson's family as a son-in-law. The first Mrs. McAdoo died in February, 1912. The next year McAdoo began to court Eleanor Wilson, youngest of the President's three daughters, and they were married in the Blue Room of the White House in 1914. McAdoo was Secretary of the Treasury at the time and offered to resign because of possible embarrassment to Wilson, but the President would not hear of it. During World War I McAdoo became one of Wilson's closest advisers, serving also for a time as administrator of the nation's railroads.

In 1920 McAdoo's friends boomed him for the presidency, but they had little support either from McAdoo or from his father-in-law, who, despite his illness, harbored a desire for a third term. McAdoo refrained from campaigning prior to the 1920 San Francisco convention and discouraged all talk of his running for fear of disturbing Wilson's plans. Even at the convention McAdoo kept a low profile and his own ambitions concealed. Derisively labeled "the Crown Prince" by his critics because of his familial association with Wilson, McAdoo received 34 percent of the first-ballot vote without exerting any effort on his own behalf. At that point a word from his father-in-law might have made him the nominee. Without it, McAdoo became merely an also-ran as Cox finally seized the nomination.

After the Democratic debacle at the polls in 1920, McAdoo returned to New York. But he had never been happy there and in 1922 moved to California, where his political fortunes experienced an immediate upturn. McAdoo supporters on the Democratic National Committee had already ousted Cox's campaign manager, George White of Ohio, from control and had replaced him with Representative Cordell Hull of Tennessee. Hull, although neutral concerning the 1924 nomination, was a friend of McAdoo. McAdoo, meanwhile, aided himself by campaigning vigorously for local Democrats in a dozen western states in the elections of 1922 and built up an important cache of political IOUs. Simultaneously, local political conditions in California conspired to help. McAdoo wisely chose Los Angeles in which to live because the population trend was toward southern California. Besides, the Democrats there had been strong New Freedom supporters. James D. Phelan, a San Franciscan by background and the reigning state boss, also quickly swung to McAdoo's side and as early as December, 1922, urged him to begin thinking about the presidency. Phelan saw in McAdoo a chance for California to enter the political big time.

Phelan was no fool. He, along with others, knew that McAdoo would make a formidable candidate. The transplanted New Yorker had the mien and the tenacity for it. Tall, lean, and saturnine, McAdoo was sometimes called a "beardless Lincoln." But there the comparison stopped. In parting his hair in the middle and wearing high-standing collars, McAdoo was the personification of strait-laced rectitude and sanctimonious moral judgment. Only his heavy hooded eyes betrayed the fact that he could himself be devious when necessary. The overall impression was of a man who was self-confident, aggressive, relentless, and infallible. As with many such men, McAdoo could be vindictive and intolerant. He was too concerned with winning ever to be magnanimous. Moreover, while he was attracted to good ideas, he too often substituted passion for reason and personal prejudices for high-minded convictions. He also lacked a certain sense of discrimination. He liked money and status too much to be a true liberal, and he was often too intent on achieving results to consider the means to be used or the price to be paid. But, whatever his shortcomings, McAdoo was charismatic and had the ability to sway an audience by the force of his personality. He was able to extract a fanatical loyalty from his followers.

McAdoo's beliefs were tailor-made for the adopted area he now came to represent. He used the word "progressive" to describe his political position but he never adequately defined it. It was unquestionably rooted in Wilsonian prewar progressivism with its suspicion of monopolies and desire for monetary and rural reform. However, the specific thrust of McAdoo's progressivism was anti-Tammany, anti–Wall Street, and dry. His anti-Tammany position grew out of his early enthusiasm for Cleveland, his own unpleasant experiences in New York, and Tammany boss Charles Murphy's attempt to steer the 1912 Baltimore convention away from Wilson and toward Champ Clark. McAdoo's anti–Wall Street bias sprang directly from his Hudson-tunnel activities and from his role in the implementation of Wilson's New Freedom monetary-reform policies. His prohibition stand rested on deep personal conviction.

All of these attitudes were eminently acceptable to agrarian Democrats in the West and South. To these individuals McAdoo appeared as a vigorous fighter for "traditional" values. Despite his New York exposure, McAdoo had never abandoned farm jargon and imagery to explain his views—a jargon and imagery which were readily understood throughout the South and West. Indeed, as a bone-dry native American of Anglo-Saxon stock who possessed an appeal to western and southern Democracy, McAdoo could claim to be the heir not only of Wilson but also of William Jennings Bryan.

McAdoo's enemies were as important in revealing the nature of his candidacy as were his supporters. Eastern liberals and the party's "intelligentsia" were opposed to him. Urban spokesmen reviled him. Walter Lippmann claimed that McAdoo was "not fundamentally moved by the simple moralities" and warned that McAdoo's political style came perilously close to demagoguery. As early as 1918 such journals as *The Nation* and *The New Republic* expressed caveats about his gaining the presidency, *The Nation* claiming that such an event would represent "an unqualified misfortune." Other detractors, mainly in the North and East, constantly referred to McAdoo's rural-oriented homilies as "McAdooleisms" and to his followers collectively as "McAdoodledom." Eastern business, railroads, bankers, and large industrialists remained against him because of his part in the creation of the Federal Reserve Act and in administering the railroads during World War I. In the East, only organized labor had much enthusiasm for McAdoo, largely because of his mildly pro-labor stand while he was railroad administrator.

McAdoo's campaign got off to a fast start. It was rapidly clear that he wanted the presidency and did not intend to play a waiting game. Immediately following the elections in 1922 McAdoo began to develop a highly efficient campaign organization. The early group working for him was composed of Daniel C. Roper, Thomas B. Love, Bernard Baruch, Thomas L. Chadbourne, Breckinridge Long, Bruce Claggett, George Fort Milton, and David Ladd Rockwell. Love was a Dallas attorney and had been McAdoo's Assistant Secretary of the Treasury. Chadbourne was a wealthy New York lawyer who had served on the War Trade Board. Claggett was private secretary to McAdoo, who trusted him. Long was from Missouri and had been Assistant Secretary of State prior to 1920. Milton was a newspaperman and historian who served as McAdoo's publicity director. All these men had known McAdoo from the Wilson years and were convinced that he would continue the Wilson policies.

The three most important of these early supporters were Baruch, Roper, and Rockwell. Baruch, a Wall Street financier and former chairman of the War Industries Board, became one of McAdoo's closest advisers. In February, 1923, when McAdoo told Baruch that he intended to make the race, Baruch immediately endorsed him as "head and shoulders above every man who has been talked about." Thereafter, in concert with Chadbourne, Baruch acted as chief McAdoo fund raiser, collecting $50,000 for the early campaign period alone. There was a paradox in McAdoo's having as one of his major supporters a Wall Street man and an easterner. But McAdoo needed Baruch's contacts and financial influence and Baruch, in turn, believed that the Democratic party's best chance lay with a Wilson-associated western dry. Baruch himself was a militant prohibitionist.

Daniel Roper was a North Carolinian by birth and had been collector of internal revenue under Wilson. In that position he had become acquainted with McAdoo, who was then Secretary of the Treasury. Like McAdoo, Roper was of Scotch and English extraction, and his earliest memories were of blue-coated Yankees stationed near his home to protect the rule of northern carpetbaggers. But his fondest remembrance was the image of the young Bryan assailing the gold kings in the silver campaign of 1896. After graduating from Trinity College (North Carolina), Roper, again like McAdoo, gravitated to a business career in "enemy country"— New York City. Also like McAdoo, he soon left because he hated it, and moved on to Washington, where he held a variety of minor bureaucratic jobs before being tapped by Wilson to be revenue collector.

Rockwell was the last of McAdoo's early supporters to join. When McAdoo decided to establish his central campaign headquarters in Chicago in the late fall of 1923, Rockwell was selected as national campaign manager. McAdoo had wanted to name Roper, but Roper had advised that no southerner like himself be appointed. Roper also cautioned that McAdoo should not select anyone who was associated with the Wilson years. The McAdoo staff already resembled a reincarnation of the Wilson government, which, while pleasing some, would undoubtedly alienate others. The result was the appointment of Rockwell, an Ohio lawyer who had been the floor manager of the Cox forces in 1920. A skilled organizer, Rockwell nevertheless was bull-headed, too sensitive to criticism, and conceited. More than once McAdoo would have reason to regret this decision.

McAdoo officially opened his drive in early December, 1923. Almost immediately thereafter, Henry Ford's disclaimer encouraged the Californian and buoyed his hopes. For McAdoo, all this represented the beginning of a struggle which he enthusiastically accepted and expected to win. He acted as if he were going to war. To one daughter, who was at

Bryn Mawr, he wrote: "I am going to make the best of it, and do the job . . . even if it takes my life." To another daughter he said: "One has to sacrifice himself for his country in civil affairs as well as on the battle-field." To a relative in Knoxville he claimed disingenuously that he was being "dragged back into politics," but added, "In that event I think we can clean up the enemy."

McAdoo was plunged suddenly into more of a battle than he had bargained for. The first shots came from a totally unexpected quarter. The Senate Teapot Dome oil investigation was currently underway in Washington. Chief investigator Thomas Walsh had been pursuing leads which had finally brought him to suspicious monetary dealings between Interior Secretary Albert Fall and wealthy oilman Edward L. Doheny. On January 24, 1924, Doheny disclosed under oath that he had made a "loan" of $100,000 to Fall just prior to Fall's granting him leases on certain naval oil lands. This was startling information, but Senator James A. Reed of Missouri, a renegade Democrat, was not satisfied that Doheny had told the committee the whole truth and demanded that he be re-called for further testimony. On February 1 Doheny appeared again and spattered oil everywhere. Fall was not the only federal official with whom he had had dealings, testified Doheny, and proceeded to name no fewer than four Wilson cabinet members to whom he had paid retainers for their services at one time or another. Among this group was William Gibbs McAdoo, who allegedly had received $250,000.

The motivations of the main characters in this drama were interesting. Doheny, who had possessed close ties with the Wilson administration, was nettled because none of his Democratic friends had offered to help him escape Walsh's net. Senator Reed nursed an ambition to run for the presidential nomination in 1924 and correctly guessed that further testimony by Doheny might hurt McAdoo. Senator Walsh was an innocent bystander. It was especially ironic that the disclosure about McAdoo should have come at Walsh's hands. Years before, Doheny had taken Walsh into his own home for recuperation after Walsh had been mentally shattered by the death of his wife. Walsh was also one of McAdoo's strongest supporters for the presidency, regarding him as a superb ad-ministrator and a brilliant Secretary of the Treasury. This episode, there-fore, was a double tragedy for Walsh. He later admitted that he all but wept because of what his pursuit of Republican wrongdoing had done to a personal friend and to his own choice for the 1924 Democratic presi-dential nomination.

Although Doheny later clarified his testimony by stating that the New York firm which McAdoo had worked for had received only $100,000 in legal fees and that McAdoo himself had received only $25,000 a year for two years as a special counsel to Doheny's oil company, the damage had been done. Public reaction was swift. Already repelled by the evidence of Republican corruption, most observers now maintained that McAdoo's Democratic presidential ambitions were ruined. With the Harding scandals as an emerging campaign issue, it was unthinkable that the Democrats would risk naming a candidate like McAdoo. Eastern newspapers, which opposed McAdoo anyway, welcomed the opportunity to deflate his chances. The Baltimore *Sun,* the New York *World,* and the *New York Times* all declared him dead politically. Top Democrats such as Josephus Daniels and Colonel Edward House asked him to withdraw, while Bryan admitted that McAdoo was injured "seriously, if not fatally." More important, Senator Walsh, who still retained the highest regard for McAdoo personally, reluctantly wrote him: "You are no longer available as a candidate."

McAdoo was in Los Angeles when the Doheny testimony broke but was preparing to leave with his wife for Washington, D.C., because of the news that Woodrow Wilson lay near death. McAdoo entrained on Saturday, February 2, the very day that the Doheny disclosures were being reported in the press. At Albuquerque the McAdoos received a wire that Wilson had died, prompting some wags to state that McAdoo would arrive in Washington in time to attend Wilson's funeral as well as his own.

The burial of a father-in-law and ex-President was important business, but it was not the most pressing matter that William McAdoo had on his mind when he arrived in the capital and was met by a worried campaign staff. From the outset, the Doheny testimony had prompted frantic communications between Roper, Rockwell, Long, Chadbourne, and Baruch. Roper was despondent and Long was panicky. Baruch waspishly complained that McAdoo should have followed his earlier advice against taking rich clients: "If you want to be President," Baruch once warned him, "you'll have to remain poor and maybe your wife will have to take in washing." All agreed that an immediate strategy conference was necessary, and Wilson's body was barely in the grave before a series of meetings were arranged. Meanwhile, on February 7 McAdoo wrote Irvine L. Lenroot, chairman of the oil investigating committee, requesting permission to testify. In his letter McAdoo emphasized that it was imperative that he appear promptly "because the newspapers throughout the land have blazoned my name on the front page in glaring type in the most unfair and libelous manner as though I were involved in some way in [the Teapot Dome] scandal."

During the evenings of February 7 and 8 the McAdoo staff probed every aspect of the problem. Crucial to the outcome of these discussions were the attitudes of Baruch and Chadbourne because it was upon their shoulders that the burden for raising further campaign funds rested. Neither was in favor of going on. Roper believed it was a mistake to continue to push McAdoo if public opinion was clearly against him. Long was already toying with the idea of switching his allegiance to Carter Glass of Virginia. At one point Roper, Long, Baruch, and Chadbourne agreed that it would be better if McAdoo withdrew and attended the convention merely as a delegate working for progressive goals.

But they reckoned without McAdoo and Rockwell. Rockwell was not prepared to capitulate so easily. He believed McAdoo could make a recovery. As for McAdoo, he was angry and displeased with the luke-warm attitude of his advisers. After the February 8 meeting, Breckinridge Long wrote in his diary: "McAdoo is mad. He is full of fight. He is swearing mad. He is just as profane as I get when I get mad. He is cursing and swearing, damning every opponent and every obstacle." Long was so impressed by McAdoo's performance that he wired McAdoo men in Missouri that very night: "There will be no withdrawal and will be an aggressive fight."

Long's telegram was somewhat premature because the final decision was neither so definite nor so militant. At the concluding meeting on the morning of February 9 in Chadbourne's rooms in the Shoreham Hotel, McAdoo paced rapidly back and forth, still saturating the air with oaths. Baruch fidgeted with his cuffs and looked grim. Long sat rigid with fear that McAdoo might yet pull out and make him look ridiculous in Missouri. Chadbourne, just up from Palm Beach and feeling the cold, kept his feet propped on a radiator. After further discussion, McAdoo agreed that he would first defend his reputation before the Senate committee. Then he would reevaluate his candidacy in the light of public reaction. If it was demonstrably unfavorable, he promised that he would withdraw.

Wilson's death and his funeral ceremonies came at a propitious moment for McAdoo because the Doheny disclosures were temporarily pushed off the front pages of the newspapers. This gave the McAdoo forces a chance to catch their breath. It also afforded McAdoo the opportunity to "cool down" and to prepare his testimony for the Senate committee carefully. On Monday morning, February 11, he appeared before that group and calmly answered all questions. Yes, he had accepted employment with Doheny but only after he had left public office and only to represent Doheny against the unjust confiscation of certain oil properties by the Mexican government. Yes, he had received $25,000 a year for two years from Doheny but was no longer in his employ. Yes, it was possible that the successful litigation of the Mexican matter might have brought additional fees to McAdoo and to McAdoo's law firm. No, he had not lobbied in Washington at any time for Doheny on any matter relating to naval oil leases and had no knowledge of them. Yes, he had represented Doheny briefly before several bureaus of the government and in certain tax cases before the Treasury Department. This latter, said McAdoo, was perfectly normal, since no modern lawyer could have a wealthy client without being involved in such litigation at one time or another.

McAdoo came away from the session feeling exonerated, but his friends were not sure. The suspicion lingered that McAdoo's fascination for money had clouded his judgment and that he had been retained by Doheny not so much for his legal ability as for his influence. Indeed, when McAdoo again met with his small group of organizers for a postmortem on the evening of February 11, he was handed a prepared statement for the press written by Baruch which amounted to a withdrawal. Chadbourne, Roper, and Joseph Tumulty (Wilson's former private secretary who also happened to be there) agreed that he should release it. Rockwell was unconvinced, and McAdoo absolutely refused. After an angry discussion, Roper finally switched to McAdoo's side, while Baruch consented to await the outcome of public response to his testimony. Chadbourne reluctantly went along but ominously indicated that he would not be able to be as free with his money in the future as he had been in the past. McAdoo, meanwhile, was assigned the responsibility of "proving" to the group that he still retained public confidence.

Breckinridge Long, who had admired McAdoo's tenacity throughout, asked him after the meeting what he intended to do. "Why, hell," said McAdoo, "fight, of course. That is definite and final." McAdoo indicated that he now would ask his supporters in the various states to meet in Chicago on February 18 to voice their opinion on his remaining in the race. The implication was that if such grassroots sentiment proved antagonistic, he would retire. But McAdoo had no intention of withdrawing, and in issuing his call for this meeting loaded the dice by charging that "eastern bosses and other sinister influences" were trying to sabotage him. Even so, Long privately confided to his diary that McAdoo would have to do something truly spectacular or he was beaten.

McAdoo arrived in Chicago on February 17 and went into seclusion in the Blackstone Hotel. The gathering of McAdoo supporters was set for 10 A.M. the next morning in the Great Northern. All was carefully staged. After the proper atmosphere was created by several pro-McAdoo spellbinders, Bruce Claggett introduced a resolution to the three hundred assembled delegates, calling upon McAdoo to remain in the contest and "accept the leadership of the Progressive Democracy of the nation." The highlight of these preliminaries was the reading of a telegram from Senator Walsh, whose interest in McAdoo had been rekindled and who now claimed that the Californian was "untouched by any revelation made before the Senate committee investigating the naval oil leases." Suddenly, with consummate timing, McAdoo appeared and, accompanied by the frenzied cheering of his followers, made a fighting speech laced with numerous invectives against Wall Street and containing promises to support farm relief, railway reform, a soldiers' bonus, and other such "progressive measures." To huzzahs of joy McAdoo concluded: "You command me to accept the leadership. I accept the command."

McAdoo considered the conference a huge success. To one son in Los Angeles he wired: "Marvelous meeting here today with forty states represented. Tremendous enthusiasm." To another son in New York City he telegraphed: "Wonderful meeting. . . . No one has ever seen anything like it." Roper, who watched the proceedings in awe, wrote to a friend: "The McAdoo conference at Chicago was a wonderful success. . . . The delegates returned home inspired with new zeal and convinced that he can be nominated and elected." Still, signs remained that McAdoo's political fortunes had suffered a severe blow. Despite the display of enthusiasm at Chicago, there was no longer a rush to the McAdoo banner. Although there were as yet no mass defections, there was a growing tendency on the part of some southern and western Democrats to consider alternatives. Rockwell, Claggett, Roper, and Long exchanged worried correspondence about this situation while simultaneously telling McAdoo supporters that "progress is occurring in all parts of the country." All of these men were forced to redouble their efforts on McAdoo's behalf, causing Long to complain to one friend, "I have simply been living on the railroad trains." But the slide from McAdoo could not be stopped, and by the end of February Long was writing in his diary, "There is no denying the fact that McAdoo is losing ground. This 'oil' propaganda, tho he is innocent of any wrongdoing, is breaking us down."

McAdoo remained as confident and pugnacious as ever. Immediately upon returning to his Los Angeles office from the Chicago conference, he sent out a flurry of combative letters to friends and backers, denouncing those weak-kneed Democrats who refused to rally to his standard as playing the game of "vicious and malignant reactionaries." At the same time, in order to allay the rumors concerning the size of the "additional fees" that would have been paid to his law firm had the Mexican litigation proved successful, McAdoo defiantly told the press that the sum would have been $900,000. Shortly thereafter Doheny gave a press interview in which he claimed that there was nothing illegal about this arrangement. The McAdoo firm, said Doheny, would have more than earned the $900,000 since the value of the oil properties to be saved from confiscation was over $400 million.

Despite the various explanations and justifications given, this further information involving such a huge sum of money caused new concern among McAdoo followers and created additional difficulties for the McAdoo drive. Frank E. Frazier, office manager of the Chicago headquarters, quit in March after issuing a round-robin letter claiming that McAdoo was finished. Long, one of McAdoo's most consistent champions, considered recommending that his own state of Missouri send an uninstructed delegation to the convention rather than one pledged to the Californian. Tumulty and Colonel House, both McAdoo admirers, turned cautious. Indeed, House quietly began to push John W. Davis. Chadbourne, who was already lukewarm, became more so, while Baruch, who once had feared that McAdoo might not be nominated, began to wonder whether he should be. Even James Phelan, who prior to this time had remained loyal and had already secured a commitment from California Democrats to send a pledged McAdoo delegation to the 1924 convention, began to doubt. While in Washington on a short trip in March, he wrote home to a friend: "I have been up and down and across, talked with McAdoo's own friends here, and NO WHERE and from NO ONE do I get a single word of encouragement. . . . They say a McAdoo leadership would put the party on the defensive."

More disastrous to the McAdoo cause was the final withdrawal of Senator Walsh's support. Despite his telegram of February 18, Walsh had remained skeptical of McAdoo's chances. Nine days after his endorsement was read to the Chicago conference, Walsh predicted privately that even if McAdoo continued to run "it will be impossible to nominate him." Still, Walsh temporarily continued to support McAdoo because he feared the demise of his candidacy would trigger a disintegration of "progressive forces" and increase the possibility of the nomination of a "conservative or reactionary candidate." However, on April 3, after further mulling the situation over, Walsh sadly notified McAdoo that he could no longer back him and suggested that he withdraw. McAdoo bluntly replied "No," and in a lengthy letter told Walsh that, despite what his friends might do, he would not cut and run. Concluded McAdoo, "Of one thing you may be sure: If I go down, it will be with the enemy's bullets in my chest and not in my back."

By April, 1924, the McAdoo drive was sputtering and previous hopes for a McAdoo bandwagon were dashed. This fact was not lost on all those Democratic leaders who had been sitting quietly by, watching the McAdoo campaign for clues to their own best course of action. Although McAdoo remained a power, there was now ample room for other contenders. The press reflected this feeling by constantly parading a host of other possibilities before its readers. As John W. Davis explained the situation in a letter to an English friend, McAdoo "was clearly in the lead" and might have "sewed the nomination up." But in view of the Doheny disclosures his selection was not likely and "it was anybody's guess who might emerge."

3

One man had long since reached the conclusion that the Democratic party needed another candidate instead of William McAdoo. Even before the Californian had officially declared his candidacy, Alabama senator Oscar Underwood had offered himself as an alternative. Underwood did so because he did not believe that McAdoo would attract southern voters or represent the best interests of the South.

Underwood possessed imposing political credentials. Born in Louisville, Kentucky, the year after the Civil War began, Underwood had been educated at the University of Virginia and since 1895 had represented Alabama in national politics. Widely recognized as the "first statesman of the South," Underwood had served in the House for ten consecutive terms before becoming U.S. senator, a post he had held since 1915. He had had a tariff named after him, had been a presidential contender in 1912, and had served the New Freedom faithfully.

To a large extent the Underwood candidacy stemmed from southern and state pride. As early as summer, 1923, Alabama Governor William W. Brandon began writing all important state Democrats requesting their support for Underwood. When Underwood indicated in August that he was willing to be drafted, Brandon stepped up his efforts and that fall opened an Underwood-for-President headquarters in Washington, D.C. Handouts were simultaneously circulated all over the South soliciting help. Also pushing for the Alabama senator were influential alumni from the University of Virginia, who boosted him as a "true Jeffersonian from Jefferson's own institution." One alumni circular asked: "Will you not join with other alumni of the University in doing your best to put him in the White House?"

Despite superficial appearances, Underwood's candidacy was not in the hands of political amateurs. In 1923–24 a majority of the Democrats in Congress were holdover southerners from the Wilson era. Among this group there was considerable support for Underwood, and in late 1923 a professional organization to conduct his campaign began to be formed. The leading voice was Representative Charles C. Carlin of Virginia. Carlin was owner of the influential Alexandria *Gazette* and had been A. Mitchell Palmer's campaign manager in 1920.

Underwood's supporters claimed that their man, not McAdoo, was a "true" Wilson progressive, and sought to win voters to this belief. Underwood had championed low tariffs throughout his life and had firmly supported Wilson's League of Nations and the World Court. But Underwood was a strong states'-rights man who, finding much to admire in the early New Freedom, had turned against the centralizing activities of the late Wilson years. He was opposed to "big" government and especially resented the growing power of the presidency. Underwood personally was wet but his stand on prohibition was fully compatible with his states'-rights views: let local option decide. More shrewdly than most southerners, Underwood correctly perceived that if laws on a national scale could be passed concerning drinking, why not concerning the social rights of Negroes? On woman's suffrage his position was clear: women should not be allowed to vote.

In his economic views Underwood was basically pro-business. His low-tariff stand was not designed to undercut the business community but to promote those economic enterprises best suited to the South. Underwood belonged to that new breed of southerners who were far removed from the stereotype of hog-wallow politics. He believed that northern investment and business expansion in the South were essential, but that the process should proceed logically and carefully. He was one of those upper-middle-class opponents of monopolistic malpractices who still retained a belief in the advantages of industrialism and business efficiency. While he often gave lip service to aiding the southern farmer, Underwood certainly was no friend of his. He believed the average southern farmer was too saddled with prejudice and too immune from innovation to provide the means for a rejuvenated and "progressive" South.

Such Underwood views were both an asset and a liability. They brought him some support outside the South, particularly in areas where McAdoo was anathema. But they also lost him the backing of numerous parochial southern elements and, as the winter months of 1924 warmed into spring, Underwood was increasingly seen for what he was—a conservative pro-business candidate. George Huddleston, Democratic representative from Alabama and a champion of the farm bloc, fought an unsuccessful but bitter fight against the Underwood candidacy on Underwood's home ground. William Jennings Bryan denounced Underwood for his "anti-progressive" views, even calling him a "tool of Wall Street" and "a New York candidate living in the South." Bryan was especially angered by Underwood's prohibition stand. Senator Joseph T. Robinson of Arkansas and Senator Kenneth D. McKellar of Tennessee flatly asserted that Underwood was "too conservative" to give the voters any real choice. Numerous other southern politicians were also reluctant to come to Underwood's aid, some because of Underwood's beliefs and some because they did not think *any* southerner could win.

Underwood's basic strategy to gain the nomination was simple. He hoped to attract delegates from most of the southern states by being a sectional candidate first. Then he hoped to acquire "second choice" backing in many northern areas by appearing as a pro-business moderate southerner. However, in wooing such diverse support Underwood ran headlong into the Klan. Believing that the Klan was representative of the malaise that had weakened the South since Civil War days, Underwood openly opposed the organization and in one famous speech in Houston in October, 1923, castigated it as thoroughly antidemocratic and illiberal. Klansmen, already attracted to McAdoo and representing those segments of southern society for which Underwood had little appeal anyway, immediately declared war on him. To the Klan he was the "Jew, jug, and Jesuit" candidate.

With McAdoo's emergence as a contender in December, 1923, Underwood had nothing to lose by continuing his battle with the Klan and he did so with relish. He believed that the Klan actually was weak politically and that its support would do a candidate more harm than good in the long run. Hence, on January 22, 1924, in a fiery speech in Cleveland, Underwood announced that he intended to sponsor a platform plank at the party's June convention which would condemn the Klan. He stated that such a resolution would put the Democratic party on record as championing freedom of religion and favoring no religious barriers to officeholding.

Contrary to his hopes, Underwood's bitter opposition to the Klan generally damaged his prospects, and in the face of the McAdoo drive his campaign sagged. It might have collapsed completely had it not been for the Doheny disclosures. Underwood was visibly cheered by McAdoo's misfortune, and his friends gleefully claimed that Doheny's charges now made Underwood "the leading candidate." Admittedly, Underwood's chances temporarily improved. William H. May, secretary of the Underwood national committee, told the *New York Times* in March that the situation was definitely "looking up" and that by convention time Underwood would control the delegations of at least nine southern and border states.

May was dreaming. Although the Teapot Dome investigation wounded McAdoo, it did not make Underwood healthy. In reply to a feeler from Governor Brandon concerning a possible switch in his support to Underwood, Senator Walsh said that he did not believe "the nomination of Senator Underwood would be at all wise." Even within Underwood's own state of Alabama there continued to be opposition. Although Underwood ultimately succeeded in capturing all twenty-four of Alabama's delegates in the state primary, the Klan and dry forces badly battered his reputation. His enemies in the Klan circulated charges that he was actually born in the North, that his ancestors had worn the Union blue (they had fought on both sides), and that he was a Roman Catholic who got his orders from the Pope (he was an Episcopalian). Bryan even entered the state on one occasion to speak against him—an action which infuriated Underwood supporters.

The Underwood candidacy faced its most crucial test in the Georgia primary in late March. The McAdoo forces had selected this same primary as a showcase in McAdoo's attempt to bounce back from the Doheny affair. In this head-to-head encounter, Underwood emphasized his southern background and called upon Georgians to "stay with the South." Before the polls closed McAdoo hurried to the state and made a whirlwind speaking tour through Atlanta, Augusta, Macon, Savannah, and Marietta, his own birthplace. McAdoo also played on his southern genealogy in his speeches and recalled how his great-great-grandfather had held Indians at bay outside of Savannah, just as he was now preparing to defend the entire nation against modern "sinister forces." McAdoo baldly appealed to Georgia state pride and covertly accepted the support of the Georgia Klan. It was a typical McAdoo *tour de force* which Underwood could not match.

McAdoo overwhelmed Underwood with a two-to-one majority and captured the entire Georgia delegation to the national convention. McAdoo followers were "wonderfully cheered" by the result. David Lawrence, a veteran political observer, saw signs that the McAdoo campaign had "taken a new lease on life." However, most pundits agreed that the Georgia victory did not restore McAdoo to his pre–Teapot Dome luster. As for Underwood, friendly Alabama newspapers claimed that Georgia was not really a true test since McAdoo could logically be expected to win in his "native" state. Underwood personally believed that he had been defeated by the Georgia Klan and fastened on McAdoo the label of a Klan-sponsored candidate. Underwood consoled himself that McAdoo's Georgia victory had lost him more votes in the North than he had gained in the South. Still, almost all observers agreed that the Georgia primary had sounded "the death-knell of Underwood's hopes" and that if McAdoo was to be stopped it would not be by the Alabama senator.

4

New York was neither Alabama nor Georgia and had a political milieu that was dependent upon an entirely different set of circumstances. One of the most important factors in that set of circumstances was Charles Francis Murphy, boss of Tammany Hall.

Murphy, one of eight children, was born on June 20, 1858, in a New York City tenement in the so-called Gas House area. Educated in the public schools until age fourteen, Murphy regularly attended mass in the

Catholic church and was at various times a driver of a crosstown Blue Line horsecar, a semi-pro ball player, and an owner of a small saloon at Nineteenth Street and Avenue A. Ultimately Murphy acquired the capital to open three more such bars, all catering to Gas House people—dockworkers, day laborers, and longshoremen.

It was not long before Murphy began to combine his saloon business with politics and rose from being the boss of the Gas House area to being leader of all Tammany. Significantly, at the time Murphy began his rise more than a third of the population of the Gas House district were foreign born, while 44 percent were first-generation Americans. Murphy, therefore, was typical of all Tammany bosses in the late nineteenth century—second-generation Irish who still appealed to recent and new immigrants through ties of language, custom, and religion. Murphy, however, was far more puritanical than the other claimants of Tammany leadership. He side-stepped both crime and blatant political bribery. As a saloon keeper he maintained a rigid code which separated drinking and sociability from gambling and prostitution. Murphy did indulge in "honest graft," but in a way that preserved his sense of morality.

Murphy succeeded Richard Croker as Tammany's leader in 1901. The New York reform Fusion campaign of that year, which swept President Seth Low of Columbia University into the mayor's office, caused Tammany to look for a new leader to replace the graft-ridden Croker. Croker subsequently skipped to England to breed thoroughbred racehorses. Murphy was selected to refurbish Tammany's image, tighten up its internal administration, and bring it respectability.

This Murphy did. Arriving at Tammany Hall every morning around nine dressed in a subdued pin-striped suit, vest, and bow tie, he would hold court at his roll-top desk, tight-lipped and impassive, directing underlings and officeholders at will. Always calm and imperturbable, Murphy presented a solid and even solemn image. He spoke in short, jerky, low sentences, seldom over twelve words long. Yet he exhibited an aura of power, or as one observer put it, "the boys always thought he had something in reserve." Murphy was insatiable for facts and engaged in careful interrogations of all visitors. He was best when the fighting was hardest and he possessed uncanny political foresight. During political campaigns he was "all business."

In his later years Murphy did not keep a rigid working schedule, moving his base of operations to the well-guarded second floor of Delmonico's Restaurant at Fifth and Forty-fourth, where he lunched every day, arriving in his Fiat at a little before noon. Looking by this time like a bespectacled Buddha, Murphy had bought a Long Island estate called "Good Ground" near the lighthouse at Shinnecock Bay, where he played golf and spent his weekends. Murphy had found no time to marry until he was forty-four and then selected a widow his own age who had also been raised in the Gas House district. He had no children of his own but adopted his wife's ten-year-old daughter.

Murphy was the first Tammany boss since Tweed to dominate New York State politics. But, unlike Tweed, he used Tammany as a training ground for respectable men who actually governed the state rather than looted it. Demolishing the Fusion forces in 1903, Murphy held undisputed sway over New York City politics until 1910, when his attention shifted to Albany. From then until his death in 1924, Murphy placed a Tammany-backed man in the governor's chair every election year. As Will Rogers once remarked to Murphy about his local political influence: "The man you run against ain't a candidate, he is just a victim."

Nationally it was a different matter. Since Bryan's day Tammany had been used in every national convention to scare western and southern rural delegates into an anti-eastern coalition. Even ambitious easterners like Cleveland had employed attacks on Tammany to corral western and southern convention votes. Any alliance with Tammany was regarded by most non-easterners as tantamount to being in league with the devil. It was a proven fact that outside of New York it was better to have Tammany as an enemy than as a friend.

During the Progressive era, Boss Murphy had wisely co-opted a few reformers into the ranks of Tammany and by 1912 had even allowed the organization to acquire a slight reformist tinge. But Tammany was not keen on New Jersey's Woodrow Wilson, and at the Baltimore convention in 1912 Murphy held New York in the camp of Champ Clark of Illinois. Bryan, meanwhile, violently anti-Tammany and anti-Murphy, moved southern and western forces to Wilson. Significantly, McAdoo was a renegade member of the New York delegation in 1912, supported Wilson, and even tried to wean the New York delegation from Murphy's control. While McAdoo emerged from the Baltimore convention as one of the top leaders in the ensuing Wilson administration, Murphy and Tammanyites were left to lick their wounds.

Tammany suffered under the Wilson administration. Tammany men were not welcome at the White House nor were their opinions valued. At best, an uneasy truce was maintained between the administration and the leaders in New York. Tammany continued to give lukewarm support to the New Freedom with the understanding that the administration would do nothing to alter the local situation in Empire State politics. However, during the late Wilson years Secretary McAdoo attempted to direct an anti-Tammany anti-Murphy strategy from Washington. With Colonel House he sought to encourage the development of an anti-Tammany faction in New York with the underlying motive of helping his own presidential ambitions. He even tried to gain help from Franklin Roosevelt, currently Assistant Secretary of the Navy, who was anti-Tammany but not particularly anti-Murphy. All such attempts misfired. But the Tammany tiger did not forgive. In 1920 the organization set out to neutralize both Bryan and McAdoo by naming a candidate itself. Its stalking horse was New York Governor Al Smith and, to the tune of "The Sidewalks of New York" (first heard in the 1920 convention and thereafter inextricably connected with the name of Al Smith), Tammanyites enthusiastically shouted and paraded for their candidate even though they knew his cause was hopeless. After forty-three ballots they switched their support from Smith to Cox, who was also opposed to and opposed by Bryan and McAdoo.

Cox was merely a temporary expedient for Tammany. The poor showing of Cox in New York in 1920 indicated that political realities in the Empire State required not only a Democratic presidential candidate who could be supported by Tammany, but one who could identify with Tammany's local concerns. Murphy, therefore, intended to have considerable say about the 1924 nominee.

He began to lay the groundwork as early as 1922 by forming an entente cordiale between himself, George Brennan (Democratic boss of Illinois), and Thomas Taggart (Democratic leader in Indiana). Both Taggart and Brennan were anti-McAdoo. Brennan was an old-time Bryan hater as well. Possessing keen intelligence and a lively wit, and looking the stereotype of the heavy-set, big-city ward heeler, Brennan had fought his way to the top in Illinois politics from the bottom of a coal mine. As a boy he had lost his leg and thereafter sported a wooden one, making his bulk seem all the greater and adding color to his personality. Brennan's rise in Democratic politics had been simultaneous with that of Bryan, whom he regarded as erratic and out of touch with the urban masses. Tom Taggart was an opponent of McAdoo (and, indirectly, of Bryan) more out of necessity than conviction. Taggart had been born in County Monyhan, Ireland, in 1856 and five years later migrated with his parents to Xenia, Ohio. He ultimately became president of the French Lick Springs Hotel in Indiana and was elected mayor of Indianapolis three times after 1895. The recognized Democratic leader in a predominantly Republican state, Taggart perceived that a McAdoo-Bryan victory would cause a shift in control of the Indiana party which would be detrimental to his personal interests.

This triumvirate of bosses first met at Taggart's French Lick hotel in 1922 and agreed to consult regularly thereafter on common candidates and on ways to block the influence of Bryan and McAdoo in the party. By mid-1923 word had leaked out that these men were attempting to form a permanent coalition which would include other bosses such as Michael J. Curley and John F. Fitzgerald of Boston and Frank Hague of Jersey City. The purpose, it was claimed by nervous rural leaders, was to advance the welfare of the urban centers and reduce the influence of southern and western elements in the Democratic party. All this, however, remained in the rumor stage since the bosses refused to talk, especially Murphy, whose secret purpose was to gain support for Al Smith.

5

To everyone Alfred Emanuel Smith was "Al." "Al" was not used in the same way as the affectionate "Teddy" for Theodore Roosevelt, since no one called Roosevelt that to his face. But Smith was hurt if people did not call him "Al." He was always "Al," whether he was in the Fulton Fish Market, the New York State assembly, or the governor's chair.

Smith was born in New York City on the third floor of a three-story wooden tenement on South Street in the Fourth Ward on December 30, 1873. Like his native New York, Smith was an ethnic meld. His immediate ancestry contained German and Italian as well as Irish blood. As a boy Smith swam naked in the East River, witnessed the brawls of drunken sailors along the docks, took walks to the Battery (which was then filled with lilacs), and went to City Hall Park to hear concerts by a brass band. As a boy Smith also watched the Brooklyn Bridge rise majestically above his neighborhood. The New York tower was anchored almost in his backyard and was completed the year he was born. The pounding of the rivets as the rest of the span was being built was a sound familiar to him, and the structure stirred him in a way he later found

difficult to describe. As he once said: "The Bridge and I grew up together."

Middle-class visitors to Smith's neighborhood might have worried
about the effect such an environment would have on a young boy, but for
Smith it provided excellent training. His Lower East Side neighborhood
was respectable although poor. There the local St. James Catholic Church
became the focal point of his adolescent world, and there he played in
amateur theatricals, served as an altar boy, and pumped the organ for the
organist. There he also first came into contact with Tammany's political
influence and met its local lieutenant, black-mustached Tom Foley, who
with a big smile threw pennies to the kids and gave the community one
of its biggest yearly events—Tom Foley's Annual Outing. Few there were
in the Fourth Ward who did not want to be like Foley, or at least wield
his power.

Leaving school in the eighth grade Smith worked in various jobs, such
as assistant bookkeeper at the local Fulton Fish Market, and shipping
clerk for the Dawson Steam Pump Works. Then at age twenty-two he
became a process server for the Commissioner of Jurors. For almost seven
years he held this post, earning no more than $1,000 a year. After acquir-
ing a wife and a family and needing more money, he was about to take
another job when Tom Foley, who was searching for someone to run for
state assembly, asked Smith to make the race. Smith accepted and in
1903, wearing a shiny blue serge suit, he nervously appeared before the
Democratic caucus for its endorsement. Once that was given Al began his
meteoric political rise.

Smith later joked that his alma mater was "FFM" (Fulton Fish Market). Actually it was the New York assembly. Smith once said about the
assembly: "It has been my school and my college; in fact the very
foundation of everything that I have attained was laid there." When first
elected to the assembly, Smith was thirty and had never been out of New
York City. He knew nothing about legislation or the legislature and took
his seat in the last row as a member of the minority. He voted the way
Foley told him to, never spoke on the floor, and occupied his seat for over
three months before he was even introduced to the Speaker. Although
reelected in 1904 and 1905, Smith still remained in the last row and
received no greater recognition than being appointed to the Committee
on Banks and Forests, causing him to remark wryly: "I have never seen a
forest, and I have never been in a bank except to serve a jury notice." All
the while, however, Smith was learning, and in his fourth term he was

appointed to a Special Committee on Revision of the Charter of Greater New York. Through his intimate knowledge of the city, he immediately won the respect of the assembly and finally moved off the last row. For the next eight years he was the assembly's expert on New York City matters.

In an age of progressivism Smith's constant agitation for social and industrial legislation also struck a popular note, and when the Democrats secured a majority, in 1911, Smith at thirty-eight became party floor leader. As floor leader he supported passage of labor codes and worker protection laws and not only bucked Tammany opposition to them but ultimately persuaded Tammany to go along. By now Smith had found the secret of how to be a Tammany-backed regular yet at the same time act independently. This skill caused him to be selected speaker in 1913, and thereafter he bent both Tammany and the legislature toward his views. As speaker he continued to support social, industrial, and labor legislation and in 1915 was one of the sponsors of a constitutional convention to modernize the machinery of New York State government. As one of the delegates to that convention Smith held his own against the best minds New York had to offer, displaying a fantastic knowledge of such intricate matters as the state budget, home rule, and taxation. Although he still retained his East Side accent and indulged in Bowery-style aphorisms, his reasoning was sharp. He once received a standing ovation when he supplied from memory a detailed history of previous legislation on the control of public-service corporations.

The constitutional convention of 1915 so enhanced Smith's popularity that Boss Murphy began to take serious notice. Smith had definitely outgrown the simple ward elections which kept returning him to the state legislature, and Murphy first decided to test Smith's strength in a county-wide election by inviting him to run for sheriff of New York. Two years later Smith became the Tammany-sponsored candidate for president of the New York City Board of Aldermen. After serving only four months of a four-year term in this position, he was nominated by the Democrats for governor of New York. In a close election in which Tammany support spelled the difference, Smith was elected over his Republican opponent.

Nineteen-nineteen found Al Smith in the governor's mansion in Albany, his stiff hair graying at the temples and becoming thin. But his complexion was still as ruddy as when he was a young man and his walk just as spry. Now, however, he dressed more meticulously ("I feel spiffy when I'm dressed just right," he would say) and carried himself with assurance and dignity. He was certainly not the uncouth fishmonger that his enemies often made him out to be.

As governor, Smith sponsored a mild reform program, which included, among other things, compulsory education for children, Americanization of foreigners, aid to adult education, economy in government, woman's suffrage, home rule for cities, and local option for Sunday motion pictures and baseball. Constantly championing the growing demands of the urban masses, Smith also advocated such measures as municipal ownership of traction lines and public utilities, rent controls, low-cost housing, and more stringent maximum-hour legislation. An avid supporter of individual freedom, Smith opposed the expulsion of five Socialists from the New York assembly at the height of the Red Scare in 1920, and vetoed the Lusk legislation which called for teacher loyalty oaths and other anti-civil-liberty procedures.

Although Smith's nomination for the presidency in 1920 was little more than an anti-Bryan, anti-Wilson gesture, the demonstration for him was one of the genuinely enthusiastic events of the San Francisco convention. Even so, he never received more than New York's ninety votes and a scattering from Illinois and Massachusetts. Certainly he was not the national political figure that McAdoo was, and he emerged from the convention without any substantial following. His political star momentarily waned when he lost the 1920 New York gubernatorial race by a narrow margin to Nathan L. Miller. However, considering the magnitude of the Harding landslide in that year and the fact that Smith ran almost a million votes ahead of the national Democratic ticket in the state, his loss was not crippling. In 1922 he returned to defeat Miller handily with a 387,000-vote plurality.

On the very day that Smith was forty-nine years old, December 30, 1922, he was back in Albany, and by virtue of that fact he automatically became a factor in the Democratic presidential picture of 1924. By this time he had proven not only his vote-getting ability, but also his relative independence from direct Tammany control. Yet Smith remained a Tammany man at heart and the machine was prepared to use its full power to help him. Besides, there were a growing number of Tammanyites in 1922 who began to entertain serious thoughts about an Irish Catholic from the New York East Side moving into the White House.

Foremost of these schemers was Charles Murphy. When Smith first met "Silent Charlie," the Tammany boss had just turned fifty, had become a millionaire, and was getting used to gentlemanly living at Good

Ground. Smith liked Murphy and always saw him as a kind of benign big brother who was genuinely interested in promoting legislation for the benefit of little people. Beginning in 1922 Murphy saw Smith as President. Happily, Murphy had always kept Smith from undue embarrassment or involvement because of his Tammany connections. As Franklin Roosevelt once told Frances Perkins, "Murphy always made it a point to keep Al honest. He never let Smith get smeared or tangled up with any of the dirty deals . . . because he thought he was a capable fellow and could go far." Yet the Tammany stigma clung to Al and, outside of New York City itself, it hurt him. Frances Perkins later recalled first meeting Smith in 1910 in Albany and having him introduced to her as "the gentleman from Tammany." Regardless of what Smith or Murphy might do, this label stuck.

In 1923–24 New York was the nation's most populous and richest state. It was always a power in any national convention, controlling by far the largest single bloc of votes. Its governor was perennially a potential national leader, and governors of New York always had their "spyglass trained on Washington." While only Martin Van Buren, Grover Cleveland, and Theodore Roosevelt had been successful in gaining the presidency as New York sons, four others—Samuel J. Tilden, Horatio Seymour, Alton B. Parker, and Charles Evans Hughes—had been nominated only to lose the election.

Smith was no stranger to presidential ambition and honestly admitted that the man who did not have aspirations for that office "would have a dead heart." During 1923 and early 1924, however, he let his friends work for him while he studiously ignored their efforts. Smith was fortunate in having a group of dedicated and loyal advisers surrounding him, the most important being Robert Moses, Joseph M. Proskauer, and Mrs. Belle Moskowitz. Moses was a Phi Beta Kappa graduate of Yale who had gone to Oxford and then returned to Columbia to write a Ph.D. dissertation on the British civil service. He began as a Republican, but had been recruited into the Smith camp and thereafter became an adviser to the governor on a unified plan for parks and state roadways. Proskauer was born in Mobile, Alabama, of Confederate Jewish parents, but was educated in New York. In 1899 he was graduated from Columbia Law School and practiced in the city until Governor Smith appointed him to the New York Supreme Court in 1923. Proskauer managed Smith's gubernatorial campaigns in 1920 and 1922, and Smith relied on him to insert in his speeches "some highbrow college stuff."

Of all Smith's early advisers, the most energetic was Belle Moskowitz. The widow of Charles H. Israels, a New York architect, Mrs. Moskowitz met her second husband, Dr. Henry Moskowitz, in 1912 at the Madison Street Settlement House where both worked for a time. She had broad contacts among university women and the New York reform element in general. She did not meet Smith personally until 1918, but thereafter became the center of a group of intellectuals, including Frances Perkins, who advised him on matters concerning social welfare. Smith, in turn, relied on Mrs. Moskowitz to feed him ideas on a whole variety of subjects. Tammany was always suspicious of her and was nettled by the fact that newspapermen used to quip: "Let's go up and see Belle and see what's on Al's mind today." In any event, Mrs. Moskowitz was one of the prime movers behind the early Smith presidential movement. This Madonna-faced Jewish matron was intrigued by the prospect of a Roman Catholic being President of a Protestant nation.

Though Al Smith possessed many strengths as a potential presidential candidate, he had some weaknesses which Boss Murphy and his close advisers tended to ignore. To the public Smith appeared as a blunt, cocky Irishman with a pugnacious set to his jaw and mannerisms which could be abrasive and offensive. He had a quick temper and often gave in to it; he was intolerant of opposition and very sensitive to slights to his religious and ethnic background. Proskauer claimed that his raucous voice and his famed derby hat were largely theatrical accessories, and that his frequent mispronunciations, such as "foist," for "first," and "orspital," for "hospital," were part of his political technique. But Smith's advisers did not sufficiently realize that though such mannerisms, along with his constant cigar chomping, may have put Smith in tune with the sidewalks of New York, they jarred on Main Street. Moreover, Smith's persistent use of the phrase, "Well, let's look at the record," and his bluntness in charging his opponents with passing out "baloney," repelled as much as they beguiled.

Then too he was intensely parochial. As William Allen White asserted, Al Smith was "city born, city bred, 'city broke,' city-minded, and city hearted." More specifically, he was *New York* born, bred, "broke," and minded. Smith exhibited fully as much insensitivity toward the values and mores of small-town and rural America as many of his detractors from these areas did toward his New York urban background. As for his pride in New York City, it bordered on idolatry. Smith once said, "I'd rather be a lamppost on Park Row than Governor of California." Such narrowness affected Al in many ways, not the least of which was his inability to speak knowledgeably on a number of national problems. On matters concerning public health, maternity insurance, workmen's compensation, and child labor (none of which had much appeal for the rural and non-urban members of the Democratic party), Smith was at home. But on the soldiers' bonus, the Fordney-McCumber tariff, the Mellon tax policies, and farm relief, Al was at sea.

Far more debilitating were Smith's religion and his stand on prohibition. Belle Moskowitz saw Smith's Catholicism as the only real barrier to his candidacy and anguished over it. It worried Charles Murphy too, but he was anxious to take the gamble. Most eastern observers agreed that Smith's religion presented a serious hurdle. Mark Sullivan went so far as to tell his readers in *World's Work* in late 1923 that if Smith were not a Catholic, "it would be universally recognized that Smith would be the Democratic nominee."

Prohibition was an even more serious matter. The Eighteenth Amendment had been ratified by New York in 1919. A year later the assembly had passed a bill permitting wine and beer of not more than 2.75 percent alcohol to be made and sold in the state. As governor at the time, Smith had approved this bill, but it was immediately declared unconstitutional by the Supreme Court as being contrary to the Volstead Act, which had set the national alcoholic limits at one-half of one percent. Subsequently, in 1921, a Republican-dominated assembly enacted the so-called Mullan-Gage Bill, which was simply a state version of the national Volstead Act. Angered by this action, moderate wets in New York forced the Democratic state convention in 1922 to insert in its platform a plank favoring a national amendment to the Volstead Act which would permit light wines and beer. At the same time these wets also mounted an attack on the Mullan-Gage Law and by 1923 succeeded in getting the assembly to pass a repeal bill.

Governor Smith was placed under heavy wet pressure to sign the Mullan-Gage repealer. Drys clamored for a gubernatorial veto. Smith was not a prohibitionist. He drank and, according to some observers, drank rather heavily; Oswald G. Villard claimed that he had as many as four to eight highballs a day. Whatever his liquor consumption, Al was no hypocrite. He was a wet and admitted it. Yet there were serious political consequences to any action he might take on the repeal bill. Franklin Roosevelt, representing upstate opinion, advocated a veto on the ground that the state was morally obligated to support federal enforcement. Besides, Roosevelt believed that Smith would materially lessen his chances for the 1924 Democratic nomination if he did not veto it. Other Smith friends counseled the same. But Charles Murphy advocated signing the repealer, claiming the issue of prohibition might as well be faced now and that sentiment in the Empire State was clearly against it.

Smith finally signed the repeal bill, laboriously working over his message and emphasizing the fact that prohibition enforcement was a federal problem, not a state one. The federal constitution, he claimed, did not place an obligation on any state to enforce any of its amendments unless it specifically said so. The Eighteenth Amendment, noted Smith, contained no such provision. Thus, he sought to duck the moral aspects of the prohibition question and base his action solely on its constitutionality. Nonetheless, the moment that Smith affixed his signature to the Mullan-Gage repealer, he became the recognized leader of all the anti-prohibition forces in the nation. At the same time he became the drys' chief *bête noire*. The Anti-Saloon League immediately called for his impeachment, and the high priest of prohibition, William Jennings Bryan, denounced him by saying: "Governor Smith has simply dishonored his office and disgraced himself; he cannot lead the nation back to wallow in the mire."

The Mullan-Gage controversy placed a temporary blight on the budding Smith candidacy and caused even his most enthusiastic advisers to have second thoughts. Indeed, the Smith movement faltered noticeably in late 1923 and early 1924 as the McAdoo bandwagon picked up speed. Then came the Doheny testimony. Immediately the Smith camp took heart. "There ain't no oil on Al" was a phrase so frequently heard that it quickly became a slogan. Smith's supporters gloated over McAdoo's misfortune. On February 4, 1924, just three days after Doheny first uttered McAdoo's name, a Smith-for-President club was opened in New York's McAlpin Hotel. When told of this in Albany, Smith said, "I don't know a thing about it," but admitted that there were "a lot of people who are enthusiastic for my nomination." On February 5, the odds on Smith's chances, which prior to the Doheny disclosures were not even quoted by New York bookies, were listed, although at a prohibitive 15 to 1.

Smith's advisers, meanwhile, experienced a resurgent zeal. Moves were now initiated for support outside of New York. Proskauer urged closer alliances with the New England area. Feelers were put out into the industrialized states of the Midwest. Norman E. Mack, a Buffalo editor and New York national committeeman, offered himself as a liaison man with the Brennan organization in Illinois. By mid-April pro-Smith enthusiasm in New York was running so high that the Democratic state convention in Albany endorsed Smith by acclamation as the Empire State's favorite son. Boss Murphy was there, of course, smiling, shaking hands, and moving ubiquitously among the delegates, assuring everyone that Smith would be the national convention's eventual nominee. In accepting the New York endorsement, Smith spoke briefly and was frequently interrupted by wild cheering and Tammany war whoops. Four days later, on April 19, when Al appeared with his wife and three of their children at John Ringling's circus in Madison Square Garden, the crowd gave him a standing ovation and hailed him as "the next President." Reporters saw great significance in the fact that Smith took particular delight in feeding peanuts to the elephants.

Murphy was naturally pleased by this turn of events and became all the more convinced that in Smith Tammany had a presidential winner. Still, he felt no need for haste. Smith was relatively young and could, if necessary, wait another four or even eight years. For the moment Murphy was mainly interested in keeping Al's name before the public and maintaining him in an advantageous position for whatever might develop. The next meeting of Democratic bosses scheduled for French Lick, Indiana, was now only a few weeks away, and Murphy intended to present Smith's case there, hoping first to gain George Brennan's and Tom Taggart's support and then eventually win over others. His desire was to weld together an urban-eastern-Chicago bloc that could control at least one-third of the national convention. Smith would be their candidate and with luck might emerge the nominee.

These plans were still locked in Murphy's mind when the late-afternoon New York papers on April 25 greeted their readers with huge pictures of the rotund face of Tammany's Grand Sachem, announcing that he was dead. Early that morning in his midtown home on East Seventeenth Street, the sixty-five-year-old Murphy had awakened with acute indigestion and had called his doctor. When the latter arrived he found the Tammany chief lying on the bathroom floor in agony. Failing to respond to any sort of treatment, Murphy died at 9:05 A.M. His last words to the doctor were, "Don't tell the Mrs. I was so sick." At the moment Mrs. Murphy was in Atlantic City and the news of her husband's illness was phoned to her. Returning immediately to New York, she was not told that he had died until she reached the front door to their home, whereupon she collapsed.

Al Smith met the news of Murphy's death with deep emotion. Notified of it at his desk in Albany, he at first refused to believe it and called Murphy's New York home himself. When the news was confirmed tears streamed down his face and his only comment to reporters was "Isn't it awful!" Three days later, still shaken and distraught, Smith was among the chief mourners at Murphy's funeral. Fifty thousand New Yorkers lined the streets for the event, paying homage to a man who had never held a single elective office. Six thousand filled St. Patrick's Cathedral for the final mass. Every important Democratic boss was there, including Brennan and some fifty Democrats from Chicago. At Calvary cemetery the flowers and wreaths formed a hedge six feet high. Among the pall-bearers was Governor Smith. There was not a sadder one.

Murphy's sudden death sent shock waves through New York politics. Tammany never recovered. The organization could not even agree on a successor until later in the year. By then it was clear that no one could actually replace Murphy. As Arthur Krock correctly said, when Murphy died "the brains went out of Tammany Hall." As for the Smith candidacy, there was general consensus that it had been dealt a severe blow. With Murphy, Smith's chances were held to be slim. Without him, they were considered nil. There were a few who saw advantages in Murphy's death for Smith. He now was the undisputed leader of the New York Democratic party and could dance to his own tune. No longer, it was said, would he appear to be a creature of Tammany, and there was a greater possibility that the true character of his candidacy could "be seen more clearly by delegates from the West and South." Belle Moskowitz, whose contempt for Tammany was well known, believed that Murphy's demise was "the best thing that could have happened for the Governor" because it now forced him to conduct his own fight.

But even those who saw advantages in the situation for Smith admitted that Murphy's political skill and shrewdness would be missed. Some observers later claimed that if Murphy had lived the Democratic convention of 1924 would have been better managed and much of its difficulties would have been avoided. In any event, Murphy's death not only removed a clever tactician from the Smith camp, but it also severed a critical bond with other urban boss-controlled organizations. At the time of his death Murphy was just beginning to pressure not only Brennan and Taggart but Cox (Ohio), James M. Guffey (Pennsylvania), George S. Silzer (New Jersey), and Albert C. Ritchie (Maryland) to support Smith. Now several of these men, especially Silzer and Ritchie, began to think of themselves as possible candidates. Even the Brennan-Taggart alliance showed signs of coming apart. Taggart began to take a greater interest in Senator Ralston from his own state and adopted a more cautious attitude toward the Smith candidacy. Only Brennan remained fully committed. The Illinois boss was seen talking earnestly with Smith on several occasions at Murphy's funeral, and it was assumed that if there was to be a successor to Murphy in the Smith campaign it would probably be Brennan.

What was critically needed, however, was someone to head up the Smith drive who could give it better balance and a broader appeal. Brennan certainly could not do it; neither could any other "boss." The selection finally devolved upon Franklin Roosevelt, who had been sidelined from politics since 1921 because of his polio attack. Prodded by his wizened and asthmatic private secretary, Louis Howe, to move back into the political arena, by 1924 Roosevelt had recovered his health enough to think again of his own political future. As an upstate New Yorker, he had usually identified with rural interests and had been anti-Tammany. In 1920, even though he had given a seconding speech for Smith as President, Roosevelt had voted for McAdoo on some of the ballots. But Smith's overwhelming gubernatorial victory in 1922 caused Roosevelt to reevaluate the situation, and when the Doheny disclosures spattered McAdoo with oil, Roosevelt moved in Smith's direction. Only Smith's "wringing wet" stance on the Mullan-Gage repeal bill gave Roosevelt reason for doubt.

In 1924 Roosevelt finally came out for the New York governor as a way of regaining some of his own former national visibility. Thus, the Smith-Roosevelt arrangement was not a one-way street. Early in the spring of 1924 Boss Murphy had traveled to Hyde Park to ask Roosevelt if he would undertake to round up some delegates for Al through his association with "the federal end of things." Both Smith and Murphy already realized that Roosevelt would make a formidable ally because of his previous connections with the Wilsonians in the party. Roosevelt agreed and, although he did not believe that Smith had a chance for 1924, thought that "we might be able to get him the nomination in 1928." Louis Howe remained discreetly silent about the latter date, because he secretly hoped that by that time Roosevelt himself might be ready to take the plunge.

With Murphy's death Smith's need of Roosevelt markedly increased, and with shrewd insight Smith named him to run his national campaign. Anti-Tammany, politically (although not personally) dry, and a Protes-

tant, Roosevelt was the perfect choice. At first Roosevelt feigned a reluctance to accept, causing Smith to make a personal pilgrimage to Roosevelt's New York City home on East Sixty-fifth Street to extract from him
at least the promise to think about it. Roosevelt agreed to consider it. A
day later Roosevelt phoned Smith his acceptance. When the appointment
was announced on May 1, 1924, Roosevelt's official title was given as
Chairman of the New York State Committee for the Nomination of Alfred
E. Smith for President.

Although Roosevelt was placed in nominal charge, the basic work of
the Smith drive was still handled by Moskowitz, Moses, and Proskauer,
while the chief lieutenants in the field were Brennan, Norman Mack, and
James J. Hoey (vice-chairman of the Smith-for-President committee).
Bankrolling the Smith campaign were such men as Robert E. Dowling
($6,000), James W. Gerard ($10,000), and Martin T. Manton ($2,500).
During the pre-convention period Roosevelt remained mainly a figurehead and was important more for propagandistic purposes than for setting strategy or lining up delegates. Unquestionably, his anti-Tammany
reputation helped defuse some of the animosity toward Smith. Conversely, New York Catholic Democrats, who heretofore had been suspicious of the Episcopalian country squire from Hyde Park, now began to
warm to Roosevelt. Sometimes Roosevelt's publicity endeavors for Smith
redounded so much to his own advantage that it produced jealousy and
friction with such Smith partisans as Proskauer and Moskowitz. With
Howe keeping a watchful eye on Roosevelt's own career, the Roosevelt
office handled a mountain of correspondence and issued daily press releases on Smith's behalf, all of which emphasized that the New York
governor was aware of the problems confronting a modern industrial
society and was the only candidate who could solve them.

The general strategy of the Smith forces was simple. As Roosevelt
wrote to a friend in early June, 1924, McAdoo "would not make any kind
of a run in the East or the Middle West, and we want somebody who can
win in November. That's where Smith's strength lies. He can carry almost
all the East and a good part of the Middle West, and even the Far West."
Smith's advisers realized that the first requisite was to keep Smith's home
base of New York covered, and to this end they carefully scrutinized
every member of the New York delegation. Next, an all-star group of
New York Democrats was enlisted in the work of the Smith committee—
men such as Mayor John F. Hylan (New York City), Mayor William S.
Hackett (Albany), and Mayor John H. Walrath (Syracuse). At the same

time a first edition of 25,000 copies of a pamphlet entitled *What Every-body Wants to Know About Alfred E. Smith* came off the press in early May and was sent to all convention delegates from the East.

As a corollary to the above actions, Roosevelt announced that Smith would make "no deals," would enter no primaries, and would fight no favorite sons. Smith's advisers, particularly Proskauer and Moskowitz, realized that he had officially entered the campaign too late to make a serious effort for delegates elsewhere, and therefore they made a virtue out of a weakness. Besides, by observing McAdoo they perceived that strong-arming favorite sons was a risky business which Smith could not afford. Smith's support at the convention, said Roosevelt, would be spontaneous, and to encourage it he manufactured glowing accounts of pro-Smith sentiment in all parts of the country. Such claims were avidly reported in the New York press. Indeed, in mid-May the New York *Tribune* headlined a Roosevelt assertion that Smith was "leading all his rivals" and had emerged as "the leading candidate" for the Democratic nomination.

This was nonsense. Roosevelt, Proskauer, and Moskowitz had already learned that selling Smith outside of the Northeast and certain sections of the Middle West was extremely difficult. To remove some of this difficulty Roosevelt had tried to play down Smith's Catholicism and his anti-prohibition stand, and had cautioned all Smith supporters against stirring animosities on either of these matters. Roosevelt knew that Smith's prohibition views were far too strong for nationwide appeal. As for Smith's Catholicism, Roosevelt's files soon bulged with letters warning him of disaster.

In neither of these respects did Smith help much. On the liquor question Al did attempt to soften his earlier Mullan-Gage position by stating: "No matter what we think of the Volstead Law, it is the law of the land and we must support it." Even the New York press saw through this charade and commented: "It is pretty late in the day for Governor Smith to try to redeem his reputation as an anti-Prohibitionist." As for the religious question, Al, backed by Proskauer and Moskowitz and contrary to Roosevelt's advice, saw no reason to dodge it. Smith was not worried by the warnings or the Klan-inspired anti-Catholic letters being received. He could not believe that such views were held by many Americans and took pains to answer some of these correspondents in his own hand, pointing out their prejudice. Prior to June, 1924, it did not occur to Al that local religious beliefs were as compelling a factor in influencing politics in Iowa or in Texas as they were in influencing the political actions of his followers in Tammany Hall.

Events soon showed Smith otherwise. By mid-May Norman Mack, who had been given the assignment of divining political sentiment in the South, found no Smith support whatever. Brennan, meanwhile, was meeting with little success outside of northern Illinois and northern Indiana. Except for the populous areas in Ohio and Michigan, the outlook in the Midwest was bleak. Letters to Smith headquarters revealed that he could not carry a single southern state and most western states were doubtful. One sample letter advised Smith "to let Texas alone as this State is full of the Ku Klux Klan." If the Smith forces wanted to do something, said this writer, "help Underwood. . . . He is the only one who has a chance to beat McAdoo."

At this stage of his campaign Smith's problems were not only his wetness and his religion but also his obvious parochialism. In typical Tammany fashion Smith knew intimately what was occurring in New York; yet he remained generally oblivious of conditions elsewhere. He had not developed a national approach. Roosevelt tried to help him but even Roosevelt was stymied because at the moment there was no unity among Democrats on major national issues. Smith remained ambiguous on the League, he was unclear about taxes, he was not sure about the tariff, and he drew a blank on farm problems. Roosevelt once urged Smith to "read up" on agricultural affairs, but Smith took no interest in them. The result was that the South, the Midwest, and the Middle Border states could not work up any positive enthusiasm for him, quite apart from his religion or his views on prohibition. By the summer of 1924, Governor Smith had come a long way since his Lower East Side days, but he still was a local candidate.

6

Democratic party confusion, along with the faltering McAdoo drive, not only caused a flurry of activity in the camp of Oscar Underwood and Al Smith, but also encouraged others to enter the race. By convention time there was hardly a state that did not have a favorite son to present to the nation. Most of these were not really serious contenders but they provided the means whereby a state delegation could go to the convention, vote for their favorite son on the early ballots, and await future developments. All favorite sons, of course, hoped the lightning would strike and tried to hold on to their delegations' support as long as possible. Among this group were Governor Cox of Ohio, who already was a proven loser; Governor Jonathan M. Davis of Kansas, whose heart was said to "beat for the masses"; Governor Silzer of New Jersey, who hoped to make the nation as wet as the Atlantic Ocean; and Governor Albert Ritchie of Maryland, whose manner was so formal that no one ever called him "Al."

More serious were the claims of other favorite sons, who not only were supported by their own states, but who attracted some modest support outside—Carter Glass (Virginia), Samuel Ralston (Indiana), Charles W. Bryan (Nebraska), and John W. Davis (West Virginia). Glass was the senior statesman of the group. He was a little man physically, with flaming red hair, a big nose, conspicuous pouches beneath his eyes, and possessed all those idiosyncrasies that endear certain politicians to cartoonists. It was claimed that mounted on stilts he could walk under the dresser to find a collar button. If he were President, one wit said, trundle beds would have to be installed in the White House. Glass had a trick of talking with his lower lip curled down so far that it dragged the rest of his face to one side. One old classmate once commented that he was the only man in the world who could whisper in his own ear. An easy butt for jokes though he was, Carter Glass was foremost a shrewd politician. Except for the brief year that he had served as successor to McAdoo as Secretary of the Treasury, he had held elective office since the turn of the century. In Congress he had specialized in currency and banking and successfully shepherded the Federal Reserve Act through that body. By 1920 Senator Glass was widely respected and was considered a formidable opponent even though he never uttered anything stronger than "Dad bum it!"

In 1924 Glass, who was an ardent Methodist and dry, became Virginia's favorite son. Although Glass differed with McAdoo on the League and on the soldiers' bonus, he had vigorously backed the Californian until the Doheny disclosures, but thereafter he was badgered by friends to make the race himself. Possessing impeccable "progressive" credentials, Glass was loath to wage a pre-convention fight and did not seek committed delegates. Even by convention time he retained a personal inclination toward McAdoo and discouraged active campaigning on his own behalf. Nevertheless, his entry into the presidential sweepstakes was a decided disadvantage for the McAdoo forces, especially since the Virginia State Democratic Convention ordered its delegation early in June to support Glass "as long as his name is before the Democratic Convention."

Samuel Ralston, another of the important dark-horse favorites, was a former governor of Indiana and also a senator. Ralston looked like Grover Cleveland, weighed over three hundred pounds, was sixty-six years old, and was not in good health. He had achieved national notoriety by defeating Republican Senator Albert Beveridge in the congressional elections of 1922. Before that, his record as governor of the Hoosier state had been excellent, not too radical to displease conservatives and not too conservative to offend liberals. The only blemish on his career was his relationship with the Indiana Klan. In a Klan-inspired fight over parochial schools, Ralston as governor had appeared to be sympathetic to the Klan's position and thereafter the Klan had embraced him. This was certainly no drawback in Hoosier politics, but it caused him embarrassment on the national level and prompted the eastern press to designate him, along with McAdoo, as "a Klan candidate."

Ralston's principles were basically Clevelandesque. A "middle-of-the-road" Democrat, Ralston opposed extremes in both the social and economic realms. He rejected either corporation rule or dictation by organized labor. A supporter of the League of Nations, he also backed the Eighteenth Amendment and was himself personally, although not militantly, dry. Ralston came of midwestern Scotch-Irish stock and, because he had been raised on a farm, knew of the farmers' problems firsthand. But he had also risen to be head of the Indiana bar and knew something about the business world as well. Ralston had very few enemies.

Because of Ralston's late induction into national politics, most observers dismissed him as a "blank page." But Boss Taggart did not think so, and when the French Lick coalition began to disintegrate after Murphy's death, Taggart seized upon Ralston as a presidential possibility. Actually, the Ralston candidacy got underway in late March, even before Murphy's demise, when Taggart indicated that he might eventually turn to the Hoosier senator if it became clear that neither McAdoo nor Smith could make it. Murphy's death reinforced Taggart's doubts about Smith and by May he was openly supporting Ralston. Taggart's reasoning was simple. He did not believe that any of the other candidates could win because they were either too conservative, too radical, southern, or wet. This left Ralston. Moreover, Taggart had faith in his own ability to control a last-minute situation. In 1912, his move in throwing the Indiana delegation to Wilson at the right moment had helped Wilson gain the nomination and gave Taggart the opportunity to place Indiana's favorite son, Thomas R. Marshall, in the vice-presidency. This time Taggart believed that he could dictate the top slot.

By far the most colorful and controversial of the favorite sons was Charles Wayland Bryan, younger brother of William Jennings Bryan. Aside from their bald pates, which they covered with black skullcaps to ward off the light, there was little physical resemblance between them. Charles, whom William referred to as "Brother Charley," was six feet one. William Jennings, whom Charley called "Double-ya Jay," was five feet ten. Unlike W. J., who was deliberate and smooth, Charley was quick in movement and rapid in speech. His staccato speaking style was accompanied by short, sharp gestures and did not in any way rival his older brother's magnetic, soaring, melodious oratory. Nor did Charley ever seek to charm his enemies. Instead, C. W. Bryan was intensely combative. Given his feisty personality, Charley's scraggly mustache and his oval rimless glasses seemed out of character. As for the black skullcap, one observer commented that it "seems about as appropriate as a monocle on a wildcat."

Born seven years after his older brother, Charles Bryan had followed W. J. to Nebraska from their birthplace in Illinois and worked at various jobs in Lincoln until W. J. tapped him to be manager of his weekly, *The Commoner*, in 1900. For the next fifteen years Charles devoted himself to this task, building circulation to a remarkable 275,000. Then, in 1915, he was elected mayor of Lincoln and in 1922 became governor of Nebraska. As governor, Bryan proved to be a bitter partisan, constantly castigating the Republican legislature which the voters had quixotically given him. It was claimed that when it rained Charley Bryan took the credit, and that he blamed all droughts on the legislature. To Bryan even a minor skirmish was an Armageddon where no neutrals were allowed. While governor he fought for cheaper gas, ice, coal, and gasoline and achieved a modest reduction in taxes. Talk, however, was Charles Bryan's main occupation, and throughout his term he commented on or about anything to anybody. The story was told about an Omaha follower who once telephoned Charley but was bankrupted by the toll charges before he could get the conversation stopped. In any case, Bryan acquired the reputation of being a "do something" governor. As one observer explained the favorable reaction of Nebraska voters to him: "The state's ears are afflicted, but its pocketbook is spared, and it cares more for its pocketbook than for its ears."

In the East Charles Bryan's candidacy was treated as a joke. It was assumed that the younger Bryan was merely a stand-in for his brother and that the two of them would declare for McAdoo at the proper time. Charles Bryan's favorite-son status, however, was as much his own idea as that of his brother and betrayed the conflicting cross-currents in western politics. As the Bryan candidacy indicated, by the spring of 1924 McAdoo had not yet completely conquered western Democracy, and even without the oil scandal he would have faced opposition in some of the farm states.

Of all the favorite sons, the most potentially formidable was John W. Davis. Davis was the Charles Evans Hughes of the Democratic party, without whiskers. As with Hughes, Davis's bearing was distinguished. He possessed an open Scotch face, his eyes were frank and steady, his facial lines sharply chiseled, and his high forehead punctuated by arched eyebrows. His most distinctive feature was his protruding and resolute jaw, which gave him a commanding look. Davis was somewhat of a paradox. Except for Underwood or McAdoo, Davis was known to more public men than any of the other candidates. Yet he was much less known to the general public. The story made the rounds that when one New Yorker first heard his name mentioned he exclaimed: "Davis? Jeff Davis is dead."

John William Davis was born in 1873 in a modest frame house on Mechanic Street in Clarksburg, West Virginia. Like Thomas Jefferson, he entered the world on April 13 and, like Jefferson, he came from Virginia and Maryland frontier forebears of Anglo-Celtic ancestry. Davis's mother, a Kennedy of Maryland, was a cultured woman who allegedly interrupted her reading of the last volume of Gibbon's *The Decline and Fall of the Roman Empire* to give birth to her son. A strong advocate of women's rights and of prohibition, Mrs. Davis possessed a BA degree from the Baltimore College for Women at a time when not one woman in a thousand could boast such training. Fluent in French and German, she also possessed a scholarly knowledge of Latin and Greek. In her declining years she took up Hebrew as an aid to Biblical exegesis. She passed this interest in learning on to her children, inspiring them so much at home that the public schools could not contain them. As one of her daughters later said, "We cannot remember when we could not read." Young John, for instance, matriculated at Washington and Lee University in Lexington at age sixteen and was admitted as a sophomore.

Davis's father, John J. Davis, had also been born in Clarksburg, before the Civil War when West Virginia was still a part of Virginia. John J. was a forbidding man, stern, a Presbyterian covenanter, who stood six feet two and possessed a beard which turned white and reached to his chest as he grew older. When attired in a long black coat and a gray hat, he was an imposing figure. Around Clarksburg he was referred to as "the old Jeffersonian." One of the best lawyers in town, John J. had been a Unionist member of the Virginia legislature when war broke out and then became a leader in the secessionist movement that created West Virginia. Thereafter he was twice elected to the U.S. House of Representatives and was an aggressive anti-Reconstruction Democrat. He violently opposed the Fourteenth and Fifteenth amendments, was a free trader at heart, and in the closing years of the century switched his allegiance from Grover Cleveland to William Jennings Bryan.

Graduating from Washington and Lee Law School, John W. Davis ultimately was enticed from a law partnership with his father into state politics and in 1910 was elected as a U.S. representative like his father before him. He immediately became part of the liberal Democratic majority which controlled the Congress during the early Wilson years and wrote the New Freedom program into law. As a member of the House Judiciary Committee, he helped draft the Clayton Antitrust Act, including the pro-labor anti-injunction section of that measure.

But Davis was never really happy as a legislator and threatened to return to his law practice in Clarksburg. Because of his reputation as a progressive, the Wilson administration was loath to see him leave Washington and in mid-1913 appointed him Solicitor General. During the next five years he argued sixty-seven major cases before the Supreme Court. As a result of this work he became one of the leading candidates for a post on the Supreme Court, a position he very much coveted. But fate forestalled that possibility. In 1918 President Wilson sent Davis to Switzerland to serve as High Commissioner for the exchange of war prisoners with Germany. While Davis was there, Walter Hines Page asked to be relieved of his post as ambassador to Great Britain and, at the urging of Secretary of State Robert Lansing, Wilson offered the position to Davis. At first Davis balked because of the financial burden of being an ambassador, but he finally accepted. He returned to the United States in March, 1921, almost penniless.

He had made a superb ambassador. The British liked and respected him. When Davis left Southampton for the United States, forty British destroyers accompanied his ship down the channel as a mark of British esteem. Upon his departure the London *Times* remarked, "Englishmen love him because his head is right and his heart is right. . . . It is of such stuff that Presidents should be made." But money, not the presidency, was on Davis's mind as he arrived home, and when an offer came to join the prestigious New York law firm of Stetson, Jennings, and Russell (the firm to which Grover Cleveland once belonged), he quickly accepted. He subsequently founded his own law practice (Davis, Polk, Wardwell, Gardiner, and Reed), and became counsel for such businesses as American Telephone and Telegraph, Standard Oil of New Jersey, and J. P. Morgan and Company. All this rapidly permitted him to enter the world of eastern wealth. Ultimately he acquired a four-acre estate on Long Island, a town house in New York City, and a driveway filled with two Fords, a Buick, and a Packard limousine. In 1922, when he was only forty-nine, he was elected as one of the youngest presidents in the history of the American Bar Association.

It was natural that Davis's home state of West Virginia should be proud of him. As early as 1920 she had supported him as her favorite son, but few others had come to his banner, and at the San Francisco convention he never received more than a scattering of votes. Nevertheless, after the convention the Davis-for-President clubs in West Virginia disbanded only temporarily, and they were quickly reactivated in late 1923. Tirelessly promoting Davis's cause was a group of his friends led by Clement L. Shaver, Democratic boss of Marion County and leader of the so-called northern wing of the party in West Virginia. Although Shaver faced some local coolness toward Davis because Davis had settled in New York rather than returning to Clarksburg after leaving England, he neutralized it by appealing to state pride and by pointing to Davis's outstanding public record. Shaver also outflanked some pro-McAdoo sentiment in the Mountaineer State by reminding West Virginians that McAdoo, too, had once lived and worked in New York City.

Davis was not a party to his friends' actions, and once when he was in Clarksburg he protested to Shaver. "This is our affair," Shaver told him curtly, and added, "You are not responsible for what your fool friends do." After the Doheny testimony in February, such friends redoubled their efforts and not only expanded their local Davis-for-President clubs but seeded some outside the state. Davis, meanwhile, recognized the developing confusion in the Democratic party and kept his options open. As he wrote to a minister friend in mid-February: "I am being considerably bedevilled just now on the political side. I begin to think that possibly I may be called upon."

By the spring of 1924 there was a growing clutch of Davis supporters both inside and outside West Virginia who believed that he might be the party's best choice. From the beginning the *New York Times* championed Davis, greeting his endorsement by the West Virginia Democratic state executive committee in January with the statement: "What American would not think it exhilarating to have such a man as John W. Davis made a candidate for the Presidency?" Colonel House, who by April despaired of McAdoo's success, began to move toward Davis, claiming that even the businessmen of the country might desert the Republicans to vote for him. Frank Polk and Robert Lansing, both State Department colleagues of Davis during the Wilson years, urged his nomination.

Such endorsements, however, underscored one of the chief weaknesses of the Davis candidacy. He was known to the readership of the *New York Times;* he was known to the inhabitants of Wall Street; he was known to West Virginia folks and to his former Wilsonian friends. But his face was not well known to the American public, and his name was anything but a household word. Besides, his Wall Street connections and his big legal fees, some allegedly as high as $350,000, did not help him. If McAdoo was suspect because of Doheny, what about Davis and J. P. Morgan? Davis met all such criticism with the blunt statement that a lawyer's clients were his own business; he would not forsake any client to suit the "gust of popular opinion." That his avid pursuit of a lucrative career worked to his disadvantage apparently did not bother Davis at all. To those who wanted to push him more aggressively, he replied as late as April that he was not an active candidate and stated that "any decision to the contrary must come from the party and not from myself." As for a favorable party decision, Davis said that he would not decline the nomination if it was offered, but that he would not seek it either. With characteristic blandness he explained his final position: "If Fate is headed for me, I must stand in the middle of the road and see whether she comes on or whether she doesn't."

7

Neutrality in political matters and reliance on fate were never hallmarks of the career of William Jennings Bryan. For almost thirty years he had been at or near the center of American politics. Although the White House had eluded him, he had thrice been the Democratic party's nominee for the presidency. Even when he had not been the candidate himself, he had played a major role in the selection of those who had made the race.

But by 1924 Bryan was disgusted with the Democrats. Not only was his own political power within the party waning, but he believed that the organization was moving away from those principles that had made it great. He was particularly upset by the emerging influence of the urban bloc, whose goals he could not support. The defeat of his "bone dry" plank in 1920 and Governor Cox's nomination at the San Francisco convention had represented more than mere setbacks for Bryan. After that convention he lost some of his enthusiasm for politicking and concentrated instead on his religious activities. This "laboring for the Lord" focused Bryan's attention increasingly on moral issues. But for Bryan all issues, including moral issues, ultimately became political ones. After 1920 he simply increased the frequency with which he used religious rhetoric to support his particular political beliefs. Under such circumstances compromise with his political opponents became less and less possible. More fervently than ever he embraced Biblical passages, literally applied, as his guide for political conduct, thereby causing many of his detractors, especially in the East, to regard him as a case for a psychoanalyst rather than as an inspired leader in the field of either religion or politics.

Bryan reentered the political arena in the congressional elections of 1922 by energetically stumping for "progressive" Democratic candidates. Blending politics with fundamentalist and prohibitionist pronouncements, he thundered through the farm country in his alpaca coat and his wide-brimmed hat, calling for the election of "the right kind of Democratic leaders." As for himself, he declared, "I am not out of politics," causing many political pundits to scurry to their typewriters to warn the American people that Bryan might again run for President. At the moment Bryan's aims were less personal and more general, and he greeted the results of the 1922 elections with joy. It showed, he said, that the nation was returning to "traditional Democratic principles."

From 1922 to 1924 Bryan was never off the stump. He always emphasized three themes: the need for rural reform, the need to curb Wall Street, and the need to enforce the Volstead Act. Bryan ignored the rising Klan. He opposed fighting fire with fire; the organization, he said, would go away if left alone. Bryan refused to believe that the Klan might split the Democratic party, admitting only that it might have "some influence" on the next election. Such views were exactly what many in the agrarian West and South wanted to hear. More than McAdoo, Bryan was still their moral and spiritual champion, and throughout 1923–24 thousands in those areas took scratchy pens or broken pencils in hand to pour out their fears and frustrations to the Great Commoner. Their plea to him was always the same: defend prohibition, spread the fundamentalist "word," and protect the farmer against the evil machinations of the East.

The Harding scandals not only reinforced Bryan's disdain for Republican pro-business policies, but they also encouraged him to become cautious in giving his personal endorsement to any particular Democratic presidential candidate. McAdoo should have been Bryan's choice. But, even before the Doheny disclosures, Bryan had been noncommittal on McAdoo. This added fuel to the speculation that Bryan himself wanted to be the nominee. As Bryan saw it, no Democratic victory was possible in 1924 without the West, and certainly none was likely without the West *and* the South. Bryan was convinced that no Democrat could carry the eastern states against the Republicans; therefore the East should be abandoned. Further, no "conservative" or "middle-of-the-roader" could appeal to the West and South. Only a bona-fide dry, anti–Wall Street "progressive" could do that. "No wet and no reactionary will have a chance," he once remarked; "at all costs" a wet plank had to be kept out of the Democratic party's platform.

For all these reasons, no candidate mentioned by the time of the Doheny testimony really suited Bryan. McAdoo had "distinct possibilities," but his New York connections and his backing by Chadbourne and Baruch made him suspect. None of the eastern governors was acceptable, and all of the midwestern ones (except for Brother Charley, whom Bryan did not think had a chance) possessed drawbacks. Davis had the "Morgan taint," which, said Bryan, "sufficiently describes his connections and his political views." Glass was too "non-assertive" to be a good candidate. Underwood, Bryan believed, would ultimately drop out and support Smith. Besides, Underwood was wet.

Of all the candidates Al Smith was Bryan's major worry. His verdict on the New York governor was direct and simple: "Smith is, of course, out of the question." Yet it is interesting that in 1924 both of these men were champions of political protest—Bryan representing the overmortgaged, beleaguered rural area; Smith the underpaid, discriminated-against melting pot. In a sense, Smith was an urban Bryan. Nor was Bryan any more of a "national" leader than Smith. Neither man was aware of his own ethnocentrism or the narrowness of his angle of vision. The same myopia that caused Bryan and his agrarians to confuse Smith's roles as machine politician and as urban reformer caused Smith and his urbanite followers to misunderstand Bryan's dual role as fundamentalist and agrarian reformer. An unbridgeable social and cultural chasm divided them. In the 1890s Bryan had opposed the leaders of New York Democracy (Cleveland and David B. Hill) because he believed that they would disrupt life in that part of the country with which he identified. In the 1920s Bryan fought Smith for much the same reason.

Although Bryan had always been thought of as a westerner, he was actually more of a southerner by 1924. In 1912 he had taken his ailing wife, Mary, to Miami for the winter on the advice of doctors. Thereafter winter in Miami became an annual affair. Finally, they built a winter home, Villa Serena, outside Miami. At about the same time Bryan also built a summer home in Asheville, North Carolina, and subsequently divided his time between the two. At least once each year Bryan returned to Nebraska, usually in November to vote, and he still maintained official residence in that state until 1921, when he changed it to Florida. Committed at last to Florida's future, he rapidly mixed into her local politics and invested heavily in Florida real estate.

By 1923–24 the Palmetto State had become as interested in Bryan as he was in it. It was a marriage of convenience. Florida craved publicity and Bryan wanted to go to the 1924 Democratic convention. In early 1924 Bryan announced that he would run for delegate-at-large in an attempt to become one of the state's twelve delegates. At the same time he began to look around for a candidate to support. The possibility of Bryan's entering the presidential race himself was briefly considered. Wayne Wheeler of the Anti-Saloon League begged him to run, and so did his brother, Charley. But whatever presidential ambitions Bryan may still have had, he assessed his own chances correctly. To all such entreaties he replied that conditions for his own nomination were not likely to arise "with so many younger men so well qualified for leadership."

Unable to give his allegiance to any of the named contenders, Bryan's search fell outside the main current of American politics. Among the possibilities he mentioned to the press were Josephus Daniels of North Carolina, Governor Clifford M. Walker of Georgia, Governor Elbert Lee Trinkle of Virginia, Braxton Bragg Comer of Alabama (seventy-six years old), and Governor Pat M. Neff of Texas. In particular, said Bryan, Dr. Albert A. Murphree, president of the University of Florida, would make an excellent candidate. Bryan's naming of numerous southern governors was obviously designed to neutralize southern support for Underwood. His mention of Murphree could only be explained as a gesture to Florida state pride. The eastern press, of course, met the Murphree suggestion with ridicule, the *New York Times* remarking that it was "received with a smile in Washington political circles." But even in Florida there was some chagrin; the Miami *Herald* stated that such a suggestion by Bryan could only serve to "lower public opinion as to his political sagacity."

From February to May, when he was officially endorsed as a delegate-at-large from Florida, Bryan undauntedly kept pushing Murphree's name forward, claiming that "his popularity will grow as he becomes known." Despite this strong endorsement, it quickly became clear that the only convert Bryan won was Murphree himself, who, unable to cope with this unexpected fame, fawned over Bryan. As for Bryan, he was actually no more committed to this "great and wise southern leader" than he was to anybody else, for at the very moment he was pushing Murphree he was also insisting that his brother Charley get into the presidential race. Why? Well, wrote W. J. to Charley, "It will not hurt." Besides, added the older Bryan, since the Doheny testimony the field had become "an open one."

Despite the Murphree fiasco and the general manner in which Bryan conducted himself prior to the convention, the Great Commoner emerged as an increasingly dominant figure in the 1924 nominating process. Doheny could be thanked for this, because his wounding of McAdoo had made the latter all the more dependent on Bryan. Bryan's chief base of support was also McAdoo's, and an open split between the two men could prove disastrous for McAdoo. It was no secret that McAdoo endorsed Bryan as a Florida delegate even as Bryan was prattling about supporting Murphree. McAdoo believed that Bryan would ultimately stop this nonsense and come over to his side. McAdoo even spread the rumor that Bryan was secretly committed to him and that Bryan's candidate-hopping was merely a façade to mask his pro-McAdoo feelings. Bryan did finally admit in early June, after McAdoo won the Florida primary, that he was "more attracted" to McAdoo than to any of the other front runners.

Along with most observers, McAdoo and his forces sadly misread Bryan in the late spring and early summer of 1924. The precise candidate was relatively unimportant to the Great Commoner. Bryan's crusade transcended nominees. He was more worried about the Democratic party, its ideology, and its composition. For Bryan, the Democratic party was supposed to sustain and protect a non-urban, non-industrialized America by reestablishing "progressive" policies of late-nineteenth-century rural reformism, by restoring the economic arrangements of small-scale entrepreneurialism, and by retaining the social and cultural mores of the Protestant countryside and small village.

Within this setting Bryan's religious fervor and his moral beliefs merged to form an amalgam of assumptions which were impervious to logic and suffused with fear. He saw Wall Street pushing Underwood in the South and John W. Davis in the North. He claimed that the "wet forces" were attempting to capture the nation through eastern governors, especially Al Smith. He suspected that the urban bosses, and particularly Tammany, were planning to extend their "evil immigrant rule" throughout the country. He often asserted that religion ought not play a role in deciding the 1924 nominee but charged that Catholics were making religion an issue because of their support of Smith. The KKK, Bryan believed, was a red herring whose existence as a political issue grew solely out of the loud cries of its eastern opponents.

As for prohibition, Bryan was adamant about its importance, and if there was any one key to his political behavior in 1924 this was it. After the 1920 San Francisco convention had defeated his dry plank, Bryan had exclaimed, "This is not my kind of convention. Four years from now it will be my kind of a convention." He had not made this promise lightly. Now, just before the 1924 convention, he remarked to a group of friends: "I don't think there is a busier man than I am. I have got to keep the Democratic party straight, and I have got to see that prohibition is enforced." His statement was prophetic.

8

The chairman of the Democratic National Committee is theoretically elected by all the national committeemen of the party, but actually the last presidential nominee usually appoints him. One of the chairman's jobs is to issue the call for the next convention and, at the proper time, officially notify state and county chairmen to initiate procedures for selecting delegations. Under the direction of the national chairman, the national committee then appoints the temporary officers of the convention and decides where it is to be held. Accordingly, in March, 1924, Cordell Hull, the long, lanky Tennessean who currently held the chairman's post, formally issued the convention call and requested the various states to begin selecting their delegations.

Struggles over the composition of those delegations had already begun, involving both the holding of state convention-caucuses and presidential primaries. Presidential primary victories traditionally had not been a favored way for a candidate to gain the nomination in either the Democratic or the Republican party. Democratic and Republican leaders had generally taken a negative attitude toward such primaries; indeed, not until after 1948 would primaries become important in either party. But McAdoo, willing to bludgeon his way to the nomination in 1924 if necessary, decided to exert pressure everywhere and in every manner. In those states where presidential primaries were held, he made a fight for delegates. In those where primaries were not held, he relied on his campaign organization and on his friends to force the state conventions or caucuses to appoint delegates favorable to his cause.

Despite the debilitating effect of the oil scandal, this double-barreled approach achieved a measure of success. In the southern and southwestern contests for delegates McAdoo captured Georgia, Texas, Kentucky, Tennessee, and Florida, while Underwood secured only his home state of Alabama. In North and South Carolina McAdoo won by default since Underwood did not oppose him there. Although Virginia endorsed Carter Glass and Arkansas sponsored her own favorite son, Senator Joseph T. Robinson, a majority in both these delegations favored McAdoo as their second choice. Oklahoma, meanwhile, adopted a resolution supporting McAdoo and Mississippi selected a pro-McAdoo slate. Only Louisiana proved obstreperous, selecting an anti-McAdoo delegation.

Elsewhere in the country McAdoo's success was mixed. Prior to the convention he picked up the delegations of Idaho, Montana, and New Mexico, and, although Iowa's delegation remained uninstructed, eighteen of its twenty-six members were known to favor him. Kansas decided to stay with her favorite son, Governor Jonathan M. Davis, but indicated strong second-choice sentiment for the Californian. Indiana remained under Boss Taggart's thumb, but there was still some Hoosier support for McAdoo.

Prohibition-weary Wisconsin, on the other hand, leaned away from McAdoo and toward Smith. Minnesota and Colorado finally decided to leave their delegations uninstructed because of violent internal opposition to McAdoo; indeed, Colorado endorsed its own favorite son, Governor William E. Sweet, rather than bow to McAdoo pressure. In Michigan such a donnybrook developed between McAdoo and Smith forces that it too finally decided to support a favorite son, seventy-one-year-old Senator Woodridge N. Ferris.

In the Middle Atlantic states and in the Northeast McAdoo fared worst. As expected, Maryland went for Ritchie, New Jersey for Silzer, and little Delaware declared for its own ex-Senator Willard Saulsbury. The Northeast remained solidly pro-Smith except for Connecticut, where Homer S. Cummings, former Democratic national chairman and a strong McAdoo man, forced the state convention to send an uninstructed delegation. In all the area east and north of the Ohio River only Pennsylvania was a McAdoo bright spot. Of the Keystone State's seventy-six-member delegation, thirty-five were for McAdoo, thirty for Smith, two for Underwood, and nine scattered.

While the relentless McAdoo drive for delegates gave him some strength in almost all areas of the country except the Northeast, it also left hard feelings and anger in its wake. This was particularly true in Missouri, Illinois, and Ohio. In each of these three situations the McAdoo forces committed some egregious blunders. In the case of Missouri, McAdoo's lieutenant, Breckinridge Long, naturally wanted to see his own state in the McAdoo column and opened a vigorous drive for McAdoo there. But Missouri's bull-headed senior senator, James Reed, had different ideas and in late January, 1924, announced his own availability as a favorite son. Just how sincere Reed's presidential aspirations were is open to conjecture. It is clear, however, that the prohibition-hating Reed despised McAdoo and wanted to deny Missouri to him. Under the circumstances, Long wisely advised McAdoo to forget about

Missouri and stay clear. McAdoo foolishly accepted the Reed challenge.

The contest was vicious. The Klan, the Anti-Saloon League, and the WCTU came out strongly for McAdoo. The Klan circulated scandalous rumors about Reed's private life. Reed, who was known for his acerbic wit and stinging tongue, lashed McAdoo in turn with charges of duplicity and corruption. He asserted that McAdoo was as guilty as Fall in handling governmental affairs and urged his fellow Missourians "to drive the clinching nail in the political coffin of William G. McAdoo."

On primary election day Reed ran far behind McAdoo in the total vote cast, yet there was no such clear-cut decision involving the specific delegates selected and, as a result, the Missouri State convention shortly thereafter voted to send an uninstructed delegation to the national convention. Since the Missouri delegation was to be bound by the unit rule and a bare majority of the group was favorable to McAdoo, it was assumed that all of the state's thirty-six votes would be announced for him at the convention. Nevertheless, in view of the acrimony of the primary contest, the unflattering press coverage, and the close nature of the outcome, McAdoo won at best only a pyrrhic victory in Missouri.

A similar situation occurred in Illinois. This was Brennan territory. For strategic reasons the Chicago boss had decided to take an uncommitted delegation to the convention, leaving him the opportunity of throwing support to Smith at the proper psychological moment. David Rockwell, McAdoo's manager, believed that it would be excellent publicity for McAdoo to contest the Brennan organization and perhaps upset Brennan's plans. At the least it would boldly dramatize McAdoo's "anti-boss" stand. The McAdoo forces had nothing to lose, reasoned Rockwell, since they had not counted on Illinois anyway.

Happy to strike at his enemies anywhere anytime, McAdoo agreed. It was a mistake. Neither Rockwell nor McAdoo realized that by such action they antagonized others besides Brennan. The effect spread far beyond Illinois, giving McAdoo the image of a grasping competitor. Moreover, it did not change the political situation in Illinois. Running unopposed because Brennan scornfully chose to ignore his challenge, McAdoo's statewide showing was dismal and a slate of unpledged delegates was still elected. Indeed, pro-McAdoo delegates lost so heavily in the Chicago area that Rockwell charged vote fraud and threatened to go to court. Brennan now more than ever was determined to kill McAdoo's nomination chances.

Rockwell said later that the decision to enter the Illinois primary was "possibly the most momentous one in the entire McAdoo campaign." Fateful as it was, however, it was not so disastrous as the experience in Ohio. Here Governor Cox was maintaining a pretense of neutrality by running as a favorite son himself rather than having the state go to the convention pledged to another candidate. Although he had an outside chance at the 1924 nomination, Cox was actually more interested in playing the role of kingmaker and was known to lean toward Smith, whom he regarded as the most talented governor in the nation. Of all the major candidates Cox liked McAdoo least, and it was no secret that his favorite-son candidacy was in part a ploy to withhold any Ohio support from the Californian. Cox was not so much disturbed by the Doheny disclosures as by the fact that McAdoo had opposed Cox's own nomination in 1920 and now was conniving with the Klan. In any case, it was the height of folly for McAdoo to contest Cox on his own home ground. Entering the Ohio primary in April, McAdoo ran a slate of delegates in every Buckeye congressional district. As in other areas where McAdoo confronted favorite sons, the Anti-Saloon league and the Klan marshaled their forces to support him.

It was a debacle. The primary vote was Cox 74,183 and McAdoo 29,267. Every Cox delegate, including delegates-at-large, was elected. As a result the entire forty-eight-member Ohio delegation became anti-McAdoo explicitly rather than implicitly. Prior to the election there had been some McAdoo sentiment in the Buckeye State, especially in southern Ohio, and it was even said that second-choice support for Smith and McAdoo was about equal. But McAdoo's frontal assault on Cox made it impossible for such McAdoo sentiment to survive. Naturally, it reconfirmed Cox in his own anti-McAdoo position.

If the three primary battles in Missouri, Illinois, and Ohio further prejudiced McAdoo's cause, they also gave heightened visibility to the two issues of prohibition and the Klan. In each of these primary battles the Klan and prohibition forces joined to support McAdoo and attack his opponents. Hence, these primaries further enhanced the belief that McAdoo was the chief prohibition and Klan candidate. McAdoo did little to dispel this belief. Although warned time and again about accepting Klan support, McAdoo did not listen. Indeed, he alone of the major Democratic candidates did not denounce the Klan prior to convention time. Knowing that his political strength rested primarily in the South, McAdoo was unwilling, perhaps fearful, to make any statement which might hurt him there.

McAdoo, of course, had far more than Klan support. The composition of his own campaign organization indicated the rather widespread nature of his appeal. James Phelan, his California champion, was a Catholic. Bernard Baruch, his primary financial angel, was a Jew. In the South he received backing from a number of anti-Klan newspapers. In Indiana the Klan was supporting Ralston, not McAdoo. Still, general Klan interest in McAdoo was keener than in any other candidate. As early as 1923 Imperial Wizard Evans had indicated a preference for McAdoo and had urged Klansmen to work for him. The Grand Dragon of Arkansas, N. Clay Jewett, was an outspoken McAdoo supporter. U.S. senator and Texas Klansman Earle Mayfield was one of the prime movers behind the McAdoo campaign not only in the Lone Star State but in the entire South.

McAdoo unquestionably made a mistake in not at least mildly rebuking the Klan prior to the convention. He had little to lose. Where else but to McAdoo did Klansmen really have to go? Silence was certainly no answer since anti-Klan Democratic party members in the industrial Midwest and the East absolutely required some kind of assurance. When McAdoo refused to give it, anti-McAdoo forces, especially the Smith camp, made capital out of his failure.

Smith had problems of his own as the convention approached. If McAdoo had the Klan to plague him, the New York governor still had the twin difficulties of rum and Catholicism. Although Smith had not entered any primaries, by convention time he had picked up the support of delegates in Pennsylvania, Wisconsin, Michigan, Minnesota, and in all the New England states. As his delegate total grew, so did his opposition. The Klan, in particular, sharply increased its anti-Smith propaganda. To Klansmen Smith remained "that Catholic" from "Jew York." Everywhere speakers of the KKK emphasized Smith's religion and warned that no Catholic should be allowed to become President.

Not all of the mounting religious opposition to Smith prior to the opening of the convention was Klan inspired. The expansion of the Smith campaign in May and early June had the momentary effect of helping McAdoo since many complacent or indifferent Protestants now scurried into the McAdoo camp. These persons would never have run a Catholic out of town on a rail, but they were opposed to a Catholic for President. The effect was to further polarize the religious issue, causing Catholics themselves to become increasingly militant and to assume that all such opposition *was* Klan-directed. Just before the convention Smith was besieged by Catholic voters who urged him to "do something about the Klan or they will rule the U.S.A." Even though he continued to downgrade the Klan's importance, Smith was obviously affected by this Catholic pressure and by the growing assault on his religious beliefs. By convention time he was as angry as many of his followers.

The major problem for Smith, however, remained his wetness. The liquor question cut both ways, of course, and Smith received some support because he was wet. The Wisconsin and Minnesota primaries illustrated this fact, both states opposing prohibition and both inclining toward Smith. Smith, himself, was surprised by the Wisconsin vote, remarking, "I don't even know anybody way out there. I've never been there, nor in Minnesota." Nonetheless, prohibition, especially when coupled with the religious issue, had a continuing deleterious effect on Smith's chances. Had Smith been dry but Catholic and small-town, or had he been wet but western and Protestant, the two factors would not have been so damaging.

Just prior to the convention the issue of prohibition fueled the political fires in both the Smith and McAdoo camps and encouraged a torrent of propaganda and oratory. The Klan attacked Smith for his wetness, but his religion interested them more. It was the Anti-Saloon League and the Protestant churches which concentrated on Smith's prohibition views. Nothing Roosevelt could do, nor any belated attempts at hedging by Smith himself, could remove the New York governor from being considered the champion of the liquor interests. Next to the churches and the Anti-Saloon League, the Hearst newspapers were most instrumental in emphasizing Smith's anti-prohibition stand. The Democratic convention simply had to reject "any candidate representing 'booze and boodle,'" said Hearst. The country would not survive the "bootlegging and bartending faction of Tammany" which Smith represented.

Despite the charges directed against him, it was neither Smith nor his followers who first threatened to make either the Klan or prohibition "official" matters involving the 1924 national convention. That task fell jointly to Bryan and Underwood. As the convention neared Bryan increased his insistence that the Democratic party denounce any attempt to change the Volstead Act or modify prohibition enforcement. Bryan made it clear that he intended to press for a nominee who stood four-square on the Eighteenth Amendment and seek an explicit dry plank in the party platform. To suggestions that he should take a more flexible stand, Bryan curtly replied, "If a strong fight is made for dry planks, it is easy to keep out a wet plank."

Meanwhile, Underwood expanded his fight against the Klan. He never got over his loss to McAdoo in Georgia in March, remaining convinced that the Klan had sealed his doom. Subsequently, as other southern delegations were swept into the McAdoo fold, he lost all ability to discriminate between actual and apparent causes and saw the Klan as the *sole* reason for McAdoo's success everywhere. As a result, Underwood announced on May 12 that he intended "to press the Klan issue" before the resolutions committee of the convention and if that failed he would "carry the fight to the floor." In a later statement, Underwood's campaign manager, Charles Carlin, avowed that the Underwood forces would "lead the fight against the machinations of the Klan" and hoped "that other aspirants for the nomination will join hands with [them] in this movement."

Rank-and-file Democratic opinion seemed to support Underwood in announcing this fight. But most professional politicians were aghast and devoutly wished that the Klan issue would not be raised. Understandably, the Underwood forces took this position to embarrass and strike back at McAdoo. Mostly, though, Underwood's anti-Klan tactic was an act of simple frustration. To charges that Underwood was purposely creating a difficult situation for the party, Carlin replied that the Klan was actually to blame. "Whether or not it should be, the Klan is an issue," said Carlin. "It has made itself one of its own volition."

9

On the eve of the Democratic convention of 1924 the party not only possessed a plethora of competing and wrangling candidates, but a number of politically dangerous issues which were apparently insoluble. This did not prevent rosy claims from being made. A week before the convention Rockwell declared that McAdoo would receive as many as 500 votes on the first ballot and shortly thereafter would gain the additional number required to give him the necessary two-thirds (a total of 732) for the nomination. McAdoo was certainly acting and talking like a winner. Just before the convention he wrote to one of his sons: "The fight seems to have narrowed down to Governor Smith of New York and myself. I have been winning victories right along—feel confident that we have more than a safe majority of the Convention and that I shall secure the nomination."

The Smith forces were of a different mind. Roosevelt maintained that the convention would ultimately turn to Smith. If Roosevelt doubted Smith's chances, as his private correspondence later indicated, he never acted like it or displayed any public doubt. Instead, he told reporters that Smith was ahead of McAdoo and would win. He branded all claims by the McAdooites of 500 votes as "extravagant" and "exaggerated." Smith, meanwhile, relying serenely on his strength in New York, glimpsed victory ahead. His daughter Emily later said that her father sincerely believed that he might win and that his family surely thought he would. Shortly before the convention opened, Smith was all smiles to newspapermen and told one of them, "We are sitting pretty." To another he said, "I believe that when they get around to naming the real man after distributing the complimentary votes, I'll be nominated."

Impartial observers knew better. McAdoo had only 270 pledged delegates, Smith 126, and the various favorite sons controlled at least 220. The remainder of the more than 1,000 delegates were uncommitted. Speculation therefore centered not on a quick victory by either McAdoo or Smith, but on the "deals" that might be arranged. It was rumored that Glass of Virginia, Robinson of Arkansas, and Charles Bryan of Nebraska would ultimately move into the McAdoo column after making a bid for second place. Some said the McAdoo forces would settle for a McAdoo-Ralston ticket. There were rumors that Cox would throw the Ohio delegation to Smith and then arrange a coalition ticket with Charles Bryan as Smith's running mate. Taggart, it was said, would give Indiana to the New York governor in exchange for an "Al and Sam" slate. One strong rumor was that Underwood would go to Smith and take second place on the ticket.

No matter how one figured the possible combinations, the two major candidates still could not muster the necessary two-thirds. The only way that could happen was if most of the favorite sons decided to withdraw and concentrate their strength on one candidate. This had become increasingly unlikely, however, as the relative weakness of the front runners began to show. Clearly, as convention time approached, the key to the outcome rested not with McAdoo or Smith but with the favorite sons. A quick success by McAdoo was possible only if he could persuade several of the more important ones to abandon the race and switch to him. But McAdoo had already antagonized many of them and was finding this goal elusive. Smith, on the other hand, was encouraging the favorite sons to remain in the struggle in order to block an early McAdoo bandwagon. For these reasons, guesses concerning the convention's outcome grew cautious as opening day neared. Most prophets realized that, as the recurring phrase went, "McAdoo is too oily and Smith is too wet." Yet no other candidates were seen as having the strength or the ability to forge a winning combination.

On one fact almost all political pundits agreed. The 1924 convention would be a long and acrimonious one. On June 19, five days before the convention convened, the *New York Times* bannered the headline: "Longest Convention on Record Forecast." It was likely, said the *Times,* that this convention would exceed the forty-four ballots taken to select Cox in 1920 and even the forty-six required to nominate Wilson in 1912. Stanley Frost, political analyst for *Outlook,* said that the only way for the Democrats to avert disaster was to keep the convention from starting. Aside from the knotty problem of selecting a candidate, Frost stated, the Klan issue, in particular, would be "like a keg of powder" which the convention would be "sitting on all the time, whether it goes off or not." As for the final result, Samuel Blythe, staffman for the *Saturday Evening Post,* warned his readers that, despite all the talk and rumors of deals, "Nobody . . . had any more idea than a snowbird of who the candidate will be—nobody."

PART III

★

THE PRELIMINARIES

1

New York City had a poor record as a political convention site. The last time it had hosted a major party convention was in 1868, when Horatio Seymour was nominated in Tammany Hall by the Democrats. Since then the nation's largest city had been passed over in favor of others.

It was determined not to be overlooked in 1924. Herbert Bayard Swope, executive editor of the New York *World,* began as early as 1923 to trumpet the virtues of New York as a convention city, and he was joined by a host of other New York advocates. Foremost among them were Charles Murphy and Norman Mack. These men applied pressure on the Democratic party's top councils while a group of New York businessmen raised a fund of $255,000 to outbid any other contenders.

By the summer of 1923 New York was clearly the odds-on favorite to win the 1924 Democratic convention. Its claims were impressive. Not only had it been ignored numerous times in the past, but it was one of the staunchest Democratic areas of the country. Just the year before, in 1922, its voters had elected a solid phalanx of Democrats to the state assembly in Albany and the Congress in Washington. City Hall itself had consistently remained in the hands of Democrats, thanks to Boss Murphy and Tammany. Besides, there was that fund of $255,000—a sum which loomed large to a party starved for money.

When the national committee met in Washington to decide the matter in January, 1924, there were only four cities in contention—Chicago, St. Louis, San Francisco, and New York. San Francisco was in a weak position because of just having had the convention in 1920. St. Louis offered too little money. Chicago rested its case on geographic accessibility and a bid of $200,000. New York presented by far the best package. Norman Mack skillfully marshaled support among his national committee colleagues and emphasized the fact that New York wanted the convention if for no other reason than to dispel the notion that the city was a "cold and unfriendly place." As for rumors that New York might not be respectful to all candidates, Mack dismissed them as unworthy of discussion. No candidate, said Mack, would have a better or worse advantage if the convention were held there.

That New York's neutrality should be questioned at all was indicative of the suspicions and animus that permeated the party by 1924. From the beginning the McAdoo forces were uneasy over the possibility of New York's being selected. They had wanted San Francisco but, after realizing the hopelessness of that site, had turned to St. Louis. In the end they reluctantly went along with New York, believing that it would make no difference. Indeed, after New York was picked, Roper issued a press statement that the McAdoo forces were actually "glad New York got the convention."

When the committee's decision was announced on January 15, Al Smith was not yet a serious contender and, although both Murphy and Mack considered the selection a boon to the Smith forces, few outside New York regarded the matter as significant. Then came the oil disclosures on February 1. Had the Doheny testimony occurred two weeks earlier, there probably would have been a bitter fight over the New York site. Now, as the McAdoo campaign staggered, the selection acquired new meaning. The Smith campaign immediately derived strength from the fact that the convention was to be held in the governor's home town. Meanwhile, anti-Smith groups became convinced that he had acquired an unfair advantage. Western and southern elements, never keen about New York anyway, were especially glum over the prospect of trusting their candidates' destinies to the vagaries of that "evil" city.

2

Of the $255,000 which New York had offered for the 1924 convention, $55,000 had been pledged by George L. ("Tex") Rickard, sports promoter and owner of Madison Square Garden. Also as part of the New York package, Rickard had promised to give to the Democratic party the use of the Garden free of charge "for as long as the convention lasts." Rickard shrewdly calculated that he would easily recoup his investment through concessions alone and even grandly announced that he would permit the Democratic party to retain all the profits that he would make above $55,000.

Madison Square Garden had been built in 1890 and was once called "the most beautiful building in New York." A masterpiece of architect Stanford White, this red-brick edifice had commanded an unobstructed view when first erected and St. Gaudens's "Diana," which perched atop its ten-story tower, was New York's most elevated work of art. Situated in the block bounded by Twenty-sixth and Twenty-seventh streets and by Madison and Fourth avenues, the Garden had witnessed some stirring political events, including the oratory of William Jennings Bryan and Woodrow Wilson; but it was much more accustomed to horse shows, six-day bicycle races, circuses, and prize fights than to affairs of state. Its history was primarily of crowds crying for blood or oohing at the tricks of aerial artists. Perhaps the Garden's most sensational single event had occurred in 1906 when Harry K. Thaw, a wealthy playboy, shot and killed Stanford White in White's Garden tower apartment in a fit of jealousy over a chorus girl. This scandal alone had made "the Garden" a household word.

Splendid for yesterday, Madison Square Garden was neither especially large nor beautiful in 1924. By then St. Gaudens's soaring "Diana" was hemmed in on all sides by taller and more imposing structures, and the Garden itself was about to make way for a huge office building for the New York Life Insurance Company. A new Garden, with twice as many seats, was slated to be erected on the old Eighth Avenue car-barn site at Fiftieth Street. Actually, the Democratic convention was to be the last scheduled major event before demolition began.

Even to serve its final function, the Garden needed a face lift, like a dying old lady putting on makeup in preparation for the end. Fittingly, such remodeling had to wait until the Barnum and Bailey Circus, which had come into the Garden in early May, was over. When the last elephant departed, architect Henry I. Cobb moved in with a crew of almost 200 men on June 1, ripping out the Garden's insides and adding to its seats. The changes were striking. The big room in the southwest corner where the freaks lived when the circus was in town was made into an attractive restaurant. An elevated speakers' platform was placed on the north side midway between Fourth and Madison avenues. Built to hold 300 persons, this platform was fronted by a space for 750 newsmen. Delegate seating was provided on the floor itself, but behind them on every side were spectator galleries which rose to the roof. The ugly steel rafters were masked by $15,000 worth of flags and bunting, giving the ceiling the appearance of the inside of a striped candy box. Refreshment stands were wedged in the areaway running all around the outside of the hall.

In the basement, thirty-six rooms were built to house the various press associations and a special light-snack restaurant for newsmen. In addition a small hospital, a women's reception room, a post office, a sergeant-at-arms room, and elaborate telegraph and telephone facilities were provided. This would be the best-covered convention in history. Eight hundred telephones were installed and over a million feet of telephone and telegraph lines were strung. A duplicate system of loudspeakers was dotted around the hall, controlled from the speaker's stand so that if one set went out the other could be instantly activated. Since this was the first convention in history to be carried in its entirety by radio, special arrangements were provided for this equipment. The American Telephone and Telegraph Company and the Radio Corporation of America set up competing broadcast facilities, and by the end of the first week in June radio stations all over the nation were signing up for their services.

By Saturday, June 21, the various renovations and installations had been completed and the Garden awaited the delegates. There were still too few seats and not enough restrooms. The latter condition was ultimately remedied after the start of the convention by the building of additional sanitation facilities just outside the hall in Madison Square Park. But nothing could be done about the number of seats. The national committee had hoped that the architect could jam 20,000 spaces into the remodeled Garden but he could provide for no more than 14,000. Nonetheless, within three weeks after the circus closed, a construction miracle had been performed. While making a final inspection of the Garden on June 21, National Chairman Cordell Hull remarked that it was "the most beautiful convention hall" he had ever seen. One New York old-timer, also seeing the Garden on the weekend before the convention opened, exclaimed, "I've known the old Garden since the days when a freight station was here. And it never was slicked up like this before. I guess it beats even the Horse Show."

3

It was no horse show that New York was preparing for, and it took its host role very seriously. In truth, the metropolis reacted to the coming of the 1924 convention like a small town. William Allen White, who knew something about small towns, called New York "Hickville-on-the-Hudson" in its pre-convention "boosterism" and in its feverish attempt to outdo anything that any city had done before. The preparations were lavish and involved almost everyone. Immediately upon being awarded the convention, the New York Board of Estimate set aside $100,000 for use by various committees in preparing for the convention, and before the end of May the board was forced to revise this figure upward to $200,000. New York hotels, meanwhile, pledged not to raise their room charges during the run of the convention and to provide maximum facilities for the delegates. Restaurants also agreed to keep their food prices steady and to cater to the delegates' every whim. Restaurateurs promised fried chicken, Virginia ham and waffles for southerners; hot tamales and chili con carne for southwesterners; steamed sweet potatoes, butterscotch pie and boiled turkey for westerners; and egg noodles and wiener schnitzel for midwesterners.

Chairman of the general entertainment committee was Thomas Chadbourne, who ultimately had fifty-four other committees working under him. A separate entertainment committee was assigned to each delegation to greet it when it arrived in New York and thereafter keep it happy. Percy S. Straus of R. H. Macy and Company, for example, was head of the committee for the Georgia delegation; Nicholas Murray Butler, president of Columbia University, was chairman of the committee for the New Jersey delegation; and so on. As Butler described the purpose of this entertainment committee system: "[In this way] we can show our friends from other parts of the country what sort of a place New York really is and how it feels, in contrast with some of the things that are said about us."

Women delegates and the wives of delegates were made the specific responsibility of a committee under the direction of New York national committeewoman Elisabeth Marbury. This group organized special church services, special art and museum exhibits, and special tours for women. The largest and most elaborate social functions planned by the women's committee were a reception and dance at the Hotel Commodore on the opening night of the convention (June 24), and a breakfast the following morning in the same hotel at which Governor and Mrs. Smith were to be the guests of honor.

Similarly, the Greater New York community planned events to coincide with the convention or altered its operation to serve the delegates. Coney Island announced that it would remain open "around the clock" if necessary. The Coney Island Business Men's Association set up a string of activities beginning on Monday night (June 23) with a parade of local Democratic organizations, including Tammany, and ending on Saturday night with a bathing beauty contest and the crowning of "Miss Democracy." Broadway and the entertainment world also geared themselves for the convention. Movie houses and theaters announced that they would save their best seats for the delegates at no increase in prices. Much was promised for the delegates to see. At the cinema there would be Cecil B. De Mille's *Ten Commandments,* Douglas Fairbanks in *The Thief of Bagdad,* Harold Lloyd in *Girl Shy,* and Rudolph Valentino in *The Sainted Devil.* If movies were not to their liking, delegates could go to the legitimate theater and enjoy *Abie's Irish Rose, George White's Scandals,* Eddie Cantor in *Kid Boots,* or Will Rogers in *Ziegfeld Follies.* If nothing else appealed, a delegate could always go to the Polo Grounds to watch the league-leading Giants play or to Yankee Stadium to cheer up the Yankees, who were currently in second place because Babe Ruth was in a batting slump.

Even under normal circumstances New York offered so many diversions and so great an opportunity for individual indulgence that the programming of some of this entertainment was superfluous. As one observer said, if a delegate wasn't careful he would never see the inside of the Garden. New York attempted in every way possible to make the delegates feel "at home." Wet, and not normally worried by it, the city even tried to reduce any embarrassment to dry delegates by discouraging bootlegging during the convention. Its success was only minimal. The *New York Times* warned shortly before the convention that the delegates would probably "not find New York City entirely free of liquoral humidity." Indeed, despite all efforts, bootleggers and the rum fleet off Montauk Point were so busy in late May and early June that prohibition authorities grudgingly admitted New York during the convention would be "a very wet town."

The city also attempted to crack down on its criminal element just prior to the convention, especially pickpockets. Known thugs were picked up and put in jail without bail until the convention was over. The pickpocket squad and the bunko detail were doubled. Blunt notice was served that petty thieves and criminals from other areas should stay away from New York while the convention was in progress. Warnings were also issued that all those caught prior to and during the convention would be given a three-to-five-month summary sentence in order to keep them out of circulation.

The police laid elaborate plans for the Garden itself. They organized into teams to protect the delegates and handle any emergency. Ironically, the headquarters for the twelve hundred convention policemen was placed in the basement of the Society for the Prevention of Cruelty to Animals at Madison Avenue and Twenty-sixth Street. A sub-headquarters was established under the speaker's platform in the Garden itself. All streets surrounding the Garden were cleared of all traffic and parking was not allowed in a zone bounded by Twenty-third Street on the south, Twenty-ninth Street on the north, Fifth Avenue on the west, and Lexington Avenue on the east.

In such detailed and elaborate manner, New York City prepared for the 1924 Democratic convention. Aware of suspicions about its hospitality and extremely anxious to prove them unjustified, the city sincerely strove to make the delegates' stay a rewarding one. The New York press was especially pleased about the planning and predicted that the delegates, even McAdoo delegates, would be overwhelmed by the reception prepared for them. New York, they agreed, had extended itself to make this the finest Democratic convention ever. All that remained was for the delegates to arrive.

4

They came from everywhere and in every manner. The first delegates to appear came from Puerto Rico. Led by National Committeeman Henry W. Dooley, they stepped off their boat on June 15, were met by their entertainment committee, and were taken to their quarters in the Hotel Belmont. Throughout the following week New York was deluged by arriving delegations. Among the last to reach the city was the Texas delegation. Traveling by special train from Dallas, the debarkation of these 103 pro-

McAdoo supporters on Sunday evening, June 22, was the signal for light-
ing the "Avenue of States," the most expensive illumination ever under-
taken in the city. Fifth Avenue suddenly became "a lighted way," with
gold bulbs in the lampposts instead of white ones, and streamers of
orange and blue lights running down each side of the avenue from Sixty-
second Street to the Washington Square arch. There a battery of searchlights threw multicolored rays into the sky. Each block along this strip
was dedicated to an individual state or territory, was festooned with its
flag or banner, and contained six eighteen-foot pylons decorated with its
name and seal. Beginning with Alabama in the block between Waverly
Place and Eighth Street, the names continued to the block between Fifty-
seventh and Fifty-eighth streets, which was dedicated to Wyoming.

The candidates were almost too busy to notice all this hoopla. The
1924 convention was unique in that all of the major candidates except
Ralston were at the convention or in New York City and were in personal charge of their campaign strategy. Smith arrived in the city on
Thursday night, June 12. Accompanied by George R. Van Namee (his
personal secretary) and Judge Proskauer, Smith went directly to his suite
in the Biltmore Hotel. While emptying his luggage, which had been
packed by his wife, he grumbled that she had included enough clothes
"to take an ordinary man to Europe for a month." Asked by reporters
whether he was now prepared to receive political visitors, Smith laughingly said no. "Do you see this bathing suit?" Smith asked. "Well, I'm
going swimming." Then, picking up some golf balls, he added, "I'm also
going to shoot some golf."

Smith would do both before the convention opened, but everyone
knew that this was not the reason he was in New York. After settling
down in his private quarters in the Biltmore, he created a command post
in a room on the top floor of the Manhattan Club, directly across the
street from the Garden. Simultaneously, a "workshop" was established in
the Prudence Building at the corner of Madison Avenue and Forty-third
Street, from which printed pro-Smith propaganda could quickly find its
way onto the floor of the convention. While Smith continued to sleep at
the Biltmore and took his breakfasts there, the rest of his time was spent
in the Manhattan Club in constant communication with Roosevelt, Moskowitz, Proskauer, and his other advisers.

Three days before Smith arrived in New York, Rockwell moved the
main McAdoo headquarters from Chicago to a lavish suite in the Hotel
Vanderbilt on Park Avenue. McAdoo planned to leave Los Angeles on

June 12 and arrive in New York on June 16, but his train did not get in until June 18. Two brass bands and 2,500 of his supporters wearing "Mc'll Do" hatbands met him at the station. Accompanied by his wife, who was still dressed in mourning for her father, McAdoo smilingly acknowledged the cheers, told his followers that there was no doubt about the outcome, and departed for his private rooms in the Vanderbilt. There he and the California delegation resided in isolation throughout the convention. The main convention hotels were the Belmont, Pennsylvania, McAlpin, Imperial, and Commodore, where as many as ten different delegations stayed. But no one used the expensive Vanderbilt except the Californians, occasioning considerable comment in view of lingering suspicions about McAdoo and big oil fees.

Other candidates, their managers, and their delegates arrived with less fanfare but with undiminished determination. Tom Taggart arrived on Friday night, June 20, and immediately went to the Waldorf, where he set up a Ralston-for-President headquarters. Claiming that he was uninterested in any deals, Taggart stated that he was for Ralston "to the bitter end." He knew, however, that the odds were against his candidate, and the Indiana delegation was not in town an hour before it was fighting rumors that Ralston was seriously ill and dying. To such rumors the Hoosiers shouted "Nonsense" and referred all skeptics to Ralston's brother-in-law, who was at the convention and who said Ralston "looked pretty husky . . . when I saw him last, day before yesterday. He was just hitching up a horse to a hayrake."

John Davis also was in New York but discreetly remained at the home of Frank Polk on East Sixty-eighth Street. There he maintained frequent contact with the head of the West Virginia delegation, Clem Shaver. Shaver had reached New York with his small delegation two weeks prior to the convention. Possessing only limited funds, he set up headquarters in the Waldorf in a reception room off the main corridor. At the entrance a modest sign was hung, "Davis-for-President Home Town Club," and West Virginia flags were draped around the walls. Here and there a portrait of the handsome Davis was strategically placed to attract delegate attention.

Senator Underwood did not arrive in New York until Sunday night, June 22. As promised, he immediately declared war on the Klan. He reaffirmed that he intended to make the Klan the dominant issue and said that he would release a more definitive statement about his intentions from his headquarters in the Waldorf the next day. True to his word, on

Monday, June 23, Underwood announced that the Alabama delegation would formally introduce to the convention platform committee a resolution to condemn the Klan. To a group of cheering followers Underwood stated: "The party is either for or against the Klan. Of course, we should name the Klan. Why not?" Naturally, the New York press gave prominent coverage to these Underwood pronouncements, but most southern and western delegates dismissed him as a poor loser. Dry delegates thought it particularly appropriate that Underwood's New York headquarters was situated in what once was the famous Waldorf bar.

By the time Underwood issued his challenge to the Klan on Monday morning, June 23, the situation was clearly deteriorating. The first casualty was the attempt by New Yorkers to impress the delegates. Instead of promoting party harmony, the city itself encouraged heightened acrimony. As one delegate claimed, "I became conscious of it almost as soon as I arrived." McAdoo said he felt it, but in his case he was as much instigator as victim. Even before he arrived in New York, McAdoo had been busy damning the city which had been his home for thirty years. He and Rockwell constantly charged that the McAdoo cause would not be able to get a fair hearing in New York. This claim was widely disseminated by the southern and West Coast press, and accepted as true by western and southern delegations even before they arrived in the city. McAdoo himself alighted from his train making new charges. The New York press, he said, was purposely distorting the news to undermine his position. He specifically condemned the New York *World*, which he claimed was engaged in a drive to slander him. To reporters he revealed that he believed much of his pre-convention campaign trouble had emanated from the eastern press and he vowed that he would make eastern journalists "eat their words" before the second or third convention ballot was over. To dramatize his feeling about the city's alleged anti-McAdoo atmosphere, he refused to attend the dinner given for all delegates and their wives on Monday evening, stating that it was "stacked" for Smith. Instead, he attended a dinner the night before, given by William Randolph Hearst, which was openly anti-Smith.

McAdoo's complaints would have had less impact had it not been for the fact that New York was failing in its attempts to satisfy visiting delegates. Everything seemed to conspire against a better New York image. On Sunday, June 22, it was hot and muggy, the temperature shooting into the high eighties. It was a good day for the beach—providing one could get there. The Coney Island buses were mobbed and out-of-towners quickly lost out to rude natives, who were much more practiced at yelling and shoving. Those visitors who persisted and finally got to Coney Island were bewildered by the crowds and came away convinced that back home was better. Those who did not go to the beach but wandered downtown to Fourteenth Street to gawk at Tammany Hall with its ancient Indian above the door reacted as if they expected to see an ogre come popping out. Others who journeyed uptown to the Riverside or Madison Avenue churches were offended to hear ministers like Harry Emerson Fosdick or Henry Sloane Coffin condemn fundamentalism as stupidity. Other delegates, taking a stroll up Wall Street and past the Stock Exchange, were intimidated by the mute and imposing buildings and had their fears about money conspiracies and financial cabals reinforced. Many delegates, especially those from the great West, were bothered by the physical strictures of the city, which made them feel hemmed in and trapped. As one said, "I'd sure hate to be a dog or a boy in New York." Many visitors confessed to a lost feeling, a sense of disorientation and loneliness. Pointing to the general surliness of New Yorkers, midwesterners were convinced that New York was a far less friendly place than Chicago. Almost all delegates were dismayed by the New York traffic, the noise and the hustle, and frequently repeated among themselves the old saw that New York was a great place to visit but not to live in.

The press in the rest of the country, especially in the West and South, reported all the various drawbacks to New York but none of its advantages. Stories were constantly carried about delegates being "robbed" by hotels, restaurants, and taximen. Further, it was said that the city's hospitality often took the form of plying unsuspecting dry delegates with liquor. McAdoo was supposedly very bitter about the fact that some of his best men "have been hopelessly drunk ever since they landed in New York." Although New York officials denied all this, it was rapidly believed in most areas of the trans-Mississippi West that their delegates were the helpless victims of unscrupulous and immoral city slickers. Certainly it did not help New York's reputation for sophistication when it became known that a group of church-seeking fundamentalist Texans found on that first Sunday that the block of the "Avenue of States" dedicated to the Lone Star State contained St. Patrick's Cathedral.

Not surprisingly, by Monday, June 23, the McAdoo forces, as well as those of many southern and western favorite sons, were openly antagonistic toward New York. Their reasons were often paradoxical. On the one hand they claimed that New York was a cold, inhospitable, selfish, mercenary place; on the other hand they constantly warned their followers against New York's warm display of hospitality because it was a trap. At the heart of the matter, of course, was the fact that New York represented everything that was alien to the supporters of McAdoo and certain other favorite sons. Here more than three-quarters of the white population were either foreign-born or the children of foreign-born. Here was the largest concentration of Jews and Catholics in the country. Here was the home of Wall Street, of Sunday baseball and boxing, of Tammany Hall, and of religious modernism. And here was the Sodom of the prohibitionists—a place where such infamous nightclubs as the Silver Slipper, Rendezvous, and the Cotton Club existed, where "the suckers" came to hear the throaty songs of Helen Morgan or suffer the insults of the brassy Texas Guinan, and where liquor was easier to get than water.

To counteract these evil influences, two groups set immediately to work—the Anti-Saloon League and the Ku Klux Klan. Spearheading the dry crusade in New York was the Anti-Saloon League. The general counsel of the League, Wayne Wheeler, was there and aiding him was his assistant, Ira Champion, a well-known Democrat from Alabama. Also present were Bishop James Cannon, Jr., who spoke for some three million Southern Methodists, and, of course, William Jennings Bryan. Bryan pulled into New York on Sunday, June 22, reiterating that his major goal was to secure a dry candidate and a strong enforcement plank. Both Cannon and Wheeler took rooms in the Herald Square Hotel and were in constant communication with each other. They did not always see eye to eye on dry strategy and there was even some jealousy between them. Bishop Cannon believed Wheeler's Republican bias showed too often. Wheeler, in turn, preferred to work through Bryan rather than through Cannon, much to the Bishop's displeasure. More than once Cannon felt it necessary to warn Wheeler against feeding Bryan's presidential ambitions and becoming too deeply involved in Democratic party politics. Still, the two had a common cause which bound them together and they pursued it relentlessly.

Mainly their efforts took the form of word-of-mouth directives to friendly delegates or open letters to the press and to delegations as a whole. In these propaganda activities Wheeler and Cannon acted not as formulators but as reinforcers of dry delegate opinions. Neither of them coerced or duped their followers into an anti-wet stance. They merely gave it focus. It was estimated, for example, that the entire delegations of certain southern and southwestern states were composed of Anti-Saloon League members or those sympathetic to its cause. The majority of the delegates from most states of the Midwest and the Far West were similarly inclined. Such delegations were promising territory in which Wheeler and Cannon could operate.

At the outset Bishop Cannon released an open letter to the press stating that dry southern Democrats would never agree "to be driven like a herd of branded cattle into a corral which has 'Democrat' over the entrance and has 'wet' placarded all over the walls." Simultaneously, Wheeler circularized all delegations, warning not only about Smith's candidacy, but also about the possible substitution of "a coalition candidate who probably will not be offensively wet." The Wheeler circular said that the "Smith-Tammany-Underwood-Wall Street leaders" wanted a convention deadlock so that they could select a candidate who would work "under a collusive agreement" with them. Other League-sponsored material was equally frenzied. Just prior to the opening of the convention, dry delegates were asked to watch out for "cheering sections and attempts to stampede the convention" and for "Tammany hospitality" (liquor) dispensed in the name of Smith. Dry propaganda also charged that the convention seating arrangements were controlled by Tammany and that an attempt would probably be made to pack the galleries for Smith.

Since all these statements had an anti-Smith thrust, they were welcomed in McAdoo headquarters, which at times became a sub-headquarters for the Anti-Saloon League. By mid-June many Anti-Saloon Leaguers were openly working in the McAdoo headquarters. L. B. Musgrove, chairman of the executive committee of the League, actually issued official League statements from there. One of these charged that Smith was using the issue of his Catholicism as a smoke screen to turn attention away from his prohibition stand. Rockwell, perceiving the emotional and political impact of such propaganda, began to rely heavily on the League and to emphasize McAdoo's dryness. To delegations, to the press, to everyone, Rockwell spoke of McAdoo's "progressive" prohibition position as contrasted with that of the "reactionary" pro-Smith wets.

In the week prior to the opening of the convention the Klan was also busy. Because of the Underwood challenge, its most pressing problem was to prevent the gathering from naming it in a condemnatory resolution. But the selection of a dry candidate and the adoption of a strong prohibition plank were also among the Klan's basic concerns. Far more than the Anti-Saloon League, the Klan linked these two desires to a virulent anti-Catholicism. And, unlike the League, whose statements and activities were visible for all to see, the Klan worked by stealth and indirection.

From the beginning the Invisible Empire had representatives at the Democratic convention. Imperial Wizard Evans and his advisers set up their headquarters in a five-room suite on the fifteenth floor of the Mc-Alpin Hotel. There, under heavy guard, Evans received daily reports from such Grand Dragons as Walter F. Bossert of Indiana, Nathan Bedford Forrest III of Georgia, and James A. Comer of Arkansas. Virgil C. Pettie (delegate-at-large from Arkansas), Hollins N. Randolph (chairman of the Georgia delegation), Swords R. Lee (delegate from Louisiana), and Senator Earle Mayfield (delegate-at-large from Texas) also worked on behalf of the Klan.

The actual number of delegate Klansmen at the convention was relatively small, but there were enough to give rise to wild rumors and exaggerations. It was said that the Florida delegation was "full of Klansmen." The Georgia delegation was allegedly "all Klan." Texas, Oklahoma, and Arkansas were supposedly under its thumb. Ohio, it was said, "had to listen to the Klan." By the time of the opening of the convention it was even believed that William Jennings Bryan was a representative of the Klan. Most of these rumors originated with the New York press, especially the New York *World*, which asserted that there were "more than a thousand" Klansmen in New York and that at least three hundred of them were official delegates. Indeed, the *World* claimed that every delegation, with the exception of three or four, contained from two to thirty Klan members or sympathizers, and that three, and perhaps as many as six, Democratic national committeemen were Klansmen. Allegedly, they were all under orders to "remain quiet and vote hard."

The Klan downplayed its importance at first, denouncing such speculation as ridiculous and contending that there were "no Klansmen" in attendance. However, perceiving the fear and consternation that such exaggerations produced among its enemies, the Klan soon fell in with the game. By Saturday, June 21, it claimed that it controlled at least 50 percent of more than a dozen delegations. It said that 85 percent of the Georgia delegation, 80 percent of the Arkansas, Texas, and Kansas delegations, 75 percent of the Mississippi delegation, and at least 50 percent of the Missouri, Ohio, Iowa, Kentucky, Michigan, Tennessee, and West Virginia delegations were Klansmen.

Whatever its actual strength, the Klan's propaganda was insidious.

Thousands of copies of its menacing publication, *The Fellowship Forum*, were distributed, making a deliberate appeal to religious prejudice and viciously assaulting the Catholic Church. Further, numerous Klan-sponsored letters were circulated among southern and western delegates urging the defeat of Smith and signing off, "Faithfully yours in the Sacred Unfailing Bond." Significantly, just before the convention opened the Klan listed Al Smith's major drawbacks in this order: (1) his Catholicism (2) his wetness, and (3) his Tammany background.

The reaction of New Yorkers to all this pre-convention animus was a combination of urban chauvinism, surprise, amusement, confusion, and sullen anger. Even before the first delegate arrived, the New York press, as McAdoo charged, showed itself to be hopelessly pro-Smith. Even those newspapers which were not supporting Smith for the nomination, such as the *New York Times,* were anti-McAdoo. Although the New York press always gave the McAdoo candidacy ample coverage, its editorial policy was overwhelmingly unfavorable to him. McAdooites were pictured in the worst light and their complaints were brushed off as the fantasies of the deluded. Frequently the New York press went out of its way to taunt the McAdoo forces and loved to point up the connection between McAdoo followers, the Anti-Saloon League, and the Klan.

New Yorkers, in turn, rallied around their favorite son in a burst of civic pride. In the week prior to the convention every motion-picture theater in the city showed films of the New York governor. Everywhere there were Smith banners, Smith buttons, and Smith posters. Subway walls, elevators, downtown billboards, even traffic signs, were plastered with the name "Smith." Cab drivers urged their fares to vote for Al. Babe Ruth advertised Al as his candidate. Eddie Cantor, who had been an East Side boy on Catharine Street when Smith had lived nearby on South Street, once interrupted a scene in *Kid Boots* to make a personal pitch for Al. All this was contagious. On Monday night, June 23, in the Forty-ninth Street Theater where *The Melody Man* was playing, a pro-Smith partisan shouted out, "Al Smith, of course," at a point in the script where one actor asks, "Who is Alfred?" This prompted so much cheering and foot-stomping that the play was brought to a halt. The Tin Pan Alley song "The Sidewalks of New York" was heard and played constantly and soon grated on the ears of visitors from the mountains and the prairies, especially its new lyrics which went:

> Al, my pal, a nation's falling
> In the war 'tween might and right.

Al, my pal, your country's calling,
   Lead us onward in the fight!
Al, my pal, to you we're turning,
   Through dark clouds will shine the sun.
Al, my pal, for you we're yearning,
   Lead us on to Washington!

Not only did anti-Smith delegates become further alienated under the pressure of all this, but New York's parochialism and resentment at being spurned began to show. As complaints against the city grew, New York became waspish. Maids and hotel managers were soon complaining that out-of-towners knew little about tipping and that many were reneging on their bills. Cabbies claimed that instead of paying their fares visitors would frequently say, "Charge it to the convention!" If Al Smith and his Bronx-born wife reminded many western and southern delegates of the popular comic-strip characters Maggie and Jiggs, such delegates were soon referred to by New Yorkers as "apple knockers" and "turd kickers." New Yorkers began to mock southerners and derisively imitate the drawl of western Americans. This disdain was shown not only by the downtown common folk but by sophisticated uptown New Yorkers as well. The city's inhabitants simply stopped their ears against Bryan's admonition, given shortly after his arrival: "You New Yorkers are always forgetting that there is quite a bit of country outside of this State." New Yorkers even reacted with pride, not chagrin, to the comment of one disgruntled Oregon delegate: "They don't know whether Portland is in Oregon or Oregon is in Portland."

Such misunderstandings and antagonistic attitudes would have remained little more than an interesting social phenomenon had it not been for their impact on the candidates and on their tactics in the 1924 convention. The effect was particularly pronounced on McAdoo and Smith. McAdoo, of course, was reinforced in his belief that all the forces of the East and of the liquor interests were arrayed against him. Smith and his followers, on the other hand, felt demeaned and threatened. Prior to this time Smith had been surprisingly nonmilitant, taking far more than he gave. Vulnerable on the liquor issue, he had spent most of his time parrying the thrusts of prohibitionists. Now on his own turf and increasingly nettled by the personal attacks made on him by the Anti-Saloon League and the Klan, Smith decided to strike back. Just as the McAdoo forces found prohibition to be their strongest issue against him, the New York governor belatedly realized the political importance of the Klan issue against McAdoo. Over Roosevelt's objections he moved increasingly toward a hard anti-Klan line, and by the opening of the convention the naming of the Klan was as much a Smith goal as an Underwood one. Smith correctly sensed that by encouraging an anti-Klan coalition he could produce a turnabout by which wets could assume a moral stance on religious toleration to match that of their militant prohibition adversaries on the liquor question. Besides, in lending his support to the anti-Klan drive, Smith was not only fighting for himself but in an indirect way was also defending the battered honor of his native city.

5

Several other matters arose prior to the opening of the convention which served to heighten animosities and harden positions. The first was convention organization.

Actually, the contending factions within the party managed to resolve this particular problem with minimum turmoil largely because of the skillful maneuvering of Cordell Hull. A Tennessee representative to the 60th through the 66th congresses, Hull had been a member of the Democratic national committee since World War I. He had first served under Homer Cummings of Connecticut, who had been chairman of the national committee during the last stages of the war. When Cummings's successor and Cox's campaign manager, George White, was unseated by pro-McAdoo elements in 1921, Hull had taken the post of national chairman with considerable misgivings. His first task was to pay off the horrendous 1920 campaign debt and regroup the party's shattered forces. For the next two years he stumped the country, wheedling funds wherever he could, even using his own money to keep a skeletal party headquarters afloat. At the same time he created a publicity bureau in Washington, D.C., to encourage and sustain Democratic enthusiasm. These efforts had paid off handsomely in the congressional elections of 1922.

Although Hull was no ideological leader and had no personal following, he was highly respected and wielded considerable influence in the party by 1924. Hoping to retire from the chairmanship and reclaim his position in the House of Representatives as soon as this convention was over, Hull intended to remain on good terms with everybody, and one of his primary goals at New York was to assure that the organization of the convention would be as unbiased as possible. To some extent this was beyond Hull's control. For example, by 1924 McAdoo sympathizers held a majority on such important convention committees as credentials, resolutions, and rules. This was not true, however, on the arrangements committee, where the McAdoo group did not have a majority. As a result, when the question of a keynoter and temporary chairman arose at this committee's first meeting in April, there was an immediate demand by anti-McAdoo elements that he not be pro-McAdoo. So much squabbling ensued that Hull almost despaired of a compromise, but finally got the committee to accept the name of Senator Byron Patton (Pat) Harrison of Mississippi as keynoter and temporary chairman. Harrison was not the sponsor of any candidate.

Similarly, with Hull's help, the sticky matter of a permanent chairman was resolved relatively amicably. None of the various factions wished to see an unfriendly face in this position and argued for their own choice. McAdooites insisted on J. Bruce Kremer of Montana, an ardent McAdoo man and vice-chairman of the national committee. Favorite-son supporters and Smith men demanded that the permanent chairman be uncommitted. Under Hull's prodding the McAdoo element finally offered the name of Senator Walsh of Montana, and the anti-McAdoo groups quickly accepted it. As a hero of the oil investigation Walsh would make a marvelous symbol; besides, he was no longer pro-McAdoo, and he was Catholic. Smith forces, in particular, were pleased by the Walsh selection. Although a Catholic, Walsh was not supporting Smith, but he was a bitter foe of the Klan.

Agreement on these organizational matters was seen as a good sign by many, including Hull. But their hopes were soon dashed. Other convention procedures were not so easily resolved, especially the disposition of the two-thirds and unit rules. The two-thirds rule had a long history. It had originated in Andrew Jackson's day to show broad convention support for the nominee, but it had been a source of friction ever since. Minorities and states'-rights advocates had clung to it. This two-thirds rule had been the major cause for the lengthy balloting at many Democratic conventions and was the reef upon which so many presidential aspirations had foundered. By means of the two-thirds rule, for example, the South had defeated Martin Van Buren's nomination in 1844, Stephen A. Douglas's in 1860, and Champ Clark's in 1912.

The unit rule also represented an archaic and troublesome procedure.

Under it a state delegation could cast *all* its votes in the name of the candidate who controlled the majority of the delegation. This practice had come into being naturally rather than as a result of any official party action. Traditionally the Democrats had permitted each state convention or party caucus to instruct its delegation whether it was to use the unit rule or not. Democratic national conventions had never exercised any monitoring control over the matter and had to accept whatever decision the individual local bodies had reached in this regard.

In 1924, because of the two-thirds rule, 732 votes were necessary for the nomination. Only 550 of the 1,098 official delegates would have been required for a simple majority. As for the unit rule, a hands-off convention policy still applied, each delegation being subject to its own instructions. These facts presented the various candidates with different problems. McAdoo strongly supported the unit rule because some delegations in which McAdoo men had majority control operated under it, thereby placing the whole state in the McAdoo column. However, Mc-Adoo was opposed to the two-thirds rule. Although he claimed on the eve of the convention that he would eventually acquire a two-thirds majority, his chances for securing a simple majority were infinitely better. He well remembered how he had helped block Champ Clark's nomination in 1912 by means of the two-thirds rule even though at one point Clark had a majority of the convention.

As early as January there were discussions in the McAdoo camp about the feasibility of changing the two-thirds rule. Some favored it and some did not. Breckinridge Long and Roper feared that a move for its elimination would be taken as a sign of McAdoo weakness. Rockwell was not sure. Ultimately, Roper issued a statement in McAdoo's name that he would not seek a change. However, after the Doheny testimony and the softening of McAdoo support in March, April, and May, the question was again raised. By mid-June McAdoo was convinced that an all-out assault on the two-thirds rule had to be made. Again, Long and Roper counseled caution and suggested that no action be taken until general party opinion could be ascertained.

Almost to a man favorite-son candidates and their supporters wanted retention of the two-thirds rule. Underwood was opposed to any change. So were Franklin Roosevelt and the Smith element. If any modification of the two-thirds rule was sought, said Roosevelt, the Smith forces would initiate action to abolish the unit rule also. Brennan, Taggart, and other urban bosses indicated that they, too, would fight to preserve the two-thirds rule. More important, numerous southern conservatives who were McAdoo backers also balked. McAdoo was therefore in a dilemma. Although the two-thirds rule was a serious obstacle for him, he could not afford a bitter fight over it. A loss on the issue might irrevocably damage his prospects. Besides, to press for this change might also open the question of the unit rule—a rule which was currently being used by eighteen delegations in which he possessed majority strength. Finally, after unnecessarily raising hackles over the possibility of a change and further alienating many favorite sons and their followers, McAdoo decided to abandon the struggle.

Even more significant than the rule changes in promoting animosities immediately prior to the opening of the convention was the matter of seating arrangements and the handling of admission tickets. Each delegation wanted to occupy the "best" seats and it was only after a bitter battle that a special seating committee decided that those states with "real candidates" would be seated as much as possible on the center aisle. New York was positioned five rows to the left of the center aisle starting nine rows from the front. California was placed on the opposite side of the aisle, its rows overlapping part of the New York delegation. Behind California was Alabama, also on the aisle. Bryan's Florida, Carter Glass's Virginia, and Ritchie's Maryland were seated far to the rear, much to their displeasure.

The inability of the architect to build more seats onto the floor of the Garden now became a critical problem. The traditional formula for delegation size in Republican conventions had been twice the number of a state's congressional allotment plus a few bonus votes for delivering that state for the party's nominee in the last election. Not so with the Democrats. They had long since permitted unconscionably large delegations by allowing a certain number of delegates to share votes. Usually these were half votes, but some delegations even permitted quarter votes to be cast. The theory was that this procedure allowed more people to participate in the work of the convention. In 1924 this meant that instead of the 1,098 official delegates planned for, some 1,436 showed up to cast these 1,098 votes. Some delegates were therefore forced to sit in sections reserved for alternates, and some alternates were pushed into the public galleries.

Simultaneously, a shortage of tickets developed. As early as January, 1924, before the tickets were even printed or a plan for their distribution was announced, New York scalpers were promising future delivery at $200 apiece. By April the pressure for tickets was so great that elaborate

Madison Square Garden decorated and floodlit for the 1924 Convention.

Thomas Taggart (Indiana), and Charles F. Murphy (New York), boss of Tammany Hall, laying plans for the upcoming convention.

The Democratic National Convention assembled at Madison Square Garden.

Senator Oscar W. Underwood and his wife, just after he announced as the first official Democratic candidate for the presidency in 1924.

William G. McAdoo and his wife, arriving in New York in June 1924 for the convention. David L. Rockwell, McAdoo's campaign manager, is on Mrs. McAdoo's left.

Tammany Hall, decked out for the convention.

Democratic National Committee Chairman Cordell Hull calls the convention to order on June 24, 1924.

The Permanent Chairman, Senator Thomas Walsh, stands by his state's standard.

Underwood

William Jennings Bryan and Brother Charley listen to a broadcast of the convention in a Waldorf-Astoria suite.

Al Smith in a characteristic campaign pose.

Underwood

Franklin Roosevelt consulting with New York delegate Nathan Straus during the proceedings.

A typical group of women delegates. These ladies are from Missouri.

precautions were created to prevent them from being counterfeited. It was also decided that not a single ticket would be given out until Sunday, June 22. At that time one ticket for each $100 contributed to the party was to be assigned by lot to contributors while the distribution to delegates and alternates was to be handled by the sergeant-at-arms. He was to call on each delegation and surrender the tickets only after each delegate showed him a certificate of election. No tickets were to be placed on general sale.

On Friday, June 20, the convention tickets, resembling small dollar bills with Jefferson's picture on the back and the date "1924" imprinted in the upper left- and right-hand corners, were driven to the Hotel Astor in an armored car. There they remained under guard until Sunday afternoon, when they were distributed to eligible contributors and delegates. Immediately some delegations, especially Ohio, charged that they were short-changed. Since J. Bruce Kremer, Homer Cummings, and Isidore M. Dockweiler were in primary charge of the tickets and were McAdoo men, it was claimed that they were holding some back for the benefit of McAdoo followers. At the center of this squabble was Edmond H. Moore, national committeeman from Ohio, who appeared in person at the ticket offices of the national committee and loudly demanded redress. Specifically, the trouble centered on a block of 2,900 tickets which were earmarked for the supporters of all the candidates.

Rockwell immediately denied Moore's charges that the McAdoo forces had more than their share, complaining instead that *they* had been cheated. They had been promised 1,000 tickets, he said, but had received only 200. The Smith delegation, Rockwell countercharged, "had tickets to burn." These lies about tickets, added Rockwell, represented "as raw a deal as has been handed the McAdoo organization since it arrived in New York City."

By June 26, two days after the convention opened, the ticket controversy had died down. Tickets suddenly appeared from somewhere and all factions found that they had enough. But if the furor subsided, the recriminations did not. Smith forces claimed that as a result of their complaining the McAdoo tickets had been smoked out. McAdoo men still asserted that Smith men had "stolen" the tickets for their own use. In any case, these ticket difficulties added to the bitterness felt by many of the candidates and their followers and made the attainment of convention harmony even less possible.

6

Opening Day, Tuesday, June 24. New York City was hot and humid—the temperature rose to 83 by noontime. McAdoo spent most of the day deep in consultation with his advisers, interrupting their sessions only briefly to talk with Bryan and a few other Democratic leaders. Al Smith was in Sea Gate, Long Island, caught by photographers and reporters while taking a swim, seemingly unconcerned about the convention's outcome. In the Garden itself, seven tons of chemicals had not completely eradicated the smell of lions as the delegates slowly began to gather. The redecorated hall was already acting like a huge sweatbox, its high ceiling shielded by the bunting and even its ventilators closed off by red and white streamers. Shortly before noon ten thousand tiny flags were released through apertures in the roof and held in suspension by suction fans while lavender and blue spotlights played on gigantic pictures of Jefferson, Jackson, Cleveland, and Wilson. It was a stirring sight, but nothing for long could take the delegates' minds off the stifling heat.

A planned parade of delegates to the Garden had earlier been canceled because of the humid weather, but some delegations marched to the Garden anyway. The first to enter was the Pennsylvania delegation, which had trooped down from the Pennsylvania Hotel accompanied by the 165th Infantry band. But there was little spirit as most of the other delegates arrived. Some said the lavish feast given for them the night before by the women's entertainment committee had made them logy. One of the largest meals ever served in New York City, that dinner had been attended by 3,500 guests, who consumed, according to the statistic-happy New York press, 320 steers, 5,250 pounds of chicken, 1,900 pounds of salmon, 10,500 rolls, 25 gallons of olives, and 24 quarts of maraschino cherries.

The convention was supposed to convene precisely at noon, but at that time many seats were unfilled and a decision was made to wait. Those who had arrived grew restless, getting up, walking around, and talking. Now and again there was a scattering of applause. Supporters of Smith clapped when George Brennan entered to take his seat with the Illinois delegation. A buzz went around the hall when Tom Taggart appeared and sat down with his Indiana colleagues. The Massachusetts delegation, headed by Senator David I. Walsh, led a weak cheer for

Smith and not long afterward the Georgia delegation self-consciously sang a song for McAdoo to the tune of "The Battle Hymn of the Republic." The greatest excitement occurred when Babe Ruth was seen in the gathering crowd. The Babe had dropped in for only a few minutes before going on to the ball park. He had gotten his ticket at the Smith headquarters that morning, having stopped by to give Smith a bat so that the New York governor could "knock out a nomination."

As more and more spectators and delegates arrived, the heat, which had been bad, became worse. An increasing number of delegates were seen coatless and collarless, with bright suspenders gleaming. Only the fastidious remained fully clothed in their Palm Beach suits. Soon fans, covered with the peace slogan "Law, Not War," began to appear. Humorous "gag" campaign buttons also began to show up on the shirt fronts and lapels of some delegates: "Charlie Chaplin for President," "Tom Mix for President," and "Ben Turpin for President." Reporting on these opening-day events the next morning, the New York *World* said that it was going to give its vote to cross-eyed Ben Turpin because he, of all the candidates, "could keep an eye on things."

At 12:45 P.M., with the galleries and the delegate section still not full, Cordell Hull stepped to the podium and gaveled the convention to order. Until the last minute it was not certain that Hull would be there because he had collapsed the day before in nervous exhaustion from his constant effort to keep all factions pacified. Now he introduced Patrick Cardinal Hayes for the invocation, causing a brief moment of embarrassment by first calling him "Cardinal Gibbons" (who had died three years before) and then "James Cardinal Hayes." Few persons west of the Hudson caught the last error. Much to the relief of the sweltering gathering the cardinal prayed for only four minutes. Next, Anna Case, dressed in a white lace gown and wearing a black picture hat, moved forward to sing "The Star-Spangled Banner." Even though she and the band were not synchronized, the convention liked it so well that they demanded an encore. This time the crowd sang along as the thousands of little flags held in suspension were allowed to float down on the delegates, who could scarcely wait for the anthem to end before scrambling for them.

By now the delegate section was full, offering observers their first opportunity to assess the group that would make the Democratic presidential nomination. The first scrutiny focused on the number of women. Although this was not the first convention which women attended, there were a sufficient number here to affect its color and tone. In the 1920 convention there had been 93 women delegates and 206 alternates. In 1924 there were 199 delegates and 310 alternates. In order to encourage greater participation by women, the party had given permission for each state to send as many as 8 one-half delegates, at least one-half of whom were to be women. About half the states had complied. Moreover, this was the first convention in which women served equally with men on the national committee, causing one woman delegate to comment somewhat indelicately that no longer did the men gang together—"on the contrary, they consorted openly with their feminine cohorts." Admittedly, there were some male chauvinists present who complained about this growing female influence, but they were in the minority.

Throughout the convention, the women appeared to take the experience much more seriously than the men. As the latter waved, smiled, joked, gamboled, and razzed each other, the women were attentive. It was obvious that they were new to politics. Indeed, as the convention progressed, they proved to be far less compromising than the men, carried grudges longer, and took offense more readily. McAdoo would rely heavily on female support to keep his forces from buckling. Smith, on the other hand, would take little notice of women, which was ironic since one of his chief advisers was female. In 1924 politics was still a man's game. Mark Sullivan might claim that the appearance of so many women at this convention sounded the death knell for "the older type politician," but such claims were largely wishful thinking. Although the influence of women was growing, the men who were the professional politicians "still operated the works." As one woman delegate later observed in the *Saturday Evening Post:* "Women have but laid hold of the hem of the garment; they have not altered the fabric or the fashioning of the robe."

Besides the presence of women in 1924, another fact about the assembled delegates was readily obvious. They were all white. There was not a black among them, or among the alternates. This was certainly not a convention where black interests were directly represented. Other characteristics of the delegates were apparent—here was a dignified courtly gentleman with a heavy southern accent, wearing a gold watch chain laden with fraternal emblems; over there was a raw-looking, ten-gallon-hat wearer from the cattle ranges; back there was the weather-beaten, countrified face of someone from the wheat belt. But the most important facts about the assembled delegates were not that easily discernible. It was impossible to tell merely from looking at them who was wet and who was dry, who was Catholic and who was Protestant, who was a captive of the unit rule and who was not, and who was controlled by a local political machine, or the Anti-Saloon League, or the Klan.

After the national anthem was finished, delegates and spectators settled in their seats as the traditional opening activities began. Hull read the list of the temporary officers. At the name of Pat Harrison the Mississippi delegation rose and cheered while Harrison strode to the speaker's stand to deliver the keynote address. Keynoters are usually selected for their oratorical ability and Harrison was no exception. He could talk on anything. As one political commentator assessed him, Harrison could in Detroit give so effective a campaign talk on Kosciusko that it would "cause all the livers of all Poles to tremble" yet the next day could deliver a speech on Lee in a Confederate cemetery that would "melt the tombstones themselves." Wearing a bow tie and a soft collar, and having a high forehead which belied the fact that he was the second-youngest member of the Senate in 1924, Harrison gave the convention a gourmet sampling of his forensic talents. Rolling his words about in his mouth to give them both an Irish and a southern coating, Harrison engaged in hyperbole so extravagant that even the most militant delegate was satisfied. Calling his colleagues "Dimmicrats" and the Republicans "the innimy," he expressed "utter amazemunt" at the degradation of the government in Washington. As he zeroed in on the Teapot Dome oil scandal the Georgia delegates in the front rows, who had been interjecting "Atta boy, Pat, give it to 'em!," fell temporarily quiet, but rediscovered their voices as soon as he returned to safer ground. New Yorkers, amused at the obvious discomfort of the McAdoo men during Harrison's recital of the oil corruption in Washington, were themselves embarrassed a short time later when the galleries met Harrison's call for a new Paul Revere with much cheering in the mistaken notion that he had said, "What this country needs [is] real beer."

Throughout his speech Harrison shouted his words as if there were no loudspeakers, constantly mopping his face and running his fingers across his head. Up in the galleries his rolling "r's" sounded like strikes in a bowling alley, and such alliterative phrases as "petted and pampered puppets" shattered eardrums. Young men seated at telephones reporting to the control room on how the speaker's voice was coming through were seen frantically talking but to no avail. The only respite came when a demonstration started approximately two-thirds through Harrison's speech when he called for the convention to choose another Wilson. At the mention of Wilson's name, the Georgia delegation lifted its banner amid yipes and howls and started around the hall. Others followed. Ironically, only New Jersey, which had sent Wilson to the White House, did not participate, being unable to get into the line of march because of a jam-up somewhere.

The demonstration for Wilson not only allowed the delegates to let off some steam but permitted Harrison to rest his voice and the galleries to rest their ears. After twenty minutes the parade degenerated into a meaningless crush of people, who finally returned to their seats by whatever route they could find. Still mopping his brow, Harrison prepared to resume his speech only to see Anna Case stride forward to lead the delegates in "The Battle Hymn of the Republic." Exhilarated by the convention's reception of the opening "Star-Spangled Banner," Miss Case was too bumptious to pass up this new opportunity to show her talent. As Anna's voice soared and swooped, Harrison first smiled at the lovely lady. But as she launched into another verse, and then another, and finally a chorus, he hitched forward so far that her right hand barely cleared his head as she directed the audience. Finally sensing his mute appeal, she wrung one more "Glory, glory, hallelujah!" out of the delegates and then returned the convention to him. Harrison never quite got into the swing of things again. The last third of his hour-and-fifteen-minute address was anticlimactic, dealing mainly with the need for party harmony. At its conclusion only a very brief demonstration occurred as the convention's official band, the thirty-two-piece Seventh Regimental under the direction of a Lieutenant Sutherland, played "It's a Long, Long Trail." The song was prophetic; Harrison's hope for harmony was not.

The remainder of the opening day's proceedings was largely perfunctory. Mayor Hylan of New York followed the keynote address with a few welcoming remarks. Appearing before the delegates as "a great Mayor of a great city in a great state," Hylan began by coughing and clearing his throat, almost rupturing the eardrums of those in the galleries. His sparse build caused whispered comment among southern and western delegates that he did not "look like a Tammany man." Hylan was not fat enough. His speech was mercifully short, unnoteworthy except for a curious oblique attack on Wall Street and an invitation to the delegates to enjoy themselves. His announcement that all delegates and their alternates would be passed through police lines with the utmost dispatch and that "New York's finest" had been ordered to assist them in every way brought cheers from the convention. "That's the best thing I've heard today," said a voice directly below the rostrum. Another remarked to his neighbor,

"I'm gonna get drunk tonight." He was wearing a huge McAdoo button.

After Hylan left the speaker's stand a few isolated resolutions were adopted and the convention adjourned at 3:10 P.M., its first day's labor completed. Reaction was mixed. Most delegates said they were satisfied with the day's happenings, McAdoo and Smith men agreeing that Harrison had been properly neutral. Most newspapers, however, believed that the day had been unexciting. Except for the Wilson demonstration, the delegates had seemed lethargic and inattentive. Much of the time they had whispered among themselves, strolled around, and were apparently oblivious of what was occurring on the platform. The galleries stumbled away from the Garden, their ears still ringing from the faulty loudspeakers. The radio audience was frankly disappointed. Beginning at noon, Graham McNamee, who was responsible for convention radio coverage, did his best to keep listeners interested by telling the home folks what the galleries looked like, how the hall was decorated, and what strategy was being planned by the various candidates, but even he could not compensate for the rather uninteresting opening performance.

Only the New York police seemed completely happy with the first day's proceedings. No one was seen violating the prominently displayed "No Smoking" signs, not a single fight was reported, not a single arrest was made. There were not even any complaints. It was, said one police inspector, "the best behaved big crowd I have ever seen." In view of the pre-convention tension that had been building in the city for over a week, newsmen could not believe it. Being cynics, however, they assumed it would not last long. To an English visitor impatient for things to happen, one American reporter quietly said, "Just wait, those are Democrats down there."

7

The delegates were extremely slow to arrive in the Garden on the morning of June 25, and Harrison was unable to call the convention to order until 11:45 A.M. The primary business of the second day was to receive the reports of the major convention committees, listen to an address by the permanent chairman, and begin the nominating speeches for President.

After a brief invocation, the credentials committee made its report.

The chairwoman of the committee, Mrs. Leroy Springs of South Carolina, moved to the rostrum to the tune of "You Great, Big Beautiful Doll," and indicated that her committee had had little to do. Despite the intra-party tension and acrimony, only very minor delegate adjustments had been necessary. Next, Thomas H. Ball of Texas delivered the report of the committee on permanent organization, recommending that Senator Walsh of Montana be made permanent chairman. A ten-minute demonstration ensued as Walsh was escorted to the platform. When order was restored, Walsh began his speech.

Walsh had been brought to the rostrum as the Sutherland band played "Smile, Smile, Smile." But the Montana senator rarely smiled. His image was consistently dour. His mustache was stubby but drooped at the edges, pulling his mouth down at the corners. His eyes were piercing behind a jungle of eyebrows. The stark contrast between his graying hair and his jet-black mustache was immediately noticeable. Calm, fair, and judicious, Walsh possessed the air of a cold intellectual. Always neatly dressed, he wore a coat and a vest throughout the convention despite the hot weather, causing one joker to claim that he slept "fully costumed and wakes with creases undisturbed."

Walsh's speech was a lawyer's brief against the Republican opposition. Concentrating on the microphone before him, his words were heard by the radio audience but not by all the delegates. The only spot of interest occurred halfway through when, temporarily carried away by his condemnation of the oil-bespattered Republicans, Walsh defied the world to name a Democrat who was tainted by corruption. In the embarrassed silence that followed, Smith delegates began to snicker, causing Walsh to add quickly, "while he was in office." That made matters worse, and giggles rippled through the hall while Walsh struggled on quickly.

Except for this brief moment the delegates were mainly inattentive, wiping hankies under their wilted collars, fanning themselves, and reading newspapers. As on the day before, the noon sun had made the Garden a steam bath. Yet the delegates mustered enough energy to give Walsh a half-hearted accolade at the close of his speech, which was accompanied by the release of a pigeon symbolizing the Dove of Peace. The poor bird flew bewildered and frightened toward each of the hall's twelve searchlights before finally seeking refuge among the steel rafters. Its continued presence there caused nervous glances to be cast heavenward by the assembled delegates.

Following Walsh's address, the committee on rules made a recommendation that the convention proceed immediately to the nominations for President since the platform committee was not yet ready to report. Because of the large number of nominations to be made, the Smith and McAdoo forces had already agreed that this session should last at least through California on the roll call of states. Thus, at 1:25 P.M. and amid stifling heat, Alabama's name was read and a nomination marathon began which would extend over the next three days.

Fortunately the delegates did not know this; otherwise the air of expectancy that met Forney Johnston as he stepped forward to nominate Senator Underwood would have quickly evaporated. Johnston was a young, trim, good-looking southerner who was a practicing attorney in Washington and the son of a former Alabama senator. He delivered a rather scholarly address whose main theme was that Underwood was a champion of freedom of speech and religion. As he spoke the convention was quieter and more attentive than at any previous time because it sensed that Johnston's entire effort was an implied censure of the Klan. When Johnston mentioned the 1856 Democratic plank which had condemned the Know Nothings, there was great applause, and some delegates, thinking this might be their only chance to register their feelings on the subject, jumped to their feet. Walsh vigorously gaveled them down. But shortly thereafter, when Johnston suggested that a similar resolution be placed in the 1924 platform condemning the Ku Klux Klan, the convention broke loose.

No sooner had Johnston's mouth begun to form the words "Ku Klux Klan" than half the delegates were on the move. As the band struck up "America," the Alabama delegation rushed into the aisle, followed closely by the New York delegation, with state senator James J. Walker at its head. Massachusetts and the other New England states quickly joined as did Maryland, New Jersey, Ohio, Illinois, Minnesota, and Wisconsin. But eighteen delegations, mainly supporting McAdoo and referred to by the press as "McAdoo Alley," remained seated amid taunts of "Come on, stand up, you Kleagles." Kansas sat sullenly by her banner. So did Oklahoma, the Carolinas, and Georgia. Texas wobbled only briefly. Arkansas and Mississippi did not move. In Colorado and Missouri there was extreme confusion. When John Keegan of Missouri grabbed his state's standard, delegate-at-large Frank H. Farris jammed it back into place and a wrestling match ensued, during which Mrs. Milford Riggs, an elderly woman, came to Farris's aid. As Keegan shoved her away, a two-hundred-pound New York policeman moved in and gave the standard to

Mrs. Riggs, warning Keegan, "There, there, now, you wouldn't take it away from a lady, would you?" In Colorado a tangle of men fought for its standard until there was nothing left but the frame and a splintered staff. As the situation also began to degenerate elsewhere, the band hastily struck up "The Star-Spangled Banner," but not before there were more ripped coats, torn shirts, and smashed signs. When order was restored at the end of twenty-five minutes, many red-faced and angry McAdoo delegates were seen still guarding their standards and shouting insults at the wilted but militant anti-Klan marchers.

The convention was at last beginning to perform as expected, and political commentators rushed to the phone and the telegraph office to file their stories. McNamee now had something to tell his radio listeners and he did so with relish. The galleries were electrified. Most spectators rose in their seats and shouted encouragement to the marchers. When fights erupted in the Missouri and Colorado delegations the galleries yelled and hollered. When Texas and California refused to move, they jeered. After order was restored and Johnston finally got to name his man—Underwood—the galleries again cheered and applauded, not so much in support of the Alabama senator as for his courage in challenging the Klan. Walsh, meanwhile, pounded the head off his gavel in successfully preventing another demonstration. Reporters immediately descended on Rockwell to ask if the anti-Klan turmoil had hurt McAdoo's chances. Rockwell said no and claimed that the "demonstration didn't mean a thing." As much as Rockwell might deny it, however, almost everyone else agreed that the Johnston speech and the anti-Klan demonstration had removed any possibility that either McAdoo or the convention could ignore the Klan issue.

8

After Alabama, the roll of states continued. Arizona passed. Arkansas, represented by an almost inaudible speaker, nominated Senator Joseph Robinson, "one of the world's immortals." As Robinson's name was mentioned, the band started playing "Ole Black Joe." Ironically, Robinson was under suspension from the Chevy Chase Country Club at that moment for blackening the eye of a fellow golfer on the fifteenth green. A brief two-minute demonstration hardly showed that Arkansans believed in ultimate victory for their favorite son. Meanwhile, a debate occurred at the edge of the New York delegation between J. Bruce Kremer (floor manager for McAdoo) and Franklin Roosevelt. It was already 2:45 P.M. and the delegates were hot and tired. The temperature outside the Garden was 87, but inside it was at least 100. Clouds were piling up in the sky and rumblings of thunder were heard in the distance. The humidity was almost unbearable. Kremer was arguing that despite the earlier agreement to carry the roll call through California, the convention ought to be adjourned so that a fresh start could be made in the morning. Roosevelt was shaking his head "No." When Kremer persisted, James Hoey slyly suggested that Kremer put the question to the convention and see which side had the most votes. After a hasty conference among McAdoo advisers, Kremer decided not to risk a confrontation at this time and, as California's name was called, James Phelan strode to the platform.

California naturally wanted the best exposure for McAdoo and realized that a hot and tired convention, already upset by the Underwood anti-Klan demonstration, represented a poor showcase. Phelan's performance was certainly no help. In a marathon speech which sounded as if his mouth were filled with mashed Irish potatoes, Phelan made it appear that McAdoo had won World War I single-handedly and was personally responsible for Wilson's New Freedom program. McAdoo had selected Phelan to make his nominating address because he was Catholic and could neutralize some of the anti-McAdoo Catholic criticism. But whatever advantage McAdoo hoped to gain was quickly eroded. One observer said it was "the worst speech never heard"; another said it almost "stampeded the convention for Smith"; still another claimed it would have killed the nomination "of Thomas Jefferson running on a ticket with Andrew Jackson." As Phelan droned on through his fifty-minute recital, there was so much talking and shuffling among the delegates that on two separate occasions Walsh had to gavel for quiet. Long before Phelan finished, the exasperated galleries were shouting, "Name your man! Name your man!" Finally Phelan raised his arms over his head and shouted: "William Gibbs McAdoo."

Throughout, California had been paying little attention to Phelan's words. California bear flags were being passed around, women were busily dressing up in Spanish costumes and cowboy hats, and "Mc'll Do" hatbands were being donned. Directly across from the speaker's stand above a flag-draped balcony exit sat Mrs. McAdoo, who was anxiously watching the preparations. When Phelan raised his arms, it was a signal for the demonstration to begin, and California delegates led by Gavin McNab rushed into the aisle shouting, "Mac! Mac! MacAdoo!" Now the standards, which had remained stationary during the anti-Klan demonstration earlier, bounced and swayed as jubilant McAdoo supporters took over the Garden for the next hour.

It was a feverish exercise in the mass expenditure of energy. In front of the California delegation two women carried aloft a twelve-foot banner "For Wilson in 1916; for McAdoo in 1924." Four women dressed in white Grecian costumes preceded them, blowing four cornets. At the head of the entire procession was Josephine Dorman of San Francisco, allegedly one of California's prettiest girls, wearing a red, white, and blue costume, and being carried by two men. For forty minutes she kept smiling at the shouting delegates before her two supporters staggered under their load and finally fell. Shortly thereafter, when it appeared that the demonstration was beginning to lag, a male cheerleader dressed in white and waving a McAdoo banner appeared on the speaker's platform to stir things up. Joined by a young woman in a bright yellow dress, the two of them jumped and shouted and directed a women-delegate cheering section which gathered below the platform. Their favorite chant was: "We don't care what Easterners do; the South and West are for McAdoo!"

At one time or another twenty-seven state standards were counted in the McAdoo procession. This number was somewhat misleading, since Illinois's standard was in the parade even though only eight of her fifty delegates were sympathetic to the Californian. The same was true of Connecticut. In several delegations there were some tense moments as pro-McAdoo and anti-McAdoo men sparred with each other. In Wisconsin there was a scuffle as a lone giant grabbed the standard and moved into the McAdoo parade, successfully defying his colleagues to stop him. Again, Colorado became a focal point of contention. Governor Sweet attempted to carry the Colorado standard, which had been repaired from the effects of the earlier altercation, into the McAdoo parade. Suddenly he was attacked by Smith sympathizers, whose actions left the state's standard wrecked as before. A police inspector and four sergeants were finally required to break up the struggle and settle Colorado down. In the end Sweet gave up, resumed his seat, and cooled himself with a "Law, Not War" fan.

After the first few moments of the McAdoo demonstration most pro-

Smith delegates became bored. In general they retained their sense of humor, but a number of caustic remarks were passed back and forth. Sneers of "Oily nightshirts!" brought forth the rebuttal that "Everyone is for McAdoo except New York." In the galleries the situation was different. To the dismay of McAdoo supporters there was barely any enthusiasm there for their candidate. Anticipating adjournment after the McAdoo nomination, many spectators had already left, leaving huge clumps of empty seats. Those who remained were militantly anti-McAdoo. Before long, chants of "Mac! Mac! MacAdoo!" were being answered from the galleries by "Smith, Smith, Alfred Smith." "Ku, Ku, Ku Klux Klan" and "Ku, Ku, McAdoo" also were favorite gallery taunts.

At 4:27 P.M. a frustrated Walsh managed to regain control of the convention while numerous delegates as well as spectators rushed for the exits to beat the thunderstorm which was still threatening outside. George Brennan of Illinois quickly moved for adjournment until 10:30 A.M. the next morning in order to close off any possibility that the Mc-Adoo leaders might attempt to keep the convention in session and force a Smith nomination under the same unsatisfactory conditions. Next on the roll call was Colorado, and then came Connecticut, which intended to yield to New York. But McAdooites had had enough for one day and Kremer himself seconded Brennan's motion. Amid a chorus of ayes the convention broke up at 4:35 P.M., just in time for the majority of delegates to be drenched by a vicious downpour. For McAdoo supporters it was a bad omen.

9

Thursday, June 26. This was to be Al Smith's day in the Garden and New York came virtually to a standstill in anticipation. Few people were on the streets and business establishments near the Garden were shut down. Those who could not attend the convention remained close to radios. During the convention's third session the sidewalks of Manhattan, said the *New York Times,* "were more like rural Main Street on Sunday than a cosmopolitan thoroughfare."

In the Garden itself there was a capacity crowd on hand for the first time since the convention opened. No longer was there doubt about what had happened to many of the "missing" tickets. They had come into the possession of Smith supporters. Even so, many in the galleries on Thursday morning had no tickets at all, jamming their way past frustrated guards by showing pasteboards of all kinds or claiming that they were "convention workers." Obviously they were there to make McAdoo's demonstration of the day before look like a wet firecracker, and they swarmed into seats on a first-come basis, refusing to budge even when the real ticket holders showed up.

As they filled every inch of the spectators' sections, the pre-storm heat of yesterday could still be felt in the hall, but these leather-lunged Smith advocates did not mind. Holding noise makers, banners, placards, and other paraphernalia, they fidgeted anxiously as Walsh attempted to bring the convention to order. At 11:00 A.M. he made his first try but finally just shook his head and sat down. Meanwhile, Franklin Roosevelt was brought to the speaker's platform in a wheel chair and sat there nodding to friends and shaking hands. The New York delegation was in place, everything in readiness for the impending demonstration. At 11:10 Walsh tried again and by 11:20 he was already so hoarse that his voice barely carried over the amplifiers. Finally, at 11:23 he introduced the Reverend William W. Porter, who began to pray amid cries of "Shut up" and "Sh-sh-sh." By the time the Reverend got to the Lord's Prayer the convention was finally quiet for the first time that day.

The roll call began. At Colorado's name Governor Sweet came forward to second McAdoo's nomination of the day before. The New York audience, which had come to cheer its favorite son, was not in the mood to hear more pro-McAdoo oratory. From the moment Sweet opened his mouth he was met with catcalls and boos from the galleries. Almost every sentence attracted rude comments or shouts of "Oil!" or "Al." When Sweet said that McAdoo was responsible for the Federal Reserve Act, voices in the galleries yelled out, "No! No! Glass!" Twice Walsh found it necessary to step to the podium and gavel for order, but each time the noise and the jeering resumed. So rude were the galleries that one irate Texas delegate jumped to his feet and proposed "that the men disorganizing this convention be removed from the hall." Walsh ruled that such a motion was not yet required but indicated that he might later accept it if Sweet was not permitted to continue in peace.

The New York delegation was frankly embarrassed by this pro-Smith shouting. The dapper Jimmy Walker, coatless for the first time in memory, looked up at the galleries in pain. James Hoey, in charge of the New York delegation while Roosevelt was on the speaker's platform, hurriedly dispatched a squad of Tammany men to the spectator sections to enforce order. To underscore their disapproval, the New York delegation loudly applauded Walsh's warning and also Sweet's speech. Hoey's emissaries, meanwhile, were busily admonishing Smith's supporters in the galleries that they were hurting Smith's cause rather than helping it. If they would just keep quiet a bit longer their moment would come.

It did. When Connecticut was called, Thomas J. Spellacy, speaking on behalf of his delegation, started to say that Connecticut yielded "to the great Empire State of New York." But he got no farther than the word "Empire" when a wall of noise hit the Garden. The tumult increased as Franklin Roosevelt was seen moving laboriously to the speaker's podium. Except for fate, Roosevelt might not have been taking these short but important steps. Bourke Cockran, the great Tammany orator who had nominated Smith in 1920, had been scheduled to make this speech but he had died earlier in the year. It was unusual for a campaign manager to deliver a nominating address, but Smith had decided on Roosevelt in late May not only because of Roosevelt's speaking ability, but because he was not a Catholic and was not associated with Tammany Hall.

Roosevelt had prepared this speech carefully, and in the month before the convention had honed it to a fine brilliance. Actually, it represented a collective effort. The skeleton had been provided by Proskauer, who, because of his intimate connection with Smith, had supplied the facts. Then he, Herbert Swope, and Roosevelt had come together and had gone over it. The staging, however, was the brain child of Roosevelt and Howe. Howe laid meticulous plans for Roosevelt's appearance and then occupied a front-row seat in the gallery where he could watch it all. Before Roosevelt started his walk, Guffey of Pennsylvania moved forward to the lectern and tested it to see if it would support Roosevelt's weight. Then, adjusting his crutches, Roosevelt took the arm of his seventeen-year-old son, Jimmy, and made his slow way to "the pulpit" as he called it. The noise which had been deafening ceased as Roosevelt gripped the lectern with both hands, threw his head back with a smile, and began to talk.

Acknowledging the turmoil produced by the pro-Smith galleries, he first chided them. "We expect that the guests of this convention will render the same fair play to all candidates and their friends that we would expect in any other city," he said. This was applauded not only by McAdoo men but even by the galleries. The remainder of Roosevelt's address was light, well-paced, and humorous. It shunned maudlin sentiment and contained none of the usual references to the candidate's humble beginnings. Roosevelt concentrated instead on Smith's achievements as assemblyman and governor. Delegates and spectators alike were captivated by Roosevelt's grace and style. By this time the difficulties that had plagued the audio system had been eliminated and every word came through sharp and clear. In contrast with Phelan, Roosevelt was "radiogenic" and used this trait to excellent advantage. He skillfully paced himself and allowed the frequent clapping to punctuate his speech at just the right moments. About three-fourths of the way through his talk, Roosevelt made a particular hit by referring to Smith as "the Happy Warrior of the political battlefield." This phrase, taken from William Wordsworth, was a contribution of Judge Proskauer. Roosevelt had been reluctant to use it, fearing it too literary for politicians, but he left it in at Proskauer's insistence. Thereafter it became Smith's *nom de guerre*.

By common consent Roosevelt's performance was one of the best of the convention. Emily Warner, Smith's daughter, wrote later that the speech thrilled its listeners and struck just the proper note. Oswald G. Villard said that of the sixty or seventy speakers he listened to during the summer and fall of 1924, Roosevelt was at the top. Walter Lippmann was likewise impressed, writing Roosevelt afterward: "I am utterly hardboiled about speeches, but yours seemed to me perfect in temper and manner and most eloquent in its effect." Unquestionably the person who was most pleased was Louis Howe, who gripped his hands so tightly while Roosevelt spoke that his knuckles turned white. Later he said that he would not have been surprised if the convention had at that moment stampeded to Roosevelt.

As Roosevelt moved to the end of his address, tension in the Garden grew. The galleries, which had been attentive and quiet, again became unruly. Several times there were false starts by hidden bands and by noise makers in the mistaken notion that Roosevelt had finished. Once Jim Hoey stood on his chair, his face flushed and angry, and shook his fist in the direction of an outburst. Finally, as Roosevelt urged the delegates to select "this man of destiny whom our State proudly dedicates to the nation—our own Alfred E. Smith," the spring released. It was 12:33 P.M. Roosevelt had talked for thirty-four minutes. His last word, "Smith," was never heard.

The bedlam was indescribable. The Garden turned into a cauldron of sound and movement. A half-dozen bands began to play as sirens, cowbells, whistles, buzzers, and fishhorns multiplied the cacophony. Remodeled to hold no more than 14,000 persons, there were close to 17,000 in the Garden during the Smith demonstration. In from the street marched an entire procession, fully organized, carrying huge Smith pictures and banners. The aisles were jammed not only by a parade of states but by Al's New York City friends. The New York delegation, of course, was first. At the mention of Smith's name, William T. Collins, sitting in the place of the dead Murphy, scrambled past two other delegates to grab the state standard and rush into the aisle. James A. Farley, a delegate from Stony Point, New York, lugged another state banner behind Collins. For the next hour these two men carried their burdens around the clogged floor of the Garden. Behind New York came New Jersey, Alaska, Nevada, Connecticut, Massachusetts, Rhode Island, Minnesota, Wisconsin, Vermont, Illinois, Ohio, and Wyoming.

Up in the galleries all restraints disappeared when a collarless and sleeveless man, after roaring "All set!," lowered his arm and a corps of helpers hired at $3.00 an hour pressed their thumbs on the buttons of big fire sirens hooked to cases of dry batteries. This metallic din wiped out all human voices and became a nerve-racking tidal wave of sound that was in marked contrast with Roosevelt's witty and urbane speech. Men and women sitting in front of these machines were blown out of their seats and staggered around shell-shocked. Children in the audience screamed with fright. Once started, the sirens did not stop but went on for more than half an hour. Originally most of this electrical noise was concentrated in only one area of the galleries; but then orders came to fan out, and men carrying batteries with horns still blazing moved to dispersed stations. Now the sound came from three sides instead of one and new streaks of empty seats appeared in the sirens' paths.

Meanwhile, the Sutherland band was striving to make itself heard, but its "Rosie O'Grady," "Mamie O'Rourke," and "Annie Rooney" were done in pantomime. The Smith paraders tried unsuccessfully to get in some kind of order as several other bands suddenly appeared from the outside. Like the Sutherland band, their music could not be heard ten feet away. At one point the crowd around the musicians was so dense that cornetists could not get their horns to their lips and the trombones had to play straight up in the air. The confusion was terrific. McNamee told his radio listeners that the Garden was a madhouse, that the walls of the building were trembling, and that he was fearful the skylights would fall down. McNamee's own voice was drowned in the din as he attempted to read Smith's biography.

For almost forty minutes there was no letup. Happy Smith supporters claimed this was "Al's party" and the city's tribute to its native son. One reporter subsequently called it "Smithville's biggest carnival." "The Old Town," he explained, "doesn't have a county fair or an Elk's street fair down on Main Street like the great open spaces west of the Hudson." This was its substitute. Further, Smith followers were determined to make this demonstration last longer than McAdoo's. They had warned earlier that if McAdoo's lasted a week, Smith's would go on for a month. Obviously not all of this demonstration was spontaneous, but much of it was. Smith bore the same relationship to the city's urban throngs that Bryan had once borne to the impoverished western farmer. Smith was the symbol of their hope and their pride. Smith's supporters were anxious to show that Al was "the people's friend" and in the process neither eardrums nor time was important.

After the first forty minutes and the demise of most of the sirens, individual noises again became discernible and the demonstration took on more meaningful forms. The parading became more regular as bobbed-haired girls, matron ladies, and hardened politicians marched for Al. At various intervals there were men stationed with ice water to give relief to throats parched from the constant shouting. At one point a contingent of newsboys, dirty-faced and barefoot, trooped around the hall. They finally gathered in front of the speaker's rostrum. One, about twelve years old, stood on the platform itself with his papers in his hand while the band played "The Sidewalks of New York." This was staged, of course, but it was dramatic and the crowd cheered. Smith himself had once been a newsboy.

At the end of an hour many of the demonstrators began to filter back to their seats. Most of the New York delegation were already in theirs when a fresh outburst was produced by an usher presenting a basket of flowers to Mrs. Smith, who sat in a box across from the speaker's stand. As she stood and bowed, tears coursing down her face, the fire sirens took a new lease on life. So did the bands. Again the noise was deafening and again the marchers formed. For ten minutes more Al's friends paraded and cheered.

Throughout this long and noisy demonstration, most delegates retained a remarkable degree of calm. Although the fervor of the marching and the yelling made it appear otherwise, only fifteen states or territories joined in the Smith demonstration. Thirty-nine did not. Smith supporters made some attempts to get recalcitrants to join but were rebuffed. Most

McAdoo delegations stationed guards around their state standards in the fear that Tammany goons would capture them and force them into the parade. As Smith marchers wheeled past the Georgia delegation, a half-dozen husky fellows massed close to the Georgia standard, one with his hand firmly on it. "Kleagles," shouted some of the marchers. "New York bums," retorted those in the Georgia camp. There were grins on both sides but animosity underneath. In the Missouri delegation four grim-faced women watched the Smith proceedings with distaste, one a gold-star mother in black. Scornfully, they threw balls of paper down the horns of tooting bandsmen, but on closer examination could be seen teetering up and down to the beat of the music as the bands went by. In the Kentucky delegation David Wark Griffith, the movie impresario, stood on a chair to obtain a better view. Not even his fertile imagination could conceive a scene like this. On the platform, Franklin Roosevelt sat nodding and smiling, great beads of perspiration standing out on his forehead. On the floor, one of the broadest grins belonged to Tom Foley, now rising rapidly in Tammany following Murphy's death. He was witnessing something Richard Croker could only have dreamed about—a Democratic convention going wild over one of Tammany's boys.

Outside the Garden the feeling for Smith was no less enthusiastic. When Smith's name was announced, a great shower of shredded newspaper, torn telephone books, office stationery, and confetti fell from the windows of New York's skyscrapers. Some of this debris was blown through the open skylights of the Garden itself and filtered down on the delegates below. Taximen and chauffeurs honked their horns, policemen yelled, and hats soared into the air. Streetcar motormen, passing the Garden, clanged their bells. Five thousand persons standing in Madison Square Park listening to three radio wagons sang and snake-danced into the street. Both Smith and McAdoo were listening to their radios when Roosevelt mentioned Smith's name—Smith in his Madison Square rooms and McAdoo in his Vanderbilt suite. McAdoo immediately huddled with his advisers and decided to hurry the convention along toward balloting. Smith was extremely pleased by Roosevelt's "Happy Warrior" speech but turned away inquisitive reporters with the noncommittal: "There is nothing I care to say at this time."

Back in the Garden the Smith demonstration finally came to a halt. At 1:43 P.M. Walsh attempted to restore order and Franklin Roosevelt helped by holding up his arms. Anna Case, now wearing a gown of flowered silk, also offered her services and began to sing "The Star-

Spangled Banner." The crowd quieted. But, as soon as she finished, a band on the fringes of the hall suddenly gave out with "The Sidewalks of New York" and a new demonstration threatened to start. Nettled by this renewed disorder, Roosevelt's face flushed and he shouted to a group of policemen, "Stop that band!" Despite all efforts, however, it was not until 2 P.M. that Walsh was able to command the convention's attention.

Now, at last, the various favorite sons had their chance. The remainder of the Thursday session was spent listening to endless nominating and seconding speeches. Following Roosevelt on the rostrum came Senator Thomas F. Bayard, who presented Senator Willard Saulsbury's name on behalf of Delaware. Florida was next and yielded to Missouri, which seconded McAdoo as jeers filtered down from the galleries. Georgia and Idaho passed. Illinois presented David F. Houston's name. The nomination of Wilson's Secretary of Agriculture was purely a courtesy and everyone knew it. More representative of Illinois feeling was Michael L. Igoe, who seconded Smith. Igoe's contention that "no oil has touched Al" caused several McAdoo delegates to jump to their feet, shake their fists, and yell "No fair" and "Rotten," while the galleries loudly chanted "Oil! Oil! Oil!"

After Illinois, Indiana came forward to nominate dark-horse Ralston. Frederick Van Nuys, Ralston's law partner, made an excellent impression by talking for only four minutes, using twenty-seven words fewer than Lincoln's Gettysburg Address to place the Hoosier senator in nomination. At the conclusion, a brief demonstration occurred as Anna Case sang "On the Banks of the Wabash," with the whole convention joining in the chorus. Throughout all this Tom Taggart could be seen sitting under the Indiana banner, his smile growing broader and broader.

Thursday afternoon wore on. Kansas nominated Governor Jonathan Davis to a scattering of applause. Howard Bruce then presented the name of Governor Ritchie for Maryland, prompting a modest demonstration, during which the Sutherland band all but wore out "Maryland, My Maryland." Massachusetts, which was expected to pass, came next. Instead, former Brigadier General Charles H. Cole came to the platform and made yet another seconding speech for Smith. This angered McAdoo delegates, who believed that the Smith forces were overdoing it. It also incensed the favorite sons, who felt that the rest of the day should be devoted exclusively to them. But the galleries loved it and by their stomping and yelling encouraged a new demonstration for Smith. Again the sirens started. Consternation showed on Roosevelt's face as he quickly gathered his lieutenants around him. Again agents were dispatched to the galleries while Jimmy Walker and Senator Royal S. Copeland struggled to keep pro-Smith delegates in their seats. McAdoo men, meanwhile, demanded that Walsh get on with the roll call. Banging his gavel and shaking with anger, Walsh hoarsely rasped into the microphone that unless such outbursts were stopped immediately he would adjourn the convention and reconvene it in some other city. McAdoo elements greeted this statement with gleeful clapping while New York leaders redoubled their efforts to quiet the crowd.

As the roll call continued and Michigan presented the name of Senator Woodbridge Ferris, feverish consultations were held in the New York delegation and among McAdoo leaders on the floor. It had just been learned that the platform committee was locked in combat over the Klan and would not be able to report to the convention before the following day (Friday). Since it was already past 4:30 P.M., Smith leaders wanted to adjourn the convention before more embarrassing pro-Smith demonstrations could develop. McAdoo leaders, on the other hand, wanted to keep the convention going, sensing that the actions of the galleries were eroding support for Smith and hoping that at least one or two quick ballots benefiting McAdoo could be taken before the platform committee reported on the Klan issue.

Consequently, after the Ferris nomination Kremer moved that the convention recess until 7:30 P.M., when nominations would be concluded and the balloting for President begun. Representative John J. Fitzgerald of Brooklyn immediately amended this motion to adjourn the convention until 10:30 A.M. the next morning. Amid shouts of "Yes! Yes!" and "No! No!" Fitzgerald explained that Kremer's motion would be unfair to those candidates whose names had not yet been presented, since the convention was already tired from the day's activities. Besides, said Fitzgerald, to hold an evening session would disrupt the many social events scheduled for the delegates. Kremer retorted that the delegates had not come to New York for pleasure but to nominate a President. With biting sarcasm he added that the delegates could probably forgo "New York hospitality" for one night.

With both sides still demanding recognition, Walsh put the question on the Fitzgerald amendment. This was the first test of strength between the Smith and McAdoo forces and each side feverishly rounded up votes. Utter confusion resulted as most delegations had to be polled on the floor. Almost without exception the McAdoo delegations voted against the amendment. New York, Illinois, Ohio, all of New England, New Jersey, Minnesota, Wisconsin, a majority of Pennsylvania, and some others voted for it. The result was 559 in favor and 513 against. The convention adjourned until Friday morning.

It had been an exciting day. As far as New Yorkers were concerned, the high point was the nomination of Smith. A few spectators had left following the Smith demonstration, but the vast majority had remained to continue to support New York's champion. Pro-Smith enthusiasm extended even into adjournment. As delegates left the Garden, they were reminded by thousands of New Yorkers that Smith was their choice. So great was the talk of Smith that McAdoo delegates removed their badges in order to merge with the crowd and not be bothered. At adjournment time there were still some demonstrations for Smith going on outside the Garden and delegates found it difficult to push their way through. Even the policemen stationed at the Garden now allowed their New York pride and pro-Smith sentiments to show. Their usual courtesy was mixed with comments like "Don't forget Al" and "He's a regular guy." After the day's session, a police captain was seen in front of the Garden sitting on a curbstone talking to a lukewarm Ohio delegate about the merits of Smith while others were standing around listening. Cabbies, motormen, hotel clerks, vendors, ushers, ticket takers, waiters, nearly everyone put in a good word for the New York governor.

The New York press reported on the day's happenings, especially the Smith nomination and demonstration, with its usual hyperbole. The New York *World* said it was "the biggest thrill" in the Garden's colorful history—more electrifying than the howls of the mob that cheered Charles Mitchell when he hammered John L. Sullivan out of the ring, even more sensational than the killing of Stanford White by Harry Thaw. The New York *Post* called it "the greatest demonstration of its kind ever staged in a national convention," and the New York *Herald Tribune* told its readers that Smith's supporters "raised the roof, bulged the sides, depressed the floor, and shook the rafters of the Garden. . . . They marched, sang, shouted, squawked, yelled and went into frenzied fits, fantoads, and catalepsies." All New York papers expressed pride in the fact that Smith's demonstration had lasted an hour and thirteen minutes, much longer than McAdoo's fifty-five.

But seasoned political commentators took a more analytical view. They suspected that the antics of Smith's supporters had cost him votes by intensifying the provincial dislike for the Big Town's candidate. Bruce

Bliven, writing for *The New Republic*, offered the reminder that parades and demonstrations do not change or sway many convention votes. After sober reflection, a *New York Times* editorial admitted: "Yesterday's protracted outburst showed that Smith could carry New York—or more accurately, that he could carry Tammany Hall. It did not show that he could carry the Democratic National Convention." Interestingly, almost all observers suggested that perhaps the real benefactor of the Smith nomination was not Al but his campaign manager. Roosevelt, it was said, was "a man to watch." All of the metropolitan newspapers agreed that his address was masterful and that no matter whether Smith won or lost Roosevelt had emerged as one of the stars of this convention.

McAdoo men, of course, were incensed at both the nature and the length of the Smith demonstration. They believed that its sole purpose had been to belittle McAdoo. The howling and discourteous actions of the galleries confirmed their fears of a "rigged convention." New rumors now swept the McAdoo camp. It was said that Tammany intended to "pack" the galleries each day until the nomination of Smith was assured. The liquor interests, it was claimed, were funding an all-out Tammany drive to "buy" delegates and bribe McAdoo supporters. It was even claimed that "black-garbed priests" were acting as cheerleaders for Smith in the galleries and were issuing Tammany's orders through the confessional.

Whatever the McAdoo or the Smith camps chose to believe, it was still doubtful by the conclusion of the Thursday session that either of the major contenders could win. Each, in his own way, had antagonized too many elements. Moreover, in both cases, their friends had often proved to be among their worst enemies. Despite all the shouting, the destiny of the convention still remained in the hands of the minority candidates.

10

The convention opened one hour and ten minutes late on Friday morning. The weather was rainy and dreary, but, to the delegates' relief, it was considerably cooler than the day before. Because of the rain and the strenuous activities of Thursday, most delegates and spectators drifted in only gradually, shaking the water off their umbrellas and shedding raincoats. They faced a boring bill of fare. A number of minor candidates remained to be named, and a long list of seconding speeches were yet to be heard.

Chairman Walsh ordered the roll call resumed with Minnesota. For the next six and one-quarter hours the Garden reverberated to florid oratory as one speaker after another made the most of his few moments in the national political spotlight. In all, about fifty thousand words were spoken, but listeners could believe it was fifty million. Elmer Davis later contended that the windstorm that had accompanied the rain after Mc-Adoo's nomination on Wednesday afternoon was nothing compared with the "big wind" that swept through the Garden on Friday. Before the day was over not only had six more nominees been added to the list but Smith was seconded four times and McAdoo seven.

Although Friday's session was anticlimactic, there were moments of interest and humor. A delegate from Minnesota never mentioned anything east of St. Paul in grandiloquently seconding Smith, who had never been west of Syracuse. Ohio's Newton D. Baker nominated Governor Cox in a rousing address that was followed by a seventeen-minute demonstration which, like most of those for the minor candidates, was about as spontaneous and effective "as a jew's-harp quartette playing chamber music to an audience of deaf mutes." Eugene D. O'Sullivan of Nebraska, who looked and acted as if he should have been from the Bronx, was supposed to extoll the virtues of his state's nominee, Charles Bryan, but devoted most of his speech to W. J. In the twelve-minute demonstration that ensued, many joined out of respect to the elder Bryan rather than out of any feeling for his younger brother.

So the chain of nominations went on. In a surprise move New Hampshire presented the name of its governor, Fred H. Brown, whose only other claim to fame was that he had once played baseball in the National League. Because the speaker constantly referred to him as a fine product of "the Old Granite State," the Sutherland band struck up "Rock of Ages" at the conclusion. When its time came New Jersey nominated Governor Silzer as expected, and the most enthusiastic demonstration of the day followed. For twenty-five minutes New Jerseyites stomped around the Garden while songs were sung for the convention by a group of Jersey City policemen. When Pennsylvania got the floor it would not relinquish it. With its delegation badly split and possessing no favorite son of its own, the Keystone State was responsible for no fewer than five seconding speeches—one each for Smith, McAdoo, Ritchie, and Underwood; nobody ever discovered whom the fifth one was for because when this hapless speaker arrived on the platform he was howled down with such ferocity that he was forced to leave without naming his man. He was rumored to have been for McAdoo.

Claude A. Swanson of Virginia made an able speech on behalf of the Old Commonwealth's favorite son, Carter Glass, that "great little man," but his effort was offset by the fervid oratory and non sequiturs of Governor E. Lee Trinkle, who seconded Glass's nomination. Smiles appeared when Governor Trinkle claimed that no one could "point a finger of scorn [at Glass] except with pride" and that Glass as President would replace the golden tinkle of the oil gusher with the strains of "The Battle Hymn of the Republic." Moreover, there was shocked consternation at the start of the Glass demonstration when the Sutherland band began playing "John Brown's Body Lies A-Mouldering in the Grave." This gaffe almost wrecked the whole thing before an embarrassed switch was made to "Carry Me Back to Old Virginny."

The last candidate to be nominated was John Davis of West Virginia. The presentation of his name came at the end of a long day and was well handled by Judge John H. Holt, who harpooned the rival party instead of rival candidates and maintained a congenial tone throughout. He spoke for only eighteen minutes, and his speech was followed by a five-minute demonstration which involved no parading and no uproar. The West Virginia delegates merely stood on their chairs and waved flags and a few held aloft portraits of their handsome candidate. Following the Davis demonstration, Mrs. Izetta J. Brown, also of the Mountaineer State, seconded Davis's nomination in the wittiest and best-received speech of the day. After Mrs. Brown, there was a quick Wisconsin second for Smith and then Wyoming and the six dependencies passed in rapid succession. The hands of the clock were already moving to 6 P.M., and as someone said, if any territory had added to the nominations or seconding speeches at this point, it would have been sold to Japan by the unanimous vote of the convention.

As the roll call for nominations drew to a close, there were hurried conferences among the leaders of the Smith and McAdoo camps. Kremer notified Brennan that the McAdoo forces once again wanted a night session in order to begin the balloting for President. Brennan, after talking with Roosevelt, told Kremer that no balloting should occur before the platform was debated. Fresh from their victory over adjournment on the day before, the Smith men surmised that the convention would again support their position, and McAdoo men, sensing the fatigue of the delegates, wisely decided not to press the matter. Glassy-eyed from the long-winded session, delegates and spectators alike had been squirming in their seats for the past several hours as one seconding speaker after another promised to talk for five minutes only to be dragged off the platform after fifteen. Similarly, they had suffered, mostly in silence, as nominators took thirty minutes to name their man only to continue for twenty minutes more. This was no time to test their endurance further.

When the decision was reached to adjourn until Saturday morning at 9:30, the Democratic National Convention had sixteen presidential candidates before it, placed there by forty-three speakers, and accompanied by nine major demonstrations. In the running were six senators or former senators, six governors, two former cabinet secretaries, one former ambassador, and one previously defeated presidential candidate. Such nominating activities had consumed almost three days. In the process deep wounds had been reopened, insults had been traded, existing party divisions had been widened, and attacks on the character and integrity of some of the leading candidates had been made.

Yet these nominating activities were only the preliminaries. The real business of the convention lay ahead. Not only had the balloting for President not yet begun, but the nature and the wording of the platform were still to be determined. Indeed, none of the basic issues which this convention had come to New York to resolve had yet been brought before it. According to the calculations of one political observer, if the past three days were any guide to the future, the convention would still be in session in October. A marathon political happening was clearly in the making and, with considerable foresight but a noticeable lack of enthusiasm, the Sutherland band sent the delegates home at Friday's adjournment to the tune of "It May be for Years, and It May be Forever."

PART IV

★

THE MAIN EVENT

1

When the Underwood anti-Klan demonstration occurred on Wednesday afternoon, almost all observers predicted that this was merely a prelude to what would probably rock the Garden later. In view of the rumored difficulties taking place in the platform committee, such prophecies seemed well founded. Indeed, as the opening days passed and no report was forthcoming from that committee, it was obvious that serious battles were being fought out of the sight and hearing of the galleries and most delegates.

Much of the work on a party platform is completed before a convention convenes. During the convention itself, the platform committee holds hearings and listens to advocates of all sorts of planks, but in the end it makes few changes. Following this customary procedure, Homer Cummings, chairman of the fifty-four-man platform committee, called a nine-man planning group together at a pre-convention gathering on Saturday, June 21, to block out the topics to be covered. Among those invited to attend was W. J. Bryan, but he had not yet arrived at the convention when this meeting was held.

The results were a disaster. Senator Glass, who was an observer at the Saturday planning session, left in dismay, confiding to reporters that it would be impossible to construct a platform on which both Smith and McAdoo could stand. Cummings himself was shaken by the disagreements within the group and adjourned it over the weekend in the hope that it could begin afresh on Monday. Bryan, meanwhile, announced as soon as he arrived in New York on Sunday that he had brought a whole platform with him, and immediately went into conference with McAdoo for an hour and a half. He emerged from this tête-à-tête claiming that he and McAdoo saw "eye-to-eye" on the platform. Such an admission did little to enhance the image of conciliator which Bryan sought to exude.

The planning group never resumed its deliberations. Instead, the full platform committee convened at 5 P.M. on Tuesday, June 24, in the Rose

Room of the Waldorf-Astoria. Thereafter it met off and on for four days, trying to resolve its differences. Its first problem was the precise wording of a prohibition plank. Even the prohibitionists were divided on this matter. Wayne Wheeler indicated to the committee that he was opposed to any plank which would morally condemn drinking because its rejection might cause a loss in dry prestige. "We won this victory without such a plank," he said, and he preferred to leave it that way. Bishop Cannon agreed and favored, at most, a simple statement calling for the vigorous enforcement of the existing prohibition law. Bryan, on the other hand, hoped to secure an unqualified endorsement of the dry principle. So sensitive was he on the matter of liquor that when he was asked by the committee to frame a resolution regretting the death of Harding, he first proposed "Our party stands uncovered beside the bier of Warren G. Harding," but then changed "bier" to "grave" in the fear that someone might get the wrong idea.

The second matter of concern was the League of Nations. Unlike the prohibition issue, this became a problem solely because of the activities of one man—Newton Baker. A member of the platform committee from Ohio, Baker had come to the convention with the intention of recapturing the idealism of Wilson for the party. He was an ardent champion of the League and sought to persuade the committee to include a plank supporting immediate American participation. Baker believed that no other issue was as important as this one and led a parade of pro-League witnesses to testify in the hearings on Tuesday evening. One of them, ex-Judge John W. Wescott of Camden, New Jersey, argued the League's case before the committee so passionately that he collapsed in the hallway afterward and had to be carried to his room.

The Klan issue remained the big difficulty, and when the committee turned its full attention to this problem on late Tuesday night, a bitter argument erupted. Senator David Walsh of Massachusetts pointed out that Catholic and Jewish voters in the Northeast were watching the Democratic party carefully on this matter. Edmond Moore of Ohio warned that if the committee did not sponsor an anti-Klan resolution, one would be introduced from the floor. Moore capped his argument by stating: "If we do not destroy the Klan, it will destroy the Democratic Party." McAdoo men were equally vociferous in their demand that the Klan not be named. They claimed that it was unwise to give the Klan such visibility and that its dangers were exaggerated. Those from the deep South and from militant Klan areas of the Midwest asserted that it was no less political suicide for them to oppose the Klan than it was for their northern and northeastern brethren to ignore it.

Since each side refused to budge, Cummings adjourned the committee at 2 A.M. Wednesday morning with the injunction that each member secure specific instructions from his delegation on a Klan plank. Simultaneously, he appointed a drafting committee composed of himself and ten other members, including Bryan, Baker, and David Walsh, to begin writing the platform document. For a day and a half this small committee labored while the Garden reverberated to the McAdoo and Smith demonstrations. Some progress was made. Bryan finally agreed to a modified prohibition plank, accepting a simple statement for the enforcement of the Constitution and of all laws. Satisfied that a specific condemnation of drinking was not included, wet advocates did not challenge this. On the League question a variety of draft planks were proposed, none of which really suited. Ultimately a catchall statement was worked out which recommended that the United States join the League, but only if such action was preceded by a favorable national referendum. However, this was not acceptable to Baker, who warned the drafting committee that if this plank was sent to the convention he would submit his own resolution from the floor.

Again, the Klan issue caused the most difficulty. David Walsh urged the drafting committee to accept the wording of a plank submitted by Edmond Moore pledging the party "to oppose any effort on the part of the Ku Klux Klan, or any organization, to interfere with the religious liberty or political freedom of any citizen." Bryan not only opposed this resolution but also one sponsored by Underwood which would have resurrected the wording of the old 1856 anti–Know Nothing plank. Instead, Bryan advocated a Virginia proposal which would decry all attempts to limit constitutional liberties but not mention any organization specifically. This was unacceptable to anti-Klan men.

Working continuously until early Thursday morning, the drafting committee finally admitted its inability to resolve the Klan problem and threw it, along with Baker's objections to the League plank, into the lap of the full committee on Thursday afternoon. Convening at 3 P.M., this parent committee quickly accepted all of the drafting committee's work except for the planks on the Klan and the League. Over these two it argued through the dinner hour and, after a brief recess, on into the evening. Finally, at midnight, amid rising tempers and name calling, Chairman Cummings ordered the drafting committee to attempt once more to arrive at a satisfactory solution.

The drafting committee knew from the start that its task was impossible, and nothing was accomplished at its meeting on Friday. Baker remained intransigent on the League, and word was sent from the Smith and Underwood headquarters that they would accept nothing less than a specific condemnation of the Klan. McAdoo and his leaders reaffirmed their earlier decision to oppose any plank which would name the Klan. As a result, on late Friday afternoon the drafting committee returned the League and Klan issues to the full committee without either being resolved.

When the platform committee reconvened on Friday evening, positions had actually hardened. As debate on the League question began, Baker again attempted to win the committee to his position. Throughout the discussion pro-Smith men remained silent, allowing Bryan to counter Baker's arguments. Bryan justified a referendum on the League by claiming that public opinion in 1924 required it. In view of Harding's overwhelming victory in 1920, said Bryan, an unqualified endorsement of the League was politically unwise. In the end the committee voted 32 to 16 to sustain the drafting committee's position while Baker reiterated his intention of submitting a minority report from the floor.

Shortly after midnight the committee turned to the Klan issue. The debate was acrimonious, sometimes frenzied. A majority of the group believed that the religious bigotry fostered by the Klan should be condemned, but a majority also believed that the Klan itself should not be named. Anti-Klan men, however, were insistent. Fourteen in number, they represented the New England and Middle Atlantic states, plus Illinois, Alabama, and Minnesota. Again, David Walsh of Massachusetts and Moore of Ohio led the anti-Klan fight, while Bryan acted as spokesman for the opposite view. Although "principle" and "constitutionality" were constantly appealed to by both sides, ethnic, cultural, and religious considerations were mainly involved. Politics became secondary as a bitter encounter ensued based on conflicting patterns of life. Angry words, near fist fights, shouted obscenities, and personal insults punctuated the debate throughout the night.

Toward 6 A.M. on Saturday morning, as the hours of arguing dragged on, an overwhelming sense of futility descended on the platform committee. In fatigue and despair, the members decided to adjourn but held on to the slim possibility that something might occur during the day to break the impasse. Cummings was instructed to report to the convention that the committee was still working and would not present the final platform until Saturday afternoon. Bryan was so swept by emotion over the bleak prospect for success that just before the committee adjourned he turned to Judge John H. McCann, delegate from Pennsylvania and an ardent Roman Catholic, and asked him to lead the group in the Lord's Prayer. Upon its completion Bryan himself began to pray, and in a choking voice beseeched the Almighty to "Cleanse our minds of all unworthy thoughts and purge our hearts of all evil desires. . . . So guide and direct us in our work today that the people of our party and of our country and of the world may be better for our coming together in this convention and in this committee."

Bryan's "Daybreak Prayer" was indicative of what had happened to the Democratic party by Saturday morning, June 28. Bryan had often said, "I believe religion is of more importance than politics." Democrats were now beginning to know what that could mean. To Bryan's credit, as his fellow committee members staggered off for a few hours' sleep, he tried valiantly to construct a final compromise. He proposed to Moore that the convention condemn the Klan by name but not include it in the party platform. But the anti-Klan element was already gearing for a convention showdown on this matter and the Bryan proposal was rejected. Thus, when the platform committee at its final meeting early Saturday afternoon voted 40 to 14 to submit the Virginia plank to the convention, the dissident anti-Klan men announced that they would offer a minority report from the floor.

2

It was an hour past the convention's Saturday-morning scheduled opening before Walsh rapped for order. Rumors were already circulating concerning the platform committee's deadlock and Bryan's "Daybreak Prayer." It was said facetiously that the platform was "complete in all its unimportant parts," while the Bryan prayer, made after instead of before the Lord's Prayer, was dismissed by eastern delegates as Bryan's usual attempt to improve upon the Almighty. Still, Walsh surprised many in the audience by following the invocation with the observation that the convention needed "inspiration from song as well." Edith Bennett of Concord, New Hampshire, proceeded to sing "The Star-Spangled Banner," as delegates whispered anxiously to their neighbors.

The first order of business was the report of the platform committee. Cummings, who wore a pince-nez and was normally a rather sad-looking man, appeared sadder than usual as he faced the delegates. In a hoarse voice which he struggled to keep from cracking, he recounted the difficulties confronting the platform committee and admitted that it could not agree on two planks. The one, involving the League, he said, had prompted long but generally amiable discussions. The other, involving religious freedom, had caused bitter and acrimonious debate. Through the night, until 6 A.M. that morning, he stated, the committee had labored fruitlessly. Nevertheless, he explained, the majority still believed that it would serve no good purpose to have these issues debated by the full convention. Therefore, in the hope of yet finding an acceptable solution, the committee was requesting that the convention recess until 3 P.M. As Cummings finished, the buzzing among the delegates increased, but before anyone could object or ask for clarification, Walsh gaveled the convention into recess.

Spectators who held tickets for the fifth session only (Saturday morning) were crestfallen and angry shouts were heard because they felt cheated. One of those caught by the short morning session was Charles B. Lawlor who had composed "The Sidewalks of New York" some thirty years before. He was blind and for days had been listening to the convention by radio. Now, with his only ticket, he was there to "see" the excitement. It was just his bad luck, he told reporters, to pick the wrong session. Lawlor did not even get to hear his song played.

No sooner did the convention adjourn on Saturday morning than the word spread that a colossal fight was brewing for the afternoon. Consequently the largest mass of people yet seen clamored to get in the Garden. Not only were legitimate sixth-session ticket holders present but so were many disappointed patrons of the fifth session. Some of these were so indignant that the entire force of twelve hundred policemen was needed to maintain order at the gates. Adding to the confusion was the fact that some fifth-session ticket holders were just now arriving, only to be told that their tickets were no longer valid. Surly comments were directed against the police, who were not, of course, at fault; and they tried to compromise the situation by allowing many to enter who had no legal right to be there. As a result, by 3:30 P.M. the Garden was so packed that the Fire Department ordered the gates closed and stationed firemen at all exits.

This crowd even surpassed the one which had attended the Smith nomination two days before. Every seat was filled. The galleries, the floor, even the aisles were jammed. It was almost impossible to move around because of the crush of people. Every major newspaper as well as all the wire services had their crack reporters present. Additional cameramen were brought in to record the event for posterity. Continuous radio coverage was assured by the preempting of all local programming and, long before the gavel fell, Graham McNamee was giving his impressions to the radio audience. Calvin Coolidge was part of that audience; the President, his wife, and two sons were currently cruising down the Chesapeake aboard the presidential yacht *Mayflower*. On board was a new high-powered receiving set which could tune in on the Democratic convention. The first family, along with the rest of the nation, was about to get an earful.

Three o'clock—the scheduled time for the reconvening of the convention—came and passed. So did 3:30. Then 3:45. Still the sixth session was not called to order. Impatience mounted in the galleries and there was considerable nervousness on the floor. Anti-McAdoo men were seen scurrying here and there. Brennan went over to talk to Hoey; then Hoey went over to talk with Brennan. McAdoo leaders, meanwhile, were busily circulating through the delegations in McAdoo Alley. Suddenly a rumor spread that there was to be another postponement because the platform committee was still locked in combat. This brought moans, especially from those who held tickets for the sixth session only. Then Bryan appeared in the hall and received a thunderous ovation. Mounting the platform he shook hands with Chairman Walsh and with Rabbi Stephen S. Wise, who was there to offer the invocation. Bryan's presence indicated that no further delays were contemplated and that the struggle over the platform was about to begin.

Walsh finally called the convention to order. The blue movie lights, which flashed on abruptly, gave the scene an appearance of eerie unreality. Rabbi Wise, shielding his eyes from the glare, made the usual plea to the Deity to bless the work of the convention. His appeal had a special meaning this day since Wise was a Jew and the major issue was going to be the Klan. After the invocation Walsh reintroduced Homer Cummings, who began to read the proposed platform. There was a groan from the convention as he unfolded a fat bundle of broad pink sheets. Even before he finished the preamble his voice gave out and Senator Key Pittman took over. Finally, P. J. Haltigan, reading clerk of the convention, finished the task, plunging along rapidly and taking few breaths. Even so it required one and one-quarter hours to read the long, dull document, which covered a range of subjects from the Republic of Greece to the protection of migratory birds.

Both delegates and the galleries were for the most part uninterested in the reading, and only a scattering of applause occurred now and again. When the League plank was read there were a few cries of "No! No!" from League advocates, but their voices were swallowed by loud clapping. Toward the end of the reading process, as the Klan plank neared, tension mounted. Delegates and spectators alike stopped fidgeting or talking and moved to the edge of their chairs. One rumor had it that if the Klan was not named the galleries would explode and the delegates would be bombarded with objects. The police were obviously expecting something. Police Inspector William Coleman was seen standing in the main entrance issuing orders to his forces. A file of policemen quickly moved down each aisle to take up stations between the delegates while another solid line of blue separated the last row of delegates from the public boxes.

During the reading of the Klan plank there was rapt attention. Murmurs of approval were heard as the platform pledged to maintain all constitutional freedoms and condemned "any efforts to arouse religious or racial dissension." But no specific mention was made of the Klan. There was an audible release of breath when the reading was over. Those who were disappointed whispered to their neighbors but acted subdued. Everyone, even those in the galleries, realized that the matter was not settled and that the battle over the precise wording of the plank was yet to come.

As the reading of the final portions of the platform progressed, many delegates and spectators reached for their hats and coats and began to file out for dinner. Before the platform was finished, the convention was in considerable disorder. The police that had been brought in to quell a possible disturbance were now needed to keep the crowds moving and, after that chore was completed, they too disappeared downstairs and went off to eat. Meanwhile, the reading of the platform was completed and the presentation of the minority reports began. Baker was first. Smiling and determined, he presented his report advocating immediate unconditional entrance into the League. There was a scattering of applause.

Then Walsh turned to William R. Pattangall of Maine, a non-Catholic, who in clipped New England tones read the minority report on religious freedom. He moved that the majority plank be amended to include the statement: "We condemn political secret societies of—" Wild applause cut him off. Waiting a moment, Pattangall tried to resume but, because of a catch in his throat, asked the reading clerk to finish. In a strong voice Haltigan read: "We condemn political secret societies of all kinds [and] pledge the Democratic Party to oppose any effort on the part of the Ku Klux Klan—"

As these words were spoken a roar arose from the convention. Delegates jumped to their feet. Loud hisses came from the Missouri delegation. Kansas shook its fists. The galleries were shouting. Spectators in the process of leaving immediately rushed back to their seats. Those who were eating at hotdog stands or waiting in line at restrooms scurried back into the hall to see what was causing the commotion. Those few policemen who had not yet left for dinner hastily returned to their stations. Walsh slammed the desk with his gavel, demanding order. Finally, the clerk was able to continue: ". . . the Ku Klux Klan or any organization to interfere with the religious liberty or political freedom of any citizen, or to limit the civic rights of any citizen or body of citizens because of religion, birthplace, or racial origin." Again, there was much shouting as cries of "Vote! Vote!" and "Clear the galleries" were heard.

The situation might have gotten out of hand if Walsh had not quickly announced that there would be four hours of debate on the minority reports, beginning with the League. Delegates and spectators who had returned to the hall now resumed their original activities, realizing that it was going to be a long evening. Numerous others joined them, moving slowly toward the exits until only about one-third of the galleries and one-half of the delegates were left. While this migration occurred, the exact procedures for the debate on the minority reports were worked out on the speaker's platform, Cummings being assigned two hours (one for the League and one for the Klan) and Pattangall and Baker given one hour each.

Cummings chose Alfred Lucking, Henry Ford's attorney and a member of the platform committee, as the first speaker for the majority League plank. Appearing old-fashioned in his black clothes and winged collar, Lucking spoke for twenty minutes and gave a creditable performance. He was followed by Senator Andrieus A. Jones of New Mexico, a stout-shouldered man, who also spoke for twenty minutes on the majority position. Next came Baker himself to plead for his minority plank. He faced two main obstacles: the anti-League Irish element in the delegations of the East; and the professional politicians of the Midwest and mountain states who considered a national referendum the best way to skirt an unpopular issue.

Baker's speech was American political oratory at its peak. Although many delegates and spectators had little interest in the matter being discussed, they returned to the hall when the word spread about Baker's performance. Already weary from hours of arguing before the platform committee, Baker collected all of his remaining energy for this final attempt. Short and frail, he seemed to gain strength as he spoke, his enthusiasm reinvigorating him. He claimed that a referendum would take too much time, that there were no legal grounds for it, and that the country should not turn its back on the dead Wilson. He spoke of Wilson as a mystic speaks of his master, invoking visions of the martyred President at the throne of God begging America not to leave unfinished the great work of peace. "He is standing here, through my weak voice," said Baker, "his presence not that crippled, shrunken, broken figure that I last saw, but the great majestic leader is standing here, using me to say to you, 'Save mankind, do America's duty.'" By such imagery Baker so stirred the audience that, according to reporters, men and women everywhere burst into tears. It was a *tour de force,* emotional and bordering on hysteria. Baker twisted, lunged at the lectern, waved his arms, and contorted his face. Long before he was finished he could no longer see through his glasses because of the mist that covered them as sweat coursed from his brow.

Although he quickly exhausted his allotted time, cries of "Go on! Go on!" drove Baker to new heights and he spoke for almost an hour. Chairman Walsh, like the rest of the audience, was too spellbound to use his gavel. When Baker was finally through, the convention gave him a standing ovation. It knew it had heard a great speech. Ohio waved its banner. Some Pennsylvania delegates stood on their chairs. Baker stumbled back from the lectern, a wet rag of a man, almost fell, then caught himself and waved wanly to the crowd. Joseph Tumulty and Rabbi Wise rushed forward to pump his hand. Meanwhile, the crowd insisted by their applause that Baker return and, still trembling, he stepped up to the podium once more to bow and smile. The band started to play "Onward, Christian Soldiers." By now there was not a dry eye in the house.

When the convention again came to order, Rabbi Wise spoke briefly for Baker's minority report. Next came the final speaker, Senator Pittman, who served as anchor man for the majority side. Pittman had an annoying habit of standing like a prize fighter, his body tense and his fists clenched, before delivering his verbal thrusts. When he harshly derided Wilson's tactics in the League of Nations fight of 1919–20, there were a few growls from the audience. When he stated that Baker was naïve and wanted to repeat all the old mistakes, numerous cries of "Not so" and "Not true" were heard. And when he claimed that Baker had come before the convention "with tears in his eyes and his broken-down, slobbering body" to appeal to its emotions and not to its judgment, boos and hisses erupted all over the hall. Pittman, who later claimed he meant to say "tottering" instead of "slobbering," was jolted and turned to Walsh, who rapped for order. Pittman continued but never fully recovered and the audience remained openly hostile.

Such sentiment had little to do with the final vote. When the debate ended and Walsh put the question, 353½ voted for Baker's plank and 742½ against it. Delegates might hold up Wilson as a saint and regard Baker as a haggard hero, but that did not mean that they had changed their minds about the League. As expected, McAdoo delegations voted against the minority report while other delegations were divided on the issue. New York, for example, cast its ballots 35 to 55 against, and Pennsylvania voted 52 to 22 for. In any event, the convention could now move on to the matter of the Klan. The time was 8:40 P.M.

3

When the debate on the Klan began, seats which had been vacated during the League discussion were quickly filled and again the floor and the aisles became clogged. This was the event the crowd had anxiously awaited and suddenly the convention became apprehensive, sensitive, and sullen. There was something about the Klan issue which stirred a sinister spirit among delegates and spectators alike. No paradise of human understanding at best, Madison Square Garden now turned into a pit of crouching hates and simmering prejudices.

The irony of the ensuing battle was that few of the major participants really wanted it. The Klan certainly did not seek it. The organization had expected that a general plank condemning secret societies would be adopted and had indicated a willingness to live with that. Now, perforce, it reluctantly undertook to defend itself. As William Allen White said, the Klan "was willing to stand anonymous insult, but not advertised rebuke."

McAdoo had consistently hoped to skirt the Klan issue. As the show-down neared, his closest advisers grew increasingly nervous and fell to arguing among themselves. Chadbourne, Baruch, Rockwell, and Roper advised McAdoo to denounce the organization, but Breckinridge Long continued to counsel caution. The Chadbourne group argued that the Klan issue was a major weapon in the hands of the anti-McAdoo forces and that McAdoo needed to disarm them with a condemnatory statement. Long later said that he had to "fight ten times every day" to keep Mc-Adoo from doing this. Long reasoned that regardless of what McAdoo might say, Smith had the anti-Klan Catholic vote and Underwood had the anti-Klan non-Catholic vote. Hence, McAdoo's potential loss from attacking the Klan far outstripped any potential gain. According to Long, the key to success was to play the Klan issue in a neutral key. McAdoo agreed.

Not only McAdoo, but the more important of the favorite sons were wary of the Klan question and fervently wished it would go away. Davis of West Virginia, Carter Glass, and Boss Taggart (speaking for Ralston) were all equivocal on a condemnation of the Klan. Moderation was their hallmark and the Klan issue threatened to mar their compromise image. None of these camps wished to take extreme positions on anything. Davis supporters spoke of their candidate as a man who could "bridge the gap" between all the various opposing forces at the convention, while Taggart portrayed Ralston as "a conciliator and healer." In taking a cautious ap-proach to the Klan, Taggart broke sharply with other northern bosses on this issue.

The Klan question also prompted some last-minute soul-searching in the Smith high command. Some of Smith's advisers advocated that the New York governor not become too closely identified with a militant anti-Klan stand; they hoped Smith would return to the position he had taken earlier in the spring—deemphasizing, not emphasizing, the religious fac-tor. Franklin Roosevelt was particularly opposed to naming the Klan and argued strenuously with Smith's more ardent anti-Klan advisers. Smith himself later admitted that nothing was probably served in pushing for an anti-Klan plank in 1924. At the moment, however, he was swayed by his own personal feelings and by urban politicians who claimed that their constituents demanded it. Further, floods of telegrams descended on the

Smith headquarters just prior to the Klan fight, urging Smith to stick with it. Brennan, Moore, Hague, Proskauer, Moskowitz, all believed it was politically the wise thing to do. Significantly, all of these leaders were "wringing wet" and viewed the Klan struggle as a means of embarrassing the dry forces in the convention. Interestingly, some of the strongest champions of the anti-Klan plank, not only among the Smith forces but also in the Underwood camp, were neither Catholic nor Jew. But they were wet.

The first speaker on the Klan issue mounted the rostrum at 8:45 P.M. Despite the switch in the convention mood, the debate on the Klan started peaceably. Talking for fifteen minutes, Senator Robert L. Owen of Oklahoma, a clean-cut, sharp-featured man who was said to be part Indian, supported the majority plank by claiming that, although he did not approve of the organization himself, the Klan did contain many sincere members who had joined out of lofty motives. It was not fair, he said, to condemn a whole barrel because of a few bad apples. The next speaker was Pattangall of Maine. Already a hero to the galleries for having introduced the minority report, Pattangall was frequently interrupted by applause as he emphasized that the anti-Klan resolution did not condemn all those in the Klan, but only those who would interfere with the religious and political freedom of others. Pattangall purposely played to the galleries and they warmed to him. They particularly liked his assertion that Catholics, Jews, and blacks ought not be deprived of their civil rights as long as they were still subject to the military draft. When Pattangall finished and left the lectern muttering, "I hate bigotry," anti-Klan delegates and spectators shouted and clapped while those seated in McAdoo Alley stared ahead in stony silence.

As soon as the convention quieted down, another anti-Klan speaker, Mrs. Carroll Miller of Pennsylvania, spoke for five minutes, directing her remarks to women. Claiming that she would rather have the Democratic party defeated on the Klan issue than win without it, she contended that not to name the Klan was to "leave our children a tarnished heritage." Next came Governor Cameron Morrison of North Carolina, who, like Senator Owen, disclaimed any sympathy for the Klan, but defended the rights of those who had mistakenly joined the order. After Morrison, Bainbridge Colby of New York, Senator David Walsh of Massachusetts, and Edmond Moore of Ohio gave brief speeches favoring the naming of the Klan. These three men were a study in contrasts. Colby was aristocratic, imperious, and a symbol of the Eastern Establishment. Walsh was stout, spoke like an old-time orator, and flashed an Irish-Catholic temper. Moore was low-key and homey, using a folksy, midwestern, Scotch-Presbyterian idiom. But all were alike in one respect. They believed that the Klan was an evil organization which deserved to be condemned.

With each succeeding anti-Klan speaker the galleries became more demonstrative. Three speeches in a row against the Klan worked them to a fever pitch. When Moore charged in an oblique reference to Smith that were it not for his religion he would be nominated in five minutes, they roared their agreement. And when it was announced at the end of the Colby-Walsh-Moore lineup that the next speaker would be Andrew C. Erwin of Georgia, they began to hiss and catcall. Erwin was editor of the Athens *Banner-Herald* and had twice been mayor of Athens, Georgia. His grandfather had been Howell Cobb, Speaker of the House of Representatives and Secretary of the Treasury under James Buchanan. His father had been an officer in the Confederate Army and Erwin himself was Presbyterian and Scotch-Irish. There was no reason to expect that he harbored any anti-Klan sympathy.

Erwin had been allotted only three minutes but he made explosive use of them. From the beginning he looked pale and his thin voice cracked. He was so excited that sometimes when he raised his arms for emphasis no sound came out of his mouth at all. Meanwhile, hisses descended from the galleries. Then they began to come from McAdoo Alley on the floor. It was electrifying. Erwin was *condemning* the Klan, not supporting it. The McAdoo sections were stunned and the galleries were caught unawares. For the first time the McAdoo states seriously attempted to heckle a speaker. Shouts of "No! No!" and "Sit down!" came from the Texas and Oklahoma delegations. There was absolute confusion among the Georgians and many in the Mississippi delegation jumped up and down and angrily shook their fists. But Erwin kept on. The Klan had to be stopped, he said. It was not simply another fraternal organization like the Elks or the Masons. Since the South could not rid herself of it, concluded Erwin, the South needed the help of the rest of the nation.

As Erwin returned to his seat, pandemonium seized the Garden. The galleries erupted as men and women pounded each other on the backs and whistled. On the floor, northeastern delegations rose to their feet cheering and applauding. The Georgia delegation greeted Erwin's return with grim faces, only one individual standing to meet him—Marion Colley of Washington, Georgia. This snub was immediately noticed by the rest of the convention and suddenly delegations with banners came from all over the hall in a pilgrimage to this young man. One of the first persons to reach him was Hoey of New York, who shook his hand. Others from the New York delegation grabbed him and hoisted him to their shoulders, bearing him away from the inhospitality of his home state. As Erwin was carried around the hall, he passed within a few feet of W. J. Bryan, who was furiously scribbling notes and who had been about Erwin's age when a similar accolade in a different day had been showered on him for his "Cross of Gold" speech.

In all, thirty standards flocked to Georgia and followed Erwin's bearers around the floor while the Georgia delegation, as well as those from other southern and southwestern states, sat filled with wrath. Their mood was not helped when the bandmaster struck up "Marching Through Georgia." At any other time this would have been in poor taste. Now it was a monumental gaffe. Shouts of fury came from many elderly McAdoo delegates. Others, further removed from the bitterness of the Civil War, rocked with laughter. But it was black humor. Two complete verses of this ancient hymn of hate were played before the band finally sensed its mistake and shifted to the national anthem. This brought the Erwin demonstration to a halt, but not before a lady from Rhode Island rushed up and kissed him on the mouth.

It took ten minutes for order to be restored sufficiently for three more speakers to give brief remarks on the Klan, two advocating the minority plank and one requesting its defeat. At this point Walsh introduced the final speaker—"that reverend Democrat, the Honorable William Jennings Bryan." Thus far Bryan had been a power behind the scenes at the convention, but this was the first chance most delegates had to see him perform publicly. For the past five days he had sat in the Florida delegation, looking thinner than four years before and constantly cooling himself with a teardrop-shaped fan. Attired in his old-fashioned black alpaca coat, Bryan presented a stark contrast to the nattily dressed urbanites like New York's Jimmy Walker. Wearing his black skullcap, which hid his shining bald pate, and sporting a huge red "Florida" badge, which covered him from chest to abdomen, Bryan certainly did not physically resemble that brash young man who had first led the party in 1896. Yet the name Bryan still possessed magic among all Democrats and his mere presence had a suspenseful effect on any Democratic convention. Now again, in 1924, western and southern delegates fully expected this "Prairie Avenger," as Vachel Lindsay once called him, to "smash Plymouth Rock with his boulders from the west." Tammanyites, in turn, remembering

Bryan's activities in previous years, especially in 1912 when he had helped block the flow of votes to Champ Clark, had much reason to be apprehensive. When Bryan raised his hand and began to speak, there was rapt attention.

Bryan often spoke to the heart rather than to the brain, and this effort was no exception. Tired and discouraged, having had but three hours sleep the night before and having averaged only four hours a night during the past week, Bryan hoped that his words might help the city understand the plains and the deltas and reunify the party in a battle against governmental corruption and greedy monopolies. He began by saying that this was the most important occasion on which he had ever been called to speak. Why? Because a small group of willful men were insisting upon the insertion in the party platform of three little words. Even now, Bryan claimed, the minority report which they advocated could be adopted if they would but agree to strike out those three words, and he paused for emphasis before saying, "Ku Klux Klan."

It was an unfortunate way for Bryan to begin because he aroused instant hostility. No reverence for his past deeds could now protect him. Nor did it matter that he was personally opposed to the Klan. For the moment he appeared as the organization's chief spokesman, and he was forced to suffer the consequences. Inevitably, as soon as he mentioned the Klan, boos came from the floor while a torrent of catcalls and jeers rolled down from the galleries. Tammanyites would later claim that the frequent disturbances during the remainder of Bryan's speech were not Tammany inspired, but were initiated by the delegates themselves. This argument was spurious since the galleries far surpassed in rudeness anything seen among the delegates on the floor that day.

Twice Bryan was forced to halt his speech because of the shouting and the turmoil, and at the third interruption Walsh stepped to the podium and beat his gavel upon it so hard that the microphones almost fell off. In cold fury, Walsh screamed so that his voice could be heard, warning that if there was one more interruption he would order the police to empty the galleries. This threat brought barely enough silence for Bryan to continue.

The last portion of Bryan's address was a debacle. The galleries' reception had stung him and he met their hostility with increasing religious fervor. In the process he offended many who were neutral and embarrassed some who agreed with him. Amid intermittent jeers, he said that the Catholic Church needed no protection from the Democratic party and that the Ku Klux Klan was only a minor issue. It required far more courage to fight the Republicans, he claimed, than to fight this misguided organization. He warned that to continue the current divisive struggle was to ruin the Democratic party without eliminating the Klan. Finally, in a fervent peroration, Bryan asserted that the only solution to all the party's problems, as well as the nation's, was to return to the Sermon on the Mount and follow Jesus. "I call you back," Bryan pleaded, "in the name of our God; I call you back in the name of our party; I call you back in the name of the Son of God and Saviour of the world. Christians, stop fighting and let us get together and save the world from the materialism that robs life of its spiritual values. It was Christ on the Cross who said, 'Father, forgive them, for they know not what they do.' And, my friends, we can exterminate Ku Kluxism better by recognizing their honesty and teaching them that they are wrong."

Boos and hisses mixed with shouting and clapping greeted the end of Bryan's speech. Here and there isolated McAdoo delegates rose to their feet as they applauded him. But most delegates remained in their seats, relieved that it was over. Even the jeering in the galleries quickly subsided. Exhausted physically and emotionally, Bryan took a seat on the platform rather than return the long distance to the Florida delegation. He slumped forward in his chair, not sure about the effect of his performance. The band played "My Country 'Tis of Thee" while some delegations immediately polled their members on the impending question. After a five-minute recess Walsh asked for the roll call on the Klan plank to begin.

The balloting started at 11:35 P.M. For the next two hours the convention was in total confusion. Never before had there been such prolonged pandemonium in an American political gathering. The delegates engaged in fist fights, arguments, name calling, wrestling matches, and brawls, while the galleries howled and stomped their feet. One newspaperman claimed that the bitterness and hatred expressed during the Klan vote was "indescribable." Another said that, as he moved among the spectators in the galleries, he was "in terror of a rain of blows or bullets" and heard dozens of verbal duels that transcended reason. Walsh, meanwhile, failed utterly to control the convention. During the last stages of the Bryan speech, a call had gone out for one thousand additional policemen to be sent to the Garden, and only their presence now averted a full-scale riot. White-lipped and tense, they circulated through the aisles and the galleries, pulling delegates apart or preventing spectators from throwing missiles and spitting on the combatants below. Many of these blue-coated public servants were from Irish-Catholic backgrounds and had a stake in the outcome. Yet they acted with even-handed fairness and were by universal agreement the heroes of the Saturday-night imbroglio. Even McAdoo supporters later admitted this. As one grudgingly put it: "Well, at least they weren't campaigning for Smith. They were too busy."

During the Klan roll call it was almost impossible to secure an accurate count since delegation after delegation had to be polled on the floor. Toward the end of the roll call, some individual delegates wanted to change their votes and more than a dozen delegations had their votes challenged. In almost all delegations there were strange and inexplicable divisions. Mrs. Pattangall, for example, was a member of the Maine delegation along with her Klan-hating husband. He voted for the minority report; she voted against.

The classic example of confusion existed in the Georgia delegation. When that state's name was first called it could not report a vote and had to be polled by the reading clerk. Sentiment was finally determined to be 17 against and 2½ for, each Georgia delegate casting one-half vote on this issue. But, when the roll call of all states neared completion, Georgia's delegation chairman and a Klansman, Hollins Randolph, demanded that his group be polled again, saying he knew of at least three delegates who had changed their minds in the interim. The votes of two of these three were in particular doubt: Pleasant A. Stovall, minister to Switzerland in the Wilson administration, and Miss Colley, the only delegate to have befriended Erwin after his anti-Klan speech. They had been placed under tremendous pressure by their irate colleagues following their original "yes" votes, and during the ensuing repoll the burly Randolph stood glowering over them. When Stovall's name was called he changed his vote from "yes" to "no" in a weak and almost inaudible voice. But Miss Colley remained adamant. When her name was called, this dark-haired granddaughter of the Confederate general and Secretary of State Robert Toombs, murmured, "I'm against the Klan" and made no further comment. All around her were shouting, pleading men trying to hoist her from her seat, yelling the word "No!" at her. Finally, after repeated requests by the reading clerk to vote either "yes" or "no," she gasped out "No" and, amid cries of indignation and sympathy from the galleries, slumped back in her chair.

The final Georgia vote was listed as 22 against and 1 for. Only Andrew Erwin and one other stubborn delegate held out. The next day

Miss Colley told reporters who interviewed her in the Pennsylvania Hotel, "I haven't slept a wink. It was a perfectly dreadful position to be in." She said that at the time she thought her vote might be decisive because of the narrow division on the issue. "I was told," she stated, "that the future of the party was at stake; that the vote was close and if I did not change the party would be split wide open." She denied, however, that any threats had been made on her life and added that even though she had changed her vote she was still "in favor of the minority report and against the Klan."

After the Georgia recount a number of other delegations attempted to gain permission for a repoll, but Chairman Walsh could see that this would encourage endless changes and he ordered the tally to be counted as it was. Shortly thereafter he announced that 541$\frac{3}{20}$ votes had been cast for the minority report and 542$\frac{3}{20}$ against. He therefore declared the minority plank defeated by one vote. The noise in the Garden was deafening. When Lawrence F. Quigley, a delegate from Massachusetts, rose to challenge this decision, Walsh at first had difficulty hearing him and then ruled him out of order. Walsh next recognized Franklin Roosevelt, who, yelling to be heard, moved for immediate adjournment. Walsh put the question and, despite a chorus of "nays," declared the convention over until 9:30 A.M. Monday morning. Name calling and shouting continued as policemen carefully began herding delegates and spectators to the outside. It was almost 2 A.M. and both the hour and a drenching rain helped reduce further friction. Distraught delegates were now faced with the more immediate problem of finding transportation to take them back to their hotels, and spectators were too busy assembling their rain gear, avoiding puddles, or catching trolleys to continue the argument.

But not the press and the radio. During the Klan fight and for days afterward, they injected the hatred and the passions of the Garden into the homes of Americans everywhere. This made the wrangling of Saturday night all the more significant. No Republican oratory could have damaged the Democratic party's image or heightened latent general public prejudices as effectively as the on-the-spot radio accounts of the happenings on Saturday evening. Fortunately for the Democrats, freak winds and electrical storms prevented some areas of the nation from hearing the worst of the Klan struggle on Saturday night. Several tornadoes swept through the Midwest and upper Mississippi valley, creating havoc in a broad swath from southwestern Pennsylvania to Iowa and causing a disruption in radio transmissions that lasted for several hours.

The Klan fight remained the major item of news throughout the entire weekend. Every newspaper and every political pundit analyzed the struggle looking for important trends. It was generally agreed that the unit rule was primarily responsible for the defeat of the minority plank, since Arkansas, Louisiana, Oklahoma, and Texas each had possessed several anti-Klan votes which were held captive. On the other hand, there was considerable press surprise that more than one-half of the votes cast against naming the Klan had come from outside the South. Numerous delegates from Indiana, Illinois, Michigan, Iowa, Kansas, Washington, Oregon, and California had helped swell the pro-Klan total. Still, the South represented the most concentrated bloc of pro-Klan support. Of the 266 delegate votes existing in the ten southern states (excluding Texas), 231 were cast against the minority report. Of the 35 southern votes cast for it, 24 came from Underwood's Alabama alone.

Northern newspapers, particularly in metropolitan communities, bitterly condemned the Democratic party for its action. Conversely, newspapers in the South and in Klan-dominated areas of the Midwest found it almost inconceivable that some individuals were willing to ruin the party over three words. They thought the whole affair had been purposely staged to embarrass McAdoo. Professional political observers differed in their reactions. Some, like Oswald G. Villard of *The Nation,* claimed that they "got thrill after thrill in hearing men and women say out loud that they would prefer to have their party wrecked and wracked and ruined rather than have it [remain] silent in the presence of a sin that threatens the very fundamentals of our American life." On the other hand, Hendrik Willem van Loon, who hated the Klan and deplored politicians like Bryan, admitted to his readers his profound shock to discover that the anti-Klan element was just "as stupid, as bigoted, [and] as despicable" in its actions as were its opponents. But it was Will Rogers who focused the situation most sharply: "Saturday will always remain burned in my memory as long I live as being the day when I heard the most religion preached, and the least practiced, of any day in the world's history."

Naturally, the major participants in the struggle varied in their assessments. Klan officials claimed that the rejection of the minority report was a tremendous victory. Privately, however, they were alarmed that the Klan had been condemned even by those who did not want the organization specifically named. McAdoo headquarters immediately said that the Klan vote was irrelevant to the selection of a presidential candidate and deplored the fuss that had been created over it. Even prior to the vote,

McAdoo had become apprehensive about the outcome and had attempted to disassociate himself by issuing orders that his name not be used to influence the balloting. When the voting began he closeted himself in his rooms in the Vanderbilt so he could not be reached. Breckinridge Long hid in the galleries in order not to be pestered by McAdoo delegates who wanted to know how they should vote. There Long experienced firsthand New York's antipathy to the Klan—an attitude which prior to this moment he naïvely believed had been created solely by Tammany.

Smith supporters claimed that the Klan fight now made Al the necessary choice of the convention. They said the Klan struggle had proven McAdoo to be "the Klan's Kandidate" and that his selection was impossible. At the same time they expressed anger at the convention's refusal to name the Klan. A few hot-headed Smith advisers, mainly Hague, Brennan, and Guffey, wanted to call on Monday for a recount of Saturday's vote, but Franklin Roosevelt was appalled and warned that such a move would be "courting fate." Smith agreed and late Sunday night authorized Roosevelt to issue a pacifying statement: "We respect the verdict and know that we can confidently rely on our Southern and Western brothers for their traditional fair play. We shall go forward with them now . . . in the task of choosing a candidate who can win."

Bryan, meanwhile, lost any doubt about the effectiveness of his Saturday-night performance and adopted the view that if it had not been for him the party would have foundered. After the Klan vote was announced, Brother Charley bluntly stated that W. J. had provided the margin of victory. Indeed, Saturday's session was barely over before W. J. was arranging for his "Daybreak Prayer" to be printed and circulated among his enemies as well as his friends. Bryan remained convinced that he had done the Lord's work both in the platform committee and on the speaker's stand.

Whatever the reactions of the major participants, later events would show that the Klan fight hurt both Smith and McAdoo. McAdoo was actually a double loser. He was thereafter irrevocably classified with the Klan, and the inability of his forces, whether acting in his name or not, to marshal more than a bare majority on the Klan issue left the elusive two-thirds necessary for his nomination still out of his reach. Similarly, the decision of the Smith element to force the Klan matter on the convention so polarized that body that a Smith selection was now more than ever out of the question. Bryan, in turn, forfeited by his performance whatever chance he may have had to act as kingmaker. The year 1924 was not destined to be another 1912 for Bryan. He would continue to be more a tragic figure than a heroic one in this, his last appearance on the national political scene.

As for the future progress of the convention, had it not been for the Klan fight McAdoo and Smith probably would have made their run at the top prize and would have collapsed within one or two days. But the Klan struggle not only made McAdoo and Smith victories all the more impossible, but made each of their camps all the more intransigent. Southern and rural delegates, angered by the New York galleries, were determined to fight to the end. Smith followers, seeing a burning cross and a white sheet behind McAdoo, were prepared to "die in the trenches." Each of these groups now succumbed to an intense emotionalism in which moral outrage was the key factor. Particularly among McAdooites, a mental attitude of "no compromise" was so assiduously cultivated that they began to view national party defeat as an acceptable price to pay to maintain their narrow party supremacy.

In all this tumult the party platform was lost from view. At the final bang of Walsh's gavel early Sunday morning, the convention had actually adopted the most extensive platform in the party's history. Bryan claimed with some justification that it was the best platform the party had ever written. Aside from the expected praise of Wilson and the condemnation of Republican corruption, the document contained many of the proposals which numerous groups had been advocating for some time. The platform called for lower freight rates and increased government aid to the farmer, federal aid to education, abolition of child labor, rapid development of highways and waterways, tax reform, elimination of lame-duck Congresses, limitations on campaign expenditures and contributions, publicly financed publicity for candidates running for national office, retention of Muscle Shoals as a government installation, and a national referendum on war. Such a platform normally would have satisfied almost everyone. But not in 1924.

4

Sunday, June 29, was a day of recess. Again the weather was humid and hot, but at least the delegates did not have to swelter in the confines of

Madison Square Garden. Some spent the day in bed, exhausted physically and emotionally by the Klan fight the night before. Some huddled in small groups at their favorite candidate's headquarters, discussing the uncertain future and rehashing events of the previous week. Some joined forty thousand fans for a doubleheader at the Polo Grounds, where the Giants lost the opener to the Braves but won the second game 5 to 3. Some courageous souls again elected to suffer the crowds at Coney Island and others went to Miller Field on Staten Island to watch the New York Guard Aerial Circus.

Some delegates, of course, went to church. Most Catholic delegates went to St. Patrick's Cathedral. But not Al Smith. He attended a late-morning mass at St. Agnes's at Forty-third Street near Lexington, where the pastor was Monsignor John P. Chadwick, former chaplain of the battleship *Maine*. McAdoo was supposed to attend St. George's Episcopal Church at Stuyvesant Square and East Sixteenth Street, but at the last minute he decided not to go and stayed behind to look after campaign matters. At St. Paul's Methodist, West End Avenue and Eighty-sixth Street, the guest minister for the day was Bishop Cannon, and he attracted many southern dry delegates. The greatest churchman of them all, William Jennings Bryan, did not attend services anywhere, remaining in bed until 6 P.M.

Few delegates' thoughts tarried long over spiritual matters that Sunday, least of all the major candidates'. Both McAdoo and Smith held long sessions with their advisers during the afternoon, mapping strategy for the presidential balloting that was about to begin. Both sides wanted to show early strength but still keep enough votes in reserve to assure a steady increase. Smith leaders even planned to seed a few McAdoo votes in their own delegations on the first ballot in order to make it appear later that McAdoo's strength was waning. The Smith forces hoped ultimately to fall heir to the votes belonging to Cox and Underwood and then arrange deals with a few western delegations to further swell Smith's total. The capstone of the Smith plan was to encourage all those favorite sons whose votes would otherwise go to McAdoo to stay in the race.

McAdoo's strategy was twofold: first, to hold existing McAdoo delegations in line, and second, to persuade Virginia, Arkansas, Kansas, and Mississippi to drop their favorite sons and enter the McAdoo column. Rockwell and Roper were to work on these favorite-son delegations while Breckinridge Long was assigned the task of monitoring all pro-McAdoo delegates. The need for close supervision of McAdoo delegations was necessary because some delegates were beginning to lose their confidence that McAdoo could win. In order to lift such lagging spirits McAdoo scheduled a special meeting with his supporters on Sunday evening, June 29, while most other candidates were relaxing. Standing on a table before over a thousand cheering admirers in the ballroom of the Park Avenue Hotel, he gave an evangelical speech filled with warnings and exhortations. Again he cautioned his supporters against "New York hospitality" and renewed his charges against the New York press, Wall Street, and Tammany. They were all uniting to defeat him, he exclaimed, but added, "We will win!" Cries of "We will! We will!" filled the hall as Rockwell stepped up to continue where McAdoo left off. Smith was through, a combative Rockwell told the throng, predicting that McAdoo would receive at least four hundred votes on the first ballot and win by the fifth. No Smith minority could prevent it if only the McAdoo forces would hold together. Loyalty and tenacity were the twin keys to victory.

The following morning, Monday, June 30, the convention opened slowly. Monday was a working day and the galleries reflected it. The spectators who were there were unenthusiastic. Delegates on the floor looked sleepy. No one really expected more than a test of strength on the first several ballots so excitement was at a minimum.

At the start there was a brief flurry over the previous Klan vote. Before Chairman Walsh could order the balloting to begin, Lawrence Quigley of Massachusetts, the same delegate who had been overruled by Walsh at the conclusion of the Saturday-night session, rose again to contest the result. He claimed that at least one delegate had been forced to change her vote against her will (obviously referring to Miss Colley) and might now be prepared to reconsider. This prompted a chorus of boos from McAdoo Alley while Miss Colley, who was sitting in the Georgia delegation far removed from the aisle in order to escape the remarks of passers-by, vigorously shook her head. Smith leaders, caught off guard by the Quigley move, looked on in shocked surprise. Finally, Roosevelt had the presence of mind to demand the regular order of business. Ignoring Quigley, Walsh stared straight at Roosevelt and calmly said, "The secretary will please call the roll."

Thus the balloting for President began on the day the convention was originally scheduled to close. "Alabama?" read the clerk. "Al-a-bam-ah-h-h casts twen-ty fo-ah votes for Os-cah Double-yuh Un-n-n-der-wood!" replied Governor Brandon, the chairman of the Alabama delegation. This drawling announcement would henceforth lead off all but one of the 102 subsequent roll calls and would become the best-known and most-repeated phrase in the country. The reading clerk rapidly proceeded through the list of states and the first-ballot results produced no real surprises. The totals read: McAdoo 431½, Smith 241, Cox 59, Underwood 42½, Silzer 38, J. W. Davis 31, Ferris 30, Ralston 30, Glass 25, Ritchie 22½, Robinson 21, J. M. Davis 20, C. W. Bryan 18, Brown 17, and Saulsbury 7. McAdoo had votes in 34 out of 54 delegations, the solid support of 21, and a majority in two others. Only 30 of his votes came from the East, and 25½ of those came from Pennsylvania. Smith received votes from 14 delegations. He had the solid support of only two (New York and Rhode Island) and a majority in Massachusetts, Vermont, and Wisconsin. Only 41 of his votes came from outside the East, 23 from Wisconsin alone. Smith secured no votes from the South whatever.

There was a remarkable similarity between this first-ballot vote for President and the earlier vote on the Klan issue. The correlation between the delegates voting for McAdoo and against the minority plank was exceedingly high. In the case of those voting for Smith and also for the minority plank it was almost perfect. All but one of Smith's first-ballot supporters had voted to name the Klan. Obviously both of these groups were closely knit and there was little likelihood of their rapid erosion. Of the two, the Smith group possessed the greater cohesiveness; but the Smith bloc represented less than one-third of the delegates and could not exercise a veto over McAdoo without outside help. McAdoo, on the other hand, commanded only 40 percent of the convention's strength, far short of the necessary two-thirds (732). He could, however, prevent the nomination of any candidate, and it was clear that only a candidate who could elicit broad favorite-son *and* McAdoo support could hope to win.

With McAdoo possessing almost twice Smith's vote the McAdoo forces expected a rapid breakthrough. It did not materialize. Indeed, the second through the ninth ballots produced no appreciable change. By that time only one candidate had withdrawn (Ferris) and the more important favorite sons were still hanging on to their votes. As a result, at the end of the ninth roll call at 4:45 P.M. Chairman Walsh accepted a motion to recess the convention until 8 o'clock that evening in the hope that something might jell in the meantime.

When Walsh gaveled the Monday-night session to order, the galleries were relatively full and among many there was the feeling that a selection was close at hand. Just before the balloting began Bryan strode on stage looking radiant, and said to newspapermen, "Boys, I have a piece of news that you'll want." Reporters herded around him, breathless, pencils poised. Spectators in the galleries craned their necks, convinced that this signaled agreement on a candidate. Calmly Bryan handed them a sheet of paper on which was written: "A great-granddaughter was today born to Mr. Bryan. The parents are William P. Meeker and Kitty Owen Meeker, Mr. Bryan's oldest granddaughter." Smiling at his little joke, Bryan walked away before any of the newspapermen recovered their wits enough to congratulate him. The galleries were left hanging and only gradually came to realize that whatever Bryan had said it did not relate to a convention decision.

The opening ballot (the tenth) provided the only excitement of the evening. Kansas, which had been voting for favorite son Jonathan Davis, suddenly shifted its 20 votes to McAdoo. Convinced that a McAdoo bandwagon was developing, a McAdoo parade immediately formed and anxious glances were exchanged by Smith supporters as McAdoo men marched about the hall shouting, "McAdoo or thirty days!" But no sooner was the roll call resumed than New Jersey, which had been supporting favorite son George Silzer, switched its 28 votes to Smith. The timing was superb. Fourteen states now joined New York in parading, yelling, and whistling. The confidence of the McAdoo delegates visibly sagged. In the end neither the Davis nor the Silzer moves encouraged any real change and, after five more fruitless roll calls that lasted until midnight, the convention adjourned until the next morning at 10:30 A.M.

The first day's balloting was ample proof that the convention was deadlocked. After fifteen roll calls Smith had gained only 64½ votes and McAdoo 47½, and the convention was no nearer a decision than when the balloting began. But neither of the major candidates would admit this. Smith passed the day at the Manhattan Club, listening to the proceedings and conferring with his advisers. After the fifteenth roll call he retired to the Biltmore, having ordered his lieutenants to encourage the favorite sons to remain in the race. McAdoo, meanwhile, stayed at his headquarters throughout the day, where he was in contact by direct wire with the convention. When the fifteenth ballot was over he and his advisers held a lengthy post-mortem. Rockwell remained confident of final victory but, knowing that his candidate held many votes in captivity under the unit rule, warned that delegate discipline still required careful monitoring. Long urged that more pressure be put on the various favorite sons, but the ineffectiveness of the Jonathan Davis switch earlier that evening cast some doubt on this strategy. Although McAdoo agreed that the favorite sons were important and had to be won over, his mounting animus toward Smith and his desire to "punish" him began to take precedence. As a result McAdoo increasingly denied himself the two major weapons in any skilled politician's arsenal—flexibility and compromise. Unfortunately, McAdoo's strategy came to rest more and more on the mistaken assumption that, as Rockwell phrased it, "the elimination of Smith automatically means the selection of Mr. McAdoo."

So the battle continued. By Tuesday morning the major question was whether McAdoo could break the hold of western and southern favorite sons on their delegates or whether any one of them could attract sufficient support from him to consolidate their own position. Tuesday's balloting provided only an inconclusive answer. A total of fifteen more roll calls were taken (sixteenth through the thirtieth) before a tired and ill-tempered convention adjourned at 11:35 P.M. Throughout, McAdoo men attempted to woo southern and western favorite sons, especially Robinson and Glass. Instead of succeeding, they saw McAdoo unity begin to erode. Dissension erupted first in the North Carolina delegation. Then Missouri and Oklahoma abandoned the McAdoo cause and Florida dropped the unit rule. On the eighteenth ballot Florida even gave one vote to Smith—the only vote he would receive from the South. That lone Florida delegate almost gave Bryan apoplexy and was thereafter virtually ostracized by the Florida delegation. Meanwhile, Smith's chance for creating any real excitement passed when Cox of Ohio decided to remain in the contest.

Although the favorite sons emerged stronger and more confident during Tuesday's balloting, no one of them could muster enough support for a breakthrough. Only John W. Davis of West Virginia represented a momentary threat. When Mississippi switched its 20 votes to him on the nineteenth ballot and Missouri followed with its 36 votes on the twentieth, a trend seemed to be developing. But McAdoo men quickly plugged the gap since most of Davis's votes were coming from the McAdoo side. Bryan was especially active in the anti-Davis campaign. Horrified when Mississippi announced its vote for Davis, Bryan rushed over and, with sweat pouring off his bald dome, told the delegation chairman, "This convention must not nominate a Wall Street man. Mr. Davis is the lawyer for J. P. Morgan." Some nodded in agreement; others verbally disagreed. Snapped one young woman at Bryan: "And who is Mr. McAdoo the lawyer for?"

During the remainder of the balloting there were no further significant changes. At the end of the day McAdoo had suffered a net loss of 62½; Smith had experienced a gain of 18; and Davis had increased his vote by 63½, mainly at the expense of McAdoo. The totals read: McAdoo 415½, Smith 323½, Davis 126½, Cox 57, Underwood 39½, Ralston 33, Glass 24, Robinson 23, and Ritchie 17½. During the final ballot of the day it was noticed that most of the delegation leaders were absent and rumors circulated that "deals" were being made. It was said that Smith was "talking turkey" with the Cox forces. McAdoo, it was claimed, was working out "an arrangement" with Glass. Supposedly Bryan was busily killing off Davis's chances. West Virginia delegates were said to be furious at this and were pressuring all favorite sons to unite behind their candidate.

Far from deals being arranged by the major contenders, there were no attempts being made to resolve the situation at all. Smith's strategy continued to be simple—sit tight and watch the favorite sons feed at McAdoo's expense. Because of Bryan's distaste for Davis and because of the McAdoo source of many of Davis's votes, New York leaders viewed the West Virginian as a great help to the Smith cause. Whether Smith himself still believed that he could win the nomination is debatable. Certainly Roosevelt did not think so. But Brennan, Mack, Hoey, and others remained enthusiastic and counseled "no compromise." The rank-and-file of Smith supporters were likewise undaunted. They watched the McAdoo decline with undisguised glee. On Tuesday night the galleries met the loss of each McAdoo vote with raucous cheering, thereby adding to the mounting frustration in the McAdoo camp. When Smith left the Manhattan Club for his hotel following the adjournment of the Tuesday-night session, his car was besieged by over five hundred well-wishers who acted as if he had already been nominated. It required thirty policemen to keep matters under control.

There was natural concern among McAdoo followers. Already the late night editions of the New York press were proclaiming "The Decline and Fall of William G. McAdoo." In the closing ballots on Tuesday there was a noticeable depression among the McAdoo delegates. The voices announcing the votes from the various McAdoo delegations began to contain a hint of desperation. On Monday it had been so many votes "for McAdoo." Now it was "William Gibbs McAdoo" with every syllable accented. After Tuesday's adjournment the normally loquacious Rockwell refused to comment on McAdoo's situation, maintaining only that he would ultimately win.

Later, at their customary after-the-balloting meeting, McAdoo advisers again concluded that they would keep their primary attention focused on Smith while stepping up their pressure on the favorite sons, especially on Robinson of Arkansas and Glass of Virginia. At the same time, they decided to block any further defections to Davis's banner. Mainly because of a fear of Davis, they now agreed upon an aggressive McAdoo drive. To oversee it, McAdoo decided to move from his headquarters in the Vanderbilt to a "battlefield command post" in the Madison Square Hotel. At no time during this Tuesday-night meeting was there any talk of compromise. Indeed, both Rockwell and McAdoo specifically rejected *any* McAdoo representation in *any* conference looking for a solution. The setbacks of the first two days of balloting had only served to make the McAdoo forces more intractable than ever.

5

Wednesday, July 2. The Democratic National Convention had been in session for more than a week and still it had not selected a presidential candidate. By Tuesday evening many of the delegates were weary and wanted to go home. As many as one hundred had already quit New York, leaving their alternates to fill in for them. Some state chairmen were predicting that, if the convention continued much longer, they would not be able to keep a full complement of delegates on hand.

For this as well as for other reasons, McAdoo leaders regarded Wednesday as a crucial day. From the beginning of the Wednesday day session McAdoo men were extremely busy, circulating through delegations and talking with state chairmen. Bryan was particularly visible, touring the hall and concentrating especially on the Missouri, Mississippi, and Oklahoma delegates. McAdoo lieutenants were even active in such enemy territory as the Ohio delegation, where Rockwell got into an altercation with ex-governor James E. Campbell, who was incensed at Rockwell's attempted intervention in Buckeye State affairs.

Despite such activity, Wednesday's opening roll call (the thirty-first) showed virtually no change from the night before. The same was generally true of the ensuing six ballots. On the thirty-fourth both the Mississippi and Oklahoma delegations did return to McAdoo, causing McAdoo hopes to rise momentarily. But on the thirty-fifth, Oklahoma, the "flirt of

McAdoo Alley," again left the Californian. The next ballot was enlivened only by a North Dakota delegate who cast one vote for Edward L. Doheny. In like manner, the thirty-seventh was interesting only because two of New York's votes were cast for McAdoo. A smiling Roosevelt indicated that these two pro-McAdoo votes in the heart of Smith country had been expected. One, Roscoe Irwin, Democratic leader of Ulster County, was beholden to McAdoo for an internal revenue job when McAdoo had been Secretary of the Treasury. The other, ex-representative Lathrop Brown of Suffolk County, came from a KKK hotbed and was a personal friend of McAdoo. This same Brown had almost had his clothes torn off him at the San Francisco convention in 1920 when he had attempted to carry the New York standard into a McAdoo parade.

The climax of the Wednesday-afternoon balloting came on the thirty-eighth roll call. The name of Florida had been reached when a voice called out, "Mr. Chairman. Mr. Chairman." It was Bryan. "I desire to obtain unanimous consent to explain my vote." For a brief moment there was silence as this request sank in, then boos and hisses from the floor began to mingle with cries of "No! No!" from the galleries. Walsh, with tongue in cheek, said: "The chair hears no objection," and motioned Bryan forward. This caused the convention to laugh. But as Bryan made his way toward the rostrum, the protests gradually revived. Edmond Moore of Ohio resumed yelling, "I object! I object!," and various sons of Tammany gathered on the platform to remonstrate with Walsh about his decision. Meanwhile, McAdoo delegates leaped to their feet and by their cheering attempted to drown out Bryan's opponents. Only when Bryan turned to face the audience did the Garden quiet down.

The scene was reminiscent of 1912 when Bryan had also requested permission to explain his vote. On that occasion he had bitterly assailed the nation's financial interests and had condemned Boss Murphy before initiating the move to Wilson. Now his primary concern was party harmony and the elimination of an impasse. But Bryan had never before functioned as a coalition leader and he would fail now. His first appearance on the Democratic stage in 1896 had been as a partisan fighter whose goal was to defeat, not win over, his enemies. In his entire career he had never advocated a program that could command the allegiance of all Democrats. Seeing all issues from an agrarian viewpoint, he was always basically intolerant of those who disagreed with him. His constant moralizing about economic issues had frequently antagonized. Now, in 1924, when economic questions were being submerged by social and cultural issues, Bryan was even less able to act as a catalyst. Indeed, with regard to the social and cultural matters which were destroying this convention, Bryan was part of the problem, not the solution.

In the early portion of his "harmony" address Bryan received rapt attention and intermittent applause, even from the galleries, which were about two-thirds full. Bryan claimed that party victory in November was his only reason for coming forward, and he expressed the hope that his remarks might help clarify the situation. The Democratic party, he contended, had an abundance of presidential timber which could bring victory, and he asked the convention's indulgence while he named a few. First he mentioned Dr. Murphree, prompting an audible gasp on the part of both the delegates and the galleries. Murphree had not even been nominated. Someone high up in the galleries suddenly shouted, "We want Smith," and a few others took up the chant. Not to be sidetracked, Bryan continued by extolling Murphree, calling him a "scholarly Democrat." "Never heard of him," came a voice from the pro-Smith area on the floor, while someone up in the galleries shouted, "I'll bite. Who's he?" Bryan quickly retorted, "Those who have not informed themselves about the nation's great men ought to remain silent until they have had a chance to inform themselves." This won him both jeers and applause. He then proceeded to add others to his list—Josephus Daniels, Robinson, Ralston, Walsh, Meredith (Iowa), and his own brother, Charles—but he pointedly did not include Glass (who had refused to release his delegates to McAdoo), and dismissed John W. Davis as a Wall Street conservative who could not possibly win. More important, he ignored Smith altogether, and this omission thoroughly inflamed the New York galleries.

When Bryan finally mentioned McAdoo as the candidate best suited for the presidency, the convention erupted. The galleries booed and hissed and McAdoo men stood and cheered. With this statement Bryan dropped any pretense at "harmony." All levity and attempts at humorous repartee now disappeared as the convention again quickly degenerated into an intemperate shouting match. When Bryan said at one point that this was probably his last convention, the galleries broke out in sustained applause. "Don't applaud," warned Bryan, "I may change my mind." At another point when Bryan referred to Republican corruption, a member of the New Jersey delegation demanded to know about "McAdoo, Doheny, and oil." "Oil! Oil! Oil!" chanted the unruly galleries, and it was several minutes before Bryan could reply that McAdoo's business with Doheny had nothing to do with the oil leases. Renewed shouts of

"Oil!" caused Bryan to add angrily: "If any oil has ever touched William G. McAdoo, the intense, persistent, and virulent opposition of Wall Street washes all the oil away." These last words were lost in the din.

Now Bryan's face glistened. Sweat stood out on his cheekbones. He pointed a trembling finger at the screaming galleries and the shouting delegates. He had lost his audience and he knew it. As catcalls and jeers continued on the floor and in the aroused galleries, Moore of Ohio, waving his arms and standing on a chair directly in front of the speaker's stand, demanded that Chairman Walsh return to the regular order of business. Walsh replied that he would as soon as Bryan used up his allotted time. Moore and others who were now crowding the platform argued that Bryan's time was already up. One McAdoo delegate shouted, "Oh, give him time," to which a booming voice in the galleries responded, "Give him twenty years!" When Moore attempted to move that the convention return to the roll call, Walsh ruled him out of order and announced that Bryan had five minutes more. But Bryan's train of thought had been broken and he rambled, using more than ten minutes to arrive at his customary condemnation of the monopolies and wealthy eastern interests. Long before this, the hall was filled with shouts of "Put him out!" "How much you getting for this?" "Stop speaking!" "We've had enough!"

Amid taunts and some applause Bryan stepped wearily from the rostrum and, protected by two-dozen policemen, made his way back to the Florida delegation. He had been on the platform for more than an hour and had, in effect, said that the Democratic party needed a candidate who was anti-Smith, anti–Wall Street, and dry. In doing this, Bryan had not resolved the convention's dilemma, and he left the speaker's platform lower in personal prestige than when he came. His speech was far below his past standards; it lacked cohesiveness; it did not build to a peak. It did not inspire nor did it contain any of his usual verbal pyrotechnics. It irritated or at best merely amused most delegates.

Even so, his appearance on the platform caused momentary panic among Smith supporters. As Bryan started to speak there were hurried consultations among Smith men on the floor. Roosevelt scribbled furiously on a note pad while Brennan prepared a request for time to answer the Great Commoner. But as Bryan continued, the Smith men began to relax. Roosevelt was the first to regain his smile and sat calmly throughout the remainder of the address. The New York delegation remained quiet. When Bryan finished, one New York delegate was heard to remark, "This man must be for another candidate than McAdoo." Roosevelt turned to his neighbor and commented, "Mr. Bryan has killed poor Mc-Adoo and he hasn't done himself any good." Charles F. X. O'Brien, one of the leaders of the New Jersey delegation, simply shook his head and mumbled, "The same old 'Dollar Bill,' the same old 'Dollar Bill.'"

McAdoo men were divided on Bryan's performance. Baruch was embarrassed and Breckinridge Long admitted that the speech had done McAdoo more harm than good. McAdoo was pleased, especially by Bryan's refusal to be cowed by the howling New York galleries. The New York press naturally denounced Bryan. To New York reporters he was the consummate hick, who possessed an infantile view of the world and believed in miracles. Typical was Oswald G. Villard's assessment of Bryan's effort: "The futility of the man, the confusion of his talk, his terrible lack of sound political and moral education were never so demonstrated. He is now a pathetic figure, so pathetic one hates to speak of him." In the hinterland, Bryan's treatment by the New York galleries was considered little short of a national scandal. The conduct of the galleries had been shameful. Despite his calm exterior, Roosevelt had seethed inwardly over their behavior and immediately afterward issued a press release disassociating Smith's forces from their boorishness. Even hard-bitten New York correspondents were dismayed at the galleries' lack of decorum. One remarked that the events of Wednesday afternoon must have shaken Bryan in his opposition to evolution, since every time he gazed into the galleries he must have become increasingly convinced of the existence of the missing link.

Unfortunately for Smith, urban rowdyism was apparently New York's only answer to rural nativism and fundamentalism. When the New York galleries gave to Bryan what at the Polo Grounds would be called "the old razzberry," it was an act of spoiled children whose frustration at not getting their own way broke out in an ugly display of bad manners. As a result, they restored to their hated adversary, William Jennings Bryan, some of the luster and influence which he was in the process of losing because of his rambling speeches and quixotic behavior. It was remarkable how little New York in 1924 really understood the rest of the country —how egotistical was the city's own view of itself and how badly it expressed its affection for Al Smith. As the taunts of the New York galleries again spread over the airwaves and crackled into the homes of

Americans everywhere, it seemed to prove once more that New York's promises of hospitality and its claims of sophistication and tolerance were false indeed.

Whatever the long-term effects of Bryan's speech, it served to lengthen the convention stalemate. Thousands of telegrams poured in from the West and South supporting him and urging the McAdooites to fight on. Still, the speech did not create a breakthrough for McAdoo in the convention. On the resumed thirty-eighth ballot McAdoo even lost one-half vote (444½ to 444) while Smith's total stayed the same (321). Needing time to assess this situation more accurately, the leaders in all camps agreed to an immediate recess and spent the interim to 8 P.M. consulting with their champions. After talking with Roosevelt, Hoey, Mack, and Brennan, Smith decided to stand pat. McAdoo conferred with Rockwell, Kremer, Long, Roper and now Bryan as well, then ordered a new all-out drive. More important, the favorite sons—Glass, Cox, J. W. Davis, Robinson, Underwood, Ritchie, and Taggart (for Ralston)—all decided to remain in the fight.

When the convention reconvened shortly after 8 P.M. on Wednesday evening the galleries were packed. Not since the night of the Klan struggle on Saturday had there been such pushing and shoving for seats. In the intervening days of endless balloting the galleries had sometimes been only half full. But the baiting of Bryan that afternoon had again whetted spectator appetites and rumors of a last-ditch attempt by McAdoo to secure the nomination acted as a magnet, again pulling New Yorkers into the Garden. As one Missouri delegate remarked as he looked up at the galleries just before the gavel fell, "They've got out the whole gashouse gang for Smith tonight."

For twenty minutes prior to the opening thirty-ninth ballot the New York Police Glee Club entertained the crowd, concluding with "The Sidewalks of New York." This song, especially, put the swarming galleries in a playful mood and they began to sing along and clap. Meanwhile, McAdoo Alley tried to close its ears. "I've been hearing that tune for days," said one Missourian, "I'm off 'The Sidewalks of New York' for life." Sensing the growing tension, Senator David Walsh of Massachusetts, substituting for Chairman Thomas Walsh, warned that he would tolerate no outbursts of any kind during the balloting. Almost simultaneously, several squads of Tammany "anti-claque killers," as the press called them, could be seen circulating through the crowd urging proper deportment. They were there under orders from the Smith leaders. On the floor many

McAdoo delegates were still hopping mad at the afternoon's treatment of Bryan and were further angered by the possibility of a repeat performance by the galleries that night. McAdoo lieutenants were seen scurrying here and there rounding up every vote, skillfully playing on southern and western fears to keep wavering delegates in line.

The thirty-ninth ballot finally began and proceeded without incident until Missouri was called. It switched its 36 votes from Davis back to McAdoo. Shortly thereafter Oklahoma also returned to the McAdoo fold. As one after another of McAdoo's wayward delegations or delegates came home cries of anguish were heard in the galleries. Only with difficulty did David Walsh keep order while Tammany runners with megaphones moved up and down the rows of spectators trying to quiet distraught Smith rooters. By the end of the ballot McAdoo's total had jumped to 499, and when it was announced a roar of approval went up in McAdoo Alley.

Amid rising apprehension in the galleries and anticipation among McAdoo delegates on the floor, the fortieth roll call began. Both Missouri and Oklahoma stuck, as did all the others who had returned, and the Californian even managed to pick up an additional 6½ votes, two of them from Connecticut, of all places. Although this was still short of a majority (550), it raised his total for the first time above the 500 mark. When the actual vote of 505½ was announced the Garden again roared and a parade was begun by happy McAdoo followers, who chanted the now-familiar "Mac, Mac, Mac-A-Do!" Clearly a do-or-die McAdoo drive was definitely on and tension was high. Bryan was seen arguing with someone in the Missouri delegation. Rockwell was earnestly discussing something with an Oklahoman. Long was talking animatedly with a Virginia delegate. The galleries were fidgeting, some holding their heads in their hands or biting their fingernails. But Roosevelt sat calmly in the New York delegation, seemingly unconcerned. To a reporter who asked him whether McAdoo would win now that he had over 500 votes, Roosevelt firmly said "No." The forty-first ballot began.

It was anticlimactic. In spite of the best efforts of McAdoo leaders, the Californian received only 504.9. Smith kept his total steady at 317.6. Favorite sons Davis, Ralston, Cox, Underwood, Robinson, Glass, and Ritchie held on to their share. McAdoo's climb had been broken. His inability to entice any of these favorite sons to come to his aid was now killing him. Personally directing his strategy from his "command post" in the Madison Square Hotel, McAdoo desperately tried to get Glass, Ralston, and Robinson to switch. Sweating messengers came and went to the Arkansas, Indiana, and Virginia delegations, but to no avail. When on the forty-second ballot there was again no appreciable change (McAdoo 503.4 and Smith 318.6), McAdoo decided to press for an adjournment in the hope of working something out overnight. Besides, he had heard that Oklahoma was again preparing to desert him and feared that this might encourage a wholesale retreat. Smith was also anxious for an adjournment, as were the favorite sons. McAdoo had frightened them and they wanted time to shore up their defenses. Meanwhile, the New York galleries were convinced that the worst of the McAdoo drive had been contained. They met the announcement of adjournment with cheers, whistles, and yells. Some even danced jigs and paraded in the aisles. In their view the hated McAdoo had been defeated.

The crucial day of the convention had indeed come and gone for McAdoo. For a time he had hung on the lip of success. But without the defection of at least several of the favorite sons he could not hope to win. Throughout the balloting on Wednesday, support for the favorite sons had remained remarkably steadfast. Cox received 57 votes on the day's first ballot (the thirty-first) and still commanded 55 on the last (the forty-second). Underwood retained his 39½ votes and Robinson his 24. Glass varied between 24 and 28½, Ritchie between 16½ and 17½, and Ralston between 30 and 32. Only John W. Davis fluctuated seriously. The West Virginian opened the day with 127½ votes but fell to 67 at the close, proving again that most of his support came from the ranks nominally belonging to McAdoo.

By the end of Wednesday not only McAdoo but Davis too was being written off by many convention observers as a successful contender. Davis supporters were indeed disconsolate, but neither McAdoo nor his advisers showed signs of surrendering. At a late Wednesday-night meeting of his staff McAdoo decided to keep the pressure on the Arkansas, Indiana, and Virginia delegations in the hope that they might yet come over. Senator Robinson and Claude Swanson (representing Carter Glass) were even summoned to McAdoo's Vanderbilt suite for a discussion of this possibility, but both left without making any promises. Bryan, meanwhile, was assigned to persuade Taggart to switch over, but he reported back that Taggart had no intention of doing so. Taggart, Bryan said, now believed that Ralston was the most available candidate and was waiting for the proper moment to mount a drive for him. It required considerable optimism, therefore, for Rockwell to announce to reporters at a news

conference early Thursday morning that "McAdoo is going to be nominated. . . . We have got the delegates."

Smith men, who earlier on Wednesday had begun to discuss contin-
gency plans about what to do if McAdoo achieved a convention majority,
rebounded with confidence. Norman Mack said his soundings indicated
that Wednesday night represented McAdoo's "dying gasp." Hoey agreed
that the Californian was at last "finished." Roosevelt buoyantly told
reporters: "McAdoo has passed the 500 mark, and he may go higher,
but he will never pass the majority mark." In a burst of enthusiasm,
Roosevelt added that the Smith forces had not yet begun to fight and that
Smith might yet be nominated.

6

By Thursday, July 3, the convention stalemate was glacial. The determination and intransigency of the major groups was unbelievable. Both
the Smith and McAdoo forces had lost the ability even to communicate. Differing political and economic ideologies, cultural patterns, and
religious beliefs may have been the underlying reasons for the origin of
their conflict, but now vanity, obstinacy, personal pride, jealousy, and
vindictiveness took over.

Despite the optimism of some of his followers, Smith realized by
Wednesday night that he had very little hope of securing the nomination
himself. But the New York press, the insistence of his supporters, and
Smith's own revulsion at the nature of the McAdoo drive caused him to
push on. Smith continued to believe that he was the victim of a smear
campaign that was primarily religious not political, and that the Klan
was at the root of most of it. Telegrams and letters poured into Smith's
headquarters telling him that he simply *had* to stay in the struggle. One
man from Connecticut asserted that he was "the only bulwark" against
fierce repression and urged him to keep his name before the convention
"as long as bigotry and intolerance menace the party." Another wrote
him, "If we do not have a test at this election, a Catholic, a Jew, or a
colored man will not have a chance again."

McAdoo was under similar pressures. His many telegrams read:
"Never Give Up," "Stay In and Win," "Fight to the Last," and "Stick to
the End." A typical communication read: "Hope is expressed everywhere

by the common people that you will not forsake them by stepping aside for any other candidate." One letter urged him as an American patriot to help return the "bootleggers and Romanists" to the "putrid gutters from whence each came." Especially symbolic of this uncompromising attitude was the matronly lady, somewhere in her fifties, with gray hair knotted softly at the back of her head, who at the merest mention of McAdoo's name was seen in the California delegation waving a brown-and-white California bear flag. Called "the mother of the deadlock" by William Allen White, she was the personification of all that the McAdoo forces thought they were fighting for. She was, according to White, "the Lord's anointed in a holy cause."

When the balloting began on Thursday morning McAdoo continued his assault on the Arkansas, Indiana, and Virginia delegations while Smith concentrated on Ohio and Maryland. McAdoo's immediate goal was to secure a convention majority and the psychological advantage that this would bring. Smith, in turn, wanted control of at least one-third of the convention. Neither side was successful. Through nineteen exhausting ballots McAdoo proved that he could consistently retain about 450 of the convention's delegates, but he could not achieve a majority. Smith could not muster one-third (367). Each time Smith started to make a run at this figure, Mississippi, Missouri, or Oklahoma would be swung into the McAdoo column to negate the Smith effect.

The only excitement in an otherwise boring day came at the end of the afternoon session. On the forty-ninth ballot it was clear that some weary McAdoo delegates were casting about for an alternative to McAdoo. When Mississippi suddenly announced its 20 votes for Ralston it appeared that one had been found. Although there was no further change on the fiftieth or fifty-first ballots, on the fifty-second Missouri also switched all of her votes to Ralston, pushing his total to 93. At that moment Taggart was seen circulating through the Mississippi and Missouri delegations, and it was assumed that a Ralston boom was getting underway. But no further defections to the Indiana senator occurred on the next two ballots, and all sides agreed to an adjournment until 8:30 P.M.

Taggart had been playing a subtle double game and the Ralston boomlet had caught him unawares. Prior to this time he had attempted to remain friendly with both the Smith and McAdoo camps. His ties with the Smith element, however, had been severely strained by his refusal to deliver Indiana's vote for the minority plank on the Klan and by growing doubts that he had any intention of giving Smith any Indiana support. McAdoo men, encouraged by this, had applied increasing pressure on Taggart to move to McAdoo. But they too were gradually awakening to the fact that Taggart was pursuing his own plan. Surreptitiously the Indiana boss had been wooing McAdoo delegates.

Taggart used the recess between the afternoon and evening sessions on Thursday to assess how best to capitalize on this windfall for Ralston. When he paid a call on McAdoo at his headquarters on Thursday afternoon, rumors flew that a Ralston-McAdoo alliance was being formed. When he also met later with Brennan, it was claimed that a Smith-Ralston deal was brewing. In both of these conferences Taggart actually attempted to ascertain how far either McAdoo or Smith would go to block Ralston. Neither side gave him much encouragement. Taggart warned both camps that a Ralston boom was growing anyway and that it might "blow up a little rain." Brennan wryly replied, "I'll have my umbrella up when it comes."

It did not come on Thursday evening. After the session resumed there were no signs that a Ralston coalition had been effected. By the fifty-seventh ballot he had reached only 97. Then on the fifty-eighth he dropped back to 40½. Rather than being dejected, Taggart decided to wait and push Ralston again when circumstances were more favorable. Meanwhile, the balloting droned on through the sixty-first roll call with no significant changes, and a weary convention finally adjourned at 1 A.M.

At that moment, this convention had set a number of records of dubious value. Thursday's 19 ballots were the most taken on any single day of any convention in American history. The total number of roll calls (61) had now surpassed the 57 at the Democratic convention in Charleston in 1860. It also had exceeded the 53 ballots taken by the Whigs to nominate Winfield Scott in Baltimore in 1852. The Republican all-time high was only 36 ballots to select James A. Garfield in Chicago in 1880. It was perhaps merciful that the squabbling Democrats in Madison Square Garden did not know that they still had 42 ballots yet to go.

The cause for this horrendous condition was no longer merely the stubbornness of the Smith and McAdoo factions; it was also the increasing influence of the favorite sons. These latter now constituted a firm bloc—a little entente—which helped sustain the impasse. The continuation of Cox and Ritchie as candidates kept Smith from securing one-third for veto purposes, while the steadfastness of Ralston, Glass, and Robinson blocked any chance of McAdoo's gaining a majority. Beginning to realize their collective power, a few of these favorite sons began to suggest that Smith and McAdoo should withdraw so that they could mount a serious drive for the top prize themselves. Such suggestions particularly infuriated Rockwell, who, frustrated by his failure to woo these favorite sons, issued an intemperate statement following the balloting on Thursday which made McAdoo's chances for success among their delegations even less likely. It was "an outrageous travesty," he said, for any of the favorite sons to continue to run. As for the "absurd suggestions" that McAdoo and Smith should withdraw and leave the field to them, Rockwell asserted: "The withdrawing comes at the other end. If there be any withdrawals, they should of right be from among the list of favorite sons."

7

So the impasse continued. As the tenth day of the convention dawned, delegates ruefully recalled the prophecies of prolonged deadlock that had preceded its convening. But no one had expected this. Delegates dreaded the thought of sweltering on July 4 in the Garden instead of enjoying the comforts of home with their wives or husbands and their families. By now more delegates had "adjourned with their feet," leaving New York and the snarling convention behind. John Nance Garner, a pro-McAdoo delegate from Texas, was one of those who had disgustedly turned his badge over to his alternate and gone home. Caught by a reporter while carrying his own bag through the lobby of the McAlpin Hotel, Garner said the party was making a spectacle of itself. The ninth ballot, he claimed, had convinced him that the convention was hopelessly deadlocked. Asked if he thought it might end soon, he replied: "Hell, this convention won't nominate a candidate in a hundred ballots!"

The 1924 Democratic convention was clearly becoming an embarrassment for almost everyone. Supposedly it was over. The empty ticket books said so. So did the official souvenir program. All the buffets, parties, dances, luncheons, excursions, receptions, and teas had long since been held. Even the decorations along the Avenue of States had disappeared. Yet the convention remained, causing Will Rogers to complain that New York had invited the delegates as visitors, not to live there.

Living expenses were becoming a serious matter for many out-of-towners. McAdoo men charged that the Smith forces were purposely lengthening the convention in order to exhaust the means of rural delegates. To prevent this, Bryan proposed that a fund be created to help those pro-McAdoo supporters who were in distress. When Smith followers counter-charged that McAdoo leaders were preparing to bribe delegates by paying their hotel bills, Arthur Brisbane of the New York *Evening Journal* announced that William Randolph Hearst would assume the expenses of one hundred random delegates and hoped other wealthy men would follow suit. In that way, said Brisbane, no delegate would know who actually paid his bills.

Whatever the personal sacrifices, most delegates remained in New York and were present at 1:15 P.M. on Friday, July 4, when Walsh gaveled the convention to order. The first two ballots of Independence Day showed that no significant changes had occurred overnight. The next ballot (the sixty-fourth) revealed a slight movement. Taggart rose and read a telegram from Ralston withdrawing his name "from further consideration from this convention." This particular telegram had been sent to Taggart by Ralston on July 1, three days before. But Taggart had ignored it, desiring to keep the Hoosier senator in the race. Ralston had never been an enthusiastic contender and his candidacy had always been more Taggart's idea than his own. Apparently he had been willing to be Taggart's "stalking horse" as long as there was no possible chance of his selection. By July 1 he had even wearied of this subterfuge, and when his vote climbed above 90 on Thursday afternoon, July 3, he telegraphed Taggart a second time demanding that he remove his name. Again, Taggart had stalled for time, sincerely believing that Ralston might yet change his mind. When the balloting on Friday morning showed no appreciable change in the relative position of the various candidates, Taggart at last was forced to read the senator's original withdrawal telegram to the convention. This was immediately greeted with cheers, and a humorous funereal rendition of "On the Banks of the Wabash" by the Sutherland band prompted Elmer Davis to comment that "if all candidates would withdraw this convention might get somewhere."

Before the assembly could fully digest the Ralston news, Ohio announced the removal of Cox's name. Again there were cheers and much interest was expressed in where Ohio's 48 votes would go. Groans quickly followed when Ohio declared that all its votes would now be cast for Newton Baker—it was simply exchanging one favorite son for another. Indiana, meanwhile, gave 20 of its votes to McAdoo and 10 to Smith.

Thus, the withdrawal of two of the more important favorite sons did not materially advance the cause of either McAdoo or Smith. The realization emerged that even if all the favorite sons retired neither one of the two major candidates would probably benefit from the release of their delegates.

The sixty-sixth ballot signaled the opening of a new phase in the convention. While the deadlock continued, plans to relieve it began to take precedence. The first overtures came from the Smith side. Following the inconclusive sixty-sixth ballot, Brigadier General Charles H. Cole of Massachusetts offered a resolution which provided that the convention reconvene in executive session at 8 P.M. and that all candidates be invited to speak to it. This caused a commotion in the McAdoo camp. Kremer of Montana claimed that this resolution was out of order and Bryan tried to amend Cole's motion to reconvene in executive session (which would eliminate the galleries) but invite no candidates. Ignoring all such entreaties, Walsh ordered a roll call on the Cole resolution. It failed to muster the two-thirds required to suspend the rules as McAdoo Alley voted solidly against it.

After the chair announced the result, Franklin Roosevelt asked for recognition. For several days he had become increasingly discouraged about the convention's prospects as well as increasingly incensed by McAdoo's dilatory tactics. At the end of the sixty-fourth ballot he had actually penned an insolent letter to McAdoo which said, "It is incredible that you would be willing to ruin your party by [such] dog-in-the-manger tactics." Before sending it, however, Roosevelt thought the better of it and decided instead to apply pressure on McAdoo by more subtle means. As he now swung forward on his crutches toward the speaker's platform, comments about his charming personality circulated once more through the hall. Roosevelt was popular even with the McAdooites. But they did not like what he now said. Asking for suspension of the rules, Roosevelt requested that Al Smith be given consent to speak to the convention. "No! No!" shouted some alarmed McAdoo delegates, while others sought immediate clarification as to whether a Smith address would be given in executive session or with the galleries present. Roosevelt's resolution did not specify and the roll call was held on the resolution as stated. Many McAdoo delegates were undecided how to react. Aware that it would be an insult to the New York governor to refuse to let him speak, some McAdoo leaders urged their delegates to vote for the resolution. Too late they found out that McAdoo wanted them to vote against it. The final vote, however, was 604½ ayes and 473 nays, far below the two-thirds necessary to suspend the rules. Hence, the Roosevelt resolution failed. With this, the convention adjourned to 8:30 P.M., at which time the regular order of business was to be resumed.

Ironically, at the very moment the Democratic convention was voting not to hear Smith, 20,000 Klansmen and their relatives from Pennsylvania, New Jersey, and Delaware were demonstrating against him at an Independence Day outing at nearby Long Branch, New Jersey. There an effigy of the New York governor, whose left arm cradled a whiskey bottle, was battered to a shapeless pulp by hurlers who paid a nickel each to throw three baseballs at him. Later, after a bevy of Klan weddings and baptisms were held, a parade of four thousand hooded knights advertised their opposition to Smith, and a Klan official declared in a rousing speech that the Democratic convention could not possibly be "so foolish as to nominate Al."

Back in New York, Smith men left the Garden on the afternoon of July 4 thoroughly angered by the defeat of the Cole and Roosevelt resolutions. George Brennan told reporters that the McAdoo forces were afraid of Smith. Bryan twice had been accorded speaking privileges, said Brennan. Why not Smith? Some hotheads among Smith's advisers suggested that he hire Carnegie Hall and make his remarks there. Others advocated that he go to the convention and sit with the New York delegation as a sub-delegate and demand permission of the floor.

Actually the real purpose of the Cole and Roosevelt resolutions was not to foist Smith on the convention or rally it to his banner, as McAdoo men feared. The proposals were designed merely to place McAdoo on the defensive tactically. The Cole resolution was the means whereby some eastern leaders hoped to clear the galleries of the loudmouths from the Lower East Side and pave the way for a joint McAdoo-Smith withdrawal. Roosevelt's proposal was likewise intended to bring the McAdoo-Smith confrontation to a head by forcing McAdoo to agree to withdraw. Roosevelt committed a blunder, however, in not connecting his resolution with an executive session excluding the galleries, as Cole had done.

But McAdoo followers continued to suspect that these two resolutions were a plot to make Smith the nominee of the convention. Rockwell was enraged and complained bitterly to reporters about Roosevelt's "low tactics." Smith, he charged, would have used the galleries to create utter turmoil and force the convention to accept him. Although Rockwell persistently held to these beliefs, McAdoo had some second thoughts. Not that the Californian changed his mind about the insidious motivation behind these two resolutions. He merely came to believe that he had committed a tactical error, especially with regard to the Smith invitation. Splitting with Rockwell, he drafted a letter to the convention before the evening session convened, requesting unanimous consent for Smith to speak if he wished. McAdoo was anxious to prove that he was not afraid of Smith, as Brennan had charged, and that he could hold his delegates in line against any Smith stampede.

At 8:45 P.M. Walsh gaveled the sixteenth session of the 1924 convention to order. After a Presbyterian prayer, which seemed to have no greater effect on the assembled delegates than those of other denominations, Walsh read McAdoo's letter. Gavin McNab of California immediately moved for unanimous consent for Smith to speak. To the surprise of McAdoo leaders, there were loud shouts of dissent from Smith's friends; angered by the original refusal, they were not now prepared to accept any favors from McAdoo. "Who's running this convention," yelled a Smith man, "the delegates or a gentleman from California?" To keep order, Walsh banged his gavel so vigorously that the head flew off and hit a New York delegate, momentarily stunning him. Simultaneously, Michael Igoe of Illinois proclaimed in a foghorn voice that he would not grant unanimous consent, saying, "You have insulted the Governor once and you are not going to do it again."

Under the circumstances there was nothing for Walsh to do but to order a resumption of the roll call. But tempers were already frayed and bitter recriminations were being hurled back and forth among the delegates. Arizona tried to inject some humor into the situation by casting one vote for Will Rogers on the sixty-seventh ballot. However nothing could prevent the convention from degenerating into a shambles. Everyone was tired and frustrated. "How long is this going to go on?" was a common question. One woman was heard to exclaim, "I never dreamed it would be anything like this. I'm through with politics." Many delegates expressed bitterness toward their leaders, toward the unit rule, toward the candidates, and toward the fates that had brought them to this convention and this accursed city. Meanwhile, the roll calls droned on, and for the remaining four ballots of the day the McAdoo forces again exerted every effort to put their candidate across. By calling up again every available pro-McAdoo delegate, McAdoo's total climbed once more above the 500 mark and even reached a convention high of 530 on the sixty-ninth ballot. This was still 20 votes short of a majority and 202 less than the required two-thirds. On the seventieth ballot McAdoo's total again began to fade as the Smith and the favorite-son forces absorbed the shock. The band, with weary humor, struck up "What Shall I Do?" No one seemed to know.

It was now 12:20 A.M. Saturday morning. One still sane delegate, Edward Frensdorf of Michigan, rose and presented a resolution which proposed that McAdoo and Smith simultaneously withdraw and throw their support to someone else. McAdoo and Smith followers alike shouted down this proposal and Walsh fought to keep order. As name calling occurred and fist fights threatened to erupt, Taggart moved adjournment and Walsh quickly accepted. Bitter arguments were continuing when the gavel fell. Departing delegates seemingly were unable to agree except on one thing—it had been a disgusting way to spend the Fourth of July.

8

Friday had been another day of disaster for McAdoo despite his reaching his highest total of the convention. He had been outmaneuvered by the Smith leaders, and his obstinacy was increasingly regarded by many delegates as the major reason for the continuing impasse. Further, Rockwell had succeeded in antagonizing a growing number of convention participants by his intemperate remarks and his militancy. At the end of Friday's balloting, for example, he told reporters that McAdoo had "no thought of compromise" and placed the entire blame for the deadlock on "two or three delegations which are disciplined like the Tammany crowd in New York City." Asked if there was *anyone* who might persuade McAdoo to withdraw, Rockwell remarked, "I fear for the man who would approach Mr. McAdoo. He is like Gen. Grant and is going to fight it out on this line if it takes all summer."

Smith, on the other hand, had appeared to be much more amenable. If the invitation for him to speak had been granted, he had intended to defend his record and his religion before the convention and then make a formal offer to withdraw. Smith had consistently rejected talk of taking second place on any ticket or using his votes as a lever for personal bargaining. On Friday, at Roosevelt's insistence, he had personally directed Tammany runners to crack down on any outbursts in the galleries, and pro-Smith shouters, especially during the commotion over the various resolutions, were often startled by Smith beadles who told them to "Shut up!" Smith even retained his good humor when Baruch and Chadbourne called on him during the Friday-afternoon recess, apologizing for the vote against inviting him to speak. Smith told them that he was too old a hand at politics to be hurt by such rejection. But the rebuff did make him more cautious. He indicated that he would now withdraw only with a similar personal promise by McAdoo and only after the two of them met to discuss a compromise candidate. More amenable or not, Smith's goal was still to close off any possibility that McAdoo might get the nomination.

As Saturday, July 5, dawned, there was growing pressure from most delegates for *something* to be done. McAdoo and Smith were obviously through, but sentiment had not yet crystallized around anyone else. It was a dismal scene when Chairman Walsh brought the convention to order for its seventeenth session. As Governor Brandon cast Alabama's usual vote for Underwood, only half the delegates were in their seats. No more than two hundred spectators were in the galleries. At no time on Saturday were there more than three thousand onlookers present and they were as demonstrative as if they were at a public library. Most of the fun for New Yorkers had gone out of the convention—McAdoo was doomed, but so was Smith.

After the day's first two ballots (the seventy-first and seventy-second) showed no change from Friday, several plans were proposed from the floor to end the deadlock. None of these were well thought out nor did they have the support of any appreciable segment of the convention. They simply sprang from the frustrations of individual delegates who hoped somehow to hit upon a scheme that might work. The Oklahoma delegation sponsored a resolution calling for the lowest name on each ballot to be eliminated until only two names were left. This was defeated when both Smith and McAdoo men voted against it. Senator Hitchcock of Nebraska proposed that beginning with the seventy-fifth roll call the candidate receiving the lowest vote on each subsequent ballot would withdraw until only five names were left. This plan also lost. Next, A. H. Ferguson, an Oklahoma delegate, proposed that the convention adjourn and reconvene on July 21 in Kansas City. Laughter met this suggestion since Ferguson was obviously influenced by personal convenience. Ex-Governor Albert W. Gilchrist of Florida immediately moved to substitute the name of Punta Gorda (Florida), his home town, for Kansas City.

Ignoring Gilchrist's attempt at levity, Walsh asked for a vote on the Ferguson proposal. It was snowed under 82.7 to 1007.3.

Other plans circulated among the delegates—that the convention move to Cleveland, that all favorite sons be ordered to release their delegates, that the high man take the presidential nomination and the next highest the vice-presidential nomination. But the only other proposal formally advanced came from Governor Thomas H. Ball of Texas. His scheme was complex and not all delegates fully understood it. He suggested that at the conclusion of each successive roll call the lowest candidate be dropped until only two were left; then, if neither of the two received the necessary two-thirds after five ballots, the unit rule would be abolished and the candidate receiving a simple majority would be declared the winner. This plan caused consternation among McAdoo leaders, even though it was generally regarded as a pro-McAdoo arrangement. Fourteen McAdoo delegations were still operating under the unit rule and there was a fear that the Ball resolution would free as many as eighty anti-McAdoo votes. On the other hand, Smith men distrusted the elimination of the two-thirds rule. McAdoo was too close to a majority for comfort. Hence, when put to a vote, the Ball resolution was shouted down by virtually all groups.

When the balloting for President resumed, it quickly became clear that the Ball resolution had probably represented McAdoo's last chance to save his situation and he had muffed it. For days Roosevelt and the Smith forces had been working to secure enough votes to give them a convention veto. Roosevelt believed that only in that way could McAdoo be forced at last to admit that his position was hopeless. On Saturday morning Roosevelt had met with several representatives of the favorite sons in a small room under the stairway at the Twenty-seventh Street end of the Garden and urged them to "loan" Smith sufficient votes to provide a veto power. Simultaneously, Moore of Ohio had used a similar argument on Baker (formerly Cox) delegates. Both of these approaches paid off during the seventy-fourth ballot, when Ohio switched 20½ votes to Smith, increasing his total to 364. On the next three ballots Smith received 366, 368, and 367 votes respectively. The latter was the exact number needed for an absolute convention veto.

The seventy-seventh ballot, the last on Saturday, read: McAdoo 513, Smith 367, Davis 76½, Underwood 47½, Glass 27, Robinson 24, and Ritchie 16½. It was now clear that Smith could deny the nomination to

McAdoo without any further help. The impact on the McAdoo delegates was staggering. His advisers were stunned and, as Roosevelt had prophesied, began at last to cast about for an "honorable" solution.

What resulted is a study in clever political maneuvering and continued personal obduracy. As soon as Ohio broke to Smith, some McAdoo leaders leaked word that they were now ready to talk. This intelligence came first to Taggart, who more than any other individual still had access to all camps. He quickly contacted Senator Pat Harrison and together they framed a resolution calling for a "harmony conference" between all the contending groups. Taggart showed this to Cordell Hull and to Chairman Walsh and they agreed to support it. The Indiana boss next secured Walter Moore's approval for Underwood, Senator Caraway's for Robinson, and Senator Swanson's for Glass. Finally he consulted Rockwell and Kremer for McAdoo, and Roosevelt and Brennan for Smith. Roosevelt sent a copy of the resolution to the New York governor in the Manhattan Club, and Rockwell carried a copy to McAdoo at his "command post" in the Madison Square Hotel. Both candidates agreed to the proposition, although McAdoo required considerable persuading.

The "harmony conference" resolution was simple. It provided that Walsh and Hull would jointly sponsor a conference of the representatives of all candidates for the purpose of reaching an understanding. Not one voice was raised in dissent when this proposal was presented to the convention, and Senator William H. King of Utah moved immediately for adjournment until 11 A.M. Monday to allow time for the "harmony conference" to do its work. As weary delegates left the Garden for the weekend recess, they were comforted by the thought that at last "the big boys" were going to hammer out a solution. Many of these same delegates normally would have bridled at any suggestion of boss control, but now they wished for some. One of the defects of this convention had been its lack of any centralized leadership. Rampant democracy had failed and now, less than four years after they had charged the Republicans with selecting Warren Harding at a small conference in a smoke-filled room, the Democrats were officially creating one.

As provided in the resolution, Hull arranged for a meeting of the various candidates' representatives in his suite in the Waldorf-Astoria shortly after dinner on Saturday evening. Over forty men came, although the framers of the resolution had envisioned at the most only about eighteen. McAdoo, for instance, sent seven spokesmen while Smith sent six. Among those present were Roosevelt, Mack, Hoey, and Brennan representing Smith; Roper, Cummings, Chadbourne, Rockwell, and Kremer for McAdoo; Johnson and Pattangall for Underwood; Taggart for Ralston; Howard Bruce for Ritchie; J. Henry Goeke for Cox; Frank Hague for Silzer; Claude Swanson and Harry Byrd for Glass; Clem Shaver for Davis; Senator Caraway for Robinson; and W. J. Bryan for C. W. Bryan. There was some resentment that William Jennings was there to represent his brother Charley, but there was no way to prevent it.

The meeting was unproductive. Rockwell again expressed bitterness at the tenacity of the favorite sons and charged them with the primary responsibility for the deadlock. When the Smith men indicated that they would agree to a joint McAdoo-Smith withdrawal, Rockwell said that only Smith should quit. In contrast to Rockwell, Roosevelt appeared conciliatory, and when the meeting broke up on Sunday morning at 1:15 A.M. with nothing accomplished, it was McAdoo and his representatives who were saddled with the blame.

Most of the participants left the meeting with the feeling that a continuation of the discussions would prove useless and only reluctantly agreed at Hull's urging to reconvene at 4 P.M. on Sunday afternoon. At the close of the Saturday-night session, Hull told the press that "progress was being made." But reporters knew better. The talk in the major camps sounded like anything but compromise. At the very moment the Saturday-evening "harmony conference" was in session, McAdoo at a meeting in the Vanderbilt Hotel was addressing the chairmen of his various state delegations, telling them he was just warming to the fight. Concurrently, McAdoo headquarters issued a statement to the press announcing a big McAdoo rally at the Hotel Commodore for Sunday night and added: "Any assertion that Mr. McAdoo has withdrawn from or intends to withdraw from the race in which he is the outstanding candidate is malevolently false." Smith forces in response indicated that they would not budge in their drive to force McAdoo to retire. On this point, Smith said, "There isn't going to be any compromise."

On Sunday morning a seemingly unperturbed Smith, feeling "like a million bucks" and dressed in a dark suit and a Panama hat, attended 11 A.M. mass at St. Agnes's. He was almost mobbed by well-wishers, who urged him to hold fast. The sermon of the day fittingly centered on the disciples' unproductive fishing expedition and Simon Peter's complaint: "We have labored all night and have taken nothing." McAdoo attended the Brick Presbyterian Church at Fifth Avenue and Thirty-seventh Street. He came unannounced and only a few persons recognized him. He and his wife lined up with the rest of the congregation to shake hands with the minister, and then they walked down Fifth Avenue and across to the Vanderbilt with only a few glances from passers-by.

At about this same time, representatives of all the minority candidates were gathering in a secret meeting under the chairmanship of Taggart in the Waldorf rooms of the national committee. These men had decided to come together on their own since it was clear from the conference on Saturday night that neither Smith nor McAdoo was able to take the initiative. For three hours they discussed the problem and finally appointed a subcommittee under Senator Caraway to draw up a delegate-release resolution to be presented to the full "harmony conference" at 4 P.M. This "little entente" resolution was actually the brain child of Governor Ritchie of Maryland, who borrowed the idea from B. Howell Griswold of Baltimore. It involved only a simple statement which read: "The undersigned do hereby release all and every delegate from any pledge, instruction or obligation whatsoever in so far as his candidacy for the Democratic nomination for the Presidency is concerned as completely as if their names had been withdrawn from the convention."

As expected, when the "harmony conference" reconvened on Sunday afternoon, neither the Smith nor McAdoo sides showed any new inclination to compromise. Shortly before 5 o'clock, as they were arguing futilely, Caraway arrived with the "little entente" proposal. After a brief consultation with Roosevelt, Brennan immediately accepted it on behalf of Smith and joined the fourteen minor candidates in sponsoring it. Rockwell, on the other hand, insisted on speaking personally with McAdoo first. Rockwell obviously had less authority to act than did Smith's advisers. Actually, Smith was not even available for consultation during much of Sunday, having gone to Sea Gate after mass to swim. When he returned to the Biltmore around dinnertime, he was brought up to date on the "little entente" plan, immediately reendorsed what Brennan and Roosevelt had done, and asked that a draft of the delegate-release proposal be prepared for his personal signature.

Rockwell originally requested only thirty minutes to consult with McAdoo, but this lengthened to an hour. He then telephoned Hull, asking for more time, leaving the "harmony conference" to cool its heels. Finally, the various representatives tired of waiting and dispersed, to be recalled by Hull as soon as Rockwell should return. Over in the Vanderbilt McAdoo was in a quandary. He discussed the proposal animatedly, first with his floor lieutenants and then with Baruch, Chadbourne, Roper, Long, and Rockwell. All except Rockwell and a few die-hard state chairmen advised him to sign it. But McAdoo, having come so far and having fought so hard, could not do it. Long later wrote in his diary: "I begged, pled, insisted and demanded he sign it. [I warned that] the withholding of his consent put him in the role of an obstructionist." Still McAdoo would not sign. Instead he drew up an elaborate counterproposal which provided that the unit rule and the two-thirds rules be suspended, that the lowest name on each ballot be dropped until a nomination was made, and that each delegate in any state with absentees be permitted to cast a pro-rata vote in order to retain for that state the same delegation total that it had had in the beginning.

This reply, which in many respects resembled the earlier Ball resolution that McAdoo had opposed, was given to the "harmony conference" at 10 P.M. Miffed at the long delay, the conference members briefly debated the McAdoo proposal and then rejected it with undisguised contempt. They were convinced that this counterplan had been designed not to secure agreement but to forestall it. Unanimously they agreed to submit to the convention the original delegate-release plan now signed by all the candidates except McAdoo.

McAdoo's isolation was at last complete. A victim of his own vanity, overwhelmed by the righteousness of his cause, and encouraged in his obstinacy by such advisers as Rockwell, McAdoo had finally lost touch with political realities. His obdurate actions naturally prompted a continuing overreaction by Smith. Normally inclined toward political compromise, Smith was again forced by McAdoo into an equally rigid stance. As soon as McAdoo's counterproposal was transmitted to him, Smith understandably labeled the Californian a damned fool and immediately revived his plan to eliminate McAdoo all by himself. The New York governor warned that he would exercise his newly acquired veto power until Christmas if necessary in order to watch McAdoo die slowly. To a reporter, who on Sunday night commented to him that in the end he might have to compromise with McAdoo on this matter, Smith interjected, "Wait a minute, that's as far as you need go. There isn't going to be any compromise. We are not talking compromise."

At that very moment, McAdoo was addressing his previously scheduled Sunday-night rally in the Hotel Commodore ballroom. Introduced by Governor William J. Fields of Kentucky as "the next President of the

United States," McAdoo told some eight hundred cheering supporters that "victory was sure" and that he would be "the most contemptible traitor alive" if he deserted them now. "I have never run from a fight in fifty years," he asserted, and added defiantly, "I am not going to withdraw."

9

"Harmony" was scarcely an option that Walsh could offer the delegates when the convention reopened on Monday morning, July 7. But hopes ran high and a sizable crowd was on hand. The mood of the galleries was light, many coming merely to gawk at prominent politicians who by now were household names and faces in New York City. There was much cheering when the "little entente" proposal was read. However, cheers turned to groans when McAdoo's counterplan was presented. It was a dismal way for a day to start which supposedly was to see the end of the impasse. And, since neither the "little entente" nor the McAdoo plan was able to secure a two-thirds vote of the convention, Walsh was forced to order the seventy-eighth roll call to begin.

When Governor Brandon rose to announce Alabama's vote, almost everyone in the Garden joined in: "Al-a-bam-ah-h-h casts twen-ty fo-ah votes for . . ." More than showing Alabama's loyalty to Senator Underwood, this phrase now was a symbol of the convention's utter futility. Still, the weekend "harmony conference" had produced one important effect. McAdoo's totals began to decline. On the first four ballots of the day Missouri left him for Glass, Oklahoma deserted him for Owen, and Mississippi gave its votes to Ralston even though he had withdrawn.

For the rest of July 7, during both the morning and the evening sessions, the war of attrition against McAdoo continued unabated. By nightfall McAdoo's total finally settled around an irreducible minimum of 350 hard-core votes, while Smith's maximum number remained at about that same number. How long such inconclusive balloting might have gone on remains conjecture, since after the eighty-seventh roll call, which saw Smith slightly ahead of McAdoo (361½ to 336½), Walsh interrupted the proceedings to read a sad announcement. A week before, Calvin Coolidge, Jr., sixteen-year-old son of the President, had been playing tennis on the south grounds of the White House and had rubbed a blister on his big toe. It had become infected and developed into a rare case of blood poisoning. Removed to Walter Reed Hospital for treatment, young Calvin had sunk into a coma and, despite the best medical aid, had gradually slipped away while his anguished parents looked helplessly on. When Chairman Walsh at 11:45 P.M. on Monday night read to the Democratic convention, "News has been received of the death of Calvin Coolidge, Jr., son of the President of the United States," it was the first knowledge the nation had of his demise. A moan of compassion went up from the delegates and spectators. They adjourned immediately and gathered in small groups to talk in hushed tones. Frustration and rancor were suspended for the moment as a wave of sympathy swept the Garden. Silence crept over the hall. Delegates thought of their own homes and families. Suddenly their taciturn Republican opponent did not seem so remote or aloof. He too could suffer.

But Coolidge's personal problems did not solve the Democrats' dilemma, for when the convention reconvened on Tuesday morning, July 8, the deadlock was still there. Gradually this convention had become an opéra bouffe. Everywhere it was the object of caustic or humorous remarks. "A Ballot a day keeps the Nomination away," said one wag, while another suggested that the only way to stop this political marathon was to "suppress it under the nuisance ordinances and order the fellow who started it held responsible." Another said the gathering reminded him of the charge of the Light Brigade: "Half a vote, half a vote onward, into the jaws of debt, into the mouth of hell, moves the convention." Still another claimed that this was the first time in American political history that a convention ever elected a true permanent chairman, since Senator Walsh had a lifetime job.

If this convention were ever to end it ultimately would have to turn to some minor candidate. But who? One major weakness of both the McAdoo and the Smith campaigns was that they had never considered a viable alternative. McAdoo had never thought of anyone but himself and Smith had come to the convention primarily to prevent a nomination, not to help make one. There was some brief talk among both Smith and McAdoo men that the chairman of the convention, Thomas Walsh, might make a good compromise candidate. He was Catholic and dry, and might appeal not only to easterners but also to midwestern Protestants. Walsh, however, had long since indicated he had no interest in the nomination. Other possibilities were Carter Glass and John W. Davis, with renewed interest being shown by some McAdooites in noncandidate Ralston. W. J.

Bryan's name was also mentioned, and one could find Smith delegates who were convinced that a plan was underway to foist the Great Commoner on the convention.

The eighty-eighth ballot, the first of Tuesday, July 8, showed that the primary benefactor of any sustained McAdoo decline would probably be Ralston. Somehow it was fitting that this divided and bickering convention should begin giving its votes to a man who had withdrawn from the contest. For the next four ballots Ralston's total climbed as a drizzle started outside the Garden and filtered through the skylights, causing some delegates to move and others to open umbrellas. Smith leaders now ruefully remembered that Taggart had earlier prophesied Ralston's candidacy might "blow up a little rain." Indiana began to chant "Ralston! Ralston!" and "Let's go home!" Sitting in a particularly disadvantageous spot, Roosevelt was getting wet but refused to be moved and covered himself with newspapers, closely observing the balloting all the while. By the end of the ninety-second roll call, Ralston had 196.75, Smith retained 355.5, while McAdoo fell to 310.

The Ralston drive represented sheer desperation on the part of some McAdoo delegates. They could not possibly turn to Smith, but they did not want any of the other candidates either. Although the Ralston vote seemed totally unsolicited, this was only part of the truth. Tom Taggart had never really given up hope for his candidate despite Ralston's withdrawal at the end of the sixty-fourth ballot on Friday. After the failure of the "harmony conference" during the weekend, Taggart remained convinced that Ralston still would make the logical choice. On Monday Taggart's rooms in the Waldorf-Astoria again took on the appearance of a campaign headquarters as he met with a number of state chairmen and convention leaders. Also working behind the scenes for Ralston were Senators Pittman of Nevada and Harrison of Mississippi. Taggart skillfully played on southern and western desires to end the stalemate, and he encouraged the belief that Ralston was McAdoo's own second choice, quoting the Californian as saying, "I like the old Senator, like his simplicity, honesty, and record."

By Monday night everything again seemed to be moving Taggart's way—everything, that is, except Ralston. Early that morning Ralston had sent a telegram to Taggart specifically demanding that his name not be reinserted and concluding with the injunction "Please respect my wishes." On Monday afternoon Taggart had telephoned Ralston at his farm in Indiana, apprising him of the new situation and begging him to reconsider. Ralston flatly declined. Taggart still continued to pump up a Ralston boom. He was among the first in the Garden when the doors opened on Tuesday morning and was seen moving from delegation to delegation throughout the day's balloting. Taggart remained convinced that, if the convention could settle quickly on the Indiana senator, Ralston could not possibly refuse.

As the ninety-third roll call began, Brennan, Harrison, Kremer, and Taggart were seen on the rostrum arguing with Walsh. Brennan wanted a recess in order to construct a stop-Ralston coalition. Because of his tie to the Klan, Ralston was as repugnant to the Smith forces as was McAdoo. Conversely, Taggart and Harrison wanted the convention to remain in session in order to keep the Ralston boom going. Kremer did not know what to do. However, when the results of the ninety-third ballot showed that Ralston had failed to score any new gains, all the men, even Taggart, agreed to an adjournment. As the delegates filed out to dinner, the totals read: Smith 355.5, McAdoo 314, Ralston 196.25, Davis 68, Underwood 44.75, Glass 27, Meredith (Iowa) 26, Robinson 19, and Ritchie 16½.

The Tuesday-afternoon recess saw more activity than at any time since the ill-fated "harmony conference" of the previous weekend. Distressed by the continuing deadlock, mutual friends of McAdoo and Smith arranged for a face-to-face dinnertime meeting of the two men in the Ritz-Carlton apartment of Hugh C. Wallace, former ambassador to France. McAdoo was not keen about attending, but Smith accepted with alacrity. It was their first personal contact since the convention opened. Smith was accompanied by Van Namee, his private secretary, and McAdoo by Chadbourne. Also present were Cordell Hull, Thomas Walsh, Herbert Swope, and Stuart Gibboney.

For over an hour the two men talked, much of the time alone in an adjoining room. Smith told McAdoo that neither of them could win and again suggested a joint withdrawal. McAdoo said that he had no right to withdraw since many of his delegations had been elected specifically to support only him. He admitted, however, that if withdrawal did occur he and Smith should first reach agreement on a compromise candidate. McAdoo mentioned Ralston as a possibility. Smith refused. Smith named Underwood. McAdoo objected. McAdoo next proposed Meredith, Walsh, and Cummings, none of whom was acceptable to Smith. Finally the two men parted with McAdoo agreeing to "think over" a joint withdrawal and Smith agreeing to consult with his advisers about other compromise candidates. As he left Smith told McAdoo that he would spend the entire evening in the Manhattan Club listening to the convention by radio and that McAdoo should communicate with him there. Upon arriving at his Manhattan Club headquarters Smith told a group of wet-eyed supporters that "probably" he and McAdoo would withdraw, and he immediately closeted himself with Brennan and Roosevelt to prepare the appropriate statement. McAdoo went immediately to his rooms in the Vanderbilt, where he was met by a group of women delegates who, having heard about the Ritz-Carlton conference, were fearful about the outcome. Two of them rushed up to him and cried, "You will not desert us!" McAdoo replied "No," upon which one of them dropped to her knees in prayer.

When the twenty-first session of the Democratic convention opened at 9 P.M. on Tuesday evening, rumors were already circulating that important decisions had been made and that the log jam was at long last about to be broken. It was noticed that Franklin Roosevelt, who normally sat with the New York delegation, was on the platform. Further, the eight hundred or so delegates who still remained at the convention were in their seats. What transpired was not wholly unexpected. As the first order of business, Walsh read a telegram which had just been received from Ralston: "Withdraw my name from further consideration by the convention. Great as the honor would be, I do not want the nomination." Roosevelt then struggled to his feet and made this statement: "After nearly one hundred ballots it is quite apparent to [Smith] and to me that the forces in this convention behind Governor Smith, the leader in the race, and those behind Mr. McAdoo, a close second, cannot be amalgamated. For the sake of the party, therefore, Governor Smith authorizes me to say that immediately upon the withdrawal by Mr. McAdoo of his name, Governor Smith will withdraw his name also from the consideration of the convention."

Once again Taggart was without a candidate and once again the Smith element had outmanuevered McAdoo. For Taggart, the disappointment was keen. To the very last moment he had been sure that Ralston would accept the nomination if it was offered. But out in Indiana, Ralston, who had been following the convention closely by radio, had been puzzled as his name was reintroduced in the balloting and his vote totals climbed on Tuesday afternoon. He had told Taggart that he did not wish to be reinserted into the race. At the moment Ralston was far more concerned about family matters (both his wife and son were ill) and about his own health (he would die before another year was out) than he was about the presidency. But because of Taggart's persistency and independent action Ralston now found it necessary to send another withdrawal telegram. In the face of such obstinacy, Taggart had no choice but to acquiesce. Sick with disappointment and fatigue, the Indiana boss had to be assisted to his suite in the Waldorf and be put to bed before the first ballot on Tuesday evening was over. Later Taggart told reporters "We would have nominated Senator Ralston if he had not withdrawn his name at the last minute. It was as near a certainty as anything in politics can be."

McAdoo men were little better off than Taggart. Both Smith's challenge to McAdoo to retire and Ralston's withdrawal left them totally lost. As long as Ralston had remained, some of them, at least, had an alternative. Now many of them could think of nothing better to do than return to their original candidate. Indeed, Smith's challenge and Ralston's removal caused a momentary resurgence of McAdoo support. Hard-core followers begged and pleaded for their wayward brethren to "come back home." When Arizona was called on the ninety-fourth ballot, Fred T. Colter, a delegate-at-large, rose and, throwing both arms in the air, his voice breaking, exclaimed: "Before God, before Christ, we want Mc-Adoo!" In the California delegation desperate pro-McAdoo ladies stood up in a double row, waved flags, and cheered shrilly for "Mac, Mac, Mc-A-doo!" Such fervor, coupled with renewed booing in the galleries, caused the old pattern to repeat: Mississippi, Oklahoma, and others returned to the Californian, causing him again to pass Smith and make a lie out of Roosevelt's contention that the New York governor was "the leader in the race." For the next five ballots the McAdooites kept their champion's total above Smith's (once reaching 421 compared with Smith's 367½). Quietly, however, an important shift was occurring elsewhere. Some of Ralston's former votes were going to John W. Davis, whose total shot from 81.75 on the ninety-fourth roll call to 210 on the ninety-ninth. Significantly, many of Ralston's votes were *not* returning to McAdoo. They were remaining in the favorite-son area. At the conclusion of the ninety-ninth ballot the totals read: McAdoo 353, Smith 353, Davis 210, Underwood 39½, Glass 38, Meredith 37, Robinson 25, and Ritchie 17½.

It was now past 2 A.M. and not only were the galleries practically empty, but whole rows of vacant chairs in the delegate sections were mute testimony to the fact that this convention was ending regardless of what its leaders might do. Walsh suddenly announced that he had a communication to read from McAdoo. It was a lengthy statement about the necessity for keeping aloft "the torch [of] Woodrow Wilson," but the key section of the message read: "I feel that if I should withdraw my name from the Convention I should betray the trust confided to me by the people in many states which have sent delegates here to support me. And yet I am unwilling to contribute to a continuation of a hopeless deadlock. Therefore, I have determined to leave my friends and supporters free to take such action as, in their judgment, may best serve the interests of the party."

This was not the unconditional withdrawal that Smith had sought, but it was designed to help end the impasse. Waiting in the Manhattan Club as he had promised, Smith had ultimately despaired of hearing from McAdoo. At about midnight he told inquiring reporters: "I haven't heard that he has accepted [the joint withdrawal suggestion]. Up to and including this minute, the solution of the convention deadlock has been up to McAdoo. I have done the best I can." Smith never did hear from him. The Californian's only reply to Smith was this communication which was read to the convention. In releasing his delegates without formally withdrawing, McAdoo refused to the end to give Smith the satisfaction of seeing him retire.

McAdoo had arrived even at this decision with anguish. For four days he had been under increasing pressure from many of his advisers to withdraw. At a final meeting late on Tuesday night he had listened as Baruch, Chadbourne, Roper, and even Long urged him to end the struggle. Rockwell alone advocated continuing the fight. Depressed, exhausted, eyes bleary, some said even dazed, McAdoo finally asked for a pencil and pad and half reclining on a bed began in longhand to write a formal withdrawal letter. But at the last moment he changed it. Love of Texas, Kremer of Montana, Jouett Shouse of Kansas, and Bryan, who were also present, urged a delegate-release statement instead because that would still technically keep his name in contention in the event none of the favorite sons proved successful. McAdoo grasped at this suggestion and, as he was putting the finishing touches on such a statement, Mrs. McAdoo joined the group, plainly upset and worried about her husband's physical condition. McAdoo asked to be alone with her for a moment, and several minutes later handed Rockwell the completed draft for submission to the convention. Then he and Mrs. McAdoo, who was crying softly, left for their Vanderbilt suite and bed. It was just after 2 A.M.

As soon as the McAdoo letter was read to the convention by Chairman Walsh, Rockwell unsuccessfully made a motion to adjourn. Despite the lateness of the hour, the favorite sons were now anxious to see where the released McAdoo votes would go. So the one-hundredth roll call began. McAdoo dropped precipitously to 190 while Smith held at 351½. Davis gained nothing. Underwood, Glass, and Ritchie retained their modest numbers. Meredith of Iowa (a Johnny-come-lately to the list of eligibles) registered 75½ votes, Robinson increased from 25 to 46, Senator Owen reentered the list with 20, and Thomas Walsh received 52½. Obviously, McAdoo votes were not flowing to any one favorite son but were being divided. If there was any discernible trend, it was to Meredith. Besides shunning Smith, pro-McAdoo delegates were also ignoring Underwood, Glass, Ritchie, and the current leader of the favorite sons, John W. Davis.

It was now close to 4 A.M. Never before was a political convention so demoralized. Weary delegates sat numbed, many staring off into space, not even speaking to their neighbors. Others held their heads in their hands. The leaders of the various delegations were dazed. Even Roosevelt had lost his smile. In the galleries only a handful of spectators remained and they were rubbing their eyes and slouching farther and farther down in their seats. Someone jokingly remarked that it was about time for another Bryan speech.

Sure enough, as the one-hundredth ballot drew to a close, Bryan was on his feet striding toward the platform. Delegates began to elbow each other to attention and those in the galleries sat erect. A delegate in the Massachusetts delegation quickly moved to adjourn the session. This was calculated to cut Bryan off, since an adjournment motion is not debatable and takes precedence over anything else. Bryan, in the meantime, had reached the platform and was pulling on the coat of John J. Fitzgerald, the convention parliamentarian, who was temporarily in the chair. Unable to ignore Bryan, Fitzgerald announced that Bryan desired consent to speak. Already the galleries were beginning to boo. "For how long?" demanded one delegate. "Throw him out!" shouted another. Bryan raised his hands, but the boos and the catcalls both from the floor and the galleries grew so loud and were so sustained that he faltered. Finally he gave up, seconded the motion to adjourn, and sadly walked away to the accompaniment of much cheering. A *viva voce* vote closed the session.

10

Even as the convention was futilely balloting on Tuesday, its final destiny rested in the hands of a man who, until Monday, had not even been in New York. James Cox, titular head of the party, had remained at home in Dayton, Ohio, listening to the convention by radio and keeping in touch by telephone and telegraph. As the Garden struggle lengthened, repeated pleas had come to him to try to end the deadlock. As a move in that direction, Cox had ordered his own name removed from contention during the sixty-fifth ballot on Friday, July 4. He had also lent his support to the "harmony conference" over the following weekend.

With the failure of the "harmony conference," Cox had decided to come to New York himself and force a solution. Arriving on Monday, he told reporters that his presence should not be misconstrued. Under no circumstances was he a candidate, and he would refuse the nomination if it was offered. He was there only to find a way out of the stalemate. He immediately called the Ohio delegation into special session and told them that he thought they should throw their support to John W. Davis. Smith, he said, could not win whether Ohio backed him or not. On the other hand, Davis might attract votes from both the Smith and McAdoo camps. The West Virginian, Cox said, "could lift the campaign above the level of the convention," although Cox freely admitted that Davis's Wall Street connections might work against him. If Davis became impossible, Cox advised that Ohio switch to Carter Glass.

Disavowing to reporters any intention of backing any particular candidate, Cox nevertheless quietly sounded out certain other delegation leaders and held a series of personal conferences with floor managers to assess Davis's strength. Cox was not shooting in the dark in his decision to push Davis. A few prognosticators as early as June had predicted that Davis would be the convention's ultimate nominee. At that time they claimed that he was the second choice in many delegations not only of the Midwest and the South, but also of the East. From the beginning of the convention, several shrewd newspaper reporters had also been telling their readers that, of all the dark horses, Davis's chances were the best. Indeed, throughout the long balloting no favorite son except Ralston had shown the drawing power of Davis. Robinson, for example, had never displayed much strength outside Arkansas—he had started with 21 votes and had never gone above 46. Glass too had remained isolated. He had received 25 on the first ballot and never got more than 78. Senator Owen, the on-again off-again favorite son of Oklahoma, who had never formally been nominated, struggled to amass 25. Ritchie of Maryland began with 22½, reached his high mark on the fifth ballot with 42.9, and thereafter averaged less than 20. Jonathan Davis of Kansas at no time got more than 32.4. Underwood failed to attract support from his native South, let alone from the North, and Alabama remained his major source of strength. Meredith of Iowa only began to receive votes on the eighty-sixth roll call as a fall-back candidate for some McAdoo delegates.

Because of the low profile of the John W. Davis campaign and the reluctance of Davis as a candidate, Smith and McAdoo leaders had not given him much attention. Only Bryan ever considered him a threat and made his potential selection an issue. But late on Tuesday, July 8, as the West Virginian's total began to climb, a serious stop-Davis movement was initiated by the Smith element. Tammany representatives were not violently anti-Davis, but he was not their second choice. They preferred Underwood because of his anti-Klan and anti-prohibition stands. To block Davis as well as to test what kind of other support Underwood might attract, the Smith group even agreed to "loan" some of their votes to the Underwood forces on Wednesday morning.

When Davis's name was first presented to McAdoo as a possible compromise candidate, he rejected it because of Davis's "wealthy connections." But the knowledge that by Wednesday many Smith delegates were leaning toward Underwood encouraged McAdoo and his followers to look in Davis's direction. This put Bryan in a terrible dilemma. Bitterly opposed to Davis because of his "Morgan interests," Bryan ran the risk of aiding Underwood if he sought to keep votes away from the West Virginian. Bryan's quandary was all the greater since Wheeler of the Anti-Saloon League was firm about keeping Underwood off the ticket at all costs and indicated to Bryan that Davis was the lesser of two evils. Still, Bryan's opposition to Davis was so keen and so well known that it prompted H. L. Mencken, who consistently exaggerated Bryan's influence, to tell his readers: "Everything is still uncertain in this convention but one thing: John W. Davis will never be nominated."

The convention was supposed to reconvene at noon on Wednesday, July 9, but it got underway almost an hour late because of the lack of a quorum. Those present showed signs of not having recovered from the marathon session of the night before. When the one-hundred-and-first roll call began, Governor Brandon was absent and a barely audible voice cast Alabama's usual sonorous vote for Underwood. But a trend quickly appeared thereafter. Connecticut switched 11 votes from Smith to Underwood. Georgia divided its votes between Meredith and McAdoo. Indiana cast 10 of its 30 votes for Davis. Iowa went for Meredith while Kansas voted solidly for Davis. Maryland suddenly switched all 16 of her votes from Ritchie to Davis. Mississippi and Missouri both went solidly for Davis. New York produced a sensation by transferring 86½ of her 90 votes from Smith to Underwood. South Carolina declared for Davis. Virginia, which had been voting for Glass, divided her vote between Glass and Davis. Rhode Island, a former Smith backer, went to Underwood. Texas voted for Meredith. When it was over the totals read: Davis 316, Underwood 229½, Meredith 130, Smith 121, Thomas Walsh 98, Glass 59, McAdoo 52, and Robinson 22½. Clearly the compromisers in both camps were moving to Davis. Moderate southern votes were flowing in his direction; so were moderate northern votes. Former Ralston votes were also drifting toward Davis. Die-hard McAdoo votes were supporting Meredith or staying with McAdoo. Ardent Smith votes were either remaining with Smith or going to Underwood.

At the close of the one-hundred-and-first ballot there was a feeling of decision in the air. McAdoo rooters were silent. The women in the California delegation were not offering their customary chants. Smith supporters were likewise quiet. Smith buttons, noisemakers, and hats had long since disappeared from the galleries. But back in the West Virginia delegation there was mounting activity. There a little band of women were whooping it up. Mrs. Frank N. Mann of Huntington, who had proudly waved West Virginia's flag throughout the 101 ballots, now did so with renewed vigor.

For the past two days Cox had steadily intensified his activities on behalf of Davis, even loaning him the services of George White, who, along with Frank Polk and Clem Shaver, was now busily herding midwestern and southern votes into the Davis corral. Their major problem was to counteract the influence of Bryan, who was frantically attempting to construct a stop-Davis movement of his own through a McAdoo-Meredith coalition. Ashen-faced, his jaw set like granite, Bryan was seen during the one-hundred-and-first roll call rushing frenetically here and there. Just before the one-hundred-and-second ballot began, he went to the New York delegation and talked vigorously with, or rather at, Roosevelt. Next he appeared in the Kansas delegation and then moved on up the aisle. At one point he stopped to argue with three Davis women, who refused to budge. Shortly thereafter he surfaced in the Mississippi delegation, where he exclaimed: "The convention must not nominate a Wall Street man."

Already the one-hundred-and-second roll call was underway. Ignoring Bryan, indecisive McAdoo delegates continued to move into the Davis column. Indiana, Georgia, and Oklahoma gave new votes to him, but the most significant was Texas, which switched all of her 40 votes from Meredith to Davis, sending the latter's total to 415½. At that moment Bryan was seen pushing forward to the platform, and many thought that another of his attempts to speak was about to occur. But, by the time he arrived, even he perceived that his cause was hopeless. Without bothering to stop he continued on under the rostrum to Cordell Hull's private room, where he sat dejectedly as the convention "put his heart in the grave." Cornered by reporters shortly thereafter, Bryan made no statement beyond saying that he needed time to sort out his thoughts.

At about 3 P.M. the one-hundred-and-third ballot began. McAdooites were suddenly faced with nominating either an eastern Wall Street lawyer or a wet anti-Klan southerner. At this point many Smith men were ambivalent. Either Davis or Underwood was minimally acceptable. Taggart, who had recovered from his earlier fatigue and was again with the Indiana delegation, indicated the attitude of many when he flipped a coin, giving Indiana's votes to Davis. Others gradually succumbed. At the very end of the roll call Washington switched all 14 of its votes to Davis. In the sudden realization that the West Virginian was now above the halfway mark, a dozen delegation chairmen were on their feet, demanding recognition. First, Iowa withdrew the name of Meredith and gave all her votes to Davis. Then came a cascade of changes: California, Illinois, Pennsylvania. When the chair recognized New York, a crowd which had gathered around the New York standard cleared an area so Roosevelt could speak without rising from his seat. He announced 60 of New York's 90 votes for Davis. With this switch there was no further doubt about the outcome, and Taggart, who caught Walsh's eye, moved to make Davis's nomination unanimous. There were at least fifty seconds.

The official tally which gave Davis 844 votes to Underwood's 102½ was lost in the roar as Walsh declared "the Honorable John W. Davis, of West Virginia, the nominee of this Convention for President of the United States." As his gavel fell, a woman delegate in the West Virginia section was standing on her chair, a bottle of ginger ale in her hand, drinking toasts to the convention. Shaver, who had been sitting in a box opposite the speaker's platform, was seen weaving his way through the throng mumbling, "Is it true, or is it a dream?" The West Virginia standard had moved out to lead a procession around the Garden while the band played "The Battle Hymn of the Republic." In the vanguard with the West Virginia delegation was the Louisiana delegation, which had remained loyal to Davis since the early ballots, and Puerto Rico, whose gray-bearded chairman, Henry Dooley, had consistently held it in the Davis ranks. At the conclusion of a fifteen-minute demonstration, the West Virginia flag and a huge picture of Davis were taken to the rostrum, where ex-Governor McCorkle, flanked by Mrs. Izetta Brown, thanked the convention for the honor paid to the Mountaineer State.

News of Davis's selection was met with a variety of reactions. At the time of his nomination the Garden galleries, which had often been the scene of enthusiastic activity, were virtually empty. Those spectators who were present showed little emotion one way or the other. Outside the Garden there were no demonstrations and only a few auto horns tooted when the Davis selection was announced. When Clarksburg, West Virginia, heard the news there was an outburst of joy. Fireworks left over from the Fourth of July were set off and several local bands straggled together to form a parade. Far into the night crowds remained in the streets as now and again a rocket would shoot up into the sky.

Back in New York the victorious candidate had only a few moments to savor his victory. During the closing stages of the balloting a tense group had kept vigil at the home of Frank Polk on East Sixty-eighth Street. Davis was sitting alone, smoking in the reception room, when the verdict was called down to him by Mrs. Davis, who with Mrs. Polk had been listening to the radio on the second floor. "You've won! You're nominated!" she cried as he bounded up the stairs to embrace her. Within minutes friends arrived and the street outside filled with pressmen, camera crews, and policemen. Davis appeared briefly on the porch to greet reporters and to appease the cameramen by posing for them. Mrs. Davis, dressed in black for a sister who had died on the second day of the convention, blushingly murmured, "I am very proud and happy." All Davis could think of to say to newsmen was, "Well, I'm glad it's over."

Smith was listening to the radio in the Manhattan Club when he heard the news. He turned to Proskauer, who was listening with him, and ordered the judge to find out where Davis was and pledge him his wholehearted support. Smith's disappointment at his own failure was keen, but he carefully masked his feelings to the horde of reporters who suddenly descended on him. McAdoo received the news of Davis's selection in his rooms at the Vanderbilt, where he was packing in preparation for leaving for a European vacation aboard the *Homeric*. McAdoo was not in sympathy with the Davis nomination and believed basically that the party had "sold out" in making it. Bitter and resentful over his treatment in Madison Square Garden, he wanted only to leave New York as quickly as possible. He absolutely refused to talk with or see reporters. To Davis he sent only a terse telegram—"Please accept my congratulations on your nomination"—and continued his packing.

In the Garden, meanwhile, the convention's afternoon session moved toward a confused finish. It was expected that the assembly would adjourn until evening, when vice-presidential nominations would begin. But no sooner was the Davis demonstration over than cries of "Walsh! Walsh! We want Walsh!" were heard. Mark Sullivan claimed that it suddenly seemed as if every delegate in the hall was yelling the chairman's name. Already during the parade for Davis there had been a few shouts of "Walsh for Vice-President." Now the demand was universal. Dozens of men were in the aisles demanding recognition, among them Igoe of Illinois. "For what purpose does the gentleman from Illinois rise?" asked Walsh. "For the purpose of placing in nomination the Honorable Thomas J. Walsh of Montana," replied Igoe. Turning a solemn face to the convention, Walsh declared, "The gentleman is out of order," and, as protests thundered over the hall, Walsh arbitrarily declared the convention adjourned until 8:30 P.M. When the protests continued, Walsh left the rostrum. As he descended the steps, a priest said to him, "Remember, Mr. Senator, every seventh Vice-President becomes President." Walsh merely shook his head and continued on. With Walsh gone, there was nothing for the delegates to do but leave also.

Reluctantly most delegates moved toward the exits, hopeful that the vice-presidential matter could somehow yet be settled, making their return to the Garden unnecessary. Now that Davis had been chosen, they wanted an immediate conclusion to the entire affair. They certainly needed no new reminders that this convention had long outlived its usefulness and antagonized virtually everyone. Yet they could not end it. As they dispersed to their hotels or to dinner prior to another session, they rode in taxicabs which still bore the inscription: "Al Smith—1924." Defiant to the end, New Yorkers were still committed to their favorite son.

11

When the twenty-third and final session of the Democratic convention began on Wednesday evening, July 9, Representative Alben Barkley of Kentucky was in the chair. Everywhere row after row of empty seats indicated that even those delegates who had remained in New York through the Wednesday-afternoon session considered this night meeting anticlimactic. The evening began innocuously enough. After the customary opening exercises, a suspension of the rules was requested in order to permit Cox to address the meeting. He came to the platform amid warm applause for his role as a harmonizer. Full of praise for Davis, Cox warned the Republicans against assuming that the bitterness of this convention would affect Democratic success in the fall, and symbolically handed to Davis the mantle of party leadership. A series of resolutions followed the Cox speech, among them an invitation to the presidential nominee to address the convention sometime during the evening. This was endorsed with much anticipation since many of the delegates had never seen or heard John Davis.

Finally the convention knuckled down to the business of selecting a Vice-President. To begin, Barkley read a letter from the absent Walsh, which again disavowed his interest in the vice-presidency and concluded: "Deeply grateful for the esteem manifested in the acclamation that attended the adjournment of the last session, I am reluctantly forced to advise you that I cannot accept the nomination yet to be made by the convention." Walsh obviously had asked Barkley to chair this session so that he could escape any further pressure to change his mind. The Walsh announcement brought groans from the delegates since no one in sight had Walsh's following. How ironic it was that this convention, after suffering through ten days of acrimonious controversy based in part on religious grounds, should have literally begged a Catholic to be Vice-President, with only his refusal preventing it.

Again the Democrats returned to punishing one another. The first spokesman for a vice-presidential candidate was W. L. Barnum, national committeeman from Arizona. He wound on so long that the booing of the delegates drowned out his man's name when he finally mentioned it—John C. Greenway, a former member of Teddy Roosevelt's Rough Riders.

In a fury, a Kansas delegate moved that vice-presidential nominating speeches be restricted to five minutes. This was adopted by acclamation. There followed a parade of five-minute candidacies: Alvin M. Owsley of Texas (former commander of the American Legion), George L. Berry of Tennessee (a labor-union executive), George Silzer of New Jersey, Mrs. Leroy Springs (delegate-at-large from South Carolina), Jonathan Davis of Kansas, Bennett Clark of Missouri (son of Champ Clark), Mayor Hylan of New York, Edwin Meredith of Iowa, William S. Flynn (governor of Rhode Island), and, finally, James W. Gerard of New York (former ambassador to Germany).

Tedious as these nominations were, the process was interpersed with several events which kept the delegates from dying of boredom or lashing out at each other in anger. Following the Meredith nomination, Norman Mack requested the privilege of the floor for Al Smith and, unlike in the earlier incident, it was quickly granted. Smith had several purposes in coming before the convention at this time. He wanted to reiterate that he would support Davis and would not sulk in his tent as McAdoo apparently was going to do. He also desired to prove to southern and western delegates that he was not the head devil. Underneath, however, Smith was still piqued by the convention's earlier rebuff and he was determined to appear before it prior to its closing. After all, he reasoned, the convention was being held in *his* city and *his* state.

Hurrying to the Garden floor from his Manhattan Club rooms close by, Smith was greeted with a magnificent ovation. There was much craning of necks as he appeared, and a general buzzing swept through McAdoo Alley as the half-empty galleries rose to their feet. Very few of the delegates from other than the New England and Middle Atlantic states had ever seen the New York governor. Standing there on the platform with his arms raised and his head nodding, he was a definite curiosity. Attempting to be humorous, Smith began by saying, "If you have been annoyed in any way by the various people with whom you have come into contact, in their zeal to explain to you why in their opinion I am the greatest man in the world, overlook it." This received some laughter and applause. Then he launched into a sixteen-minute harangue, extolling himself, his record, the state of New York, and New York City. Claiming that he had done "nothing toward securing the nomination" (which caused mouths to drop open in McAdoo Alley), he left the unmistakable impression that he ought to have received it because of all that he had done for women, children, criminals, the poor, veterans, factory workers, and so on. His final pledge to "take off my coat and vest" and work for Davis did little to soften the sharp edges of his speech.

Few men have failed as miserably as Smith did in addressing this last session of the 1924 convention. Understandably he was worn out, disappointed, and hurt. But his performance was much too aggressive and contentious. The New York press thought the speech was wonderful, but they were in the minority. The wild cheering of the galleries as he spoke, his raucous voice, his lack of grace and charm, all combined to place him in a bad light. Smith too easily shook his fist, waved his arms, and wagged his head. He dwelt too much on his New York achievements and too little on the broader concerns of the party. He justified his enemies in thinking of him as merely a local chieftain and not a national leader. He may have proved that he did not have horns on his head, but he did little to show the West and the South that he was not just another New York wise guy. Even some of his supporters were dismayed by his performance. At the conclusion of his address, one pro-Smith man was heard whispering to a southern anti-Smith delegate: "I take it all back. Al's not yet ready for the White House."

Smith also suffered by comparison when Davis put in his appearance a short time later. If Smith was better than he looked or sounded, Davis seemed too good to be true. Tall, handsome, his ruddy face crowned by a shock of snow-white hair, Davis was introduced to a cheering convention at 11:45 P.M. He wore a black suit, black shoes, and dark blue tie, and carried a stiff straw hat and a walking cane. Poised, self-assured, and charming, Davis was the picture of the perfect candidate. Even McAdooites disheartened by their defeat perked up. Journalist Clinton Gilbert once said of Davis, "In making Mr. Davis look as he does, nature has won half the battle for him." It was true. As one convention wit commented, it would almost be a shame for Davis to be elected President because he could never live up to the first impression.

Davis spoke easily and in a clear voice, looking down only occasionally at the 8½-by-11-inch telegraph forms on which he had scribbled his speech in longhand. It took him only eight minutes to cover what he wanted to say. He immediately caught the audience's fancy by claiming that at least no one could accuse the convention of having acted in haste in making his selection. Then he thanked the convention for the honor, prophesied that a difficult campaign lay ahead, and promised to work cooperatively with all elements in the party. His theme was harmony and

Roosevelt making his "Happy Warrior" nominating speech for Al Smith. Wood-row Wilson banner is in the background.

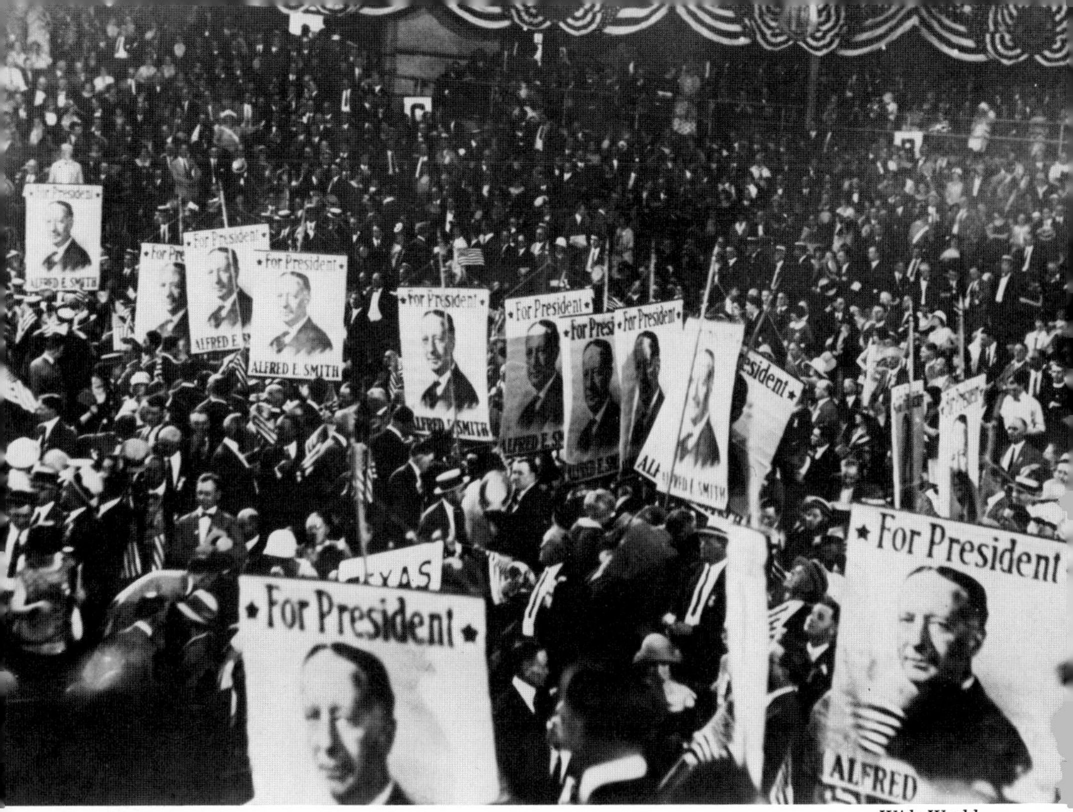

Wide World

Floor demonstration for Smith following his nomination.

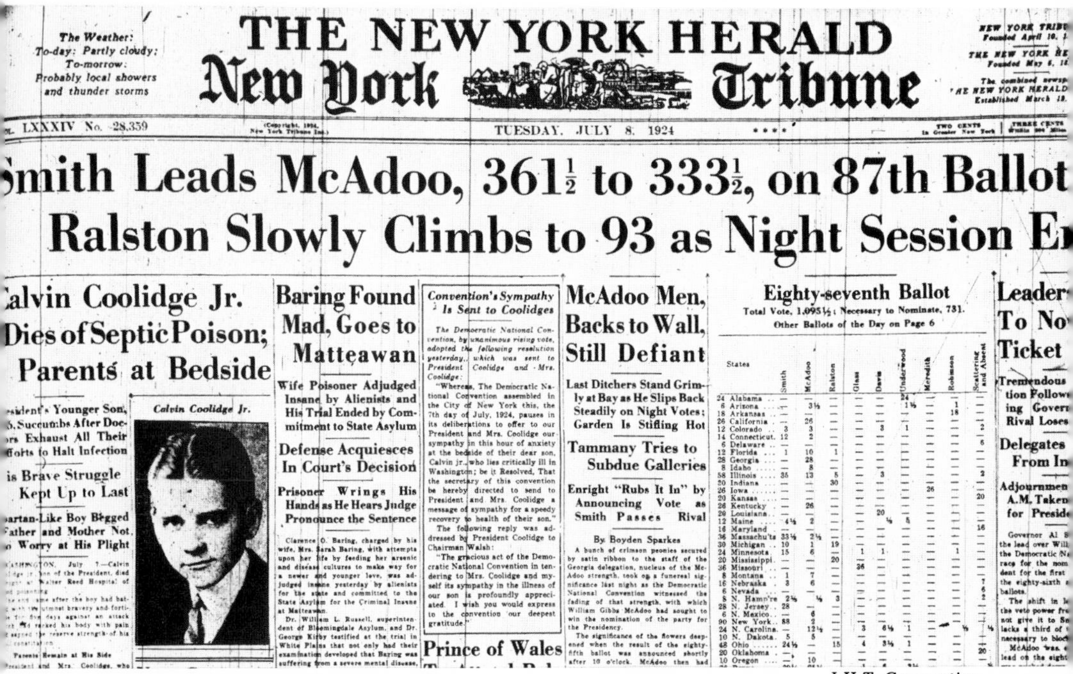

The Weather: To-day: Partly cloudy; To-morrow: Probably local showers and thunder storms

THE NEW YORK HERALD
New York Tribune

NEW YORK TRIBUNE Founded April 10, 1
THE NEW YORK HERALD Founded May 6, 18
The combined newspaper THE NEW YORK HERALD Established March 18,

LXXXIV No. 28,359 (Copyright, 1924, New York Tribune Inc.) TUESDAY, JULY 8, 1924 TWO CENTS In Greater New York | THREE CENTS Within 200 Miles

Smith Leads McAdoo, 361½ to 333½, on 87th Ballot
Ralston Slowly Climbs to 93 as Night Session En

Calvin Coolidge Jr. Dies of Septic Poison; Parents at Bedside

President's Younger Son, 16, Succumbs After Doctors Exhaust All Their Efforts to Halt Infection

His Brave Struggle Kept Up to Last

Spartan-Like Boy Begged Father and Mother Not to Worry at His Plight

WASHINGTON, July 7.—Calvin Coolidge jr., son of the President, died night at Walter Reed Hospital of ... poisoning

The end came after the boy had battled with the utmost bravery and fortitude for five days against an attack which had racked his body with pain and sapped the reserve strength of his constitution.

Parents Remain at His Side

President and Mrs. Coolidge, who

Calvin Coolidge Jr.

Baring Found Mad, Goes to Matteawan

Wife Poisoner Adjudged Insane by Alienists and His Trial Ended by Commitment to State Asylum

Defense Acquiesces In Court's Decision

Prisoner Wrings His Hands as He Hears Judge Pronounce the Sentence

Clarence O. Baring, charged by his wife, Mrs. Sarah Baring, with attempts upon her life by feeding her arsenic and disease cultures to make way for a newer and younger love, was adjudged insane yesterday by alienists for the state and committed to the State Asylum for the Criminal Insane at Matteawan.

Dr. William L. Russell, superintendent of Bloomingdale Asylum, and Dr. George Kirby testified at the trial in White Plains that not only had their examination developed that Baring was suffering from a severe mental disease,

Convention's Sympathy Is Sent to Coolidges

The Democratic National Convention, by unanimous rising vote, adopted the following resolution yesterday, which was sent to President Coolidge and Mrs. Coolidge:

"Whereas, The Democratic National Convention assembled in the City of New York this, the 7th day of July, 1924, pauses in its deliberations to offer to our President and Mrs. Coolidge our sympathy in this hour of anxiety at the bedside of their dear son, Calvin jr., who lies critically ill in Washington; be it Resolved, That the secretary of this convention be hereby directed to send to President and Mrs. Coolidge a message of sympathy for a speedy recovery to health of their son."

The following reply was addressed by President Coolidge to Chairman Walsh:

"The gracious act of the Democratic National Convention in tendering to Mrs. Coolidge and myself its sympathy in the illness of our son is profoundly appreciated. I wish you would express to the convention our deepest gratitude."

Prince of Wales

McAdoo Men, Backs to Wall, Still Defiant

Last Ditchers Stand Grimly at Bay as He Slips Back Steadily on Night Votes; Garden Is Stifling Hot

Tammany Tries to Subdue Galleries

Enright "Rubs It In" by Announcing Vote as Smith Passes Rival

By Boyden Sparkes

A bunch of crimson peonies secured by satin ribbon to the staff of the Georgia delegation, nucleus of the McAdoo strength, took on a funereal significance last night as the Democratic National Convention witnessed the fading of that strength, with which William Gibbs McAdoo had sought to win the nomination of the party for the Presidency.

The significance of the flowers deepened when the result of the eighty-fifth ballot was announced shortly after 10 o'clock. McAdoo then had

Eighty-seventh Ballot

Total Vote, 1,095½; Necessary to Nominate, 731.

Other Ballots of the Day on Page 6

States	Smith	McAdoo	Ralston	Glass	Davis	Underwood	Meredith	Robinson	Scattering and Absent
24 Alabama	—	—	—	—	—	24	—	—	—
6 Arizona	—	3½	—	—	—	1½	—	1	—
18 Arkansas	—	—	—	—	—	—	—	18	—
26 California	—	26	—	—	—	—	—	—	—
12 Colorado	3	3	—	—	3	1	—	—	2
14 Connecticut	12	2	—	—	—	—	—	—	—
6 Delaware	—	—	—	—	—	—	—	—	6
12 Florida	1	10	1	—	—	—	—	—	—
28 Georgia	—	28	—	—	—	—	—	—	—
8 Idaho	—	8	—	—	—	—	—	—	—
58 Illinois	35	13	5	—	3	—	—	—	2
20 Indiana	—	—	30	—	—	—	—	—	—
26 Iowa	—	—	—	—	—	—	26	—	—
20 Kansas	—	—	—	—	—	—	—	—	20
26 Kentucky	—	26	—	—	—	—	—	—	—
20 Louisiana	—	—	—	—	20	—	—	—	—
12 Maine	4½	2	—	—	½	5	—	—	—
16 Maryland	—	—	—	—	—	—	—	—	16
36 Massachu'ts	33½	2½	—	—	—	—	—	—	—
30 Michigan	10	1	19	—	—	—	—	—	—
24 Minnesota	15	6	—	1	1	—	—	1	—
20 Mississippi	—	—	20	—	—	—	—	—	—
36 Missouri	—	—	—	36	—	—	—	—	—
8 Montana	1	7	—	—	—	—	—	—	—
16 Nebraska	3	6	—	—	—	—	—	—	7
6 Nevada	—	—	—	—	—	—	—	—	6
8 N. Hamp're	2½	½	3	—	—	—	—	—	2
28 N. Jersey	28	—	—	—	—	—	—	—	—
6 N. Mexico	—	6	—	—	—	—	—	—	—
90 New York	88	2	—	—	—	—	—	—	—
24 N. Carolina	—	12½	—	3	6½	1	—	½	½
10 N. Dakota	5	5	—	—	—	—	—	—	—
48 Ohio	24½	—	15	4	3½	1	—	—	—
20 Oklahoma	—	—	—	—	—	—	—	—	20
10 Oregon	—	10	—	—	—	—	—	—	—

Leader... To No... Ticket

Tremendous ... tion Follow... ing Gover... Rival Loses

Delegates ... From In...

Adjournmen... A.M. Taken ... for Preside...

Governor Al S... the lead over Will... the Democratic N... race for the nom... dent for the first ... the eighty-sixth ... ballots.

The shift in le... the veto power fr... not give it to Sm... lacks a third of ... necessary to bloc...

McAdoo was ... lead on the eight...

I.H.T. Corporation

Front page, New York *Herald-Tribune,* reporting the 87th ballot and the death of Calvin Coolidge, Jr.

Crowds gathered in the rain in Madison Square Park, listening to the convention proceedings over loudspeakers.

Dr. Hiram Evans, Imperial Wizard
of the Ku Klux Klan.
Underwood

July 4th march of more than 4,000 Klansmen in Long Branch, N.J. More than 20,000 people convened at Klan headquarters in Long Branch.

Underwood

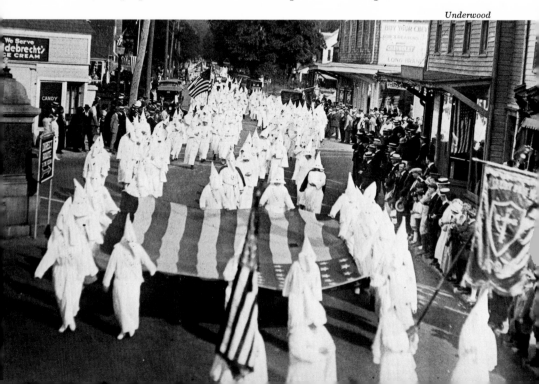

Official photographs of the Democratic (New York) and Republican (Cleveland) conventions. Note the unornamented staidness of the Republican gathering.

He's a Daredevil

Portland Oregonian

A cartoonist depicts the Democrats' dilemma eight days after the convention opened.

Kool Klammy
Kal Koolidge
Kant Kondemn the
Ku Klux Klan. You
Kan Kill the Kruel
Ku Klux by Kanning
Kunning Kwiet Kal.

Anti-Coolidge propaganda distributed supporters of La Follette.

Democratic nominees John W. Davis *(left)* and Charles W. Bryan.

Wide World

Independent nominees Robert La Follette *(right)* and Burton K. Wheeler.

Republican nominees Calvin Coolidge *(left)* and Charles G. Dawes.

Madison Square Garden is razed.

he dismissed the fights and tensions of the past two weeks as "but the thunderstorm that has cleared the clouds away and left shining on us the sun of coming victory and success." Unlike Smith, Davis retired from the rostrum to the plaudits of everyone.

It was now 12:05 A.M. Thursday morning, July 10, and the convention was still left with the problem of the vice-presidency. Jared Y. Sanders of Louisiana suddenly moved for an hour's recess, stating that this request did not come from him but from party leaders who were currently working on a solution. The motion passed, prompting some delegates to leave. Whomever the leaders picked was apparently all right with them. The majority, however, wandered about aimlessly for the next hour, talking to each other and to friends, speculating on the outcome. Meanwhile, Davis closeted himself with party leaders in the third-floor dining room of the Manhattan Club. He had already personally asked Thomas Walsh to be his running mate, but Walsh had again refused. Similarly, Meredith, who was Davis's second choice, also had declined. Stymied in his first and second choices, Davis now surrendered the decision into the hands of the party leaders.

Present at this early-Thursday-morning Manhattan Club conference were Guffey of Pennsylvania, Daniels of North Carolina, Brennan of Illinois, Cox of Ohio, Taggart of Indiana, Hague of Jersey City, Kremer of Montana, McNab of California, Smith of New York, and Frank Polk. Taggart suggested the name of former Vice-President Thomas R. Marshall as a possible compromise candidate. In view of Marshall's inept performance during Wilson's illness, this was a ridiculous proposal. Smith put forward Silzer of New Jersey, but it was quickly agreed that since Davis was from the East it would not be wise to name another easterner. Ritchie of Maryland was eliminated for the same reason. Newton Baker was mentioned but he had already indicated that he did not want it. Then Daniels mentioned Charles Bryan of Nebraska as someone who would provide balance for the ticket both geographically and philosophically. Bryan was a dry, a westerner, and a "progressive." Smith immediately objected and warned of northeastern defections if Bryan was selected. He indicated, however, that he would "go along" if Davis really wanted him. On the other hand, George Brennan greeted the proposal enthusiastically, regarding Bryan as an excellent choice who would, among other things, cement his brother, W. J., to the ticket. McAdooites, who had preferred Meredith, willingly accepted the Nebraskan. Davis, after considering the proposition for a moment, gave it his approval. As he left the Manhattan Club to return to the home of Frank Polk, word was sent to the convention to arrange for Charles Bryan's selection.

When Bryan was picked by the conference in the Manhattan Club his name had not even been placed in nomination for Vice-President. This was remedied by a delegate from Nebraska as soon as the convention reconvened at 1:10 A.M. Such action was a signal that Bryan had been tapped. Although rumors to that effect were already sweeping the hall, the news was received with incredulity. Reporters were stunned. When Charles Bryan was first told of the decision, he remarked, "Quit your kidding." His older brother was sitting disconsolately with the Florida delegation, still pondering the significance of the Davis nomination, when he was told of the selection. "It can't be true!" exclaimed the Great Commoner. "Did Davis agree to Charley?" he asked. When assured that Davis had indeed agreed, Bryan muttered, "The age of miracles has not passed." By the time Brother Charley rushed over to ask him whether he should accept, W. J. was already claiming that Davis's dry stand and his past Wilsonian associations made him worthy of Bryan support. Brushing aside Charley's qualms about "Wall Street," W. J. urged him to go on the ticket "to make it better." Newspapermen who were crowding about the elder Bryan were goggle-eyed at this rapid transformation, prompting one of them to remark, "If monkeys had votes Mr. Bryan would be a champion of evolution." Mercifully, no one mentioned that exactly twenty-eight years before to the day Bryan had begun his career by railing against Wall Street in his "Cross of Gold" speech.

The closing moments of the convention represented a comedy of errors. To the end the gathering remained divided, spiteful, and acrimonious. As the balloting for Vice-President began, the delegates had before them thirteen official candidates. Despite the fact that word of Charles Bryan's selection had spread around the hall, votes on the opening roll call were cast for thirty different persons, including three women. At the completion of this ballot George Berry, the labor-union executive from Tennessee, outpolled Bryan 263½ to 238. Confusion within the various state delegations was fantastic. West Virginia, for example, split its 16 votes among eight candidates. Tired as they were, the delegates simply refused to do as they were told. However, once their chaotic preferences were listed, a semblance of sanity returned. Before the first-ballot results were announced, Brennan asked permission to shift all of Illinois's 58 votes to Bryan. Others also began to switch, including New York with its 90 votes. But some refused to swing over. Rhode Island did not, nor did

Iowa, Louisiana, Massachusetts, Oregon, Tennessee, or Wisconsin. Most delegations were in such an uproar and so many persons were demanding recognition that Barkley, momentarily forgetting about the radio microphones, snapped at one delegate: "Dammit, can't you wait!"

After the tellers finally caught up with the action Barkley announced that Charles Bryan had 740 votes, eight more than the necessary two-thirds. This prompted some applause but also some hissing. An attempt by McNab of California to declare Bryan nominated by acclamation was angrily hooted down. "Not a chance," yelled one eastern delegate. Barkley wisely ignored McNab's suggestion and merely declared that Charles Bryan, "having received more than the required two-thirds vote," was the vice-presidential nominee of the convention. At that moment neither W. J. nor C. W. Bryan was in the Garden. Brother Charley had stepped outside for a breath of fresh air and William Jennings was already on his way to his hotel room and bed.

It took only five minutes to appoint the appropriate committees for the notification of the President and the Vice-President, and at 2:30 A.M., Thursday morning, July 10, the 1924 Democratic convention adjourned without delay on motion of Senator William H. King of Utah. The three hundred spectators who were still in the galleries moved slowly to the exits making wisecracks about the two-week-long Democratic ordeal. One of them laughingly commented that this was "the second Republican convention" while a small group mischievously began to chant: "We want Coolidge! We want Coolidge!" Weary delegates rose from their seats, the women smoothing out wrinkled dresses and the men pulling pants from sticky skin. None of them would miss the Garden. "Is it really over?" asked one California delegate of his neighbor. "Yes," came the reply, followed by a fervent "Amen!"

12

But the longest, most complicated, and most acrimonious political convention in American history was not really over. The delegates would leave and a swimming tank would be erected the very next day on the spot where Davis had acknowledged the convention's nomination. The Garden itself would shortly disappear. But the ramifications and effects of this gathering would be felt for years. Even on a short-term basis, postmortems concerning the convention filled the press for days, reminding everyone that a political event of unique significance had taken place.

In sheer statistics this convention surpassed anything before known. The 103 ballots were, in themselves, an all-time record. No fewer than sixty different persons received votes at some time during the convention, marking another record. This gathering heard more speeches, listened to more spoken words, experienced more fist fights, spent more time in committee, and witnessed more demonstrations than any other such assemblage in history. Further, it wrote a longer platform, spent more money, and went further into debt than any similar meeting. In tons of debris collected, food consumed, and soda pop drunk, it also set a record. The caterer to whom Tex Rickard gave the hot-dog and cold-drink contract made a fortune.

The national press reported such statistics with both interest and disdain. New York newspapers naturally concentrated on those matters which put New York in the best light. They contended that, despite the acrimony, this was the best-run and most carefully safeguarded convention in history. They pointed out that the emergency hospital in the basement of the Garden had treated 254 patients, but only one had died (of apoplexy) and only 12 had been sent to a regular hospital for further care. The remainder had been treated at the Garden for heat prostration, sore throats, cuts, sprains, headaches, and fainting spells, and then were returned to the floor or to the galleries. Moreover, contrary to claims of the convention's wetness, only eleven men had been picked up by the police at the Garden for intoxication. The biggest haul by prohibition agents during the convention had occurred on July 8 when they captured a runner with a dozen bottles of whiskey in a heavy traveling bag in the lobby of the Hotel Pennsylvania. He had claimed that they were for a convention delegate but he could not remember his name. Aside from the liquor problem, not one arrest had been made in or near the Garden during the long convention. And, except for the Klan fight and Al Smith day, the police had no trouble controlling the crowds. Firemen, likewise, had retained the convention's cooperation in enforcing the strict no-smoking rules and had had to close the Garden only twice to further attendees because of possible fire hazards. Garden firemen extinguished the one fire of the convention without most delegates' even knowing about it.

The substantive aspects of the convention caused continued and lively debate. Some observers claimed that excessive delegate loyalty to particular candidates had stymied the convention. William Allen White said the gathering was the victim of money, McAdoo, and the mob. According to White, the Democratic party's need for money had permitted Tammany to gain a forum in New York City and had made McAdoo a more controversial figure than he would have been elsewhere. Other pundits selected the religious factor, the Ku Klux Klan, Doheny's disclosures about McAdoo, or prohibition as the primary reason for the Garden debacle.

Certainly delegate loyalty was an important factor in the 1924 convention struggle. From the thirtieth ballot on, Smith's total did not vary by more than 13 votes lost or 44½ gained. Between the seventy-fourth and the one-hundredth ballots his vote spread was only a minuscule 13½. McAdoo's totals varied more widely but they too rested on a hard core of supporters. On all but sixteen of the roll calls McAdoo's vote was in excess of 400. The best example of delegate loyalty was Alabama, which, often alone, continued to cast its 24 votes for Underwood.

Such delegate loyalty was unfortunately not matched by managerial sagacity or ingenuity. Roosevelt was by far the shrewdest of the convention strategists, but even he permitted conditions to arise that harmed his candidate. He was much too slow in demanding a crackdown on the galleries and erred in not connecting an invitation for Smith to speak to the convention with an executive session. Rockwell was often mistaken and contributed heavily to McAdoo's defeat. He passed up a chance to impress the convention by not calling up McAdoo's reserves early enough, and then he failed to encourage McAdoo to withdraw while the Californian still had the power to act as a kingmaker. Taggart, in turn, although correctly measuring the feelings of the convention, did not know his own candidate. Even the winning manager, Clem Shaver, cannot be given high marks. Davis won in spite of, not because of, his skill.

Although many observers said so, McAdoo's connection with Doheny was not a crippling factor at the New York convention. It may have weighed heavily against McAdoo outside the convention but not in it. McAdoo had secured most of his hard-core support before the oil disclosures. True, the New York galleries made much of the "oil" issue, but the delegates did not. On the platform and on the floor McAdoo's legal connections were only rarely alluded to. McAdoo's convention opposition did not dwell on them—not Roosevelt, or Brennan, or Underwood, or Smith.

The Klan and the Klan issue obviously had an important effect. But its primacy was somewhat overestimated. Senator Thomas Walsh remained of the opinion that if McAdoo had earlier denounced the Klan he would have been nominated. Conversely, the New York press spread the belief that the Klan prevented Smith from making a better showing. Those who introduced the Klan as an issue did use it shrewdly against McAdoo. Because the convention was held in New York City the Klan question undoubtedly became more important than it would otherwise have been. But those delegates who condemned McAdoo for his reluctance to denounce the Klan opposed him for other reasons as well. The Klan issue, like the "oil" issue, merely reinforced opinions already held rather than being itself a decisive formative factor. Nor did the Klan lead many delegates away from Smith to McAdoo, or to any other candidate. A strong Protestant disinclination to support Smith existed anyway. To attribute all, or even a significant portion, of anti-Smith opinion to the Klan would be an exaggeration. The majority of Smith's opponents were not Klansmen, did not support the Klan, and even voiced disapproval of it. It is true, however, as with all hate organizations, that the Klan infected everything it touched in 1924, friend and foe alike—McAdoo, Smith, Bryan, Ralston, Underwood.

While Catholics were bitter about their treatment at the 1924 convention, the religious issue too was overstated. Smith firmly believed that he did not receive the nomination because of his Catholicism. Much was made of the fact that Smith never received more than a single vote from the South and received scarcely more than 20 votes from states west of the Mississippi. Obviously religion was a factor, but it was inextricably tied to other factors. There were numerous Catholics in western and midwestern delegations who avidly supported McAdoo. Similarly, there were Protestants in eastern and northeastern delegations who were ardent champions of Smith. Many of the most vociferous anti-McAdoo leaders were non-Catholic. Some of them were also anti-Smith. Religion was certainly not a common denominator. The convention's willingness to accept Walsh, a western Catholic, as Vice-President was indicative that more complicated factors were at work than a simple Protestant-Catholic split.

A more fundamental cleavage was wet versus dry. If a dominant issue can be found, this was it. It impinged upon every other factor that can be mentioned. It was the cement that held most of the convention alliances together. Smith's wetness, more than his religion, was of concern to westerners and southerners. Even Bryan admitted this. Except for prosperity, prohibition in 1924 was the most sensitive national issue commanding the attention of the general public. Smith's stand on prohibition and his apparent refusal to enforce the Volstead law were crucial factors to many delegates. Three years after the convention and after the heat of the 1924 battle had subsided, McAdoo admitted to a friend that his main goal in opposing Smith had been to prevent "a restoration of the liquor traffic in the United States."

Conversely, the majority of Smith leaders opposed McAdoo because he was a militant dry. McAdoo himself later stated that their main purpose in blocking him was "not because they thought I was a member of the Klan (they knew better than that) but because I was a dry and in favor of enforcing the Eighteenth Amendment." Indeed, never once did Smith or his advisers state that they believed McAdoo as President would discriminate against Jews or Catholics, or that he would be nonprogressive in economic affairs. But they often remarked that he would perpetuate a bone-dry situation. Significantly, in the closing ballots, when the Davis boom was underway, Davis's major support came from former McAdoo delegations in the South and West, which switched to him only after they were assured that he did "not smell of beer or wine." Even Bryan consoled himself that Davis was at least safe in this respect. Similarly, when it came time to select a vice-presidential nominee, the most critical requirement was not that he was a Protestant but that he was dry.

As important as the wet-dry cleavage was, it would also be a distortion to explain the 1924 Democratic imbroglio solely on that basis. The struggle actually grew out of an amalgam of all these various factors. Taken together they not only produced a convention in turmoil, but reflected a nation in the midst of traumatic changes. As already indicated, every shade of opinion, every prejudice, every fear, every division which could be found in American society as a whole was duplicated in Madison Square Garden in 1924. For that reason the convention's main event was not the selection of its presidential nominee but the ceaseless struggle between all these elements in its committees, in its galleries, and on its floor. In that struggle, which involved competing life styles, religious beliefs, social backgrounds, and conflicting moralities, partisan candidates like Smith and McAdoo elicited a fanatical response and became symbols which helped perpetuate and intensify that struggle rather than resolve it.

Marking the first concerted attempt to reach a political consensus on many of these matters, the Garden convention was a failure. But for the moment a compromise candidate like John W. Davis offered the party an opportunity to escape that failure with some honor. The reluctant third choice of many northeasterners, Davis provided hope to the urban politicians who were forging new alliances that the future of the party lay with them. Belatedly supported by the West and South, Davis also was the means whereby these beleaguered elements rationalized that they were still in control. For both sides the 1924 convention was over. But the struggle for party dominance had only begun.

PART V

★

THE KNOCKOUT

1

The donkey was the correct symbol for the Democratic party in 1924. From July 2 on, most commentators agreed that the party had made a complete ass of itself. By the time of the one-hundred-and-third ballot on July 9, so the argument went, it was no longer nominating a candidate for the presidency, but a receiver in bankruptcy. Just before the final roll calls were taken William Allen White told his readers that the result would not make a President but a job for the garbage man.

The Davis nomination caused a momentary reassessment. The press and newspapermen hardly knew what to think. Clinton Gilbert was amazed that "out of all this madness came John W. Davis, the most sweetly reasonable candidate that has ever been offered for the Presidency." Most newspapers admitted that by nominating Davis the convention had somewhat redeemed itself. "All's well that ends well," said the Springfield *Republican*.

But all was not well with the Democratic party. There were, of course, the usual messages of warm regards and praise for the decision. Ralston sent Davis his congratulations and pledged his support. Taggart told reporters: "Davis is a big, capable man, and I am for him." Governor Jonathan Davis of Kansas said that he thought the convention had selected an "excellent candidate." Other favorite sons lauded the nomination, agreed to work for the ticket, and predicted party victory in November. However, Carter Glass had no illusions about the situation and privately told a friend that Davis's nomination was not as good as "the paper it was written on." Davis himself realized the true nature of his position. When congratulated by reporter Charles Michelson just after his nomination, Davis responded with a wry grin: "Thanks, but you know how much it is worth."

The critical question confronting Davis was: could he reunite a splintered and squabbling party? Despite their relief at Davis's nomination, about the only thing the delegates could agree upon as they left the

Garden was that they never again would attend another convention in New York City. Only for a handful had the gathering been a success. Senator Thomas Walsh bore away with him the respect and admiration of almost all who had participated. Roosevelt returned to Hyde Park a much stronger and better-known political figure than when he came. Governor Brandon's voice made him so famous that a New York radio company offered him $10,000 to leave politics and become an announcer. He refused although the offer was $2,500 more than the state of Alabama paid its chief executive.

For most, the convention left wounds that would not heal. Southerners and westerners could not forget the howling New York galleries. Easterners could not forgive the religious bigotry and fanatical intransigency of McAdoo followers. Various convention scenes remained forever vividly embedded in memory. Although Smith emerged as the better sport, he remained personally very bitter about the convention's actions. Only Roosevelt's and Proskauer's constant warnings to keep calm prevented him from being consumed by his own anger. Following their advice, Smith took only one day after the convention to soothe his hurt in the Atlantic off Sea Gate and then he returned to Albany, where he threw himself back into Empire State affairs.

McAdoo continued to be inconsolable. Convinced that "sinister influences" had defeated him, he closed off his suite in the Vanderbilt to reporters and would issue no public statement about the convention outcome. He was described by friends as having suffered a crushing blow. On July 11, while Davis was still at Frank Polk's house, McAdoo appeared at the front door just before 5 P.M., alighting from a taxi still bearing Al Smith signs. The Californian had belatedly decided to pay his respects to the party's presidential nominee before leaving for Europe the next morning. He talked with Davis for over an hour but reporters could get nothing out of him except the admission that they had discussed politics. As to whether he would support Davis, McAdoo said that he might have a statement about that just before sailing, "if I can find time to prepare it." The next day, just before boarding ship, he told reporters that he would support the Davis-Bryan ticket and would try to play some part in the campaign after his return in September. When pressed for details, he brushed reporters aside petulantly. "Won't you men please leave me alone?" he said.

William Jennings Bryan left the convention to meet his wife in St. Louis, and then he returned to Florida and his prohibition and anti-evolution crusades. Despite his about-face on Davis, Bryan still had qualms about the West Virginian and constantly needed to rerationalize his support. Such continued soul-searching caused Fiorello La Guardia to comment that the Democrats had managed to nominate a ticket that even a brother could not endorse. Indeed, this convention had been most unkind to Bryan in spite of Charley's selection. The cynical East had stripped him of everything but his God. Bryan died at the Democratic National Convention of 1924. Physically he would live yet another year, but his time as a political leader had run out. Like McAdoo, he remained extremely bitter about the convention and about the way it had booed him. With tears in his eyes, he told Alabama Senator Thomas Heflin just before leaving New York, "I have never been so humiliated in all my life."

2

As the Democratic leaders and delegates left New York City on July 10 and made their way home, President Coolidge also went home. On that very day he stood bareheaded in a little churchyard in Plymouth, Vermont, and participated in a simple burial ceremony that laid his younger son to rest on a rocky hillside where generations of Coolidges had gone before. This dour silent man was the Democratic convention's primary target and, as it turned out, its primary beneficiary.

After analyzing Calvin Coolidge for fourteen pages in an introductory chapter in his *The Mind of the President* (1926), C. Bascom Slemp, Coolidge's suave private secretary from Turkey Cove, Virginia, concluded: "I have no explanation for Mr. Coolidge. . . ." Few persons did. Chief executive by accident, Coolidge's fame rested mainly on his breaking the Boston Police Strike of 1919 rather than because of anything he had done during the Harding administration. As Vice-President he had quietly presided over the Senate and had dined out about three times a week as the representative of the White House. Harding had paid little attention to him, and it is probable that only the Ohioan's sudden death prevented Coolidge from being dumped from the ticket in 1924. Possessing neither charm nor oratorical ability, Coolidge was a provincial, untraveled New Englander, whose personal reactions were sometimes unpredictable. His humor tended to be mordant and he could snap out cutting remarks with deadly effect.

Coolidge's governmental philosophy, however, was highly predictable and consistent. He was suspicious of government and believed that its major justification was to help business. He favored sound money, high tariffs, and low taxes. He believed that Congress should initiate programs and legislation and that the President should act primarily as a figurehead. While he took an inward boyish delight in being President, he shrank from the responsibilities. In his work habits he was no whirlwind. Ike Hoover, the White House chief usher, claimed: "No other President in my time ever slept so much." Later, in his own *Autobiography* (1929), Coolidge listed one rule which he considered most important: "It consists in never doing anything that someone else can do for you." As for his taciturn exterior and his silent manner, he once observed: "The things I don't say never get me into trouble."

To some people Coolidge's blandness and his aphorisms were wisdom; to others they represented smugness and stupidity. To some his peculiar humor was innocent; to others it was sadistic. But to most individuals Coolidge seemed to have "character," a trait which was in short supply in the wake of the Harding scandals. Coolidge himself did much to promote this feeling. First he yielded to congressional pressure by removing Secretary of Navy Edwin Denby and Attorney General Daugherty from his cabinet, and then he appointed a special counsel to prosecute Interior Secretary Albert Fall. Such actions not only pleased the general public, but also attracted the support of distressed and embarrassed Republicans. When, on June 30, 1924, a grand jury handed down criminal indictments against the Teapot Dome culprits, most citizens saw it as a victory for Coolidge as much as for the Democratic chief investigator, Thomas Walsh.

By late 1923 and early 1924 it was clear that the Republicans needed Coolidge fully as much as he needed them. By that time a myth of greatness had begun to spring up around him, largely as a result of the media. Coolidge once wrote: "In public life it is sometimes necessary in order to appear really natural to be actually artificial." He had ample reason to know. Newspaperman Clinton Gilbert later claimed that to offset Harding's damage to the image of the presidency, Coolidge had to be endowed with all those qualities that Americans expect in their Presidents, and "as a people we rose grandly to the task." "In a week," said Gilbert, "the only thing there was in common between Mr. Coolidge, the Vice-President, and Mr. Coolidge, the President, was his name." Whatever the reason for creating this "new" Coolidge, the change worked.

Soon Republican leaders, as well as all cabinet officers, jumped on his bandwagon and spoke of him as the party's indispensable 1924 nominee. Wall Street, especially, waxed eloquent about the need for Coolidge's remaining in the White House. Perhaps no single endorsement was as important as that by Henry Ford in December, 1923.

When Coolidge formally announced his presidential candidacy in that same month, a close-knit group of friends and associates were already tooling up his campaign. Foremost among these were Frank W. Stearns and William M. Butler. Along with Slemp, they first worked to forestall any competing candidacies. Then, since Coolidge was a newcomer to national politics, they proceeded to build a Coolidge organization from scratch. Few Republicans were bound to Coolidge by bonds of personal loyalty or devotion. There was no "Coolidge faction" in the Republican party.

Stearns, a Boston merchant who chomped constantly on a cigar, and Butler, a nonflappable businessman from Beacon Street, made an excellent team. With Slemp's help, Butler and Stearns flooded the South and the Midwest with Coolidge literature, especially those areas where disaffection among the farmers was high. Pro-Coolidge men were quickly identified in all states and were encouraged to boost his fortunes there. When the delegate lists from the various states for the 1924 Republican convention became available, Butler wrote each delegate a personal letter asking for his support. As the spring of 1924 passed, it became clear that these endeavors were meeting with success. Entire delegations from the southern states early declared for Coolidge along with many from the West and the Midwest. Only La Follette country seemed in doubt.

All this naturally discouraged would-be contenders. Only Hiram Johnson and Bob La Follette showed any desire to fight. Johnson, who claimed he was the legitimate heir to the "progressivism" of Teddy Roosevelt, entered his name against Coolidge in most state primaries, but defeated him only in one—South Dakota. Elsewhere Coolidge won by overwhelming majorities. The crushing blow for Johnson came in his own home state of California, where on May 6 Coolidge beat him by over 50,000 votes. As a result, Johnson wisely decided to "throw in the towel." La Follette continued on his way alone.

The Republican convention which met in Cleveland on June 10, 1924, was definitely a Coolidge-run affair. Most newspapers could not help but notice the shift in control there. Gone were the ruling cliques of 1920 which allegedly had played such an instrumental role in Warren Harding's selection. Gone too were the swarms of senators who had dominated the floor and the halls. Indicative of this change was the eclipse of the influence of Senator Henry Cabot Lodge, now displaced by the emerging Coolidge-Butler faction in Massachusetts politics. According to one observer, Lodge "stood around at the convention like someone unemployed." He served on no important committees and was invited to make no speeches. This was not a politician's convention but a businessman's convention, and business leadership was everywhere evident. William Butler, about to enter on his duties as chairman of the Republican National Committee, was clearly the kingpin. He wrote the convention's script and other business-oriented political amateurs like himself saw that it was acted out.

The Republicans met in the new modern Cleveland Convention Hall, which seated 15,000. The whole effect was stolid. Instead of arched steel rafters wrapped in bunting, there was a gray, sand-colored plastered ceiling with a clouded glass skylight in the center. The hall's only adornment was one great red, white, and blue wall-hanging at the back of the stage. On this hanging were suspended the portraits of Lincoln, McKinley, and Theodore Roosevelt. There was no lore about this site and no smell of circus here. It was bland and subdued in appearance and structure, much like the Republican party itself.

The delegates and spectators also reflected this. There were no outlandish hats and costumes, no extra bands, no cheering galleries, no extravagance, no "whooper-uppers." When the convention opened, the twelve hundred delegates immediately settled down to work. On orders from Butler, Senator Theodore Burton, Coolidge's fellow Congregationalist from Ohio, was made temporary chairman, and Frank W. Mondell, representative from Wyoming, was elected permanent chairman. Burton's opening speech was too long, an hour and fifty minutes—much of it a paean to Ohio, which had contributed seven of the eleven Republican Presidents prior to that time. Burton spoke for almost an hour before there was any sustained applause (with regard to prohibition enforcement), and he received only a one-minute ovation on his first mention of Coolidge. He got his greatest audience reaction when at the climax of his speech he condemned splinter groups and urged party solidarity. This was an obvious reference to the disgruntled La Follette faction. Thereafter, unity became the keynote of this Republican convention.

La Follette delegates, mainly from Wisconsin, were responsible for some disharmony. In the hearings before the platform committee they presented a complete set of minority planks signaling an all-out attack on business and private monopoly. Receiving only one vote from the committee (Wisconsin's), this minority platform was subsequently howled down on the convention floor. Its demise caused the convention band, led by the famous John Philip Sousa, to strike up "Hail, Hail, the Gang's All Here," at which point someone yelled, "All except Wisconsin!"—a cry that swept the hall like wildfire. Soon everyone was singing:

> Hail, hail, the gang's all here,
> All except Wisconsin,
> All except Wisconsin. . . .

It was the only time the convention really showed any life. For La Follette followers it was a clear indication that they were no longer welcome in the Republican party.

The Republicans blithely sailed past all those whirlpools which were to suck down the Democratic party in Madison Square Garden three weeks later. The Klan issue was settled in the platform committee and never reached the floor. After some animated debate, the group decided not to dignify the Klan by mentioning it. Instead, the committee presented to the convention a general "religious tolerance" plank, which was accepted without discussion: "The Republican Party reaffirms its unyielding devotion to the Constitution and to the guarantees of civil, political, and religious liberty therein contained." Although Imperial Wizard Hiram Evans, Grand Dragon Walter Bossert (Indiana), and some sixty other Klansmen were present in Cleveland, they exercised little influence over the convention's deliberations. The Republican decision not to name the Klan was made on the basis of practical politics. As one jokester said, "If you say 'K.K.K.' to the elephant it answers 'Ain't the moon beautiful!'; if you say it to the donkey, it kicks itself all over the lot."

Prohibition and the League of Nations proved to be no problems either. Assuming that Harding's landslide in 1920 had settled the League issue, the 1924 platform ignored it. As for prohibition, the party merely reendorsed its previous enforcement plank. So confident was Wayne Wheeler of Republican action along this line that he did not even bother to attend the Cleveland convention, but allowed Anti-Saloon League interests to be handled by his assistant, B. N. Hicks. A careful check of delegate lists prior to the convention had assured him that there was no vocal opposition to prohibition enforcement among any of the Republican delegations.

Without any acrimony or bloodshed the Republican convention accomplished by the end of the second day what it would require the Democrats a week to do. Like the later Democratic platform, however, the Republican platform was lengthy and often vague—the two "competing with each other," said the *New York Times*, "to see which can first reach oblivion." But, unlike the Democratic platform, this one rested on the Harding normalcy policies. It reaffirmed protective tariffs, endorsed the Washington Disarmament Conference, applauded the new departures in Mexican and Latin American relations, praised the elimination of the twelve-hour day, promised continued federal support for highways, urged a Great Lakes–St. Lawrence Seaway, pledged continued aid to sick and wounded veterans, reendorsed immigration restriction, reaffirmed the repayment of World War I foreign debts, and promised a continuance of the Mellon economic policies involving tax reduction and government economy.

When it came time to nominate candidates for the office of President on the morning of June 12, it was not surprising that only one name was presented. When Dr. Marion L. Burton, president of the University of Michigan, speaking without notes and cutting his prepared speech in half, mentioned Calvin Coolidge, a brief eighteen-minute demonstration followed, during which everyone participated except Wisconsin. Ignoring shouts of "Stand up, Wisconsin, stand up!," that state finally did but only because at the end of the Coolidge demonstration the Sousa band played "The Star-Spangled Banner." The delegates wanted to name Coolidge by acclamation immediately but protocol required seconding speeches, and nine of them were given before the balloting began. During the first and only roll call, 1,065 of the 1,109 delegates voted for Coolidge, 34 voted for La Follette (6 from North Dakota and 28 from Wisconsin), and 10 voted for Hiram Johnson (all from South Dakota). When these totals were announced, the delegates rushed for the exits. They had nominated a President and there was still time for lunch.

The only suspense in the entire convention occurred during the ensuing afternoon session. It centered on the selection of a vice-presidential nominee. Eight names were presented with the expectation that Coolidge would make his wishes known. But Coolidge gave no clear signals to the convention. It was rumored that he wanted maverick Senator Borah as his running mate and had even talked with him about it. In view of the Senator's known opposition to the administration, most delegates treated such rumors as unbelievable. When no concrete word was forthcoming from Coolidge, many delegates turned instead to Governor Frank Lowden (Illinois) who had earlier announced that he would not run. By the end of the second ballot, they gave him the nomination. Millions of Americans heard newscasts declaring Lowden the winner only to learn shortly thereafter that he had absolutely refused to accept.

Under these unusual circumstances the convention was forced to adjourn and reconvene at 8 P.M. in the hope of finding a new prospect. In the interim, William Butler tried to initiate a move to Herbert Hoover. Ku Klux Klan representatives pushed Indiana Senator James E. Watson. The farm bloc wanted either ex-Senator William S. Kenyon or Senator Charles Curtis. But no one was more effective in beating the drums for his candidate than Mark W. Woods of Nebraska, who persuaded most former Lowden supporters to vote for Chicago banker Charles G. Dawes. As a result, on the evening's opening ballot (the third), Dawes quickly showed strength, and by the end of the roll call his margin over Hoover, the next-highest candidate, was 682½ to 234½. Dawes's selection was a surprise to Butler, who had had things his own way prior to this moment. It was also a surprise to Dawes, who wrote to a friend that it was "about the most unexpected thing in my life." It was unexpected for Coolidge, too. He had already written Lowden a letter of congratulations.

When the Republicans disbanded on June 12, after three days' work, the result met with shrugs almost everywhere. Wall Street, of course, was happy, but elsewhere there was no great enthusiasm. The outcome was expected. However, after the Democratic imbroglio several weeks later, this convention and its work acquired new meaning. By then Coolidge was not only the recipient of general Republican party support but was also the unwitting receiver of the benefits flowing from the Democratic turmoil. Standing bareheaded on that Vermont hillside in mid-July just before the 1924 presidential election campaign began, his personal life was under a shadow, but his political prospects had never been brighter.

As for the contrast between the Republican and the subsequent Democratic conventions, even the most nonpolitical citizen could not fail to take notice. In Cleveland the atmosphere had been efficient and responsible; in New York it was chaotic and emotional. In Cleveland the convention had acted like a disciplined unit; in New York it acted like a hopeless rabble. In Cleveland the delegates had been moderate middle-of-the-roaders; in New York there were only the extremes. In Cleveland conversations among the delegates had been discussions; in New York they were arguments. These striking differences were significant and themselves became issues affecting the ensuing presidential campaign. The New York convention, Democrats claimed, showed their party "was at least alive" as compared to "the moribund Republican gathering at Cleveland." The two conventions, countered the Republicans, showed all too well who should govern the country. How could the Democrats rule the nation when they couldn't even govern themselves?

3

From the time he entered the Senate in 1905, Bob La Follette wanted to be President. His support of chief executives from Theodore Roosevelt to Calvin Coolidge had been only perfunctory, and rarely had he whole-heartedly endorsed administration policy. Now, in 1924, he was a sixty-nine-year-old sick man engaged in a race with death to satisfy his presidential ambitions.

La Follette was a dour, lonely figure who seemed constantly to be at odds with the world. His high forehead, pompadoured silver hair, and deep-seated, piercing eyes gave him a prophetlike quality. Representing that brand of agrarian thinking peculiar to the upper Mississippi Valley, La Follette usually bristled at the first sign of opposition and fought all his battles ruthlessly. Diplomacy and tact were unknown to him. He thrived on defiance. Like Bryan, he deified a mystical concept of democracy. Also like Bryan, moral judgments often took the place of sound economic analysis, and he thought he saw horns under every silk hat. Unlike Bryan, La Follette basically respected intellect, liked good books, and cared little for personal wealth.

There had been two bitter episodes in La Follette's political life, in 1912 and in 1917. In the first, progressives had deserted him to follow Theodore Roosevelt into the ill-fated Bull Moose struggle. In the second, the country had deserted him on the question of intervention in World War I. In the one, he felt betrayed by his friends; in the other, he was denounced and hounded by his friends. He was deeply hurt in both cases and never fully recovered. As one observer put it: "If no other public man in America in our times has been so savage, it can also be said that no other public man in America in our times has so suffered."

From 1917 to 1922 La Follette remained under suspicion because of his vigorous opposition to American participation in the war. Then, general disillusionment with the war following the League fight worked to his partial advantage. More important, the adverse economic situation which developed in the western farm areas after 1920 added to his public rehabilitation. As one of the stalwarts of the emerging farm bloc he was reelected as a Republican senator from Wisconsin in 1922, and continued to refurbish his image by being militantly anti-administration and pro-farmer. Inevitably, the growing political influence of the farm bloc rekindled his presidential ambitions. By 1923 he once more began to talk like a presidential candidate and by mid-year warned that if both of the major parties nominated "reactionaries," a third alternative would surely be found. By early 1924 a La Follette boom was being nurtured in the Dakotas, and most agrarians were predicting that La Follette would somehow enter the 1924 race.

There was a cloud on the horizon—his health. Beginning in 1923 La Follette experienced a deteriorating heart condition. In the summer of 1923 he entered the Battle Creek Sanitarium for rest and recuperation. That fall he made his first trip abroad, as he said, "to learn about Europe," but actually to continue his recovery. Upon his return, however, he was so ill that he missed the opening of Congress in December. In January, 1924, he at last resumed his congressional duties but had to be very careful. Meanwhile, his family and close friends pretended that nothing was amiss. Bob, Jr., who manned the Washington end of things for his father, and Philip, who kept the Senator's base in Wisconsin inviolate, maintained the fiction that their father was suffering merely from a persistent and recurring case of the grippe. Even in their letters to each other they rationalized that he would "soon be good as new." La Follette's wife, Belle, and his daughter, Fola, also participated in this gentle subterfuge. The La Follettes were a close-knit family, and La Follette, Sr.'s political career was a family enterprise in which they all shared.

By 1924 events were beginning to outrun La Follette's health. Since 1922 various liberal and labor groups had been attempting to join together for an assault on the pro-business administrations of Harding and Coolidge. The most aggressive attempt was that of the Conference for Progressive Political Action, which in a series of three meetings from

1922–24 managed to weld together a loose confederation of the railroad brotherhoods, old progressives, dissident agrarians, labor units, and socialists. Generally they favored McAdoo, but when he was smeared with oil they turned to La Follette. It was a disputed point whether they should form a third political party or keep their separate identities and simply support the Wisconsin senator as an "independent" candidate. They all agreed, however, that only La Follette could "solidify the whole Progressive movement and put to rout the forces of reaction."

This development was timely for La Follette. As his son Phil wrote him in late January, 1924: *"Take care of yourself,* Daddy—we can make a great run this year if you keep your health." Throughout the remainder of the winter and the spring of 1924 La Follette kept his name before the public by capitalizing on Teapot Dome and supporting the various Senate scandal investigations. The La Follette sons spent the spring whipping up La Follette sentiment in the western states, using such phrases as "progressive unity" and "progressive expression" as synonyms for a La Follette candidacy. As summer approached and there was talk of a CPPA convention's being held specifically to consider presidential possibilities, the La Follette sons increased their efforts. By now Bob, Sr., had an apocalyptic sense of mission. Suffering from severe bronchial congestion in May, he again required rest, but even this did not stop the La Follette drive. To Phil he wrote: "I know how much you are sacrificing for your Dad. . . . Whatever befalls we are going to make some history within the next year."

When a CPPA convention was finally called for Cleveland in July, 1924, La Follette was undecided about how to proceed. Ultimately he and his sons agreed that he should not formally initiate or endorse the creation of a third party because it would encourage local tickets, nor should he run on any platform except his own. On the other hand, they agreed that he should do nothing to discourage the CPPA convention from nominating him. In short, La Follette hoped to maintain a balance between retaining full freedom of action and simultaneously securing the endorsement of the Cleveland group. Further, he wanted to keep clear of all Communist and radical support—support which had killed many an independent candidacy.

On the evening of July 3, while the Democrats were locked in battle in New York City, La Follette received a telegram at his Washington home from William H. Johnston, chairman of the national committee of the Conference for Progressive Political Action, asking him to be the

CPPA's presidential nominee. Leaders of the CPPA had been watching the Madison Square Garden struggle with profound interest. They had hoped that no one would win who would appeal to labor or agrarian interests. Now, after some seventy ballots, they were convinced that no "progressive Democrat" would be selected and that a candidate like La Follette would attract the support of *all* progressives. La Follette was in a dilemma. Since he did not wish to fall into a third-party trap, he did not give Johnston an immediate reply. Instead, he decided to announce his candidacy as an independent just before the CPPA acted.

The CPPA convention opened on Independence Day in the same Cleveland auditorium that the Republicans had recently vacated. Six hundred delegates were in attendance, representing socialists, laborers, farmers, intellectuals, and a host of other groups. There were, however, no Communists present. Seeking to forestall any La Follette embarrassment on this score, the convention maintained tight security. For example, William Z. Foster, head of the Communist Workers Party of America, was turned away by the doorkeeper, who would not allow him in even as a spectator.

Heralded as a convention of the "plain people," this assemblage was a peculiar blend of the old and the new. Jacob Coxey was there as were other old-time Populists. So were the "Yipsils"—members of the Young People's Socialist League. Everywhere there were purveyors of panaceas and nostrums, and the gathering contained a definite lunatic fringe. There were even some disgruntled Republicans present, like urban maverick Fiorello La Guardia, who said he represented a different urban America than Broad and Wall. Interestingly, in this so-called people's convention there was only one black, and women played no role whatever. If one could say the Republican convention was a gathering of Babbitts and the Democratic convention one of southern fundamentalists and northern boss politicians, this one was a collection of students. The majority of the delegates were under forty and large contingents were present from Columbia, Yale, Harvard, Dartmouth, Barnard, Vassar, and Union Theological Seminary. These collegiate claques were there to support La Follette's nomination.

This convention had no band, little organization, and none of the hoopla associated with political gatherings. Yet there was much enthusiasm and a sort of self-imposed discipline which carried it briskly through the afternoon's opening exercises. Then, shortly before 5 P.M., while some confusion developed over what exact procedures to follow, Bob La Fol-

lette, Jr., strode to the speaker's stand and was introduced to an expectant audience by Chairman Johnston as "a chip off the old block." As
the cheers died, Bob read a statement from his father announcing that he
would be "an Independent Progressive candidate for President." With
this, the delegates jumped to their feet and would have nominated him
on the spot, but the convention managers indicated that the time for that
was still twenty-four hours away.

During the night recess of July 4, a bitter debate raged in the CPPA's
organization committee. The socialist delegates insisted that a bona-fide
third party be formed, presenting a complete ticket for all national offices.
But Bob, Jr., bluntly told them that his father would not run under such
circumstances, and this ended the argument. The next day, July 5, La
Follette's independent candidacy was endorsed by the CPPA convention,
and a La Follette-written platform, which Bob, Jr., read to the assembly,
was quickly accepted. A model of brevity compared to the hefty Republican and Democratic documents, its very first sentence set the central La
Follette theme: "The great issue before the American people today is the
control of government and industry by private monopoly." The platform
then went on to call for tariff and freight-rate reductions, abolition of the
Mellon tax policies, governmental aid and subsidies for the farmer, public
ownership of water power and the railroads, the right of labor to unionize
and bargain collectively, elimination of labor injunctions, a soldiers'
bonus and a raise for postal employees, direct election of the President, a
popular referendum on war, ratification of a child-labor amendment, ten-
year terms for Supreme Court justices, and legislative veto over judicial
decisions.

So dominated was this convention by La Follette that it adjourned
without even selecting a vice-presidential nominee. It assumed that La
Follette would handpick him. But La Follette made no decision for more
than a week while he mulled over the possibilities. He wanted Justice
Louis D. Brandeis and sounded him out, but Brandeis said no. Finally,
he named Senator Burton Wheeler. Elected as the junior senator from
Montana in the Democratic landslide of 1922, Wheeler had arrived in
Washington determined to make a name for himself. His primary vehicle
had been the 1924 Senate investigation of the Justice Department, which
he conducted with more zeal than skill. A political adventurer, young and
aggressive, he was one of the first to condemn the Davis-Bryan ticket and
announce his unwillingness to support it. "When the Democratic party
goes to Wall Street for its candidate," he said, "I must refuse to go with

it." Such an attitude made him acceptable to La Follette, who believed that Wheeler would add fire to his ticket. Wheeler accepted with alacrity, but made it clear that he was not renouncing his Democratic party affiliation. "I am a Democrat," he insisted, "but not a Wall Street Democrat."

From the beginning the La Follette-Wheeler independent ticket produced mixed emotions. Although the Socialist party finally endorsed it, many socialists and others on the left were disappointed in the CPPA convention and were put off by La Follette's maneuverings to disassociate himself from parties. The Communists refused to have anything to do with him, condemning his platform as "the most reactionary document of the year." Conservatives, on the other hand, claimed that "raw, red radicalism" was involved in the La Follette candidacy and denounced his platform as "Wisconsin Bolshevism."

La Follette followers, of course, were overjoyed, but their enthusiasm tended to run away with their reason. The battle they were fighting in 1924 was still the battle of 1896 and 1912. The La Follette platform said nothing about the Ku Klux Klan or civil rights. It did not mention prohibition and ignored foreign affairs. It was notable only for its nostalgic call to attack special privilege and monopoly. In this respect, La Follette was little more than a Republican Bryan. Further, the CPPA convention hardly showed itself opposed to "boss" domination or "controlled" politics. It was no example of enlightened democratic action. The delegates had been perfectly willing to follow one man's every wish, even to the extent of adopting a platform in whose construction they had had no part. Oswald G. Villard contended that the La Follette nomination, unlike those of the Republicans and the Democrats, was the result of "an honest convention" in which there were "no political bosses, no ward heelers, no Harry Daughertys, no Tom Taggarts." Maybe so. But there was La Follette.

4

At the beginning of 1924 the Republicans had looked forward to the presidential campaign with apprehension and distaste. By mid-July both their outlook and their chances had improved markedly. Although suffering from some disunity, the party was not the confederation of feuding, disparate groupings that the Democratic party was. As Walter Lippmann correctly observed, although the Democratic party was stronger in its various parts, the Republican party was much stronger as a whole, and it capitalized on that fact. Moreover, the scandal issue, which had inundated the Republicans in midwinter, had receded by midsummer. Because of their sometimes misguided zeal to uncover wrongdoing, Democratic senators like Burton Wheeler had even wearied the country by their excessive activities. Meanwhile, Coolidge had steered a wise course. Taking advice from such senior statesmen as William Howard Taft, who told him "to do nothing" and give the public "a rest from watching Washington," he kept out of sight and let returning prosperity do its work.

The Madison Square Garden convention provided the Republicans with a tremendous lift. As one GOP official put it: "Well, the Democrats might have disbanded and gone home. But short of that they've done about all they could for Coolidge and Dawes." Still, the Davis nomination represented a potential danger and most Republican leaders admitted it. McAdoo had been their choice because his nomination automatically would have neutralized the corruption issue, freeing them once again to attack Wilsonism as they had in 1920. Now an "honest conservative" was running—one who could attack corruption and conceivably split the middle-of-the-road vote. In Republican eyes, Davis was a far more formidable candidate than McAdoo and one of the few men who had any chance to revitalize the Democratic party.

Republican campaign strategy was formulated accordingly. A joint effort of Coolidge and his campaign manager, William Butler, it involved avoiding the corruption issue and keeping prosperity foremost. The sixty-three-year-old Butler organized the campaign like the businessman he was. Finances were handled expertly and a smoothly operating campaign machine was created. Butler was a severe taskmaster. He kept check on every phase of Republican campaign activity. "I am interested in a personal way in the success of Calvin Coolidge," he once said, leaving no doubt that he intended to secure an ultimate Coolidge victory.

Coolidge fitted the Butler-run campaign perfectly. He stayed close to his presidential duties, remained outwardly serene and calm, and spoke as little as possible. As Coolidge once told the press: "I don't recall any candidate for President that ever injured himself very much by not talking." Coolidge even began his campaign late and in a muted key. His acceptance speech on August 14 was typical. On critical issues he said almost nothing. His sole goal, he claimed, was a "government of common sense" and he defended all existing administration policies. The Democratic press denounced such Coolidge efforts as "limp and inadequate." But others did not think so, especially such arch-symbols of American business and technology as Henry Ford, Thomas Edison, and Harvey Firestone. They agreed that the United States was lucky to have a man like Calvin Coolidge.

What Coolidge did not say or do for himself, Butler did for him. His publicity for Coolidge was masterful. It made virtues out of weaknesses and assets out of liabilities. Truth and myth were mingled skillfully. Coolidge's silence, it was said, hid "a powerful and original mind." One campaign leaflet described the Coolidge phenomenon this way: "He has more on the shelves and puts less in the show-window than anyone in the country." Coolidge's efficiency, honesty, integrity, and frugality were constantly emphasized. His reliability and his "safe" qualities were lauded. With hyperbole, but also with some truth, C. Bascom Slemp later said, "President Coolidge was the whole Republican campaign of 1924. He was all the issue there was, and all that was needed."

Coolidge himself gave the campaign almost no attention. Early on, Stearns wrote Butler the advice: "Personally I hope the President will not make any strictly political speeches, except possibly one. I hope that he will make very few non-political speeches, away from Washington—not more than three or four at the most—I mean before election." This advice was heeded. During September and October Coolidge made several set speeches on such neutral topics as "The High Place of Labor" and "The Genius of America" without even alluding to his candidacy or taking notice of his opponents. Then, on November 3, the evening before the election, he went on nationwide radio, urged all citizens to vote, and closed his brief remarks by saying "Good night" to his father up on the farm in Vermont.

In such manner Coolidge proved to be a master at destroying issues rather than debating them. Consciously or unconsciously, he employed dullness and apathy as political weapons, meeting every yawp with a yawn. How much the death of his son affected his campaign is difficult to say. Just before the election Coolidge wrote his father that when Calvin, Jr., had died "the power and the glory of the Presidency went with him." We do know that in his *Autobiography* he devoted only a single paragraph to the entire 1924 campaign and concluded by saying: "The campaign was magnificently managed by William M. Butler and as it progressed the final result became more and more apparent."

Candidate Dawes presented a different picture. Some twelve years before, Dawes too had lost a son under tragic circumstances, a twenty-one-year-old junior at Princeton, who had drowned in Lake Geneva. But there the similarity with Coolidge ceased. Dawes was a pipe-smoking, bombastic, energetic, aggressive, outspoken middle westerner. He came from a long line of fighting men. One of his ancestors was Manasseh Cutler, the founder of the Ohio Company; another was William Dawes, Paul Revere's riding companion in warning Middlesex farmers about the British in 1775. His own father was General Rufus R. Dawes, commander of the famous Sixth Wisconsin Brigade at Gettysburg. Dawes himself had served as a brigadier general in World War I—a most unorthodox officer, coat open, forgetting to salute, and calling his superiors by their first names. He was perhaps best known for being Harding's tight-fisted and garrulous director of the budget.

While Coolidge advocated remaining nonspecific during the campaign and emphasizing nothing but prosperity and economy in government, Dawes indicated a strong desire to hit hard at La Follette and his "radicalism." Moreover, while Coolidge and almost all Republican leaders thought it wise to ignore the Klan question completely, Dawes early stated that he would speak out on it when necessary. He once said about the Klan: "If I trim, I'm gone." It is questionable if many voters made their way into the Coolidge camp because of Dawes's more aggressive attitudes. His brand of economic conservatism and his career as a banker attracted neither liberals, laborers, nor dissident farmers. Sometimes Dawes was even an embarrassment for the Republicans. Hoover warned Butler to keep him out of California, and proper Bostonians were aghast when Dawes on a speaking tour in Maine "lit his pipe right on the stage and sat there puffing in the faces of the ladies who sat next to him." Butler's main problem was keeping Dawes from becoming too expansive and ebullient.

Ebullient was hardly the word for it. In 1924 Dawes became one of the most vigorous and peripatetic vice-presidential campaigners in history. He made over one hundred speeches and traveled some fifteen thousand miles, slashing at his opponents. An early exponent of the "give 'em hell" style which Harry Truman later made famous, Dawes was in wide demand. As one humorist said about the Coolidge-Dawes combination: "Coolidge and Dawes, Coolidge and Dawes; one for the freezes, and one for the thaws." Certainly Dawes never lost votes by sounding like an "egghead" or a boring college professor. He would talk on any subject, anytime, anywhere. His delivery was electric. It was said that he was the only man in the world who when he spoke could keep both feet and both arms in the air at once. During the campaign he constantly hammered on the theme of conservatism versus radicalism, aiming his blows chiefly at La Follette. He generally ignored the Democrats, characterizing them merely as being somewhere between "the forces of progressive conservatism" (Republicans) and "red radicalism" (La Follette Progressives).

This calculated preoccupation with La Follette permitted the Republicans to skirt most of the issues in American political life raised by the turmoil in the Madison Square Garden convention. In the face of the La Follette candidacy, matters like the Klan and prohibition were given lesser priority. For example, Butler claimed throughout the summer and fall of 1924 that there was *no* religious issue. Coolidge said not one word on the Klan, and even Dawes finally avoided it as much as possible. In only one speech, in late August in Augusta, Maine, did Dawes devote much time to it and then he handled it in a manner that caused La Guardia to claim, somewhat unfairly, that he had "praised it with faint damn." Nor did prohibition receive much Republican attention. Again Coolidge ignored it while Dawes and other Republican speakers concentrated only on the constitutional requirement of enforcing the law, not the moral question of whether the law itself was correct. In this way the Republicans were able to keep the prohibition debate at a much lower temperature than the Democrats, especially in those areas where the issue's impact was strong.

To the end, the Republicans massed almost all of their fire on La Follette. They attacked his pacifism and his wartime record. They denounced his "ties to Bolshevism." They bemoaned his anti-judicial attitudes and charged him with attempting to tear down American institutions. As a final shot the Republicans raised the fear that not to vote for Coolidge would throw the election into the House of Representatives. There La Follette followers would forestall a presidential selection while the Senate, controlled by La Follette Progressives and Democrats, would elect Charles Bryan as Vice-President. With the House unable to agree on a President, so the Republican scenario went, Bryan would automatically function as the chief executive. This was a prospect calculated to turn any undecided intelligent voter's hair white. "The struggle," warned Butler at the close of the campaign, "is not over the methods of government but the abolition of government. The issue is to save the country." As one of the most effective Republican slogans read, it was "Coolidge or Chaos."

Where was John W. Davis in all this? Commented *World's Work:* "The spectacle of a Republican candidate for the presidency coolly ignoring his Democratic opponent is the one novel feature of the contest. Nothing like it has ever been known."

5

Although the La Follette campaign always possessed a disturbing Alice-in-Wonderland quality, it prompted much comment and attracted wide interest. As expected, a galaxy of former liberals and reformers immediately announced their support for the Wisconsin senator—John R. Commons, Jane Addams, John Dewey, Helen Keller, Florence Kelley, Oswald G. Villard, Louis Brandeis, Norman Hapgood, and Felix Frankfurter. Their support, however, rather than strengthening his cause, was more a testimony to how far some of them too were currently out of touch with popular American political interests.

At the beginning La Follette considered Davis the man to beat, primarily because of his Wall Street connections; and he ordered his running mate, Wheeler, to spare no energy in attacking him. La Follette, meanwhile, intended to emphasize the progressive planks in his platform and articulate progressive philosophy. But he could not long refrain from battling Wall Street either, and soon lapsed into his usual oratory associated with the early progressive era.

The La Follette crusade got off to a fairly good start. The Wisconsin senator was the only one of the three major candidates who fully comprehended the emerging importance of the media, and he opened his campaign on Labor Day with the first political address ever delivered exclusively over radio. Sitting alone at the microphone in a studio, La Follette watched through a glass to the outside, where Bob, Jr., with prearranged signals indicated how his voice was coming over. Then, on September 18, La Follette began a personal speaking tour by appearing in Madison Square Garden. Demolition work on the Garden was already in progress and the colonnade in front was gone. This did not prevent a sellout crowd of fourteen thousand from hearing him speak. Thereafter he traveled through the eastern Atlantic and midwestern states, striving to put his progressive message across. His campaign was not extensive—neither his health nor his finances would permit it. But he did visit thirteen states and made twenty major speeches. Of these, four were devoted entirely to monopoly, and every one of them mentioned this as "the supreme issue." By taking this approach La Follette minimized his advantages and maximized his defects. It was the same old "Battling Bob," complained one writer, "flaying the trust and nailing the pelt up as he had for twenty years." Others complained that he was "fighting shadows" and that on this issue he was as cracked as the Liberty Bell which he had authorized as his ticket's official emblem.

On those matters about which the Republicans chose to say little, La Follette did not help himself either. He was so equivocal on prohibition that neither wets nor drys could support him. In his youth he had imbibed, then later took the pledge. He had advocated a national referendum on the prohibition question, was in a quandary what to do about the Eighteenth Amendment, but finally voted against the Volstead Act. At base, he really believed in local option. Wayne Wheeler and the Anti-Saloon League naturally opposed him. But even the Association Against the Prohibition Amendment refused to endorse him for the presidency. La Follette flatly repudiated the Klan, then minimized the significance of this position by claiming that the Klan was really "an unimportant issue." In no way, he said, could the threat of the Klan be compared with the danger of private monopoly—"the one dominant, all embracing issue in this campaign." As for foreign policy, La Follette was avowedly isolationist—he was anti-war, anti-League, and anti-international finance capitalism.

Ironically, Senator Wheeler, who was belatedly added to the ticket, was a far shrewder and more effective campaigner than La Follette. Wheeler did not believe that Davis was the primary opponent. Coolidge was. Moreover, not private monopoly, but corruption was the central issue. Wheeler early realized that it was impossible to arouse the public about the defects of the corporate system when most people were currently reaping economic rewards at its hands. Governmental corruption, on the other hand, he believed had real possibilities, and through seventeen thousand miles and twenty-six states he made effective use of the Harding scandals, especially Teapot Dome. Brash and possessing a kind of boyish smile, Wheeler was alternately charming and cunning on the stump. He had a knack for seizing his opponent's jugular. His most effective and famous ploy was to debate an empty chair, which he addressed as "President Coolidge." After firing embarrassing questions at it, he would say, "There, my friends, is the usual silence that emanates from the White House."

But it required more than a Wheeler to save the Progressive campaign from general ineptness. Despite some voter enthusiasm at the beginning, the La Follette campaign never caught on. La Follette's own personality worked against it. He did not receive anything like the volume of mail Bryan got in 1896 or Roosevelt secured in 1912. La Follette was too earnest, too zealous, too serious. As one writer reminded his readers in 1924, "In thirty years La Follette has not raised one laugh." Nor could La Follette's campaign organization make up for these personal shortcomings, as Coolidge's did. Efforts by the CPPA, by La Follette's sons, and by John M. Nelson (La Follette's general campaign manager) to breathe more life into the struggle were continually hampered by mismanagement and lack of coordination. Before the first month of the campaign was over Bob, Jr., despairingly remarked: "There are too many bosses in this organization."

More critical was the dearth of money. The task of financing the campaign was placed in the hands of a committee headed by Herman L. Ekern, attorney-general of Wisconsin. It began with the belief that millions of dollars would pour in from poor people to help Bob fight the predatory interests. But "poor people" make poor campaign contributors —a fact that La Follette fund raisers rapidly discovered. Soon they were begging for free advertising and scrabbling to scrape together a few hundred dollars here and there. Before the end of July campaign manager Nelson had to admit, "We are at present practically without funds."

Simultaneously, the disparate groups which supported La Follette made hash out of attempts at concerted action at the local level. Dilettantes, labor leaders, old Progressives, dissident farmers, radical militants, amateur politicians, all talked loudly for La Follette but went their separate ways. La Follette's earlier insistence on remaining independent and not founding a third party did not help. The effect was crippling. In early September, La Guardia wrote to Nelson at the Chicago headquarters, "I am so damned discouraged that only my interest and love for Senator La Follette keeps me going." Especially debilitating was the confusion over how to list La Follette on local ballots. Phil La Follette worked desperately on this problem and in the end La Follette-Wheeler electors were placed on the ballot in forty-seven states. But there was no uniformity. In some places they were listed as Socialist, in some as

Farmer-Labor, in others as Non-Partisan. Everywhere there was perplexity about the ticket's official designation.

By the close of the campaign the entire La Follette movement was playing into Republican hands. La Follette himself began to ignore Davis and, like Wheeler, concentrated on Coolidge and Dawes. By maintaining that every voter on Election Day would be "either in the Conservative Republican party, or in the Radical party of protest," La Follette gave support to Republican claims that the real contest lay between Coolidge and himself. In the process many moderate progressives began to lose some of their zeal. The executive council of the AF of L early decided to endorse La Follette. However, the decision was not unanimous and by the end of October many AF of L leaders were apologizing for it. Some labor leaders, like John L. Lewis and William Hutcheson, never supported him. Liberal churchmen like Harry Emerson Fosdick and Reinhold Niebuhr came out for him, but no major church journal did. While La Guardia backed the ticket throughout, other liberals, such as James G. Garfield, Frank Knox, Raymond Robins, Chester Rowell, and fifty other former 1912 Progressives declined to aid the La Follette campaign. Neither Senator Borah nor Senator Norris, La Follette's closest farm-bloc colleagues, gave him any assistance.

Such important holdouts were damaging to the La Follette drive and caused grave concern among La Follette supporters and campaign leaders. Yet almost to the end La Follette deluded himself about the extent of his voter appeal and the success of his movement. So did his sons. Phil consistently wrote Bob, Jr., glowing letters about pro-La Follette response while La Follette himself contended: "The reports from every part of the United States are encouraging beyond my best expectations." At the very end, though, there were creeping doubts and budding pessimism. Bob, Jr., especially, revealed in a few of his letters home that the presidential prize was probably going to elude them. Coolidge, he noticed belatedly, was "gaining strength every day."

6

"I am buried fathoms deep under letters and telegrams, and having no preliminary organization you can imagine my state of mind. . . . Pray for me." So wrote John W. Davis to a close friend immediately following his nomination. Davis needed divine aid. Despite the widespread praise for his selection and the claim that a new opportunity emerged from the Madison Square Garden chaos, Davis knew he faced a thankless task.

His first problem was to develop a staff and create a well-oiled campaign machine. Colonel House urged him to make appointments only after consulting with McAdoo, Walsh, W. J. Bryan, Ralston, Smith, and Underwood, in order to "soothe the sensibilities of the different factions." Others advised that he surround himself only with the best organizational politicians the party had to offer—men like Homer Cummings, Dan Roper, and Robert Woolley. But Davis had a deep sense of loyalty to those who had worked for his nomination, and when Cordell Hull indicated that he did not wish to continue either as campaign manager or as national chairman, Davis appointed Clem Shaver, the original Davis-for-President man, to take his place.

It was a poor choice. Shaver had felt that his task was over when Davis had been nominated, and he really did not want the job. A shy, odd sort of man, Shaver was quieter even than William Butler of the Republicans, and lacked his political acumen. Shaver liked to delve into Indian lore, to breed cattle, and fish more than engage in politics. He possessed few attributes of a leader and was totally lacking in aggressive qualities. To his West Virginia neighbors he was known as "Pussyfoot." Yet he had one basic trait that made him attractive to a presidential candidate who had a divided party behind him. As Roper said to Davis: "While [Shaver] is somewhat inarticulate and not as active or aggressive as you might wish, you won't have to lie awake nights worrying about sins of commission. You know he will be loyal."

Named to aid Shaver were a number of relative unknowns, among them Samuel B. Amidon of Kansas and Emily Newell Baker of Missouri. More important for plotting strategy were Walter Lippmann, Carl Vance, Lansing P. Reed, and Allen Wardwell. Of them all, Frank Polk remained Davis's shrewdest and most efficient adviser, but even his talent could not make up for the mediocrity elsewhere. In the end, the Davis high command was no match for its task. Senator Key Pittman once remarked in disgust, "From the chairman down most of them are incompetent and inexperienced."

As for general campaign organization, it was a disaster. Davis should have been especially sensitive to this problem because in 1920 he had written to friends that one of the prime reasons for Harding's landslide victory over Cox was a "superior organization." In 1924 Davis presided over one that was a shambles. The Democratic publicity bureau was always inexpertly manned even though Robert Lansing had specifically warned both Davis and Shaver that "without them [the media] behind you, victory is out of the question." Shaver did not even appoint a chairman for the finance committee until sometime after the campaign began. The three speakers' bureaus (in Washington, New York, and Chicago) were continually understaffed. By the last week in July there were complaints from all parts of the country that the organizing of the campaign was too sloppy and that Davis's prospects were being hurt as a result. Four weeks later, at the end of August, Joseph T. Davis, one of the managers of the Chicago headquarters, wrote to Polk: "The campaign work is moving very slowly and rather ineffectively. It seems to lack decisiveness, initiative, and proper cooperation." By September Shaver still had not been able to energize many local headquarters. Actually, in some areas the Davis campaign never got off the ground at all. As late as November 3, there were reports of "the complete breaking down of the national organization work" in numerous local districts. "The result," confided Colonel House to his diary just before the election, "is about the worst managed and most confused campaign that I have ever had any knowledge of."

Not all of this was Davis's or Shaver's fault. As Davis once complained, "Every time I'd reach out into the Eastern group, personalized by Al Smith, the McAdoo group would run away from me. Then, when I'd reach out and try to get the McAdoo group somewhere back in the corral, the Smith group would run away from me." It was true that after the debacle at Madison Square Garden almost all of McAdoo's supporters and a large number of Smith's followers went home and sat on their hands. Some of these gradually came around but not before valuable time was lost. Almost all of the favorite sons and their supporters aided Davis immediately. Governor Silzer, Governor Ritchie, Governor Davis, Senator Robinson, and Senator Underwood gave yeoman service to the Davis-Bryan ticket. Of them all, Governor Cox worked the hardest. Significantly, Senator Walsh never campaigned for Davis at all, nor did he work for his Montana senatorial colleague, Burton Wheeler.

Despite his intermittent confusion and doubt, W. J. Bryan also devoted considerable energy to the 1924 campaign. In the period from Labor Day to Election Day he gave almost a hundred speeches in fifteen western and southwestern states. In these areas Bryan support was important not because it brought votes to Davis, but because it kept waver-

ing voters from defecting to La Follette. However, there was little
contact between either one of the Bryans and Davis during the campaign.
Davis rarely consulted either W. J. or Brother Charley. He trusted the
motives of neither, especially W. J. He regarded the elder Bryan as an
exhorter rather than a logician and believed he belonged more in the
ministry or in the theater than in politics. The only man, said Davis, who
rivaled Bryan as a master of the mechanics of voice was Caruso. Still,
Davis needed W. J. Bryan and, although he kept aloof from him, he did
nothing to offend him either.

Though Davis was given little chance of making much of a showing in
the East, he came to rely most heavily on Al Smith and his followers.
Davis had a high regard for Smith and soon discovered that he could
work better with the Smith faction than with the Bryan-McAdoo element.
Of course, Davis's hope of carrying New York (which he needed to win)
depended directly on the cooperation of Smith. Smith gave it, though not
as vigorously as Davis would have liked. Smith stumped briefly for him
in New England in October but it was clear that Al was more concerned
with retaining Democratic control of New York State than with putting
Davis in the White House. Despite Smith's endorsement, some dissatis-
faction with Davis was always apparent in the East. On Election Day
numerous "Coolidge Democrats" appeared at the polls. Even on the sidewalks of New York City one could hear support for "Cal and Al." This
encouraged subsequent charges that Tammany sold out Davis as President in order to keep Smith as governor. Actually, many Democratic
voters in New York City split their tickets contrary to Tammany's wishes.
Conversely, some Republicans in the city, especially those with ethnic
attachments, voted locally for Smith but nationally for Coolidge.

McAdoo die-hards never came around to Davis. For these individuals,
McAdoo's political demise was, as one California supporter phrased it,
"like dropping an elevator 12 stories from in under them." They simply
did nothing during the campaign. They continued to feel betrayed and
retained their conspiratorial theories about unscrupulous eastern politicians. McAdoo also set a poor example. He remained extremely sensitive
about the 1924 convention in particular and Democratic political affairs
in general. Even before reaching Europe on his post-convention vacation
he was brooding deeply about the events that had made Davis the
Democratic nominee. All his shipboard and European letters to friends
were at once self-pitying and belligerent. His complaint was always the
same—a few crooked bosses, backed by the liquor interests, had trumped

up a fake religious issue and had thwarted the will of the party by rejecting him. Hence, while Rockwell ultimately moved behind Davis and even endorsed him as "the best candidate for the presidency that has been presented to the American electorate in my time," McAdoo remained apart.

The Californian did not return from Europe until the middle of September and then spent a short time in the Johns Hopkins Medical Center in Baltimore for minor surgery. On October 4 he wrote Davis that he regretted he had been unable to help him but hoped that after October 15 he could give him some aid. On October 18, however, he sent a letter to Senator Swanson of the speakers' bureau indicating that "for health reasons" he would not be able to participate in the campaign. In the end McAdoo did make three brief speeches for Davis—all from the rear platform of the train that was bearing him from the East Coast back to California. None of these addresses was effective. Davis, who privately blamed McAdoo for much of the Democratic party's troubles anyway, was not particularly surprised by such inactivity. But he was hurt. The Davis high command was extremely angry and let McAdoo know it. Defiant to the end, McAdoo later claimed, "If I had made a thousand speeches, it would not have altered the result," and he labeled such Davis disapproval as "a base exhibition of ingratitude."

Crippling as these matters were to his campaign, Davis himself represented a drawback. More gregarious and more affable than Coolidge, he still was not an extrovert or a "personality." He did not make good newspaper copy. Reporters, trying to encourage public interest in him after the convention was over, could turn up nothing novel. When quizzed about his early life by reporters, one of his former professors at Washington and Lee could only say, "John W. Davis was simply a normal young man."

What many Democrats hoped for in 1924 was a leader of the Wilson type who could inspire a splintered party. They expected too much from Davis. The same qualities that prevented the West Virginian from being better known to the public prior to his nomination now hampered him in the campaign. His moderate manner, his shyness, his humility, coupled with a certain diffidence, made the task harder. Like Coolidge he needed an image maker, but unlike Coolidge he did not have one. All agreed that Davis was a "gentleman" and would run a "gentleman's campaign." "What else can you expect from a man who owns twenty-three walking sticks and a pair of black satin knee breeches," commented one Republican sarcastically. Perhaps no candidate in history ever conducted a higher-minded drive than Davis—and few contenders have remained so far removed from intimate contact with the electorate. Davis was never able to play the ethnic game which was so important to Democrats in the East, and he was as totally out of place at a Nebraska farm rally as at a Jersey City bar mitzvah. Few in the public could really identify with him. No one would have dreamed of calling him "Jack."

And Davis was no orator. He never got a thrill out of speaking. He often remarked about "sweating blood" over his campaign speeches, which frequently contained words like "fustian" and "sedulous" and quotations from Samuel Johnson and Rudyard Kipling. Even his most partisan friends admitted that he needed more emotion, more warmth, and more common language in his talks. Claude Bowers once told Davis's advisers that "he must slug more and purr less if he is to make an impression on these times." But Davis consistently failed to do so. The net result was damaging. As the Chicago *Tribune* once reported during the campaign: "John W. Davis spoke here a few days ago. He used meticulous English but didn't hold the crowd. Senator Wheeler spoke here last evening. He murdered the King's English but got the crowd."

From the beginning the Davis campaign strategy was faulty. He first attempted to concentrate on economic issues like the tariff, Mellon's tax policies, and agricultural reform. The results of the congressional elections of 1922 caused him and his advisers to make this mistake; they did not realize voters were not interested in attacks on high tariffs and low taxes at a time of emerging national prosperity. Besides, it was quickly clear that Davis was not markedly different from Coolidge on most economic matters. Fearful of expanded governmental powers and deeply committed to the retention of private property, Davis offered no real alternatives. He would reduce the tariff somewhat, allow a broader tax base, and expand farm loans, but his whole philosophy rested on voluntary, cooperative, state, regional, and local resolution of most social and economic issues. Davis certainly offered no hope to those who wanted the inequalities of wealth readjusted by the policing power of the federal government.

Still, Davis attempted to convey that he was a liberal and to portray the Democratic party as "the progressive party of the country." In his acceptance speech in mid-August he used the words "I indict" or "I charge" eleven times. But the substance of that speech revealed no plan for clearly differentiating the Democrats from the Republicans. Then, as later in the campaign, he failed to make corruption the important issue that most Democrats hoped it would be. Instead, Davis treated Teapot Dome rather gingerly. Although he mentioned it in almost every speech, as the campaign wore on he alluded to it only obliquely. His problem was that Coolidge seemed untouchable on this matter. Much to the displeasure of his more militant supporters, on more than one occasion Davis was forced to say, "I make no charges against the honesty and integrity of the present occupant of the White House."

Doheny's February testimony concerning his financial arrangements with various famous Democrats was still having a deleterious effect on the fortunes of the Democratic party by the time of the campaign of 1924. However, it was mainly Davis's own association with Wall Street that caused him to downplay the scandals. To alleviate this problem, Davis resigned all his directorships at the start of the campaign and even cut his ties with Stetson, Jennings, Russell, and Davis. But it did not help. He continued to be attacked for his rich and presumably corruptible connections. His attempts to emphasize his humble beginnings and his West Virginia background rather than his recent New York past only caused snickers and encouraged jokes about his being a "poor little barefoot Wall Street lawyer."

On other issues Davis fared no better. Although he knew Europe and European problems, he failed to make foreign policy a matter of importance. The party had muddied the waters concerning the League to such an extent that Davis hardly knew where to begin on that question. Prohibition too was a problem. Although Davis was dry and believed in enforcement, he had never been keen on the amending process as a way of controlling manners and morals. The Constitution was too sacred to be demeaned by additions relating to drinking habits. As a result Davis often spoke of "home rule" as the proper solution. Thus he satisfied neither wets nor drys. The Republicans delighted in badgering him on this issue, and at almost every Republican rally signs appeared reading "Davis: Wet or Dry?" One writer characterized Davis on the prohibition question as "shifting uneasily from dry foot to wet foot and ending on his knees."

The Klan likewise proved to be bothersome. Pressure concerning the Klan issue quickly shifted from the Garden to the candidate himself. Davis's mail was saturated with opinions on what to do. Letters from northern non-Klan areas urged him to speak out on its dangers. Those from Klan-dominated midwestern and southern states begged him to remain silent. His close advisers cautioned him to choose his words very carefully on this subject. Finally at Sea Girt, New Jersey, on August 22, Davis condemned the Klan, but then after doing so, he worried about it. Following the speech he even contacted Bryan for his reaction, anxious to keep the South and the Klan-infected Midwest in line. Bryan replied that in view of New York and Middle Atlantic attitudes it had probably been necessary for him to say something, but he added pointedly, "Now that your position has been so emphatically stated, they [the public] will not expect you to divert attention from other issues by continuously mentioning it."

Thereafter Davis alluded to the Klan rarely and only in "safe" areas where it would not adversely affect his western and southern vote. In the end he was scarcely more forthright on the Klan issue than were the Republicans, making Coolidge's silence less glaring. The Klan, meanwhile, made matters easier for both the Republicans and the Democrats by singling out La Follette as its *bête noire*. On the very day that Davis made his Sea Girt speech, Imperial Wizard Evans asserted that La Follette was "the arch-enemy of the nation." In running against him, concluded Evans, both Coolidge and Davis were "aides of the Klan" and for that reason "the Klan will take no part in the political struggle as far as they are concerned."

Even in areas where the Democrats should have had an edge Davis was unable to deliver. The West Virginian, for example, remained anathema to organized labor because of his Wall Street associations even though labor grew increasingly restive with La Follette. The AF of L endorsement of La Follette naturally caused bitterness in Democratic ranks. The Davis high command believed that the AF of L had acted unfairly and too precipitately. Davis had tried unsuccessfully to meet with Samuel Gompers earlier in the summer to head off the La Follette endorsement but had failed to do so. The injured feelings on both sides did not diminish during the campaign.

The black vote was another missed opportunity for Davis. Aware of growing Negro disenchantment with the Republicans, Davis exhibited a sympathetic attitude even though the Democratic party platform ignored the black man completely. Prodded by northern urban politicians, he paid lip service to expanded rights for blacks when he addressed northern urban audiences. But Davis always had to protect his southern white flank and had to tread very cautiously. As a result, black organizations such as the NAACP denounced both major parties as basically insensitive to the needs of Negroes. The NAACP condemned the Democratic party for being controlled by racists and southern Bourbons, and the Republican party for going back on its many earlier promises. La Follette, in turn, gave so little attention to the black man that most Negroes and their organizations did not even consider him a factor.

In the final analysis, Davis's own running mate, Charles Bryan, was more of a liability than an asset. Although Bryan could, and did, speak the farmers' language, his value diminished as La Follette became a central issue and as many grew to fear a possible House decision on the presidency. The existence of Bryan on the ticket virtually precluded any Republican cross-over votes, which the Democrats in the Midwest and West badly needed. Further, it was difficult to know who was disliked and feared more in certain circles of the East—Charles Bryan or La Follette. Bryan's campaign rhetoric, like La Follette's, was reminiscent of a bygone day and betrayed a lack of knowledge of modern economic problems and modern business. Bryan spoke so constantly about the "predatory interests" and warned so against "all the favor-seeking, privilege-hunting corporations" that the Republicans could fire off rebuttals in any direction and hit either Bryan or La Follette. Dawes was especially successful in linking Bryan and La Follette together in the public mind as dual evils that had to be avoided at all costs.

As the campaign progressed, Davis himself concentrated more and more of his efforts on La Follette as if to prove that the Democrats, in spite of Bryan, were as conservative as the Republicans. La Follette, he said, would destroy the Constitution, upset the system of checks and balances, eliminate the power of the courts, and undermine the law. In making such attacks Davis came perilously close to becoming an open ally of his Republican opponents. By the beginning of October, Davis did begin to have some second thoughts about this vigorous assault on La Follette. Belatedly suspecting that he had fallen into a trap, he urgently asked a number of correspondents: "Do you think it good or bad policy for us to attack La Follette?" Some, like former Attorney General A. Mitchell Palmer, who had never quite recovered from the Red Scare of 1919–20, urged him to continue; others suggested caution. Davis was inclined for the remainder of the campaign to "leave La Follette and Dawes to fight it out with each other while I make an effort to debate the 'strong, silent man' in the White House." But Coolidge never gave him the chance. Besides, Davis's own visceral reaction to La Follette's heretical ideas on judges and the courts did not really allow him to relinquish this battle.

By early November, the Davis campaign resembled the ill-fated Davis-for-President blimp, which, suspended over the New York Polo Grounds in preparation for the Army–Notre Dame football game, exploded and fell, subsequently burning off thirty feet of the stadium roofing much to the anger of J. W. Coogan, the owner. The Democratic candidate continued to the last to feed the fear of a La Follette victory, and as a result, rather than prompting votes to fall away from the Progressive party, he caused them to fall away from his own. La Follette, by lumping his Republican and Democratic opponents together, made them appear alike as "two peas in a pod." This situation naturally redounded to the benefit of the GOP. Despite the Davis campaign, the real choice was between Coolidge and La Follette, as most observers claimed. Just before the election H. L. Mencken succinctly put it this way: "Dr. Coolidge is for the Haves and Dr. La Follette is for the Have Nots. But whom is Dr. Davis for? I'm sure I don't know, and neither does anyone else."

7

Just prior to Election Day there was a wide range of opinion concerning the outcome. Each of the participants and their supporters professed confidence and predicted victory. But among professional observers the only matters in doubt were the size of a Coolidge win and the relative strength of the Davis and La Follette votes. By the close of the campaign, New York bettors were offering odds of 10 to 1 on Coolidge and getting few takers. The final *Literary Digest* poll showed a 56.5 percent vote for Coolidge, 21.2 percent for Davis, and 21.3 for La Follette. *Current Opinion* commented that if the vote on November 4 showed a smashing victory for Coolidge, no one would be amazed; if it resulted in a drawn election requiring congressional action, there would be some surprise; and if it produced either a Davis or a La Follette victory, "the news will be received with well-nigh universal astonishment." William Allen White summed up the general feeling more simply: "In a fat and happy world, Coolidge is the man of the hour. Why tempt fate by opposing him?"

Not many did. When the polls closed, Coolidge had received

15,718,211 votes, Davis 8,385,283, and La Follette 4,831,470. The Prohibition party, Socialist-Labor party, and Communist party between them secured less than 130,000 votes. The electoral margin was 382 for Coolidge, 136 for Davis, and 13 for La Follette. Coolidge received 54 percent of the popular vote, Davis 28.8 percent, and La Follette 16.5 percent. Both houses of Congress went Republican. The new Senate was composed of 50 regular Republicans, 40 Democrats, 1 Farmer-Laborite, and 5 La Follette Republicans. In the House the Republican margin was even greater—232 regular Republicans, 183 Democrats, 2 Farmer-Laborites, 2 Socialists, and 15 La Follette Republicans.

Reaction was swift. Joyous Republicans naturally congratulated themselves. Horace D. Taft wrote to his famous brother, William Howard, that "the election is all that we could ask." Both Progressives and Democrats were chastened and downcast. Davis told one friend, "I was quite prepared, when the campaign closed, for an unfavorable result, although I confess, I did not appreciate the magnitude of the disaster that was impending." William Jennings Bryan admitted, "We have suffered a very severe defeat—much greater than I had any idea was possible." La Follette at first did not want to believe the returns and came to accept the verdict only gradually. He finally consoled himself that he had run as well as he did. The Democrats, in turn, ultimately took comfort in the thought that not only had La Follette been defeated but that he had come in a poor third.

A careful analysis of the outcome revealed some sobering yet interesting facts. Despite a nationwide campaign by all parties to "get out the vote," the contest had failed to attract to the polls more than 51 percent of the eligible voters. This was slightly better than the 49 percent who had marked their ballots in 1920, but it was far below the 70.5 percent who went to the polls in 1916. Moreover, despite the Nineteenth Amendment, only 35 percent of those who did vote were women. As for money, the Republicans spent $4,270,469 on the campaign, the Democrats $903,908, and the Progressives $221,977. This amounted to 27 cents per vote for the Republicans, 11 cents for the Democrats, and 4 cents for the Progressives. Ironically, the Democratic party attracted more large contributors than the Republicans, but far more Republicans than Democrats gave in the $1,000-to-$5,000 range. As usual, the Republican party ended the campaign with a surplus; the Democrats were in debt; the Progressives were bankrupt.

At the polls on Election Day Davis carried not a single state outside the South except for Oklahoma, and he failed in every border state except Tennessee. Significantly, the Davis-Bryan ticket lost in Nebraska (Bryan's home state), West Virginia (Davis's home state), and New York (Davis's adopted state). In the latter, Davis received only 950,796 votes, while his Republican opponent garnered almost double that number (1,820,058). In four states (California, North Dakota, Wisconsin, and Minnesota) Davis got less than 10 percent of the total vote—an unbelievably poor showing for a major candidate. Yet the overall performance of the Progressives was even worse. La Follette ran first only in Wisconsin and second only in California, Idaho, Iowa, Minnesota, Montana, Nevada, North Dakota, South Dakota, Oregon, Washington, and Wyoming. Elsewhere he was a distant third. In only one state, Wisconsin, did La Follette manage to get over 50 percent of the vote. Davis got more than 50 percent in eleven states and Coolidge more than 50 percent in twenty-two.

Although La Follette's 4.8-million popular votes were viewed by some pro-La Follette observers as a sign of the resurgence of pre–World War I progressivism, they were no such thing. Rather than being a positive indication of continued prewar liberalism, they were mainly a symptom of party confusion and voter discontent. Moreover, while Teddy Roosevelt's 4.1 million votes in 1912 represented 30 percent of the total votes cast, La Follette's 4.8 million in 1924 comprised less than 15 percent. La Follette's effect on the two major parties was not general, as would have been the case if his appeal had been universal, but instead was highly selective. The Democratic party was more injured by him on the Pacific Coast and in the mountain and Atlantic states; the Republicans were hurt most in the midwestern states and in New England. The best estimation of the composition of the La Follette vote was about one million Socialists or pro-socialists, about 2.5 million agrarians, and a little over one million eastern liberals and laborers. By any standards, La Follette's acceptance among both farmers and laborers was much less than expected.

The Klan, whose very existence had threatened the life of the Democratic party in 1924, seemed not to be a factor in the voting. Some Democrats expected that Davis's Sea Girt speech would hurt him where the Klan was strong. But no such development occurred. Davis lost no state because of Klan activity nor did Coolidge win one. In such a strong Klan state as Arkansas, for example, Davis got 87,743 votes to 40,036 for Coolidge, surpassing even Cox's majority in 1920. Similarly, Davis carried Oklahoma in an overwhelming victory and won Texas with six times

Coolidge's total. In 1920 Cox had not doubled Harding's vote in Texas. In 1924, all southern states that traditionally went Democratic still fell to Davis; all midwestern states that traditionally went Republican voted for Coolidge. In a few local areas the Klan did ride into power on the tail of the Coolidge landslide. Klan-endorsed governors were elected in Indiana, Colorado, and Kansas, but the Klan could not defeat Al Smith in New York or Senator Walsh in Montana. Nor did it bring about the downfall of numerous other anti-Klansmen. Texas, for example, elected a female anti-Klan governor.

As for the real reasons for the Coolidge victory and the staggering Progressive and Democratic defeat, La Follette followers could not reach any conclusion and remained confused and disoriented. The Democrats offered all sorts of suggestions. The main reason for their own debacle, some Democrats said, was "the terrible weight" of Charles Bryan on the party ticket. William Jennings Bryan charged that the "eastern money power" plus "the treachery of Tammany" had wrought this defeat. Easterners asserted that the Democratic ticket had been stabbed in the back by the "slackers and deserters" in the West. The fact that Davis had received less than 10 percent of the presidential ballots cast in California, McAdoo's home state, was taken as proof of this. Others pointed an accusing finger at Davis, deploring his style of campaigning, or at Clem Shaver, condemning his loose campaign management and inefficiency. Clem Shaver claimed that the major reason was "money, money, money." The Democrats had not had enough, said Shaver, otherwise Davis would have won. In a flight from reality, Shaver asserted to W. J. Bryan three days after the election, "The country did not want Coolidge, does not want him now."

Less partisan observers believed that a complex and interrelated combination of factors—returning prosperity, the prohibition vote, Coolidge's "safe" personality, fear of La Follette "radicalism," failure of the corruption issue, and rising agricultural prices in the farm areas—had wrought La Follette's and Davis's defeat. And on one further fact *all* observers agreed—Madison Square Garden had been too heavy a burden for the Democratic party to carry. If the election of 1924 had provided the knockout blow, the Democratic party was already on its knees as a result of that convention. It had cast a pall over all that followed and helped seal the party's fate. Davis freely admitted it. So did Senator Walsh and Cordell Hull. Under any circumstances and with any candidate, the Democrats might have lost to Coolidge anyway. But, as H. L. Mencken said, the Democratic party in the hot New York summer of 1924 had gradually gone insane and then tried to commit suicide by naming Davis as its nominee. Arthur Krock summed it up this way: "When the debris began to fall, somebody looked underneath the pile and dragged out John W. Davis, who then showed that he was not in his right mind by extricating Charles W. Bryan. And Davis confirmed the fact that he was a gassed casual by putting his hand and that of Bryan's into the warm and honest, but weak and faltering, clasp of Clem L. Shaver and, with the bland smile of a Chinese angel, went forth among the electorate for incredible slaughter." It was true. Not even the most partisan Democrat could deny it.

PART VI

★

REMATCH

1

"Business seems to be in the saddle," said *Harper's* in early 1925. "Let us see what it can make of the job." This was perhaps the most significant result of the election decision of 1924. In the midst of the turmoil of social, cultural, religious, ethnic, and demographic changes, a business civilization emerged triumphant. As both major parties demonstrated an inability to adjust to—sometimes, even an unwillingness to discuss—these other matters, national economic concerns acquired precedence.

Already identified with the middle and upper-middle classes, and pursuing policies which were beneficial to the business-oriented North, the Republican party was the logical custodian of the ensuing business boom. Calvin Coolidge, now President in his own right, nursed this development along by continuing the Harding normalcy policies. In view of the 1924 election he could take such action without fear either of much internal opposition in his own party or serious opposition from the outside. After all, both the pro-Coolidge vote and the pro-Davis vote had represented basically an endorsement of the status quo and, as Robert Lansing analyzed it, a condemnation of "the tendency of the past decade toward novel theories of government."

The trend was apparent at once. After 1925 Coolidge, more than Harding before him, packed regulatory boards and agencies with economic conservatives and pro-business men. McAdoo had earlier prophesied that, given a chance, Coolidge would prove to be "a more useful servitor of the interests than Harding was." Indeed, the *Wall Street Journal* was foremost among the joyful when Coolidge was elected in 1924. Coolidge's lackluster message to Congress in December, 1924, was highly praised in business circles precisely because it recommended no substantive changes and merely reaffirmed what had already been done. "It isn't essential that we should have a great amount of legislation," wrote Justice Taft approvingly to Elihu Root. "What we need is stability and not movement at the present time."

Political inactivity now permitted a new breed of bureaucratic and political managerial talent to take hold. Such famous GOP professional politicians as Harding, Knox, and Penrose had recently died. Before the year 1925 was out, Lodge would follow. Already stepping into their places were men like Stearns, Butler—and Hoover. Herbert Hoover, in particular, became the spokesman for the new emerging business age. Secretary of Commerce and, as one critic said, "assistant secretary of everything else," he popularized not only business prosperity but also the need for business responsibility. His own successful career had not been built on the ruthless individualism of a savage economic past, but on the humanitarian-oriented individualism of a cooperative economic system in which all could share. With his ideas of welfare capitalism and business-labor partnership, Hoover now strove to transform the anti-corporation thrust of the old Wilsonian progressivism into a "modern progressivism" of business expansion and scientific efficiency. Along with numerous others he believed that capitalism could transcend mere materialism and become socially-oriented and even spiritual. Not merely by coincidence did advertising executive Bruce Barton's best-selling *The Man Nobody Knows,* which portrayed Christ as the world's foremost salesman-businessman, find a receptive audience when it first appeared in 1925. Such a positive economic "faith" was already permeating the churches, the courts, the colleges, the press, and even intellectual circles. By late 1925 *Nation's Business,* the organ of the United States Chamber of Commerce, could truthfully report that the businessman had become "the most influential person in the nation." Similarly, the *Wall Street Journal* could confidently claim, "Never before, here or anywhere else, has a government been so completely fused with business."

Though difficulties concerning religious intolerance, the political allegiance of blacks, prohibition, labor inequities, and so on continued to plague various sections of the country, especially the urban communities, the nation as a whole cheerfully made way for the business-dominated "wonderful nonsense" of the ensuing period, with its ticker-tape parades, famous murder trials, flagpole sitting, and bunion derbies. In this race for notoriety, pleasure, and quick riches Wall Street became the chief listening post for much of American society. Trading and feverish activity at the lower tip of Manhattan indeed became one of the country's major concerns. As long as this continued, the Republicans could not only ignore most of the unresolved social, cultural, and moral problems of the day but appear statesmanlike in doing so.

There is little doubt that some of the driving force which might have been directed toward reform and increased political activity in the post-1924 period was siphoned off in profit making and economic action. The new capitalism first bred and then fed a spreading political indifference. It was a dispirited Republican insurgent and Democratic minority, for example, that returned to the Capitol for the short congressional session in December, 1924. No business came before that session except for the annual appropriation bills. This marked the beginning of congressional doldrums which extended into the succeeding years. This is not to say that Congress lapsed into complete inactivity. Numerous solons, like Fiorello La Guardia, continued to keep a wary eye on the White House, and dissident farm elements, led by Senator Norris, continued to disrupt Republican party harmony by attacking the administration on public power and general farm policy. But even La Guardia found it expedient to resume using the "Republican" label during the period, and Senator Norris, despite his restlessness, never bolted the party. Inevitably, the power and influence of the farm bloc declined. Most Republican congressmen were content for the moment to savor their party's national success. Meanwhile, internal problems in the Democratic party kept it occupied as well as impotent. As for radical change, it was simply out of the question. As La Guardia said, "I tell you, it's damned discouraging to be a reformer in the wealthiest land in the world."

2

Reformers of the progressive type were a particularly sorry lot after 1925. Symptomatic of this was the rapid demise of the La Follette movement. Springing from agrarian discontent and nursed by La Follette's ambitions for the presidency, this crusade was supposedly designed to remedy the defects in the American economic and political system as a whole. But it was not only singularly unsuccessful, it was remarkably impermanent. Few reform coalitions have collapsed so quickly. As the *New York Times* said about the La Follette drive when the 1924 returns were announced, "Instead of committing murder, it has committed suicide." Indeed, the Socialists disengaged from the La Follette movement immediately following the election. They were so weakened by the 1924 struggle that when they held their first post-election convention in Chicago in early 1925 only forty-five delegates were present. Eugene Debs set the tone of even this small gathering by condemning La Follette. Similarly, with only one negative vote, the AF of L's executive council immediately after the election returned to its traditional nonaligned policy. The council agreed that its 1924 experiment had been a mistake. When Samuel Gompers died in 1925, his position as head of the AF of L went to William Green, who in many ways symbolized organized labor during the remainder of the decade. A placid, colorless man who belonged to both the Elks and the Odd Fellows, Green wore rimless glasses, a large gold watch chain in his vest, and a diamond ring on his finger. Here was no shaker of America's political and economic foundations.

When the CPPA held its post-election convention in February, 1925, the handwriting was already on the wall, though some progressives wanted to ignore it. *The Nation,* a strong supporter of the La Follette effort, continued to claim that his campaign had been "a magnificent achievement," while John Nelson, acting as a caretaker chairman for the CPPA, tried to raise funds for a continuation of the fight. He failed. In the end, the CPPA had no choice but to justify its prior existence in a series of resolutions and then order itself dissolved. Meanwhile, La Follette Republicans elected to Congress in 1924 made big talk but soon lost choice committee assignments, suffered from patronage discrimination, and were shunned like pariahs.

La Follette militants quickly discovered that the senator's erstwhile followers in the general public were among the most mercurial elements in the electorate. Following the election they rapidly disappeared. La Follette had built no solid foundation for continued public interest nor had he left a cohesive political program for it to support. The Wisconsin senator's revivalistic reform rhetoric had imparted a temporary sense of unity to his movement, but it had not resolved its many internal differences. For the long haul, there was really nothing to hold his supporters together, and many jumped ship as soon as the election was over. Burton Wheeler, for example, immediately returned to the Democratic party.

Interestingly, some La Follette supporters shortly came to believe that Herbert Hoover, not La Follette, was the prophet of the future and gradually converted to Hoover's new capitalism. Hoover's brand of "progressive individualism," which rested not on the mere acquisition of property but upon cooperation and public service, fitted many urban liberals far better than La Follette's ancient rhetoric. Further, Hoover's emphasis on the elimination of waste and on the application of engineering methods to the solution of human problems appealed to the intellectual segment of the progressives that worshiped science and efficiency as the guiding principles for modern reform.

As for La Follette, the end was tragic. He never perceived that he had made a poor candidate in 1924 or that by looking backward he had hindered the forces of liberalism from addressing the newer and more pressing social and cultural problems of modern American society. After the election he proclaimed that he had "just begun to fight," and he was at his Senate desk at the opening of Congress in December, 1924, with plans for new assaults on "monopoly." Naturally the Republicans ignored him. But so did the Democrats. Now, more than ever, he was alone. He admitted in his diary that these were difficult days for him but he tried not to give "any outward evidence of the taste in my mouth." Meanwhile, his health grew rapidly worse. He was forced to spend part of January and February in the sun in Florida. He returned to Washington in March, only slightly improved. In May his doctor ordered him to bed, and he never left it. His diary entries during this period were heartrending, often beginning with "Very bad night last night," "Feeling weak," or "Off my feed." On June 18, 1925, he suffered a fatal heart attack. At his bedside stood Belle, Bob Jr., and Phil, who had shared in his career and were supportive to the end.

La Follette's demise merely set the tombstone of the 1924 progressive movement in place. It had already died. Actually, the "progressivism" identified with prewar America and with Teddy Roosevelt and Wilson had never survived into the twenties as a viable political alternative. The rapid emergence of an urban society, the requirements of being a world power, and the organization necessary for fighting a world war had killed it. Many historians later claimed to see a direct linear connection between the Populists, the Bull Moosers, the Wilsonians, the La Follette movement, and the subsequent New Deal, but in reality, the La Follette movement of 1924 was too brief, diverse, random, and undisciplined to be a continuity of anything. Progressive reaction and disunity in 1924 emphasized the heterogeneity, not the homogeneity, of postwar political thinking, and underscored the progressives' lack of a program, not their possession of one. In some respects, La Follette was less of a New Dealer than Hoover, more of a conservative than Al Smith. By 1924 progressivism had come to mean all things to all people, or, to put it another way, had come to mean nothing much at all.

The main problem lay with the so-called liberals themselves. They, above all others, were confused and disoriented. Walter Lippmann consistently lamented that by the mid-twenties such terms as "progressive" and "conservative" had become meaningless because liberals had been unable to find their way or redefine their position after the war. Lincoln Steffens, returning in 1924 for a visit to the United States from his self-imposed exile on the Italian Riviera, made the curious comment that Henry Ford was a new kind of "reformer without politics . . . a radical." Such confusion in terms, perpetuated largely by the liberals themselves, was debilitating. As Donald Richberg, a Bull Mooser who supported La Follette in 1924, said: "Throughout this period, the progressive forces in American political life had only the vaguest ideas of where they were going."

That was true. Some former progressives like William Allen White ultimately made their peace with the business culture and consistently supported the Republicans. Some, like Newton Baker, continued with the Democratic party. Some, like John Dos Passos, fled into the ranks of the socialists or moved even farther to the left. Others, like Carl Becker and Reinhold Niebuhr, opted out entirely, being completely disillusioned with American politics. Many simply proceeded to function as independent voters having no particular political home and waiting for a new mission. Correctly sensing this fantastic splintering, Donald Richberg ruefully admitted in 1929, "Few indeed are the progressives of my generation who have survived the bludgeoning of these years." The La Follette episode of 1924 certainly had not helped.

3

The aftermath of 1924 affected the Democrats unevenly. For McAdoo and some of his followers it meant a continued distaste for politics. Bernard Baruch vowed that he would never again participate in a nominating battle. "As far as politics is concerned," he wrote McAdoo shortly after the election, "I don't even let anybody come into my office and talk about it to me." Numerous former Wilsonians, such as A. Mitchell Palmer and Colonel House, had lost the political zeal of their youth and were now resigned to enjoying the benefits of Republican economic affluence. McAdoo returned to California and plunged into money making, generally ignoring political matters. "I am buckling down to business again with the curse of politics off me," he wrote Tom Chadbourne. Still bitter over his treatment in 1924, McAdoo's letters were filled with "I told you so's" and barbs about harvesting the seeds of destruction sown at the Madison Square Garden convention. As for the future, McAdoo remained, temporarily at least, uncooperative. To Chadbourne he wrote: "I am having a lot of letters asking my advice as to what ought to be done for the Party, but I have said nothing thus far and maybe I shall say nothing at all."

Davis, the titular leader of the party, and his friends, were scarcely more active. Some, like Frank Polk, believed that Davis had been betrayed by both East and West and they felt little incentive to aid the party. Shaver compounded his earlier error of accepting the job as national chairman by remaining in that post for the next four years. During that time the organized activity of the party fell to its lowest point ever. Davis continued to be praised as a man, although not always as a candidate. His whole performance had lifted the level of American politics, claimed *World's Work*, and Robert Lansing consoled him by saying, "You did more than any other Democrat could have done." After the election, however, Davis exercised no more aggressive leadership than he had during the campaign. Immediately following his defeat he sailed for an extended holiday abroad and then resumed his lucrative Wall Street practice. He never returned to public life, made only an occasional political speech, and contented himself with writing on legal and constitutional subjects. He consistently hoped that he would be appointed to the Supreme Court, but this was not to be. Wealth and legal prestige were his sole rewards.

By 1925 only Al Smith remained as a focal point for a possible Democratic resurgence. He alone continued in the national political spotlight. After his rejection by the Madison Square Garden convention, Smith had reluctantly given in to pleas by Davis that he run again as chief executive of the Empire State, and he vindicated that decision by running almost a million votes ahead of the Democratic presidential ticket. In defeating his Republican adversary, Theodore Roosevelt, Jr., Smith became the first New York governor in a hundred years to hold the governorship three times. Demolishing his opponent with such quips as "If bunk was electricity, young Roosevelt would be a powerhouse," Smith emerged an even bigger political figure than before. In view of the fact that the Republicans captured both houses of the New York legislature and even elected a Republican lieutenant-governor, Smith seemed to be, as one Democratic leader called him, "the eighth wonder of the world."

This showing clearly kept alive Smith's hopes for a presidential nomination someday, but it also further dampened the enthusiasm of many anti-Smith elements to work for a revitalization of the party. East Coast newspapers claimed persistently that Smith could "revive the spirit of the national party for future national victory," but southern and western newspapers remained ominously silent. They believed Smith's gubernatorial success in New York was wholly personal and contained the same cultural, ethnic, and religious ingredients that had proved to be so indigestible at the party's convention in 1924. Demolition squads might raze old Madison Square Garden to the ground, but that did not eradicate the political divisions which had surfaced there. As for Smith as the Democrats' "man of destiny," Walter Lippmann prophesied in early 1925: "One cannot say that the new urban civilization which is pushing Al Smith forward into national affairs is better or worse than that older American civilization of town and country which dreads and will resist him. [But] it seems to be the fate of this genial man to deepen that conflict and to hasten it, and to make us face the conflict sooner than we are ready."

Apart from the question of who could, or would, revitalize the Democratic party, two facts were obvious: its future was bleak and its leadership was up for grabs. Composed of militant, ultra-conservative southerners; Catholic foreign-born, working-class northeasterners; and disgruntled, nativistic western farmers, the party by early 1925 appeared to be disintegrating. Most contemporary pundits agreed that such a schizoid organization had no prospects for success. It was pointed out that in the twentieth century it had never polled as much as 50 percent in a presidential vote. From 1896 to 1924 the Republican party had consistently remained the majority party, averaging 53 percent, while the Democrats averaged only 41 percent. Both of its post–Civil War Presidents (Cleveland and Wilson) had been minority victors and had sneaked into office only because the Republicans at the moment were disunified. Most of the time it was the Democrats who were disorganized, and a Democratic nomination gained at the cost of continual splits within the party was rarely worth it. Little wonder that Clem Shaver, viewing the Democratic organization at the beginning of 1925, could only shake his head and moan, "I am appalled at the state of the Democrats of the country."

Still, bad as things were, there was some reason for hope. Despite its defects, the Democratic party remained the only national party with sizable support in all parts of the country. Further, it was the only party that contained a true cross-section of all the various ethnic, social, cultural, and economic pressure groups in American society. To many it still seemed to be the only agent capable of representing the entire electorate, and for that reason alone, according to John Davis, "its integrity and vitality must be safeguarded and preserved."

Local election results in 1924 illustrated that the Democratic party continued to be much stronger in its parts than as a whole. Considering the magnitude of the Coolidge landslide, the Republican showing in congressional races was not spectacular. Moreover, a careful analysis of the local vote in many sections of the country indicated that the Republicans were actually receding from their peak year of 1920. In industrial and ethnic-centered areas Coolidge did not do as well as Harding had four years earlier. Republican percentages dropped in Massachusetts, New Jersey, New York, and Rhode Island, and Democratic percentages increased in still other regions such as Michigan, Connecticut, and Illinois. This trend was especially evident in big-city voting. In 1920 all but three of twelve major cities produced Republican pluralities. In 1924 there was a decrease in Republican pluralities in seven of the twelve. Significantly, Davis carried 183 more counties in 1924 than Cox had in 1920 while Coolidge carried 377 fewer than Harding. More important, local trends in northern cities showed the Negro vote was slowly moving toward the local Democratic machine, despite the handicap of the Klan. In New York City, for example, Cox had received only 3 percent of the black vote in 1920, but in 1924 Davis received over 25 percent, an unprecedented showing for a Democratic presidential candidate.

What the Democratic party obviously needed was a plan of unity which would minimize its national divisions while capitalizing on its local strengths. Davis was the first to admit that the party could never again become a national power unless it stopped its internal bickering. Robert Lansing claimed that the party had to "unite on principles and not expedient issues simply to get votes in one place only to lose them elsewhere." But McAdoo, suddenly lifting his self-imposed ban on giving advice, stated: "The Democratic Party has a cancer in its head [Tammany] and cancer in its stomach [the Brennan Illinois machine]. We have got to perform a major operation and get rid of these cancers before we can ever make anything out of the Democratic Party." Bryan, meanwhile, claimed that to become truly "progressive," the party had to effect "a union between the producers of the South and West against the predatory corporations that dominate the politics of the Northeast. In 1916 we won without the aid of the East," concluded Bryan, "and we must win without its aid in 1928." Naturally, views as partisan as those of McAdoo and Bryan were hardly capable of bringing to the party the peace that Davis envisioned or of spawning the new principles that Lansing advocated. Battle-scarred and militant veterans like Bryan and McAdoo were simply not suited to act as innovators or adjudicators. Indeed, none of the party's most famous leaders, including Smith, seemed able or willing to play either role.

Into this vacuum stepped Franklin Roosevelt and his personal assistant, Louis Howe. Howe had been a political reporter in Albany when Roosevelt had first appeared there in 1910 as a freshman legislator. He had originally sized up Roosevelt as "a spoiled silk-pants sort of guy" but changed his mind when Roosevelt, by opposing Tammany, had demonstrated that he could be his own man. Thereafter Howe attached himself to Roosevelt, became his private secretary, ran his political campaigns, and lived at the Hyde Park homestead as one of the Roosevelt family. An odd-looking little man, Howe was barely five feet five inches tall, weighed no more than one hundred pounds, suffered from bad health, smoked incessantly, and was usually seen with uncombed hair and cigarette ashes all over his clothes. This unkempt appearance, however, masked a shrewd political mind. Dedicated to making Roosevelt President someday, Howe now urged him to take the lead in the quest for Democratic party unity.

Roosevelt was in an enviable position to do so. His moderate role at the Madison Square Garden convention had won him friends even among McAdooites while at the same time preserving the respect and loyalty of Smith supporters. These latter had been particularly pleased at the manner in which Roosevelt had stuck by their man. After the convention closed, Roosevelt had returned to Hyde Park in the hope of continuing his rehabilitation from the effects of polio and vowed to remain out of politics for the time being. He therefore had played little part in the Davis campaign, making only one radio speech. Davis was basically too conservative for Roosevelt's tastes anyhow. But Roosevelt found it impossible to remain aloof from Empire State politics, and helped Smith against Theodore Roosevelt, Jr. Howe and Roosevelt's wife, Eleanor, had created a minor sensation by following the embarrassed Republican candidate around the state in a car topped by a gigantic teapot—a visible reminder of Teapot Dome.

While delighted at the election of Smith as governor, Roosevelt was worried by the 1924 Democratic presidential defeat and was, like others, fearful about the party's future. He early indicated that he would lend his support to any plan which would reverse the situation. He hoped that the initiative would come from Shaver. The key to any party revitalization, he believed, would have to begin with the national chairman and central party headquarters. Only in that way could the party properly proceed to rediscover "a truly progressive program."

In December, 1924, after observing no movement at all at national headquarters, and prodded by Howe to do something himself, Roosevelt sent a circular letter to all former delegates of the Madison Square Garden convention, urging them to review Democratic party needs and send suggestions to him. The exact wording of this letter, which had as its key sentence "Only by uniting can we win," was a ticklish business. Roosevelt did not want to hurt Shaver's feelings or make it appear that he was trying to "take over" the party. Even so, his action caused some resentment. Shaver saw it as implied criticism, and several other leaders also regarded it as such. Cordell Hull even felt constrained to defend his past actions in letters to friends, but to one he frankly admitted that "there is always room for improvement in our party work."

As for the replies to Roosevelt's letter, they ranged all over the lot. Plenty of scapegoats for the party's desperate situation were found: the bosses, Negroes, Bryan, McAdoo, Smith, the "radicals," Wall Street, self-seekers, the North, the South. As for solutions, they were mixed: Bryanism was a dead weight which had to be eliminated; a "new" party had to be built in the West; organizational continuity had to be established between campaigns; more money needed to be raised; the political differences between the various wings of the party had to be compromised; a "liberal" program must be constructed; the ethnic American had to be taken more carefully into account; better publicity was required; religion should be shunned as a political factor; the liquor question had to be defused as a national issue; organized labor must receive more attention; and a "compromise candidate" had to be found who would appeal to all sections and to all types of Democrats.

This remarkable cross-section of political attitudes and responses suddenly made Roosevelt the most knowledgeable man in the country about

Democratic party problems. Acting openly now as a party harmonizer, Roosevelt in early 1925 sounded out Cordell Hull and Senator Thomas Walsh about the feasibility of convening a national conference of party leaders to consider the replies to his December letter. Simultaneously Howe tried to sell the conference idea to John Davis. Roosevelt also wrote a letter to Clem Shaver suggesting that Walsh be named the chairman of such a conference and that he call it into session for the spring. To forestall injured feelings similar to those that had resulted from his circular letter, Roosevelt inserted a blunt disclaimer: "I don't need to assure you, my dear [Shaver], that there is no ulterior motive in this letter of mine, nor do I represent any candidate or any group."

In the end the Roosevelt-Howe conference proposal fizzled. Although leaders like Hull, Walsh, Meredith, and Robinson ultimately supported the idea, others opposed it. Already confident of his front-running position for 1928 and currently receiving pledges of almost unlimited financial support from some of his New York friends, Smith gave it scant attention. Most southerners, westerners, and former McAdoo men were uneasy about the suggestion and suspicious of Roosevelt's motives. Even Shaver remained wary of "New York interests" inserting themselves into party affairs in this way. Baruch was lukewarm toward the plan. Davis also doubted its value, fearing it might revive the Madison Square Garden fight. Bryan was adamantly opposed, convinced that any attempt to integrate eastern urban Democrats into a "progressive" party was doomed to failure.

As an educational and formative experience for Roosevelt's subsequent career, this ill-fated attempt at party reorganization was invaluable. Despite the setback, he continued after 1925 to talk of the need for party unity and agreement on liberal principles. With Howe's help, he continued to send out from Hyde Park appeals for harmony and pleas for a re-creation of a "progressive program." Never did Roosevelt spell out what such a program should contain, nor did he offer any concrete proposals; but through such propaganda he remained identified with a better party stance and a moderate reasonableness. Precisely what Roosevelt may have had in mind during this period is not known. But Howe's thinking represented no mystery. At all times he worked incessantly and successfully to enhance the Roosevelt name and image.

4

A "unity" conference in 1925 probably would not have been successful because of its proximity to the divisive Madison Square Garden convention of 1924. By 1926–27 the urgency for such a conference largely disappeared since the party again staged a comeback in local and state areas. The Democratic vote cast for representatives and senators in 1926 far exceeded that cast for the party's presidential nominee in 1924. More important, the number of Democrats holding elective offices markedly increased while the number of Republicans declined. By the end of 1926 the Democrats held 22 out of 48 governorships. Forty-seven of the ninety-six senators were Democrats. As a result of the congressional elections of 1926, the large Republican majority in the House was cut to twenty-four.

Further, by late 1926, the Smith faction had become more opposed to holding a unity conference than the McAdooites. In 1926 Al was re-elected governor of New York for a phenomenal fourth term. In a Republican-dominated era, no Democrat now enjoyed the national visibility or possessed the vote-getting reputation of Smith. As a result, his nomination for the presidency in 1928 became almost a foregone conclusion. Indeed, the trend to Smith was so dramatic that by the spring of 1927 his advisers were cautioning him not to let the enthusiasm of his supporters go too far or dangerous resentment would arise.

Smith was clearly in no mood to be humble. With the shoe now on the other foot, he began to talk about the need for changing the procedures for nomination, especially the elimination of the two-thirds rule. He also encouraged the belief that another fight such as the one in Madison Square Garden would kill the party and warned his former opponents not to take up a crusade against him. Late in 1927 McAdoo materially aided the Smith cause by announcing that "in the interests of party unity" he would not seek the nomination. Just six days later, Democratic leaders from eight mountain and Pacific Coast states, all of whom had supported McAdoo in 1924, met in Ogden, Utah, and reluctantly endorsed Smith as "the only available candidate." Meanwhile, moderate southern leaders, such as Cordell Hull and Josephus Daniels, openly acknowledged that Smith could not be denied the nomination. Back in New York both

Baruch and Chadbourne came out for Smith. Significantly, John W. Davis early declared as a Smith delegate.

The 1928 Democratic convention was therefore anticlimactic. Called to order on Tuesday, June 26, in Houston, Texas, it adopted a platform, nominated Smith as President and Senator Robinson as Vice-President, and completed all its tasks in three days. The Houston town fathers were dismayed because in making their bid for the gathering they had counted on at least a six-day convention to bring the city out of the red. Certainly this was no repeat of Madison Square Garden. Indeed, the former happening in New York in 1924 hung like a sword over everyone's head. Most Democrats felt that a failure to reach a quick decision at Houston would again throw the party into chaos. The watchword was "Remember the Garden." Claude Bowers, the scholar Democrat, used this as his point of departure in his keynote address, urging moderation and selecting his words carefully so they would soothe. No one, regardless of the intensity of his feelings, showed any inclination to repeat the Garden's mistakes. Perhaps under any circumstances Smith would have won the nomination in 1928. But surely he would not have won it so easily without "that horrible experience" as a backdrop. Not only Smith's opponents, but the Smith forces themselves demonstrated that they had learned from the past. Roosevelt again gave the nominating speech for Smith, but there the similarity between the two conventions stopped. From the outset the Smith drive was orchestrated in a low key. This time Smith wisely stayed away from the convention and remained at work in Albany. At Houston there were no Tammany steamroller tactics, no shouting galleries. Smith men were constantly kept under wraps. No cases of liquor were unloaded from the train that took the New York delegation to Houston. The millions of Americans who tuned in their superheterodyne sets in 1928 hoping to hear some more fun were gravely disappointed. So were some Tammanyites, one of whom, fondly remembering the excitement of the Garden, claimed this gathering "was the longest wake any Irishman ever attended."

There was intense feeling at Houston nevertheless. It was simply not allowed to show. At the end of the first ballot, when Smith was only ten votes shy of a two-thirds majority and Ohio switched to put him over the top, no attempt was made to make the selection unanimous. Anti-Smith holdouts continued to exist in all sections of the South and West, and Smith got no votes at all from South Carolina, Georgia, Florida, and Texas. Even the naming of a dry Arkansas Protestant as Smith's running mate did not placate opposition sentiment. This anti-Smith element watched the New York governor's nomination in anguish and accepted him only by default. The Madison Square Garden struggle of four years before may have decimated the anti-Smith ranks, and Bryan's sudden death in 1925 together with McAdoo's disclaimer in 1927 may have left them leaderless and disorganized. But bitterness, fear, and frustration were still at work. Bishop Cannon, for example, reviewing the work of the Houston convention for his followers, bemoaned the fact that party control had at last fallen to men from "the foreign-populated city called New York." He promised, however, that "no subject of the Pope" would ever enter the White House.

Al Smith had won his party's nomination but he had not won his party. Commentators then, and historians and political scientists later, liked to point out that Smith's nomination in 1928 "fully admitted the newer peoples of the cities to America" and at last gave them "access to power and honours." It was, said one writer, the "first hurrah" of a new political era. Maybe so. But this cannot mask the fact that Smith in 1928 was still no more of a national leader and possessed no more universal appeal than McAdoo. Significantly, those silent anti-Smith elements which exercised restraint at Houston for fear of another Garden brouhaha, returned to their local communities, where they dropped any pretense of accepting Smith and acted accordingly.

From the outset of the presidential campaign Smith was burdened with difficulties. Some were of his own making and some were not. His first mistake was not to bend every effort to woo and disarm western and southern dissident sentiment. Regardless of all his efforts, he might have failed anyway, but there was certainly no reason to antagonize them further. Rather than continuing to rely on Roosevelt and other party moderates, Smith turned increasingly to his own coterie of New York confidants and financial backers for campaign organization and guidance. For example, he appointed John J. Raskob as chairman of the national committee to take Shaver's place. Raskob was a devout Catholic, the son of an Alsatian father and an Irish mother, and, like Smith, a self-made man. A super-salesman and an early investor in William C. Durant's auto empire, Raskob later became prominent in General Motors. He was a supporter of Coolidge in 1924 but had become alarmed by the anti-Catholic activities of the Klan and in 1928 he turned to Smith. Raskob was wringing wet, had no political finesse or experience, and desired few social or economic changes. Smith appointed him because he liked him and because he thought Raskob might help neutralize Republican north-eastern business influence. Raskob believed that the Democrats, even with the urban vote, could not win without big-business support. To assist him in wooing business backing, Raskob enlisted the aid of a num-ber of millionaires: James W. Gerard, Herbert H. Lehman, Jesse Jones, Peter G. Gerry, and William F. Kenny. Raskob, Lehman, and Kenny each contributed more than $100,000 to the Smith campaign.

The appointment of Raskob unquestionably helped keep open the wounds of 1924. So did the continued presence around Smith of such partisan advisers as Belle Moskowitz, Judge Proskauer, and Robert Moses. The Bryan-McAdoo wing was especially incensed by this blatant display of eastern and New York control. But, to some extent, all Demo-crats were put off. Roosevelt thought Smith's action in not securing a more representative staff was a grave mistake which might "perma-nently drive away a host of people in the south and west." As Roosevelt predicted, many of these—who needed few excuses anyway—now simply ignored the Smith campaign and refused to work. Daniel Roper snubbed the Smith ticket and gave it no help whatsoever. Hull, a dry southerner, found it impossible to stomach Raskob and provided Smith with only nominal aid. To show his distaste for the whole situation, Senator Owen of Oklahoma switched his support to the Republican can-didate, Herbert Hoover.

McAdoo continued to serve as the focal point for much anti-Smith discontent even though he persistently claimed he was out of politics. The Californian stayed away from Houston and remained "on vacation" during the 1928 convention and for some time thereafter. During this period McAdoo's friends fed him letters claiming that Smith was turning the Democratic party into "a saloon party" and causing all Democrats to appear as if they were "alcoholic by nature and can not live out of a fluid situation." Smith's followers, on the other hand, urged McAdoo to drop his resentment and help "the new Democratic party" which was being built. McAdoo steadfastly refused. "I am out of politics," he would reiter-ate, and then add, "I have absolutely nothing to do with the campaign now in progress."

Yet McAdoo was not finished with party politics, and he was in anguish. "I can't support Hoover," he told one of his friends, "and I can't endorse Smith's prohibition views and some of his other views. But," he admitted, "I don't want to take myself out of the party since I may have some potentialities for future service to the country that can be best preserved by using them within the party." Finally, just before the election on November 3, and long after it could do Smith any positive good, McAdoo released the ambiguous statement that he was "preserving his party allegiance." Immediately thereafter he wrote to Homer Cummings: "I suppose you were surprised . . . to read my telegram of November 3rd. . . . I doubt very much if the Tammany outfit would have done as much for me if the conditions had been reversed."

Nineteen-twenty-four was four years in the past, but along with many other Democrats, McAdoo could not forget.

<h1 style="text-align:center">5</h1>

The "Brown Derby" campaign of 1928 is a well-worn story. Like Davis in 1924, Smith had the misfortune of again running against Republican prosperity. It is doubtful if any Democrat could have overcome that liability in 1928 any more than in 1924. Moreover, Smith's opponent in 1928 was Herbert Hoover, the chief apostle of the new economic age. Despite some minor sentiment against Hoover in his own party, he had been nominated by the Republican Kansas City convention on the first ballot, and Senator Charles Curtis, a moderate farm-bloc member, was tapped as his running mate. Hoover, who was not really the favorite of either Wall Street or the farmer, was the undeniable darling of the rank-and-file and went into the 1928 campaign with virtually unified backing. Once again the Democratic party faced a Republican opponent who did not have to expend nervous energy trying to keep a warring and divisive party in line.

Much has been made of the personality differences between the two contenders in this election. They were poles apart. Hoover was aloof, cold, and introverted; Smith was aggressive, open, and bombastic. Just as the radio hurt the Democrats in 1924 by broadcasting their Madison Square Garden squabbling all over the country, so in 1928 did it give unflattering overexposure to Smith's city mannerisms, his lack of a formal education, and his exaggerated Lower East Side accent. Radio was never a friend to the Democrats until Franklin Roosevelt tamed it to his use. In 1928 the airwaves provided constant reminders not only for southern and western Democrats but for others as well that "alien forces" had captured the Democratic party. The impact on Democratic solidarity was disastrous.

Further adding to the Democratic weakness in 1928 was the continued similarity between the parties on many of the issues. Walter Lippmann commented that, just as in 1924, he could see no essential difference between the Republican and Democratic platforms except that this time "the Republican took longer to read." On the tariff, on foreign affairs, and on farm relief the two parties sounded much alike. Even on prohibition, and even though the Democratic candidate was a known "modificationist," both parties pledged to uphold the law by enforcing it. In the end, Smith, like Davis before him, was left with few substantive distinctions to talk about and was reduced primarily to convincing the country that he would not harm Coolidge prosperity.

This party similarity permitted other issues, which sprang almost exclusively from the Smith candidacy and which had been kept muted by the Davis compromise selection four years before, to assume importance. Most of these issues—especially fundamentalism, prohibition, and the Klan—bore a direct relationship to the Madison Square Garden convention and were intensified because of that experience. Not often emphasized is the manner in which the bitterness, animosities, and bigotry emanating from that convention still affected the fortunes of Al Smith and the Democratic party in 1928. It is especially ironic that some of these issues would only now achieve campaign prominence, and would do so at a time when their general appeal to the American public was actually declining. The Smith nomination of 1928 unquestionably served to perpetuate the national political significance of these matters beyond their natural time.

Years later Hoover stated that Smith "was a natural born gentleman" and that during the "Brown Derby" campaign "he said no word and engaged in no action that did not comport with the highest levels." The same could not be said for many of Hoover's supporters and, indeed, for many Democrats with regard to their own nominee. Throughout the 1928 campaign, fundamentalists raged at Smith. Actually, their Armageddon had occurred more than three years before in Dayton, Tennessee. There, in mid-July, 1925, William Jennings Bryan in his last great battle had defended a literal interpretation of the Bible against the thrusts of the agnostic lawyer Clarence Darrow, who was handling the defense of a local high-school teacher charged with contravening the anti-evolution laws of Tennessee. There Bryan had so subjected his narrow views and those of his fundamentalist followers to public ridicule that the fundamentalist movement, although it continued to survive, never fully recovered. Bryan had died suddenly a few days after the Dayton "Monkey Trial," having been "called home," said his friends, to reap his heavenly reward. Knowing Bryan's prodigious capacity for heavy, greasy food, Darrow had irreverently claimed that he died "of a busted belly."

There is no question that the Smith candidacy rekindled fundamentalist fervor. Smith's reputation as an enemy of "the old-time religion" had already been firmly fixed by the Madison Square Garden Convention, and the Bible-belt country, especially, rallied against him. Smith's Tammany connections, his urban background, and his immigrant derivations would have disqualified him in fundamentalist eyes anyway in 1928. But his wetness and his Catholicism were most crucial and all the more glaring because of the Madison Square Garden experience. The general distribution of the fundamentalist opposition to Smith seen in the Garden in 1924 was now duplicated in the country as a whole.

Similarly, the Ku Klux Klan attacked the Smith candidacy and found it a welcome tonic for its faltering cause. The Klan actually had reached its height about the time of the Garden convention and had been losing ground steadily since then. By the end of 1926 its membership was said to be only half of the 4 million it had enjoyed in 1924. By midsummer 1928 it could claim only 150,000 members. Shifting public attitudes as well as the organization's excesses had prompted this decline. But the fears and suspicions upon which it had fed lingered on, and a Smith nomination quickly intensified them. Klansmen who had found themselves powerless to do anything about a Smith selection at Houston were not so impotent during the campaign. Already conditioned by the earlier events in Madison Square Garden, previously Klan-dominated local areas were a fertile field for anti-Smith Klan propaganda. Even more than the fundamentalists the Klan made Smith's religion a campaign factor.

The Klan may have been declining rapidly in membership by 1928, but with regard to a Smith candidacy it had plenty of help. A number of southern senators campaigned vigorously against him, using scurrilous and inflammatory language. Thomas Heflin of Alabama charged that the Smith candidacy "represented the crowning effort of the Roman Catholic hierarchy to gain control of the United States." Methodist and Baptist ministers also attacked him violently and repeated the grossest lies about him. None surpassed Dr. Bob Jones, famous Methodist evangelist and fiery prohibitionist, who scared his flock half out of their wits by claiming, "I'd rather see a saloon on every corner than a Catholic in the White House." One day he even proclaimed, "I'd rather see a nigger President than a Catholic in the White House."

Just as in 1924, prohibition was probably a more critical factor than any of these others with regard to the Smith candidacy. As recent studies have shown, pro-Smith support in 1928 still had a heavy anti-prohibition base; conversely, prohibition still provided the most reliable common denominator underlying anti-Smith sentiment. And yet the prohibition movement too had passed its peak by 1928. Although both parties placed enforcement planks in their platforms, attitudes for modification were growing rapidly. The phrases "local option" and "home rule" were increasingly heard, and many local communities, while they continued to vote nationally for prohibition, were undermining it locally. At first only brewers and distillers like August A. Busch and Fred Pabst had been active in organizations like the Association Against the Prohibition Amendment and had supplied the money and the brains for the anti-prohibition movement. But by 1926–27, railroad presidents, bankers, businessmen, lawyers, and educators had joined in. Pierre Du Pont, once a strong advocate of prohibition, came out against it. So did such men as Nicholas Murray Butler, Percy S. Straus, and Elihu Root. Significantly, John Raskob as well as fifteen of the twenty-eight directors of General Motors were anti-prohibition. In 1928 Raskob was a central figure in the AAPA.

Again the Smith candidacy reinvigorated a dying crusade. Seeing their opposition growing and extremely fearful of what a Smith victory might mean, prohibition leaders refurbished their bonds with the Klan and fundamentalists. Supplanting reason with emotion and appealing to prohibition-connected cultural and ethnic prejudices, militant prohibitionists revived the worst aspects of their earlier Madison Square Garden tactics. Wayne Wheeler claimed that he had anxiously awaited this opportunity to again meet Smith and the liquor interests "head-on."

Because of such intense feeling, Smith was warned by moderates in the party, among them Roosevelt, to "soft-pedal the booze question." But in 1928 it would have made no difference. Al Smith's image as "leader of all the liquor forces" had long since been established. Inevitably, anti-Smith prohibition literature appeared everywhere. Through such outlets

as *The New Menace, The Fellowship Forum,* and *The Protestant,* prohibitionists, the Klan, and fundamentalists cooperated in flooding areas of
the South and Midwest with anti-Smith diatribes. "Will Dry Protestants
of the South Put Their Worst Foe in the White House?" one leaflet asked.
Another gave "30 Reasons Why Protestants Should Be Sure to Vote for
Alcohol Smith," among them being, "To contribute a boy to fill a drunk-
ard's grave" and "To furnish a daughter to add to the Red Light District
by the gin-fizz route." One prohibitionist cartoon showed Smith as a
ruffian driving a beer truck on which was the placard "Make America
100% Catholic, Drunk, and Illiterate." Running after the truck was a
priest shouting, "Mr. President, allow me to suggest that I will receive
your confession and advise you."

   Under such circumstances the campaign of 1928 became no contest at
all. At last the Democrats had a chance to see what happened when their
fight in Madison Square Garden was translated into the national political
arena. In many sections of the country Democrats once again became
their own worst enemies as they punished each other far more than their
Republican opponents. On Election Day Hoover received 21,391,993
votes or 58.1 percent and Smith 15,016,169 or 40.8 percent. Hoover's
electoral margin was 444 to 87, one of the largest in the nation's history.
Hoover captured 40 of the 48 states, including 5 from the Solid South. Of
these five, Florida, North Carolina, Texas, and Virginia had not voted for
a Republican since Reconstruction days. Smith carried only two northern
states—Massachusetts and Rhode Island—and even lost his home state of
New York. For Smith this last was the cruelest blow of all.

6

As in 1924, the significance of the 1928 vote did not appear in the raw
figures. The subject of careful analysis since, this vote has produced a
wide variety of interpretations. Despite Smith's defeat, it is often noted
that he received nearly twice as many popular votes as John W. Davis in
1924. Moreover, while Hoover split the Democratic South, Smith dented
the Republican North, especially the urban North. In 1920 Harding had
carried all 27 of the nation's principal cities outside the South. In 1928
Smith captured 8 of these and registered gains in all the rest. In 1924 the
Republicans had carried the 12 largest cities by a plurality of 1.3 million.

In 1928 the Democrats carried these same cities by a small majority, but a majority nevertheless.

Unmistakably there was an increasing self-consciousness in city electorates throughout the twenties and much of this stemmed from an upsurge in immigrant and ethnic participation in national political affairs. Most analysts contend that this development was hastened by the "vicarious identification" of many ethnics and immigrants with the New York governor. That Smith markedly accelerated this movement of urban ethnics and immigrants into the Democratic party and attracted their votes at the national level is beyond dispute.

But perhaps too much significance is ascribed to this shift and even to Smith's role in it. At no time during the 1920s had the Republican party depended on this element for its national victories; nor did the increase in the numbers of voting ethnics itself presage later Republican national defeat. In all areas, except the Eastern Seaboard, Hoover's margin of victory in 1928 was sufficient to have offset a far greater swing of the cities to the Democrats than actually occurred. Further, although Smith was a powerful magnet, the drift of the urban-ethnic element into the Democratic party would have continued in any event. Any "liberal" Democratic candidate would have possessed a natural attraction for them, but even the appearance of another John W. Davis would not have halted this development. By continuing to emphasize and to appeal to local issues, worker interests, and ethnic solidarity, local urban Democratic factions were emerging as more formidable by 1928 with or without Smith.

Although it is often suggested that blacks too were part of this 1928 "Smith revolution," the pro-Democratic shift in urban-ethnic populations was not matched by the same intensity among Negroes. A continuing gradual drift toward the Democrats was occurring in local elections in the black sector but, far from capitalizing on the black vote at the national level in 1928, the Democrats, like the Republicans, again missed their chance. For some time blacks had been indicating a willingness to desert the Republicans, but nothing in the Democratic platform or in the antics of many white Democrats gave them much reason to look for their salvation there. Further, Smith's refusal to mention lynching and denounce "Jim Crowism," and his poor record on black patronage while governor of New York, caused most black leaders to shun him. At the national level the tendency of many, among them W. E. B. Du Bois, was still to remain neutral.

Whatever kind of analysis is used, the inescapable fact remains that the bulk of Americans voted against Smith in 1928, many of them within Smith's own party. Not only the business-oriented middle class, but a majority of workers and a majority of farmers cast their ballots for Hoover. Aside from the obvious impact of prosperity, one of the favorite questions asked about 1928 was whether religion or prohibition sealed Smith's fate. While this has precipitated some interesting arguments and a spate of books and articles, it is really an academic question. Both factors were important but neither killed him. In 1928, as at Madison Square Garden in 1924, these two issues masked a larger struggle for Democratic party control. If 1928 was a rematch between the Republicans and the Democrats for possession of the White House, it was also a rematch between the various warring factions in the Democratic party for supremacy. And, although the prohibition and religious factors were declining in importance both in the national arena and within the party by 1928, regional (East, Midwest, West, and South), demographic (city, suburb, rural), and ethnic differences were not. It is entirely possible that some other candidate, not directly associated with the Madison Square Garden fight, might have done better than Smith in 1928. Rather than helping the party live down its divisive past, Smith re-agitated old emotions, reopened old wounds, and reemphasized cultural, religious, and social incompatibilities. He kept alive such disruptive matters without being able to resolve them. He could not capitalize simultaneously, for example, on poor southern white discontent and northern black disenchantment, on rural cultural sensitivities and agrarian economic resentment, or on ethnic aspirations and small-town frustrations.

Al Smith may have been, as some observers later insisted, the harbinger of the New Deal and the "herald of a new political order." But, if he was, he was certainly never its spokesman. Following the election of 1928 Smith took a short vacation to Biloxi, Mississippi, and then returned to Albany to transfer power to Governor-elect Franklin Roosevelt, whom he had tapped to succeed him and who had won in 1928 in New York despite the Republican presidential landslide. Smith took his own defeat very hard, causing Robert Moses to remark later, "Smith was never the same after November 6, 1928; that day was his Gethsemane." Upon leaving Albany Smith became chairman of the board of directors of the County Trust Company of New York and also president of Empire State, Inc., which just before the stock-market crash in October, 1929, let the contracts for the construction of the 102-story Empire State Building.

From 1928 on, he became increasingly involved with wealthy men, some of whom had financed his 1928 campaign, and he grew perceptibly more conservative. By 1929–30 many of his earlier friends were bemoaning the fact that Al had "gone Fifth Avenue," and, according to H. L. Mencken, was being "ruined by associating with rich men—a thing far more dangerous to politicians than even booze or the sound of their own voices."

Those Smith supporters who were worrying because Al was destroying his effectiveness to lead the Democratic party back to health were wasting their concern. Al Smith had never possessed the ability to restore the Democratic party. Although he was the undisputed "hero of the cities," he was not sufficiently representative of the broad membership of the party. At best, he still remained only a regional urban leader and as such could not provide the balance necessary to win. The rematch between Republican and Democratic forces in 1928 demonstrated that northern urban Democrats by themselves could not elect a Democratic President just as 1924 had shown that neither the South nor the West alone could do it either. A champion was required who could join the South, the West, and the North together. Smith was not that man. In 1928, just as during the Madison Square Garden struggle, Al Smith was not a solution to the Democratic party's troubles. He was a part of them.

EPILOGUE

After the election of 1928, Will Rogers, speaking as a Democrat, commented about the outcome: "Women, Liquor, Tammany Hall—all had their minor little contributing factors one way or another in the total, but the whole answer was: We just didn't have any merchandise to offer the Boys that would make 'em come over on our side of the Street." Black Thursday and the Depression of 1929 shortly supplied much of that needed "merchandise," and what the Depression did not provide Franklin Roosevelt did.

As a catalytic factor in moving the nation from the Republicans to the Democrats, the Depression had no peer. The failure of the new economic era eliminated one of the primary props that had supported Republican national victories throughout the decade. Despite local trends moving in the Democrats' favor, as long as Republican economic prosperity continued, it was unlikely that the Democrats would soon emerge as the dominant national party. This fact was widely accepted by Democratic leaders at the time even though some scholars later contested it. Many of those Democrats who had replied to Roosevelt's open letter in 1925 had predicted that only a national disaster would be likely to dislodge the Republicans from the White House. Roosevelt himself remarked in late 1924 that he did not think the country would elect a Democrat again until Republican policies had produced "a serious period of depression and unemployment."

Aside from its obvious economic impact, the Depression was also important for other politically associative reasons. It finally broke the back of the drys. After a temporary resurgence during the 1928 "Brown Derby" campaign, the prohibition movement resumed its downhill slide. Hard times after 1929 gave it the *coup de grâce*. By 1932 Democrats of almost all persuasions were able to agree on the necessity for a repeal plank. Even Republicans now admitted prohibition's failure and the feasibility of local home rule. Similarly, the Ku Klux Klan, continuing to

283

experience reverses following the 1928 campaign, was swallowed by the Depression and slipped into virtual oblivion. Religious fundamentalism, meanwhile, was left isolated as prohibition and the Klan declined, and ultimately was stripped of any national political significance.

Obviously the Democratic party had not "solved" these moral, social, and cultural issues by 1932, any more than had the Republican party. Differences over them would continue to exist and would frequently embarrass both parties. But by 1932 these issues had lost their political sting, and their removal from the center of the political arena was of maximum benefit to the Democrats. Dissident and disgruntled economic interest groups within the party, which heretofore had been prevented from coalescing because of their oversensitivity about such social and cultural problems, were now freed to arrange new alliances.

The earlier voting shifts that had begun in the 1920s suddenly acquired a heightened significance. Many previously independent concerns began to merge: the farmers' desire for government subsidies, laborers' demand for greater economic representation, reformers' hope for increased social welfare, public power advocates' dream for expanded government activity. Unaware of, or indifferent to, the aspirations of the urban masses and generally antilabor in outlook, the Republicans were condemned to watch their disappearing pluralities in the cities turn into massive majorities for their opponents by 1932. But this was only one of a number of voting shifts which were working against the Republicans by 1932. As a result of the Depression, lawyers, journalists, ministers, writers, teachers—those whom Hoover often referred to as "the intelligentsia"—were moving bodily into the Democratic column. Many of these individuals had earlier been attracted to Woodrow Wilson and the New Freedom but had been thrown off by Republican prosperity and put off by Democratic divisiveness. Undoubtedly the most significant voting trend growing out of the Depression occurred among the discontented farming and suburban middle class, consisting mainly of native, old-stock (not ethnic, new-stock) Americans, who gradually lost faith in Republican economic policies, although not necessarily in Republican social and cultural views.

None of this, of course, denigrates the role of Franklin Roosevelt in the emergence of a new Democratic coalition. Historical arguments have arisen as to whether *any* Democrat might not have won in 1932. Such arguments are unnecessary. The signal fact is that the Depression *and* Roosevelt made an unbeatable combination. From the moment that Al

Smith named Roosevelt to give his "Happy Warrior" speech in Madison Square Garden in 1924, Roosevelt, and not Smith or McAdoo, became the party's man of destiny. When, four years later, the "Happy Warrior" selected this crippled polio victim as his successor in Albany and met all objections with the curt remark, "Hell, a man doesn't have to be an acrobat to be Governor," Smith made Roosevelt's rise to the White House almost inevitable. In a strange complementary way these two men, both born in New York within a decade of each other, together determined the shape of modern American political history.

Roosevelt's subsequent gubernatorial victory in the face of the Hoover landslide in 1928 was an important achievement, but his scant 25,564-vote plurality over Albert Ottinger, his Republican opponent, did not show irresistible voter magnetism. However, Roosevelt's reelection in 1930 by 750,000 votes astonished everyone, including his mentor. Just as Smith's overwhelming gubernatorial victory in 1926 made him the front runner for 1928, so now did Roosevelt's success in 1930 project him automatically into the presidential spotlight. More in truth than comedy, Will Rogers greeted the New York gubernatorial result in 1930 with the quip, "The Democrats nominated their President yesterday."

There the similarities between Smith and Roosevelt in their rise to the top stopped. Where Smith learned little from the Madison Square Garden fight of 1924, Roosevelt learned much and put this knowledge to practical use. Unlike Smith, he immediately set out to soothe all the dissident elements in his party and skirt all matters that would sustain or promote schism. Madison Square Garden and its aftermath had taught him how to appeal to all delegates, what to emphasize and what to minimize. Neither Smith nor McAdoo had been able to do this because they were the recognized leaders of the two most affected groups. But Roosevelt, even though a Smith supporter, had successfully functioned outside them all. Non-Catholic, non-urban, non-farmer, and non-laborer, he was not identified emotionally with any particular section or faction. Also, unlike either Smith or McAdoo, Roosevelt and his advisers operated on the belief that Democratic victory was possible only if the West and the South were rejoined with the North and their collective enthusiasm for the party restored.

Throughout 1930–31, Roosevelt and Howe, with the able assistance of others like James Farley, developed a unity strategy which by 1932 paid rich dividends. Roosevelt's advisers ingratiated themselves with western and midwestern politicians, carefully avoided hurting favorite sons, but always urged Roosevelt as a possible alternative candidate. One of Farley's most important recruits was Arthur Mullen, national committee-man from Nebraska, who had fought diligently for McAdoo in 1924. Another was Burton Wheeler of Montana, who had long since rejoined the Democratic party and now began to work assiduously for Roosevelt. At all times these men emphasized economic distress to the exclusion of all other issues, claiming that the Depression was the direct result of Republican normalcy policies. Roosevelt immeasurably aided his own cause in the western areas by indicating that he might endorse govern-mental price supports for the farmer, prompting Republican George Norris at last to cross over to the Democratic side.

Concomitantly, the fact that Warm Springs, Georgia, where FDR frequently convalesced, was Roosevelt's second home, was not lost on the South. Before long, Senator Richard Russell was speaking of the New Yorker as "Georgia's favorite son," while other southerners were im-pressed by his moderate stand on a variety of issues, including prohibi-tion. By 1931 Colonel House of Texas was telling his friends that Roosevelt was the party's best bet if a repetition of either 1924 or 1928 was to be avoided. Meanwhile, Howe and Farley applied pressure on such potential northern troublemakers as Edward Flynn, the political boss of the Bronx, and lined up important northeastern financial backers like Joseph P. Kennedy.

Throughout, urban Catholic support for Roosevelt was downplayed. This was made somewhat easier because of a growing coolness between Smith and Roosevelt. The Roosevelt-Smith feud has been the subject of much analysis. Allegedly rooted in snubs given by Roosevelt to Smith as far back as the campaign of 1928, the estrangement between the two men widened until by 1931–32 it was open and bitter. In 1928 Roosevelt had indeed expressed misgivings about Smith, believing that the South had let Smith have the nomination to "get it off [their] chests," but that he could not possibly win. He also felt Smith came to rely too heavily on partisan advisers like Belle Moskowitz and "the General Motors publicity and advertising section" (Raskob). Although Roosevelt continued to sup-port Smith in 1928, he remained only on the fringes of the campaign and, along with others of Smith's friends, was saddened by his post-election aberrations. Smith, meanwhile, finding himself out of politics for the first time in years, tried to effect reentry into New York state governmental activity and looked to Roosevelt for sympathy and aid. They were not forthcoming.

Whatever the degrees of blame, the story was basically one of a protégé who rapidly surpassed his mentor—or a case of a man out of power becoming jealous of one who was in power. Of course, there were many contributing factors: Smith's vanity, Roosevelt's vanity, differences over state patronage matters, differing positions on prohibition, differing approaches to economic issues. In the end, Roosevelt came to view Smith as a busybody and a detriment to his own career. Smith saw Roosevelt as a two-faced, wishy-washy, shallow, ungrateful pupil. Howe said that Smith always "considered Franklin a little boy who didn't know anything about politics." Jim Farley later claimed that the split was no one's fault, but the inevitable result of the competition between two strong men who wanted to become President.

By 1932 Smith actually had become the focal point of a stop-Roosevelt movement. When FDR declared for the presidency in January, 1932, Smith announced his own candidacy two weeks later. Al claimed that he owed it to his friends. Whatever the reason, nothing Smith might have done could have so solidified pro-Roosevelt sentiment in many areas of the South and West. It also produced much soul searching in eastern and urban Democratic circles. In the end, only the Pendergast (Kansas City), Curley (Boston), and Crump (Memphis) machines went over to Roosevelt. Most stuck with Smith, including the Hague (Jersey City) and Nash-Cermak (Chicago) machines. Frank Hague of Jersey City not only remained a Smith partisan but also became his campaign manager.

Because of the Depression there were a host of Democratic hopefuls prior to convention time in 1932: Governor Ritchie of Maryland, who still longed for the nomination; Newton Baker of Ohio, who was fondly remembered for his 1924 convention performance; John Nance Garner of Texas, feisty speaker of the House of Representatives; Cordell Hull, now a senator from Tennessee; and colorful Oklahoma Governor W. H. "Alfalfa Bill" Murray, whose slogan was "Bread, Butter, Bacon, Beans." But the major contest lay between Roosevelt and Smith, and most pre-convention speculation centered around these two men. Senator Walsh, one of the heroes of the Madison Square Garden convention, early loaned his services to Roosevelt, even permitting his name to be presented for permanent chairman against the hand-picked Smith-Raskob selectee, Jouett Shouse. Walsh won.

When the solemn silver-haired Walsh strode forward to the podium of the 1932 Chicago Democratic convention, sharply etched memories of Madison Square Garden flooded over the audience. Almost two-thirds of the delegates in attendance at Chicago had been at New York in 1924. As the closing strains of "Happy Days Are Here Again" faded, Walsh's first words to the convention contained the hope that his task would "not prove so protracted, nor the labor of the place so arduous or delicate as those . . . that devolved upon me when I last undertook to meet a similar assignment." Reporters said that you could almost hear the audience offer a silent "Amen."

For this convention, as for 1928, the Madison Square Garden experience of 1924 was as much a conditioning factor as contemporary circumstances themselves. And, once again, the main actors were the same. Bryan, of course, was gone; but Smith, Roosevelt, Davis, Cox, Glass, Owens, Robinson, and McAdoo remained. Because of Smith's candidacy, from the outset Roosevelt was denied control over Connecticut, Massachusetts, Rhode Island, New Jersey, and two-thirds of the New York delegation. Coupled with Governor Ritchie's stranglehold on Maryland, this meant that FDR could not count on the Northeast and to amass a two-thirds majority had to attract support elsewhere. The largest and most available repositories of delegate strength were the California and Texas delegations, which were solidly for Garner. Both were much under the influence of McAdoo, who, after Smith's resounding defeat in 1928, had renewed his interest in politics and now headed the California delegation. McAdoo had at first cooperated with the Smith forces in a stop-Roosevelt movement because he hoped that Garner would emerge as the nominee. Never for a moment, however, did he contemplate a Smith victory.

For the first three ballots the forces of these strange bedfellows held. At that point the vote was FDR 682.7, Smith 190.25, and Garner 101.25. Since 769 was necessary for nomination, a recess was called to permit conferences. Later there were conflicting stories about the exact sequence of events, but the basic pattern is relatively easy to reconstruct. Garner, who was in Washington, called Sam Rayburn of the Texas delegation, telling him that he did not want to prolong the convention and asking him to sound out compromise sentiment. Rayburn later called back and said that California was willing to go to FDR if McAdoo could be satisfied and that Texas would too if Garner was made Vice-President. Said Garner later, "I didn't like the thought of taking the Vice-Presidential nomination. But I wanted another Madison Square Garden deadlock even less. . . . So I said to Sam, 'All right, release my delegates and see what you can do.'" Shortly thereafter an agreement was struck between Farley, Howe, Rayburn, and Tom Connally concerning Garner and the vice-presidency.

Meanwhile, McAdoo was under heavy pressure. Homer Cummings, J. Bruce Kremer, and Daniel Roper, all of whom still hated Tammany and were militant drys, urged McAdoo to shift to Roosevelt in order to close off any possibility that Smith might again be nominated. McAdoo, after also consulting with Rayburn, finally let it be known through Roper that he would switch if all patronage matters in California were cleared with him and if Garner was accepted as Vice-President. Roper immediately contacted Howe, and Howe called FDR in Albany, who assured Roper that these conditions would be met. Smith, who had assumed that the California and Texas delegations would remain in the stop-Roosevelt coalition, was dismayed when he heard otherwise. He tried anxiously to get hold of McAdoo but McAdoo purposely remained out of reach, nor could he contact Garner, who was refusing to answer his phone.

When the convention reconvened for the fourth ballot and California's name was reached, McAdoo strode to the platform and announced to an expectant audience: "California came here to nominate a President of the United States. She did not come here to deadlock this convention or to engage in another disastrous contest like that of 1924." Pandemonium erupted as the Cermak-packed Chicago galleries began to hiss and boo, ultimately drowning McAdoo out. Only after some minutes was he able to continue. Then he coldly added, "I intend to say what I propose to say without regard to what the galleries or anybody else think," and concluded, "I want to cause no wounds. Those of 1924 were created against my wish. . . . California casts forty-four votes for Franklin D. Roosevelt."

That did it. By the time Texas was reached it was all over. On the final ballot FDR received 945 votes and Smith, his nearest rival, only 190.5. Smith, who had finally given up trying to reach McAdoo or Garner, was in a rage, and on his direct orders the New York delegation refused to make the nomination unanimous. Charged by the Smith forces with being a traitor, McAdoo later reiterated that his sole purpose in switching to Roosevelt was "to save the party from another protracted and fractional fight which would have destroyed all possibility of success in November." Many, however, were convinced that this was not his only reason. Reporters, remembering Madison Square Garden, referred to

McAdoo's announcement as "Smith's kiss of death" and the "Payoff Pow-wow." One telegram among the many praising McAdoo for his action put it bluntly: "You sure evened up with Smith." Roosevelt, listening to the radio in Albany, blurted out when he heard the news, "Good old Mc-Adoo!"

Roosevelt did not allow this action to sidetrack him from the path of neutrality and he continued to apply the lessons learned from 1924. Although he owed his nomination directly to the McAdoo forces, he did not want to be trapped by either of the chief protagonists of the Madison Square Garden struggle of eight years before. When McAdoo wanted to pose with him for a picture following his acceptance speech, Roosevelt reneged because he feared that it would rub salt in the wounds of Smith's followers. He had no such problem with Smith. After forestalling any move to make Roosevelt's nomination unanimous, Smith remained alone with his bitterness and anger throughout the night, secluded in his rooms in Chicago's Congress Hotel. Early the next morning he packed his bags, and checked out before Roosevelt arrived by plane to accept the nomination in person. It was three months before the two men would greet each other again.

On Election Day, 1932, the Roosevelt strategy of conciliation and moderation, together with the Depression, brought an end to a decade-long series of Democratic party national defeats and frustrations. On that day, Roosevelt received 22,809,638 votes, or 57.4 percent of the total. The hapless Hoover secured only 15,758,901, or 39.6 percent. In the congressional races, in state assembly contests, and in the drive for governorships, the Democrats posted spectacular gains. From the bottom to the top of the political ladder the country was at last dominated by the Democrats. In the end, the economy, not prohibition, religious beliefs, or cultural considerations, proved the decisive factor. FDR succeeded in doing what Bryan, La Follette, McAdoo, or Smith could never have done—he became the leader of a national coalition in which all geographic sections and most economic pressure groups participated. Indeed, Roosevelt united his party in a way and to a degree that not even Wilson had achieved. FDR saw clearly what Bryan, McAdoo, and Smith had not—that big-city immigrant and ethnic groups, industrial workers, intellectuals, the professional classes, and native American whites on farms, in small towns, and in the suburbs could join to form a "progressive" entity. Only with respect to the black man did the Democrats again fail in 1932. Blacks were still not yet prepared to enter the Democratic party in droves. The Negro vote for FDR in 1932 was no greater than that for Smith in 1928.

In writing his memoirs, Arthur Mullen said: "There was a suicide in Madison Square Garden in 1924. There was a wake in Houston, Texas, in 1928. There was a resurrection in the Chicago Stadium in 1932." This statement succinctly tells the story of Democratic fortunes from the disastrous days spent in the Garden to the heady success of 1932. During those eight years Madison Square Garden stood as the nadir of Democratic prestige and served as the horrible example of how not to conduct political affairs.

No one who was connected with that experience ever really escaped its influence. For the nation, and particularly for the Democratic party, it marked the beginning of a struggle to adjust to the political realities of a predominantly urban society and to find a new, workable political consensus. For the South and West, it forced a recognition of their declining relative importance and the emergence of the urban East. For the urban East, it meant a realization that for sustained political dominance cooperation from the South and the West was absolutely necessary. For native Americans, it demonstrated that the benefits of American democracy could not long be denied to anyone. For recent and non-native Americans, it provided a reminder that parochialism and prejudice were not the monopoly of any one class but infected all. For Democratic politicians in general, the Madison Square Garden imbroglio and its aftermath illustrated that racial, ethnic, moral, social, and cultural problems were not easily resolved by the political process. The economy and economically oriented issues were far safer and far more politically productive to deal with. When elevated to the level of *national* concerns, moral, racial, religious, and cultural issues militated drastically against the chances of party success.

For the major actors in this drama the results were mixed. In his grave seven years before the Roosevelt victory in 1932, William Jennings Bryan probably would not have understood the new coalition although ultimately he might have supported it. He was perhaps better off under his tombstone in Arlington cemetery, which read: "He kept the faith." Thomas Walsh, who had acted so judiciously as the permanent chairman in 1924 and was so anxious to prevent another such debacle in 1932, was appointed Attorney General by Roosevelt. Unfortunately he died on

March 2, 1933, while en route by train to Washington to be sworn in. Homer Cummings, one of the strongest of McAdoo's supporters in 1924, was immediately named by Roosevelt to take Walsh's place. Daniel Roper, another McAdoo man in 1924 and a strong advocate of the switch to FDR in 1932, became Secretary of Commerce. Cordell Hull, the astute Tennessean who shouldered the organizational problems of the party during the difficult Madison Square Garden period, was selected as FDR's Secretary of State.

The 1924 standard bearer, John W. Davis, was at the Chicago convention in 1932 as a Roosevelt delegate, but by 1936 he had joined the anti-Roosevelt Liberty League and cast his ballot for Alf Landon. In 1940 he was a leader in the Democrats-for-Willkie movement. In both 1944 and 1948 he supported Thomas E. Dewey, and in 1952 he voted for Dwight Eisenhower, contributing $1,000 to the latter's campaign. Davis died in March, 1955, more of a Republican than a Democrat.

McAdoo followed his support of Roosevelt in 1932 with a campaign for U.S. Senator from California. Successful in his bid, he served in the Congress from 1933 to 1939. During this period he backed the New Deal, including the controversial court-packing plan of 1937, and constantly reinforced his progressive credentials. "I like movement and change," he once said in reply to the question of why he continued to support FDR. To the end of his life in February, 1941, McAdoo retained the respect of Roosevelt and other ardent New Dealers.

Al Smith, who did more to "revolutionize" the Democratic party than any other politician except Roosevelt himself, continued to be a bitter and contentious man. Annoyed that he had been unable to "win against the bigots" either in 1924 or 1928, he was doubly frustrated by Roosevelt's rise to power and his election. The gulf between the two men remained unbridgeable. Except for a brief handshake after FDR's victory in 1932, they went their separate ways. By 1936, Smith, like Davis, was an open Roosevelt hater. In his autobiography he makes only one reference to Roosevelt in connection with the events of 1924 and then only to state that he delivered the "Happy Warrior" speech. He makes no mention of Roosevelt at all in relation to his own 1928 nomination and campaign.

To the time of his death in October, 1944, a scant seven months before that of his Hyde Park protégé, Smith remained estranged from the party that had nurtured him and given him so many honors. In the end the Happy Warrior became the Democratic party's most unhappy victim. In a peculiar way, both Smith's early successes and his later failures acted as important catalysts in the final forging of the modern Democratic consensus. But, ironically, that consensus had come into being in 1932 not so much on his behalf as against him. FDR had emerged as the final alternative to Smith, not as his successor, and became the eventual beneficiary of leftover anti-Catholic and pro-Klan opinion, anti-Tammany and anti-boss attitudes, and southern and western anti-eastern sentiment. More than any other event, Madison Square Garden had made this possible.

NOTES TO TEXT

Page

xiii Warner statement: Emily S. Warner, *The Happy Warrior: A Biography of Alfred E. Smith,* 164.
Atlantic Monthly, CXXXIV (October, 1924), 530.

xiii Burner quote: in *The Politics of Provincialism,* 102.

xiii Lippmann assessment: Walter Lippmann, "The Setting for John W. Davis,"

I. THE GENERAL ARENA

3 Roosevelt quote: in Frank Freidel, *Franklin D. Roosevelt: The Ordeal,* 91.

3–4 For an analysis of the Republican victory in 1920 see Robert K. Murray, *The Politics of Normalcy: Governmental Theory and Practice in the Harding-Coolidge Era,* 1–15, and *The Harding Era: Warren G. Harding and His Administration,* 43–92. See also Wesley M. Bagby, *The Road to Normalcy: The Presidential Campaign and Election of 1920, passim.* For the most recent survey see Burl Noggle, *Into the Twenties: The United States from Armistice to Normalcy,* 179–213.

5–6 For a detailed account of the achievements of the Harding years see the two books by Murray above.

7 The Red Scare is covered in Robert K. Murray, *Red Scare: A Study in National Hysteria, 1919–1920.*

7 The best analysis of nativism is John Higham, *Strangers in the Land: Patterns of American Nativism, 1860–1925.*

7 The immigration statistics are from Roy L. Garis, *Immigration Restriction: A Study of the Opposition to and Regulation of Immigration into the United States,* 170, 183 *n.* 20, 261–62.

8 Billy Sunday quote: Burner, *The Politics of Provincialism,* 93.

9 Good in portraying some of the difficulties surrounding prohibition are Peter H. Odegard, *Pressure Politics: The Story of the Anti-Saloon League;* Herbert Asbury, *The Great Illusion: An Informal History of Prohibition;* and Andrew Sinclair, *Prohibition, The Era of Excess.*

10 The basic work on the fundamentalist crusade is Norman Furniss, *The Fundamentalist Controversy, 1918–1931.*

10–11 The Bryan comments are in Lawrence W. Levine, *Defender of the Faith, William Jennings Bryan: The Last Decade, 1915–1925,* 248–49.

11 Cannon statement: in Virginius Dabney, *Dry Messiah: The Life of Bishop Cannon,* 181.

11 In John Braeman *et al., Change and Continuity in Twentieth Century America: The 1920's,* 202–13, Paul Carter enters a caveat against generalizing too broadly about the fundamentalist urban-rural split. See also Ernest R. Sandeen, "Towards a Historical Interpretation of the Origins of Fundamentalism," *Church History,* XXXVI (1967), 66–83.

12 Cash statement: Wilbur J. Cash, *The Mind of the South,* 337–38.

12 "We are going to take . . .": Richard Hofstadter, *Anti-Intellectualism in American Life,* 132.

12 For Bryan's fundamentalist attitudes and activities see Furniss, *The Fundamentalist Controversy,* 103–61; "The Presidency in 1924; William Jennings Bryan," *Forum,* LXX (August, 1923), 1815.

13 Consult the section on Sources for the various books on the Klan. The business side of the Klan is covered best in Charles C. Alexander, "Kleagles

Page

  and Cash: The Ku Klux Klan as a Business Organization, 1915–1930,"
  Business History Review, XXXIX (Autumn, 1965), 348–67.

14 "subordinate to the priesthood . . ."; Gustavus Myers, *History of Bigotry in the United States*, 290–91.

15 "We want the country . . .": Braemen *et al.*, *Change and Continuity in Twentieth Century America: The 1920's*, 222.

15 Niebuhr comment: in The Commonweal, *Catholicism in America*, 25.

17 For the best description of the connection between the Protestant churches and the Klan see Emerson H. Loucks, *The Ku Klux Klan in Pennsylvania: A Study in Nativism*, 118–33. See also Robert M. Miller, "A Note on the Relationship Between the Protestant Churches and the Revived Ku Klux Klan," *Journal of Southern History*, XXII, No. 3 (August, 1956), 357–59.

17 The primary analyzer of the Klan as a small-town phenomenon is John M. Mecklin, *The Ku Klux Klan: A Study of the American Mind*.

18 Klan statistics are in Kenneth T. Jackson, *The Ku Klux Klan in the City, 1915–1930*, 15.

19 Heflin comment: in Stanley Frost, "Fear and Prejudice in Deadlock," *Outlook*, CXXXVII (July 16, 1924), 423. The best general treatment of the Klan and politics is Arnold S. Rice, *The Ku Klux Klan in American Politics*.

20 "It is my opinion that . . .": Correspondence, "A Defense of the Klan," *The New Republic*, XXXVII (December 5, 1923), 44.

21 Wheeler comment to Bryan: in Sinclair, *Prohibition, the Era of Excess*, 256.

21 The various Bryan statements on the 1920 convention are in Morris R. Werner, *Bryan*, 271; Genevieve F. and John O. Herrick, *The Life of William Jennings Bryan*, 331; and New York *Tribune*, June 27, 1920, p. 1.

22 Blythe quotation: in Samuel G. Blythe, "What Ho the Democrats," *Saturday Evening Post*, CXCVI (October 6, 1923), 46.

22 Walsh's warning to Bryan: in Levine, *Defender of the Faith*, 310.

24–26 For a general review of the farm bloc and its impact on the Harding and Coolidge administrations see Murray, *The Harding Era*, 90, 187–88, 202–17, 222, 288–89, 326; Murray, *The Politics of Normalcy*, 44–46, 69–70, 84–85, 90–93.

26 For books on La Guardia consult the section on Sources.

27–28 For an analysis of the Republicans and organized labor see Murray, *The Harding Era*, 227–64, 388–91.

28–29 On the Negro in the 1920s see Frances L. Broderick, *W. E. B. Du Bois: Negro Leader in a Time of Crisis, passim;* Elliott M. Rudwick, *W. E. B. Du Bois: A Study in Minority Group Leadership, passim;* Edmund D. Cronon, *Black Moses: The Story of Marcus Garvey and the Universal Improvement Association, passim;* Elbert L. Tatum, *The Changed Political Thought of the Negro, 1915–1940, passim;* and John H. Franklin, *From Slavery to Freedom: A History of the American Negroes*, 489–502. For the Negro in the early twenties see Murray, *The Harding Era*, 54, 397–402. The most recent general coverage is in Richard B. Sherman, *The Republican Party and Black America: From McKinley to Hoover, 1896–1973*.

30–31 For an analysis of the 1922 elections see Murray, *The Harding Era*, 294–321. On prohibition and the Klan as political issues see "Barleycorn's Resurrection as a Big Campaign Issue," *Literary Digest*, LXXIII (June 17, 1922), 12–14; "The Ku Klux Klan in Politics," *Literary Digest*, LXXIII

Page

(June 10, 1922), 15; "Barleycorn Fighting for Resurrection," *Literary Digest*, LXXV (November 18, 1922), 12.

31–32   Cross-section of opinion on the 1922 elections is from "As I See It," New York *Tribune*, November 12, 1922; "The Democratic Tidal Wave," *Literary Digest*, LXXV (November 18, 1922), 9–11; "Democratic Plans to Win Next Time," *Literary Digest*, LXXV (December 9, 1922), 10–11; Russel B. Nye, *Midwestern Progressive Politics: A Historical Study of Its Origins and Development, 1870–1950*, 323–25.

32   For the Harding scandals and their accompanying rhetoric see Murray, *The Harding Era*, 456–485, and Murray, *The Politics of Normalcy*, 102–29.

33   Garner comment: John N. Garner to McAdoo, January 24, 1924, William G. McAdoo Papers.

33   Baruch quote: in Burner, *The Politics of Provincialism*, 107 *fn.* 3.

33   Hull remark: Hull to Woodrow Wilson, April 21, 1923, Cordell Hull Papers, IV. Also Hull to J. H. McMillin, March 19, 1924, *ibid.*, VI.

34   The Lubell theory is found in Lubell, *The Future of American Politics*, 2nd rev. ed., 217.

II. WITH THE TRAINING CAMPS

37   *Literary Digest* poll: "Who Will Be the Democratic Nominee?" *Literary Digest*, LXXVII (June 30, 1923), 6.

38   Sullivan's comment on Ford: in Mark Sullivan, "Democratic Presidential Possibilities," *World's Work*, XLV (March, 1923), 493.

38   The Jersey City *Journal* is quoted in "Democratic Plans to Win Next Time," 11.

38   Villard quotation: Oswald G. Villard, "Why Henry Ford Should Not Be President," *Nation*, CXVI, No. 3021 (May 30, 1923), 624.

38   Coolidge's endorsement by Ford: "Figuring the Horse-power of the Ford Indorsement," *Literary Digest*, LXXX (January 5, 1924), 7.

39   The three books on McAdoo are his own *Crowded Years; The Reminiscences of William G. McAdoo;* Mary Synon, *McAdoo: The Man and His Times;* and John J. Broesamle, *William Gibbs McAdoo: A Passion for Change, 1863–1917.*

40–41   An excellent article on the political consequences of McAdoo's move to California is Robert E. Hennings, "California Democratic Politics in the Period of Republican Ascendancy," *Pacific Historical Review*, XXXI, No. 3 (August, 1962), 267–80.

42   For a survey of the McAdoo campaign see Lee N. Allen, "The McAdoo Campaign for the Presidential Nomination in 1924," *Journal of Southern History*, XXIX, No. 2 (May, 1963), 211–38.

42–43   Baruch and his early pro-McAdoo activity: Bernard Baruch, *Baruch: The Public Years*, 178–80.

44   McAdoo quotes: From McAdoo to Sally F. McAdoo, January 11, 1924, McAdoo Papers, Box 63; McAdoo to Nona de Mohrenschildt, January 11, 1924, *ibid.*, Box 63; and McAdoo to May Wiley, January 23, 1924, *ibid.*, Box 63.

45   The attitudes of Daniels, House, Walsh, and Bryan are reported in the *New York Times*, February 2, 1924, p. 5.

Page

45 Baruch quote: in Baruch, *Baruch: The Public Years,* 169.

45 Agreement on conferences is in entry, February 2, 1924, 1924 Diary, Breckinridge Long Papers, Box 3.

45–46 McAdoo's request for a hearing: McAdoo to Lenroot, February 7, 1924, McAdoo Papers, Box 295.

46 Account of the February 8th meeting is from Long's diary entry, February 8, 1924, 1924 Diary, Long Papers, Box 3.

46 Long's telegram to Missouri: Long to C. C. Oliver, February 8, 1924, Long Papers, Box 172.

46 Account of the February 9th meeting: entry, February 9, 1924, 1924 Diary, Long Papers, Box 3. See also Roper, *Fifty Years of Public Life,* 218.

47 McAdoo's testimony is in U.S. Senate, 68th Cong., 1st Sess., *Leases Upon Naval Oil Reserves,* Hearings Before the Committee on Public Lands and Surveys (Washington, D.C., 1924, 3 vols.), 2059–70.

47 There is some confusion as to the exact time of the post-hearing meeting. See Baruch, *Baruch: The Public Years,* 181–82. Entry, February 11, 1924, 1924 Diary, Long Papers, Box 3, proves Baruch's account wrong on a number of points.

47 McAdoo quote is in *ibid.*

48 Long's diary entry is February 13, 1924, 1924 Diary, Long Papers, Box 3.

48 The Walsh telegram is quoted in *New York Times,* February 19, 1924, p. 3. For Walsh's renewed faith in McAdoo see various items in Thomas J. Walsh Papers, Boxes 374–75.

48 "You command me to . . .": Chicago *Tribune,* February 19, 1924, p. 1.

48 McAdoo's telegrams to his sons are McAdoo to W. G. McAdoo, Jr., February 18, 1924, McAdoo Papers, Box 63, and McAdoo to Francis McAdoo, February 18, 1924, *ibid.*

48 Roper's statement of success: Roper to S. R. Burton, February 21, 1924, *ibid.,* Box 296.

48–49 Long's activities and statements are in Long to William Collins, February 24, 1924, Long Papers, Box 78, and entry, February 24, 1924, 1924 Diary, Long Papers, Box 3.

49 Sample McAdoo letters are in McAdoo Papers, Boxes 63–64.

49 Interview concerning "additional fees" is in *New York Times,* March 3, 1924, p. 1.

49 The reactions of Tumulty, House, Long, Chadbourne, and Baruch are found in entry, March 26, 1924, 1924 Diary, Long Papers, Box 3, and entry, April 10, 1924, Edward M. House Collection: Diary of Edward M. House, vol. 18.

49 Phelan quote: in Hennings, "California Democratic Politics in the Period of Republican Ascendancy," 273–74.

49–50 Walsh's opinions on McAdoo: Walsh to M. M. Duncan, February 27, 1924, Walsh-Erickson Papers, Box 9a, and Walsh to Albert D. Nortoni, February 16, 1924, *ibid.*

50 Walsh-McAdoo exchange: Walsh to McAdoo, April 3, 1924, Walsh Papers, Box 375, and McAdoo to Walsh, April 26, 1924, *ibid.*

50 Davis quote: Davis to Lord Shaw of Dunfermline, March 29, 1924, Davis Papers, Box 40.

51 "Will you not join . . .": Open letter to alumni, February 18, 1924, Mercer C. Johnston Papers, Box 48.

Page

51   Best on the Underwood campaign is Lee N. Allen, "The Underwood Presidential Movement of 1924," *Alabama Review*, XV (April, 1962), 86–87.

51–52   Underwood's views are found in Oscar W. Underwood, *Drifting Sands of Party Politics*, especially 378–91. The Oscar W. Underwood Papers clearly reveal his interest in the presidency but, as with most senatorial collections, they are cluttered with much day-to-day trivia.

52   Reactions to Underwood's candidacy: "Ringside Remarks as the First Democratic Hat Sails In," *Literary Digest*, LXXVIII (August 11, 1923), 15.

53   May statement: in *New York Times*, March 9, 1924, Section I, Part 2, p. 8.

53   The Alabama primary: Allen, "The Underwood Presidential Movement of 1924," 90–96.

53–54   The Georgia primary: *New York Times*, March 21 and 22, 1924.

54   Opinions on McAdoo's victory in Georgia: "McAdoo's March Through Georgia," *Literary Digest*, LXXXI (April 5, 1924), 11.

54   The only biography of Murphy is Nancy J. Weiss, *Charles Francis Murphy, 1858–1924: Respectability and Responsibility in Tammany Politics*. For a briefer treatment of Murphy see Morris R. Werner, *Tammany Hall*.

56   Will Rogers quote: Weiss, *Charles Francis Murphy*, 46.

58   For the French Lick triumvirate and their possible motives see Blythe, "What Ho the Democrats," 6; Matthew and Hannah Josephson, *Al Smith: Hero of the Cities*, 306; Warner, *The Happy Warrior*, 142.

58   For the various biographies of Al Smith consult the section on Sources.

59   "It has been my school . . .": Josephson and Josephson, *Al Smith*, 100.

59   "I have never seen . . ." Irving Stone, *They Also Ran: The Story of the Men Who Were Defeated for the Presidency*, 291.

62   Roosevelt's statement to Perkins: Josephson and Josephson, *Al Smith*, 4, 172. Judge Proskauer later claimed that Murphy was "partly responsible" for Smith's excellent record as governor since he did not allow him to be compromised. Joseph M. Proskauer, *A Segment of My Times*, 42–43.

62   Perkins's first introduction to Smith: Frank Graham, *Al Smith, American: An Informal Biography*, 136–38.

63   For the Moskowitz-Smith relationship see Josephson and Josephson, *Al Smith*, 192–97, 301–303; Henry F. Pringle, *Alfred E. Smith: A Critical Study*, 64; Lela Stiles, *The Man Behind Roosevelt; The Story of Louis McHenry Howe*, 107.

63   White's statement: William Allen White, *Masks in a Pageant*, 465–66.

64   Prior to 1924 the only Catholic to receive a presidential nomination was Charles O'Conor on a minor-party ticket in 1872. He received fewer than 30,000 votes. Moos and Hess, *Hats in the Ring*, 49.

64   Sullivan quote: Mark Sullivan, "The Democratic Dark Horse Pasture," *World's Work*, XLVI (July, 1923), 288.

64   Villard on Smith's drinking habits: Oswald G. Villard, *Prophets True and False*, 7–8.

64–65   For the Mullan-Gage repealer controversy see Alfred B. Rollins, Jr., *Roosevelt and Howe*, 210; personal files, Folder "Mullan-Gage Laws," Alfred E. Smith Papers; Alfred E. Smith, *The Citizen and His Government*, 179.

65   Bryan remark: Levine, *Defender of the Faith*, 208.

65   For the Smith quote and bookie odds: *New York Times*, February 5, 1924, pp. 1, 5.

Page

66–67   Events surrounding Murphy's death and funeral: *New York Times,* April 26, 1924, pp. 1, 2; Weiss, *Charles Francis Murphy,* p. 7; Alfred Connable, *Tigers of Tammany: Nine Men Who Ran New York,* 268.

67   Krock statement: Weiss, *Charles Francis Murphy,* 92.

67   Reactions to Murphy's death: "What Murphy's Death Means to the Democratic Party," *Literary Digest,* LXXXI (May 10, 1924), 14.

67   Moskowitz's attitude: Josephson and Josephson, *Al Smith,* 306.

68   FDR's changing view of Smith: Freidel, *Franklin D. Roosevelt: The Ordeal,* 116, 164–166.

68   Howe's role in FDR's early career: Stiles, *The Man Behind Roosevelt,* 88–91.

68–69   For FDR-Smith discussions concerning Roosevelt's selection as campaign chairman see Franklin D. Roosevelt Papers, "Scrapbooks, 1924–26," III. FDR kept voluminous scrapbooks throughout this period. The FDR-Smith correspondence in the extant Smith Papers is very limited. Much of the Smith-FDR contact was by phone.

69   Roosevelt quote: FDR to S. B. Amidon, June 6, 1924, Roosevelt Papers, "1924 Campaign Correspondence," Box 18.

70   Sample New York press coverage of FDR's assertions: New York *Tribune,* May 19, 1924, p. 1.

70   "It is pretty late in the day . . .": "A Dry Edict From a Moist Governor," *Literary Digest,* LXXX (March 15, 1924), 13.

71   "to let Texas alone . . .": Pat O'Keefe to Smith, June 25, 1923, Smith Papers, Folder 200-341.

72–73   The Carter Glass Papers are very revealing of Glass's reluctance to make the race. See also Rixley Smith and Norman Beasley, *Carter Glass: A Biography,* 259–60; Mark Sullivan, "Carter Glass—Sound Democrat," *World's Work,* XLVIII (May, 1924), 78–82; *New York Times,* June 12, 1924, p. 7.

73   The Samuel M. Ralston Papers are very helpful in showing great enthusiasm among his friends in the spring of 1924 for him to run. Also see " 'A Second Grover Cleveland' Whose Eyes Are on the White House," *Current Opinion,* LXXIV, No. 6 (June, 1923), 671–72; Stanley Frost, "The Klan Shows Its Hand in Indiana," *Outlook,* CXXXVII (June 4, 1924), 187–90. Ralston was continually angered by persistent charges that he was "the Klan's candidate."

73–74   Although Taggart's full intentions are somewhat shrouded, there are clues in various letters, April–May, 1924, Ralston Papers.

74   Various descriptions of Charles Bryan: "Charles Wayland Bryan," *Current Opinion,* LXXVII, No. 3 (September, 1924), 297; "Charles W. Bryan, of Nebraska," *World's Work,* XLVIII (September, 1924), 548–53; W. J. Bryan, "My Brother Charles," *World's Work,* XLVIII (September, 1924), 553.

74   For the telephone story, and the general reaction of Nebraska voters: "Charles Wayland Bryan," 296–97; Clinton W. Gilbert, *You Takes Your Choice,* 151.

75   "Davis? Jeff Davis is . . ." John W. Owens, "Dilemma of the Democrats," *The New Republic,* XXXIX, No. 496 (June 4, 1924), 37.

75–76   The most manageable primary source material on Davis is in his "Reminis-

Page

cences of John W. Davis" (Oral History Research Office, Columbia University). The best biography is William H. Harbaugh, *Lawyer's Lawyer: The Life of John W. Davis.*

77   The London *Times* quotation: in " 'Simply Normal' John William Davis," *Literary Digest,* LXXXII (July 26, 1924), 40.

77–78   Shaver's remark: Theodore A. Huntley, *The Life of John W. Davis,* 136.

78   "I am being considerably . . ." Davis to Rev. P. N. McDonald, February 7, 1924, Davis Papers, Box 39.

78   "What American would not . . ." *New York Times,* January 13, 1924, Section II, p. 6.

78   House, Polk, and Lansing support: entry, April 10, 1924, House Collection: Diary of Edward M. House, vol. 18.

78   Davis's rejoinder to criticism about his wealthy clients: *New York Times,* April 1, 1924, p. 1, and sample letters in Davis Papers, Boxes 39, 45.

78   "If Fate is headed . . .": "Reminiscences of John W. Davis," 149.

79–80   Bryan's reaction to the 1922 elections: Levine, *Defender of the Faith,* 183–85, 296.

80   Bryan's views on the Klan: Paolo E. Coletta, *William Jennings Bryan: Political Puritan, 1915–1925,* 234. See also sample letter, Bryan to Thomas Walsh, December 20, 1922, William Jennings Bryan Papers.

80   The letters written to Bryan by the common people of the West and the South are amazing in their sincerity and simplicity. See Bryan Papers, especially Boxes 37–40.

80   "No wet and no reactionary . . .": Bryan to G. M. West, February 13, 1924, Bryan Papers, Box 39.

81   "Smith is, of course, out of . . ." Bryan to Cordell Hull, December 18, 1923, Bryan Papers.

82   "with so many younger men . . .": W. J. Bryan to T. D. Judy, February 11, 1924, Bryan Papers, Box 39.

82   Newspaper remarks concerning Bryan and Murphree are in Levine, *Defender of the Faith,* 301, and *New York Times,* January 14, 1924, pp. 1, 4.

82   "It will not hurt. . . .": W. J. Bryan to C. W. Bryan, February 9, 1924, Bryan Papers, Box 39.

83   Bryan's implied support for McAdoo: Levine, *Defender of the Faith,* 307.

83   "This is not my kind . . .": Werner, *Bryan,* 271.

83   "I don't think there is . . .": Paxton Hibben, *The Peerless Leader, William Jennings Bryan,* 379.

85–86   Long's advice to McAdoo about Missouri: various items in Long Papers, Box 172.

86   Various Reed charges against McAdoo: *New York Times,* February 26, 1924, p. 3; *ibid.,* March 1, 1924, p. 5; *ibid.,* March 8, 1924, p. 14.

86   Rockwell's reasoning in contesting Illinois: Mrs. Kellogg Fairbanks to Thomas Walsh, April 24, 1924, Walsh Papers, Box 374.

87   Rockwell's statement on the Illinois primary: Rockwell to Breckinridge Long, January 12, 1924, Long Papers, Box 172.

87   Cox's attitude on the Ohio primary: James M. Cox, *Journey Through My Years,* 324.

87   For McAdoo's decision not to attack the Klan see various items, McAdoo Papers, Boxes, 295–306.

Page

88 Klan support of McAdoo: Burner, *The Politics of Provincialism*, 87; Charles C. Alexander, *The Ku Klux Klan in the Southwest*, 164–66.

88 For an analysis of general public anti-Catholicism see James H. Smylie, "The Roman Catholic Church, the State, and Al Smith," *Church History*, XXIX, No. 3 (September, 1960), 324–25.

89 Appeals to Smith to "do something" about the Klan are in "KKK," Smith Papers, Folder 200-341.

89 Smith remark concerning Wisconsin and Minnesota: *New York Times*, April 4, 1924, p. 8.

89 The two Hearst quotations are from Herbert Eaton, *Presidential Timber; A History of Nominating Conventions, 1868–1960*, 296, and Coletta, *William Jennings Bryan: Political Puritan, 1915–1925*, 178.

90 Bryan quote: in *ibid.*, 234.

90 Underwood statement: *New York Times*, May 13, 1924, p. 3.

90 "lead the fight against . . .": "The Klan and the Democrats," *Literary Digest*, LXXXI (June 14, 1924), 12.

90 "Whether or not it should be . . .": *New York Times*, May 14, 1924, p. 1.

90–91 For McAdoo's confidence see letters sent to both of his sons: McAdoo to F. H. McAdoo, May 6, 1924, and McAdoo to Robert McAdoo, June 11, 1924, McAdoo Papers, Box 63.

91 Sample pre-convention claims by FDR: *New York Times*, May 19, 1924, p. 19.

91 For Smith's pre-convention confidence see Warner, *The Happy Warrior*, 156–157, and Pringle, *Alfred E. Smith*, 306.

92 *New York Times* forecast: *New York Times*, June 19, 1924, p. 1.

92 Frost remark: Stanley Frost, "Democratic Dynamite," *Outlook*, CXXXVII (June 18, 1924), 265.

92 Blythe statement: Samuel G. Blythe, "A Party Up in the Air," *Saturday Evening Post*, CXCVI (May 31, 1924), 20, 145.

III. THE PRELIMINARIES

95–96 Mack's arguments for New York: *New York Times*, January 16, 1924, p. 2.

96 Roper's press statement: *New York Times*, January 22, 1924, p. 21.

96–97 Rickard's offer concerning profits: *ibid.*, January 30, 1924, p. 20.

98 "I've known the old Garden . . .": *ibid.*, June 22, 1924, p. 3.

99 White's statement is in William A. White, *Politics: The Citizen's Business*, 52.

99 Butler comment: *New York Times*, May 9, 1924, p. 2.

102 Smith remark: *ibid.*, June 13, 1924, p. 21.

103 Taggart and various Hoosier comments: *ibid.*, June 21, 1924, p. 2, and June 23, 1924, p. 4.

104 Underwood quotation: *ibid.*, June 24, 1924, p. 3.

104 "I became conscious of it . . .": "Reminiscences of Marvin Jones" (Oral History Research Office, Columbia University), 315.

104 McAdoo's arrival statements: in *New York Times*, June 23, 1924, p. 1.

105 "have been hopelessly drunk . . .": "Reminiscences of Claude Bowers" (Oral History Research Office, Columbia University), 52.

106 Bryan's arrival statements: in *New York Times*, June 23, 1924, p. 3.

Page
106–107 Wheeler's and Cannon's activities: Justin Steuart, *Wayne Wheeler, Dry Boss: An Uncensored Biography of Wayne B. Wheeler*, 199–201, and James Cannon, Jr., *Bishop Cannon's Own Story: Life as I Have Seen It*, 333.

107 "to be driven like a herd . . .": *ibid.*, 332.

107 Wheeler's circular: "Anti-Saloon League Warning," June, 1924, in "1924 Campaign Correspondence," Roosevelt Papers, Box 18.

107 Sample of dry propaganda: in *New York Times*, June 14, 1924, p. 1, and 22, 1924, p. 1.

107–109 Klan influence at the convention: Alexander, *The Ku Klux Klan in the Southwest*, 167; Rice, *The Ku Klux Klan in American Politics*, 80–81; New York *World*, June 26, 1924, *passim; New York Times*, June 22, 1924, p. 3.

109 The best example of biased anti-McAdoo reporting is in New York *World*, June 23, 1924, p. 1. See also Ernest H. Abbott, "A Party Civil War," *Outlook*, CXXXVII (July 9, 1924), 383–84.

109–110 Lyric is from Pringle, *Alfred E. Smith*, 301.

110 Sample New York chauvinism is in *New York Times*, June 19, 1924, p. 2, and July 6, 1924, p. 3.

111–112 For Hull's various activities: Harold B. Hinton, *Cordell Hull: A Biography*, 165–66; Cordell Hull, *The Memoirs of Cordell Hull*, I, 116; see also J. R. Bolling to Hull, March 1, 1923, Hull Papers, IV; Woodrow Wilson to Hull, October 27, 1923, *ibid.*, V; and Hull to W. G. Schamberger, December 21, 1923, *ibid.*, V.

112 Hull's own neutrality is revealed in many letters in *ibid.*, V, VI, and VII.

112 For the controversy over a keynoter see *New York Times*, April 23, 1924, p. 23, and May 18, 1924, p. 1.

112 On the question of a permanent chairman see *ibid.*, June 4, 1924, p. 3; Josephine O'Keane, *Thomas J. Walsh: A Senator from Montana*, 154. The various favorite sons also endorsed Walsh's selection.

112–113 McAdoo and the two-thirds rule: entry, June 1, 1924, 1924 Diary, Long Papers, Box 3; *New York Times*, June 17, 1924, p. 1; *ibid.*, June 22, 1924, p. 1; *ibid.*, June 25, 1924, p. 1.

114 The seating and ticket controversies: *ibid.*, June 20, 1924, p. 3; *ibid.*, June 21, 1924, p. 1; *ibid.*, June 23, 1924, p. 4; New York *World*, June 24, 1924, p. 1.

115 Rockwell's charges: various clippings in "Scrapbook–Political: 1924," Roosevelt Papers.

116 For an account of opening day see the contemporary issues of the New York press.

117 Comment about Ben Turpin: New York *World*, June 25, 1924, p. 6.

117–118 The number of women delegates in 1924 would represent the general level of female participation in Democratic conventions down to 1956.

118 "on the contrary, they . . .": Elizabeth Frazer, "Mrs. Delegate," *Saturday Evening Post*, CXCVII (August 16, 1924), 6.

118 Sullivan quote: Mark Sullivan, "Behind the Convention Scenes," *World's Work*, XLVIII (September, 1924), 536.

118 "Women have but laid hold . . .": Frazer, "Mrs. Delegate," 6.

119 "cause all the livers . . .": Clinton W. Gilbert, *You Takes Your Choice*, 214.

119 Harrison's speech: Charles A. Greathouse, comp., *Official Report of the*

Page

Proceedings of the Democratic National Convention, held in Madison Square Garden, New York City, June 24–July 9, 1924 contains the record of all convention speeches, resolutions, motions, and votes. Unless otherwise indicated, all quoted material from convention speeches, motions, and resolutions used hereafter in this book is taken from this source. Subsequently it will be cited as *Proceedings . . . 1924.*

121 Reaction to opening day: "The Democratic Line of Attack," *Literary Digest,* LXXXII (July 5, 1924), 10; Abbott, "A Party Civil War," 384; New York *World,* June 25, 1924, p. 2.

121 "the best behaved big crowd . . .": *ibid.,* p. 6, quoting Police Inspector Coleman.

121 "Just wait, those are . . .": Moos and Hess, *Hats in the Ring,* 15.

122 "fully costumed and . . .": New York *World,* June 26, 1924, p. 1.

124 Rockwell statement: *New York Times,* June 26, 1924, p. 7.

125 Comments on Phelan's speech: "Democracy Tunes Up on Jazz," *Independent,* CXIII, No. 3872 (July 5, 1924), 5; Eaton, *Presidential Timber,* 298.

127 "were more like rural . . .": *New York Times,* June 27, 1924, p. 8.

129–130 FDR's speech: Greathouse, comp., *Proceedings . . . 1924,* pp. 122–29.

130 Origin and use of the "Happy Warrior" phrase: Josephson and Josephson, *Al Smith,* 312–13; Warner, *The Happy Warrior,* 159–60; Proskauer, *A Segment of My Times,* 51.

130 Various reactions to FDR's performance: Warner, *The Happy Warrior,* 160; Oswald G. Villard, "An Unconventional Convention," *The Nation,* CXIX, No. 3079 (July 9, 1924), 36; Freidel, *Franklin D. Roosevelt: The Ordeal,* 176; Stiles, *The Man Behind Roosevelt,* 93.

132 "The Old Town doesn't have . . .": New York *Post,* June 26, 1924, p. 1.

133 Smith remark: *New York Times,* June 27, 1924, pp. 1, 6.

136 Various comments on the Smith demonstration: New York *World,* June 27, 1924, editorial; New York *Post,* June 26, 1924; "Bedlam Makers and Gate Crashers," *Literary Digest,* LXXXII (July 12, 1924), 52, quoting New York *Herald Tribune.*

136–137 Bliven observation: Bruce Bliven, "The Democracy Fumbles," *The New Republic,* XXXIX, No. 501 (July 9, 1924), 177.

137 "Yesterday's protracted outburst . . .": Warner, *The Happy Warrior,* 161, quoting *New York Times; New York Times,* June 27, 1924, p. 1.

137 Rumors concerning Tammany, liquor, and priests: *ibid.,* June 27, 1924, p. 6; Cannon, Jr., *Bishop Cannon's Own Story,* 335. At the close of the convention, Claude Bowers wrote to Samuel Ralston that he personally saw "priests by the dozens working on the floor—at one time as many as forty." Bowers to Ralston, July 10, 1924, Ralston Papers.

138 Elmer Davis comment: *New York Times,* June 28, 1924, p. 1.

138 "as a jew's-harp quartette . . .": "Speaking of Conventions," *Independent,* CXIII, No. 3873 (July 19, 1924), 46.

IV. THE MAIN EVENT

144 Wheeler quote: Steuart, *Wayne Wheeler, Dry Boss,* 208–209.

144 Wording of the Harding resolution: Werner, *Bryan,* 277.

Page

144   Moore quote: New York *World,* June 24, 1924, p. 1.

145   Supporting the Virginia proposal were not only the pro-McAdoo men but the followers of such minor candidates as Ralston. For Ralston's thinking on the Klan problem see Ralston to Taggart, April 1, 1924, Ralston Papers.

147   Bryan's paper: William J. and Mary B. Bryan, *The Memoirs of William Jennings Bryan,* 477; Herrick and Herrick, *The Life of William Jennings Bryan,* 332–33; *New York Times,* June 30, 1924, p. 4.

148   Cummings's explanation to the convention: Greathouse, comp., *Proceedings . . . 1924,* 224–26.

148   Interview with Lawlor: *New York Times,* June 29, 1924, p. 12.

148   Description of confusion at the gates: *ibid.,* p. 14.

150   "any efforts to arouse . . .": Greathouse, comp., *Proceedings . . . 1924,* 245.

151   "We condemn political secret societies . . .": *ibid.,* 248.

153   Vote on the League plank: *ibid.,* 278–79.

154   White comment on Klan: White, *Politics: The Citizen's Business,* 79.

154   Sample opinion of McAdoo's advisers in McAdoo Papers, Box 306; entry, July 15, 1924, 1924 Diary, Long Papers, Box 3.

154   For Taggart's approach to the Klan issue see *New York Times,* June 22, 1924, p. 3. The Thomas Taggart Papers are virtually worthless in revealing Taggart's convention plans. However, the Ralston Papers clearly show that one of Taggart's goals was to keep Ralston free of the Klan fight and reserve him as the convention's "compromise" candidate.

154–155   Opinions of Smith and his advisers on the Klan: Freidel, *Franklin D. Roosevelt: The Ordeal,* 178; New York *Herald Tribune,* June 29, 1924, p. 1; Washington *Star,* July 12, 1924, p. 4; Alfred E. Smith, *Up to Now: An Autobiography,* 284.

155–156   Pro- and anti-Klan speeches: Greathouse, comp., *Proceedings . . . 1924,* 279 *et. seq.*

156   Marion Colley is erroneously called "Cooley" in convention proceedings.

157–159   Bryan's speech on the Klan: Greathouse, comp., *Proceedings . . . 1924,* 303–309.

159   Newspapermen's comments on the unruliness of the galleries: in *New York Times,* July 6, 1924, Section VIII, p. 1.

160   "Well, at least they weren't . . .": *ibid.,* June 29, 1924, pp. 10, 14.

160–161   For a composite picture of the confusing Georgia situation see New York *World,* June 29, 1924, p. 1; *New York Times,* June 30, 1924, pp. 1, 3; Greathouse, comp., *Proceedings . . . 1924,* 310–14, 321–22, 329–31. The Colley interview is in *New York Times,* June 30, 1924, p. 3.

161   Official vote is in Greathouse, comp., *Proceedings . . . 1924,* 333–34. A recount by the convention tellers the next day gave the vote as 543³⁄₂₀ against and 542⁷⁄₂₀ for. Somewhat later, a recheck disclosed the vote to be 546.15 against and 541.85 for. In each case the anti-Klan plank lost, but by a very narrow margin. See Richard C. Bain, *Convention Decisions and Voting Records,* 222, and Appendix D.

162   For samples of southern and western charges see "The Klan Enters the Campaign," *Literary Digest,* LXXXII (July 12, 1924), 9–10; Cannon, Jr., *Bishop Cannon's Own Story,* 336.

162   Villard quote: in Villard, "An Unconventional Convention," 35.

Page

162   "as stupid, as bigoted . . .": in "The Agony of the Democrats," *The Nation*, CXIX, No. 3080 (July 16, 1924), 66.

162   Rogers quote: *New York Times*, June 30, 1924, p. 6.

163   Long's activities are detailed in entry, October 21, 1924, 1924 Diary, Long Papers, Box 3.

163   "We respect the verdict . . .": *New York Times*, June 30, 1924, p. 1.

166   McAdoo rally reported in *ibid.*, pp. 1, 2.

167   Although only sixteen men were nominated, nineteen received votes on the first ballot. The newcomers were Governor William Sweet of Colorado, who got 12, Pat Harrison 43½, Houston Thompson 1, and John B. Kendrick 6. One of those nominated, David Houston, received no votes on the first ballot. Greathouse, comp., *Proceedings . . . 1924*, 346.

167–168   Bryan's "joke" on the reporters: *New York Times*, July 1, 1924, p. 24.

168   At the end of the fifteenth ballot the totals were: McAdoo 479, Smith 305½, John W. Davis 61, Cox 60, Underwood 39½, Ralston 31, Glass 25, Harrison 20½, Robinson 20, Ritchie 17½, and Governor Bryan 11. Greathouse, comp., *Proceedings . . . 1924*, 410.

168–169   McAdoo strategy: entry, June 30, 1924, 1924 Diary, Long Papers, Box 3.

169   Rockwell statement: New York *World*, July 1, 1924, p. 1.

169   Bryan and the Mississippi delegation: Eaton, *Presidential Timber*, 301.

171   State chairmen's prediction: *New York Times*, July 2, 1924, p. 1.

173–174   Bryan's speech was reported extensively in the New York press on July 3, 1924. Verbatim account is in Greathouse, comp., *Proceedings . . . 1924*, 527–37.

175   Various comments on Bryan's speech: *New York Times*, July 3, 1924, p. 3.

175   Villard's statement: in "An Unconventional Convention," 35.

175   FDR's press release: New York *World*, July 3, 1924, p. 1.

175   Reporter's statement on the missing link: New York *Herald Tribune*, July 5, 1924, p. 1.

176   Sample letters and telegrams to Bryan are in Bryan Papers, Box 40.

176   "They've got out the whole . . .": *New York Times*, July 3, 1924, p. 2.

177   FDR's denial that McAdoo would win: New York *World*, July 3, 1924, p. 1.

179   "McAdoo is going to . . .": *New York Times*, July 3, 1924, p. 5.

179   "McAdoo has passed . . .": *ibid.*

179   Sample telegrams to Smith are in "1924 Campaign Correspondence," Roosevelt Papers, Boxes, 1–17.

179–180   Examples of telegrams to McAdoo are in McAdoo Papers, Box 306.

180   "the Lord's anointed . . .": White, *Politics: The Citizen's Business*, 106.

181   Brennan and Taggart quotes: *New York Times*, July 4, 1924, p. 3.

182   "The withdrawing comes . . .": *ibid.*, p. 1.

182   Garner's remark: Bascom N. Timmons, *Garner of Texas: A Personal History*, 108.

183   Brisbane proposal: Brisbane to Bryan, July 3, 1924, Bryan Papers, Box 40.

183   Elmer Davis quote: Eaton, *Presidential Timber*, 305. For the sequence of the Ralston telegrams see Ralston Papers.

184   Vote on the Cole resolution: Greathouse, comp., *Proceedings . . . 1924*, 685.

184   The unsent Roosevelt letter is in Rollins, *Roosevelt and Howe*, 216.

Page

185 Description of the Klan rally at Long Branch: *New York Times*, July 5, 1924, pp. 3, 5.

185 Roosevelt later said he did not specify an executive session because he did not want to imply "that the people of New York were not fit to be trusted to behave. . . ." New York *World*, July 5, 1924, interview with Roosevelt.

186 McAdoo's letter requesting permission for Smith to speak: McAdoo to Walsh, July 4, 1924, McAdoo Papers, Box 306.

186 Igoe remark: Greathouse, comp., *Proceedings . . . 1924*, 700. The stenographer of the convention recorded the word "invited" instead of "insulted," but Igoe later claimed that he had said "insulted." *New York Times*, July 5, 1924, p. 2.

187 Rockwell's statement on McAdoo's possible withdrawal: *ibid.*, July 5, 1924, p. 3.

189 Vote on the Ball resolution: Greathouse, comp., *Proceedings . . . 1924*, 762.

189 Votes on the seventy-fourth through the seventy-seventh ballots: *ibid.*, 766, 770, 774, 778.

190–191 Details relating to the "harmony conference" are reported in *New York Times*, July 6, 1924, p. 2, and New York *World*, July 6, 1924, pp. 1, 2.

191 Smith's and McAdoo's headquarters statements: *New York Times*, July 6, 1924, pp. 1, 5.

192 Events leading to the "little entente" resolution: *ibid.*, July 7, 1924, p. 2; John W. Owens, "Now That It's Over," *The New Republic*, XXXIX, No. 503 (July 23, 1924), 229.

193 "I begged, pled, insisted . . ." entry, October 16, 1924, 1924 Diary, Long Papers, Box 3.

193 Smith remark: New York *World*, July 7, 1924.

194 McAdoo statements: *New York Times*, July 7, 1924, p. 1.

195 Various examples of levity are to be found in New York *Herald Tribune*, July 5–7, 1924.

195 For interest in a Walsh candidacy see Cannon, Jr., *Bishop Cannon's Own Story*, 334; Arthur F. Mullen, *Western Democrat*, 245; Steuart, *Wayne Wheeler, Dry Boss*, 220; sample letters in Walsh-Erickson Papers, Box 9a.

196 Ninety-second roll-call vote: Greathouse, comp., *Proceedings . . . 1924*, 878.

196–197 A copy of the Ralston telegram and a notation concerning the Taggart phone call are in Ralston Papers.

197–198 Various accounts of the Ritz-Carlton meeting are given: *New York Times*, July 9, 1924, pp. 1, 3; Smith, *Up to Now*, 288–289; Coletta, *William Jennings Bryan: Political Puritan, 1915–1925*, 190.

198 "You will not desert . . .": *New York Times*, July 9, 1924, p. 3.

198 Ralston's withdrawal telegram: Greathouse, comp., *Proceedings . . . 1924*, 887.

198 Roosevelt's withdrawal proposal: *ibid.*, 888.

198–199 The details leading to the Ralston withdrawal are reconstructed from the Ralston Papers. The final telegram was dated July 8, 1924, and was sent from Ralston to Taggart. See also David Burner, "The Democratic Party in the Election of 1924," *Mid-America*, XLVI, No. 2 (April, 1964), 103 *fn.* 38. A Ralston nomination still had a Smith one-third veto gauntlet to run. Taggart

Page

gart's assessment, later claiming that he had withdrawn his name precisely never indicated how he proposed to bypass it. Ralston agreed with Tag-because "I believed I was going to be nominated." Ralston to I. T. Jones, July 16, 1924, Ralston Papers.

199 By Tuesday night eastern delegations were still at about 95 percent strength, but pro-McAdoo delegations from the West were only about 75 percent manned. In some western McAdoo delegations women alternates had virtually taken over.

200 McAdoo's statement to the convention: Greathouse, comp., *Proceedings . . . 1924*, 936.

200 Smith comment: *New York Times*, July 9, 1924, p. 1.

200 The scene surrounding McAdoo's final withdrawal decision is a composite picture drawn from New York *World*, July 8–9, 1924, *New York Times*, July 9, 1924, and various entries, 1924 Diary, Long Papers.

202 Cox's support for John W. Davis: Cox, *Journey Through My Years*, 328–329; Eaton, *Presidential Timber*, 309.

203 Mencken comment: Moos and Hess, *Hats in the Ring*, 58.

204 Vote on the one hundred and first roll call: Greathouse, comp., *Proceedings . . . 1924*, 955.

205 Bryan's reaction on the one hundred and second ballot: Burner, *The Politics of Provincialism*, 127.

206 Scene at the Polk home and the various Davis statements: *New York Times*, July 10, 1924, p. 9; Huntley, *The Life of John W. Davis*, 137–138.

207 McAdoo's congratulatory telegram: *New York Times*, July 10, 1924, p. 1.

207 Priest's comment to Walsh: Thomas L. Stokes, *Chip Off My Shoulder*, 189.

208 Walsh's rejection announcement: Greathouse, comp., *Proceedings . . . 1924*, 994.

209 For Smith's motives in wishing to address the convention see Smith Papers, various items, dated July, 1924; also Warner, *The Happy Warrior*, 163.

209–210 Smith's speech: Greathouse, comp., *Proceedings . . . 1924*, 1012–15.

210 "I take it all back . . .": Pringle, *Alfred E. Smith*, 314.

210 Various comments on Davis's appearance: "The Big Three—And 'You Takes Your Choice,'" *Literary Digest*, LXXXIII (October 25, 1924), 42.

210–211 Davis's speech: Greathouse, comp., *Proceedings . . . 1924*, 1023.

211 Smith's reluctance concerning Charles Bryan's selection: Eaton, *Presidential Timber*, 310; Smith, *Up to Now*, 290.

211–212 Final decision on Charles Bryan as Vice-President: *New York Times*, July 10, 1924, p. 1.

212 "If monkeys had votes . . .": editorial, *The Nation*, CXIX, No. 3081 (July 23, 1924), 86.

213 Barkley's gaffe: Eaton, *Presidential Timber*, 311.

217 "a restoration of the liquor traffic . . .": Coletta, *William Jennings Bryan: Political Puritan, 1915–1925*, 190.

217 "not because they thought . . .": undated typewritten manuscript, McAdoo Papers.

V. THE KNOCKOUT

221 White's comment is in White, *Politics: The Citizen's Business*, 101–102.

221 Gilbert quote: in Gilbert, *You Takes Your Choice*, 51.

Page

221 Springfield *Republican* quote is in *New York Times,* July 10, 1924, p. 5.

221 Ralston, Taggart, and Jonathan Davis remarks are in *ibid.,* pp. 1, 9, 10.

221 Glass's reaction: Smith and Beasley, *Carter Glass,* 263.

221 Davis quote: Charles Michelson, *The Ghost Talks,* 235.

222 For a sample of Smith's continuing bitterness see Smith, *Up to Now,* 287.

222 "if I can find time . . .": undated typewritten manuscript, McAdoo Papers.

222 McAdoo's farewell interview with reporters: *New York Times,* July 11, 1924, pp. 1, 2.

223 Bryan's immediate post-convention remarks and activities: Hibben, *The Peerless Leader,* 386; Arthur Mann, *LaGuardia: A Fighter Against His Times, 1882–1933,* 170; Werner, *Bryan,* 280.

224 Hoover statement: in Ike Hoover, *Forty-Two Years in the White House,* 233.

224 Coolidge quotes are from Calvin Coolidge, *The Autobiography of Calvin Coolidge,* 196. This work reveals more about the man than do his private papers. The latter are skimpy in information. As Edward Clark wrote to Harry E. Ross on January 18, 1933, Coolidge "did not follow the practice of other Presidents in trying to explain his Administration through letters to his friends." Edward Tracy Clark Papers, Box 15.

224 "In public life . . .": Coolidge, *Autobiography,* 20.

224 Gilbert quotations: Gilbert, *You Takes Your Choice,* 27.

225 For the significance of the Ford endorsement see "Figuring the Horse-power of the Ford Indorsement," 7.

225 For the Coolidge pre-convention campaign see Coolidge Papers, Reel 137, File 587, and Reel 147, File 980. Also see Clark Papers, Boxes 17–18.

226 For various impressions of the Republican convention see Claude M. Fuess, *Calvin Coolidge: The Man from Vermont, passim;* Kenneth C. MacKay, *The Progressive Movement of 1924, passim;* John A. Garraty, *Henry Cabot Lodge; A Biography,* 416–24. The official convention record is George L. Hart, reporter, *Official Report of the Proceedings of the Eighteenth Republican National Convention, held in Cleveland, Ohio, June 10–12, 1924.*

227 "If you say K.K.K. . . .": Felix Ray, "Some Like Them Hot," *The New Republic,* XXXIX, No. 503 (July 23, 1924), 241.

227 Wheeler's confidence concerning the Republican prohibition stand: Steuart, *Wayne Wheeler, Dry Boss,* 223–24.

228 *New York Times* quote: in "A Striking Contrast in Conventions," *Current Opinion,* LXXVII, No. 2 (August, 1924), 141.

228 Republican platform is in Kirk H. Porter and Donald B. Johnson, comp., *National Party Platforms, 1840–1964,* 258–65.

228–229 For the confusion over Borah's selection see Donald R. McCoy, *Calvin Coolidge; The Quiet President,* 245–246; Nicholas M. Butler, *Across the Busy Years: Recollections and Reflections,* I, 281; Henry L. Stoddard, *As I Knew Them; Presidents and Politics from Grant to Coolidge,* 527; Marian B. McKenna, *Borah,* 204, 209–11; Fuess, *Calvin Coolidge,* 345–46.

229 Dawes's selection as Vice-President: Bascom N. Timmons, *Portrait of An American: Charles G. Dawes,* 227–29; McCoy, *Calvin Coolidge,* 247.

230–231 "If no other public man . . .": William Hard, "Robert M. La Follette," *Review of Reviews,* LXX (September, 1924), 276.

231 Sample La Follette family comments on the Senator's health: in Fola and Belle C. La Follette, *Robert M. La Follette,* II, 1074, 1089. Family closeness

Page

is evident in all correspondence between Bob, Sr., Bob, Jr., Belle, and Phil in the Robert M. La Follette Papers. For excellent examples see Boxes 29–31, Series A.

231–232 For the CPPA see Nathan Fine, *Labor and Farmer Parties in the United States, 1828–1928,* 398–438, and MacKay, *The Progressive Movement of 1924,* 54–91. The quote is from *New York Times,* January 14, 1924, p. 4.

232 *"Take care of yourself . . .":* Phil La Follette to R. M. La Follette, January 20, 1924, La Follette Papers, Box 31, Series A.

232 "I know how much you are . . ." R. M. La Follette to Phil La Follette, May 7, 1924, *ibid.*

232–233 For letters relating to the La Follette strategy see *ibid.,* Box 101, Series B; see also Fola and Belle La Follette, *Robert M. La Follette,* II, 1109–10.

233 For the composition of the CPPA convention see William Hard, "That Man La Follette," *The Nation,* CXIX, No. 3080 (July 16, 1924), 65; MacKay, *The Progressive Movement of 1924,* 112.

234 La Follette platform and nomination: Fola and Belle La Follette, *Robert M. La Follette,* II, 1112–13; Porter and Johnson, comp., *National Party Platforms, 1840–1964,* 253–55.

234–235 Burton Wheeler's selection as Vice-President: Fola and Belle La Follette, *Robert M. La Follette,* II, 1115–16; Burton K. Wheeler, *Yankee from the West,* 249–51.

235 Reaction to the La Follette candidacy: Fola and Belle La Follette, *Robert M. La Follette,* II, 1115; Hard, "That Man La Follette," 66; Nye, *Midwestern Progressive Politics,* 336. An excellent article on the La Follette candidacy is James Weinstein, "Radicalism in the Midst of Normalcy," *JAH,* LII, No. 4 (March, 1966), 773–90.

235 Villard's comments: Oswald G. Villard, "Honest Convention," *The Nation,* CXIX, No. 3080 (July 16, 1924), 63.

236 Taft's advice to Coolidge: Henry F. Pringle, *The Life and Times of William Howard Taft,* II, 1019.

236 "Well, the Democrats might have . . .": Rice, *The Ku Klux Klan in American Politics,* 80.

236 "I don't recall . . .": Howard H. Quint and Robert H. Ferrell, *The Talkative President: The Off-the-Record Press Conferences of Calvin Coolidge,* 10.

237 Slemp's comment on Coolidge as a campaign issue: Slemp, ed., *The Mind of the President,* 7.

237 Stearns's advice to Butler was reported in a letter from F. W. Stearns to E. T. Clark, September 15, 1924, Clark Papers, Box 18.

237 Coolidge's election-eve speech: Fuess, *Calvin Coolidge,* 352–53.

237 Coolidge's quotes on the campaign of 1924: Coolidge, *Autobiography,* 4, 189.

238 Dawes on the Klan: Timmons, *Portrait of An American: Charles G. Dawes,* 214, 231–233; Richard J. Walsh, "Charles G. Dawes," *World's Work,* XLVIII (October, 1924), 635.

238 Dawes as a Republican "embarrassment": Herbert Hoover to William Butler, August 12, 1924, Coolidge Papers, Reel 162, File 2000; E. T. Clark to F. W. Stearns, July 15, 1924, Clark Papers, Box 17.

238 "Coolidge and Dawes, Coolidge . . .": in "Topics in Brief," *Literary Digest,* LXXXII (July 5, 1924), 20.

Page
238–239 Dawes's style and strategy: "As Dawes Defines the Issue," *Literary Digest,* LXXXII (August 30, 1924), 10.
239 La Guardia remark is in McCoy, *Calvin Coolidge,* 257.
239–240 Butler comment: Wheeler, *Yankee from the West,* 254.
240 "The spectacle of a Republican . . .": in "March of Events," *World's Work,* XLIX (November, 1924), 3–4.
240 La Follette's campaign activities are covered in Fola and Belle La Follette, *Robert M. La Follette,* II, 1115, 1127–47; MacKay, *The Progressive Movement of 1924,* 159; Nye, *Midwestern Progressive Politics,* 338.
241 La Follette and prohibition: Sinclair, *Prohibition, The Era of Excess,* 266; Steuart, *Wayne Wheeler, Dry Boss,* 225–26.
241 The clearest expression of La Follette's anti-Klan attitudes is in a letter, R. M. La Follette to Robert P. Scripps, August 5, 1924, La Follette Papers, Box 119, Series B.
241 La Follette and foreign policy: "La Follette's Foreign Policy," *The Nation,* CXIX, No. 3095 (October 29, 1924), 477–80.
241–242 Wheeler's tactic of debating an absent Coolidge: Wheeler, *Yankee from the West,* 259.
242 "In thirty years La Follette . . .": is from "When La Follette Carried Water to the Elephant," *Literary Digest,* LXXXII (August 9, 1924), 42.
242 "There are too many . . .": R. M. La Follette, Jr., to Herman L. Ekern, August 6, 1924, La Follette Papers, Box 119, Series B.
242 Problems of coordination and fund raising are revealed in correspondence with John M. Nelson and W. T. Rawleigh, *ibid.,* Box 100, Series B. See also William H. Johnston to Mercer G. Johnston, July 28, 1924, Johnston Papers, Box 49, and James H. Shideler, "The La Follette Progressive Party Campaign of 1924," *Wisconsin Magazine of History,* XXXIII, No. 4 (June, 1950), 453.
242 La Guardia quote: Fiorello La Guardia to John M. Nelson, September 6, 1924, La Follette Papers, Box 99, Series B.
242–243 Sample letters complaining of ballot problems are in *ibid.,* Boxes 31 and 101, Series B.
243 La Follette's AF of L endorsement: Philip Taft, *The AF of L in the Time of Gompers,* 483–85.
243 For lack of "liberal" support see Robert M. Miller, *American Protestantism and Social Issues, 1919–1939,* 28; McCoy, *Calvin Coolidge,* 259; Fola and Belle La Follette, *Robert M. La Follette,* II, 1121; MacKay, *The Progressive Movement of 1924,* 196; Chester H. Rowell, "Why I Shall Vote for Coolidge," *The New Republic,* XL (October 29, 1924), 218–23.
243 "The reports from every . . .": R. M. La Follette to Phil La Follette, September 8, 1924, La Follette Papers, Box 31, Series A.
243 "gaining strength every . . .": R. M. La Follette, Jr., to Rachel Young, October 30, 1924, *ibid.*
243 "I am buried fathoms . . .": Davis to H. S. Dulaney, July 11, 1924, Davis Papers, Box 46.
244 Sample advice on party organization: House to Davis, July 10, 1924, House Collection, Folder 14, "John W. Davis, 1919–1928," Drawer 6.
244 Roper comment on Shaver: Roper, *Fifty Years of Public Life,* 226.
244 Pittman remark: in Burner, *The Politics of Provincialism,* 135 *fn.* 7.
244 Davis's analysis of the 1920 Democratic defeat: Davis to House, September

Page

29, 1920, House Collection, Folder 14, "John W. Davis, 1919–1928," Drawer 6.

245 Lansing's warning about the media is in Lansing to Davis, November 6, 1924, Davis Papers, Box 54.

245 "The campaign work is moving . . .": Joseph T. Davis to Polk, August 30, 1924, Frank L. Polk Papers, Folder 29, Drawer 86.

245 "the complete breaking down . . .": George E. Sevey to Davis, November 3, 1924, Davis Papers, Box 53.

245 Colonel House statement: entry, October 25, 1924, House Collection, Diary, vol. 18.

245 Davis's complaint about the Smith and McAdoo factions: "Reminiscences of John W. Davis," 151.

245–246 The Charles W. Bryan Papers amply illustrate Bryan's western contribution during the period July to November, 1924. However, they also reveal a woeful lack of communication and cooperation between the two Democratic candidates.

246 Examples of Smith's and FDR's modest help are in "1924 Campaign Correspondence," Roosevelt Papers, Boxes 18–26.

246 "like dropping an elevator . . .": P. M. Abbott to Thomas Walsh, July 11, 1924, Walsh Papers, Box 373.

246 Contrary to the mass of evidence contained in his private papers and letters, McAdoo later claimed in his autobiography, "Defeat, when it has come my way, has never left me sour or disappointed." McAdoo, *Crowded Years*, 528.

247 McAdoo's various promises of help for Davis during the campaign: McAdoo to Davis, October 4, 1924, Davis Papers, Box 52; McAdoo to Claude Swanson, October 18, 1924, McAdoo Papers, Box 306.

247 McAdoo's defense of his meager aid: McAdoo to Chadbourne, November 13, 1924, *ibid.*, Box 309; McAdoo to S. R. Bertron, August 6, 1928, *ibid.*, Box 339.

247 "John W. Davis was . . .": in " 'Simply Normal' John William Davis," 35.

247 "What else can you . . .": in "John William Davis," *Current Opinion*, LXXVII, No. 3 (September, 1924), 290.

248 Bowers's advice: Claude Bowers to Thomas Walsh, August 21, 1924, Walsh Papers, Box 373; "Reminiscences of Claude Bowers," 55–56.

248 The Chicago *Tribune* is quoted in Wheeler, *Yankee from the West*, 257.

249 Davis quote concerning Coolidge's honesty: Stone, *They Also Ran*, 334. For a good account of the impact of Teapot Dome on the campaign see Burl Noggle, *Teapot Dome: Oil and Politics in the 1920's*, 152–76.

249 "poor little barefoot . . .": Harold L. Ickes, *The Autobiography of a Curmudgeon*, 252.

249 Davis's stand on prohibition: Davis to Wayne Wheeler, February 14, 1923, Davis Papers, Box 12; Sinclair, *Prohibition, The Era of Excess*, 265.

249–250 For Davis's correspondence on the Klan see Davis Papers, Boxes 48–53.

250 Bryan's comment is in Bryan to Davis, August 25, 1924, Bryan Papers, Box 40.

250 Evans statement: *New York Times*, August 23, 1924, p. 3.

250 Davis and labor: Samuel Gompers, *Seventy Years of Life and Labor: An Autobiography*, II, 537; "Mr. Davis as a Friend of Labor," *Literary Digest*, LXXXII (August 23, 1924), 11–12; *New York Times*, July 10, 1924, p. 6.

Page
250–251   Davis and blacks: Robert L. Jack, *History of the National Association for the Advancement of Colored People*, 88–90.
251   The Democrats and the farmer: "Democracy as the Farmers' Friend," *Literary Digest*, LXXXII (August 30, 1924), 9–10; "The Vice-Presidency," *World's Work*, XLVIII (October, 1924), 579–80.
251   Davis's doubts about how to handle La Follette: Davis to Palmer, September 24, 1924, Davis Papers, Box 51; Palmer to Davis, September 30, 1924, *ibid.;* Davis to Gilbert Hitchcock, August 28, 1924, *ibid.*, Box 50; "Reminiscences of John W. Davis," 151.
252   Mencken quote: McCoy, *Calvin Coolidge*, 260.
252   Opinion just prior to Election Day: "2,386,052 Straws Forecast Tuesday's Tempest," *Literary Digest*, LXXXII (November 1, 1924), 6–7; "Campaign Party Cries and Alarums," *Current Opinion*, LXXVII, No. 5 (November, 1924), 553.
252   White quote is in William A. White, *Forty Years on Main Street*, 245.
253   The vote used here is from Svend Petersen, *A Statistical History of the American Presidential Elections*, 86–87; for slightly varying figures see Edgar E. Robinson, *The Presidential Vote, 1896–1912*, 46.
253   Horace Taft quote: Horace D. Taft to William H. Taft, November 8, 1924, William H. Taft Papers, Box 568, Series 3.
253   Davis comment: Davis to Martin T. Manton, November 12, 1924, Davis Papers, Box 55.
253   Bryan remark: Levine, *Defender of the Faith*, 320.
253   Analysis of the vote: Hugh L. Keenleyside, "The American Political Revolution of 1924," *Current History*, XXI (March, 1925), 833–40. At no time during the 1920s was the female vote 40 percent of the total cast. Those women who did vote avoided "radical" candidates and gave proportionately greater votes to strong prohibition candidates.
253   Analysis of 1924 campaign expenditures and contributions: U.S. Senate, 68th Cong., 2 Sess., *Campaign Expenditures*, Senate Report No. 1100 (Washington, 1924); Louise Overacker, *Money in Elections*, 139.
254   For the vote in the various states: Petersen, *A Statistical History*, 86–88.
254   The La Follette vote: Keenleyside, "The American Political Revolution of 1924," 833–40.
254–255   The Klan impact on the vote: Alexander, *The Ku Klux Klan in the Southwest*, 173–74; "Klan Victories and Defeats," *Literary Digest*, LXXXIII November 12, 1924), 16.
255   The various reasons given for the defeat are drawn from the Bryan Papers, especially a letter to Clem Shaver, November 17, 1924, Box 40, and from the Davis Papers, Box 53.
255   "The country did not . . .": Shaver to Bryan, November 8, 1924, Bryan Papers, Box 40.
256   Krock quote: Krock, "The Damn Fool Democrats," 261–62.

VI. REMATCH

259   *Harper's* quote is in Nye, *Midwestern Progressive Politics*, 348.
259   Lansing statement: Lansing to Davis, November 6, 1924, Davis Papers, Box 54.

Page

259 McAdoo remark about Coolidge: Noggle, *Teapot Dome*, 59.

259 Justice Taft's comment: Taft to Root, September 19, 1924, Elihu Root Papers, Folder "1923–1928," Box 166.

260 *Nation's Business* is quoted in Arthur M. Schlesinger, Jr., *The Crisis of the Old Order, 1919–1933*, 61.

261 La Guardia quote: in Tucker and Barkley, *Sons of the Wild Jackass*, 398.

261 *New York Times* statement is in "Coolidge and Dawes Spike Enemy Guns," *Current Opinion*, LXXVII, No. 6 (December, 1924), 681.

262 For a firsthand account of the troubles of the progressives see John M. Nelson to R. M. La Follette, February 2, 1925, La Follette Papers, Box 102, Series B.

262–263 For an interesting analysis of the progressives and the new economics see Paul Glad, "Progressives and the Business Culture of the 1920's," *JAH*, LIII, No. 1 (June, 1966), 75–89.

263 La Follette's post-election attitudes: Fola and Belle La Follette, *Robert M. La Follette*, II, 1150–51.

263 La Follette's declining health and death: *ibid.*, 1168–73; various entries, Diaries for 1924 and 1925, La Follette Papers, Box 1, Series B.

263 For the most recent assessment of the progressives in the immediate postwar period see Noggle, *Into the Twenties,* especially chapter IX. I have read in manuscript form Stuart Rochester's *The Fallen Garland: Disillusionment in the American Liberal Community, 1914–1920* which will be published shortly by the Pennsylvania State University Press. Rochester shows conclusively that progressivism died in the war.

263 MacKay in *The Progressive Movement of 1924* is one of the originators of the "continuity" school. Generally in agreement with him is Arthur Link, "What Happened to the Progressive Movement in the 1920's?," *AHR*, LXIV, No. 4 (July, 1959), 833–51. Otis L. Graham, Jr., *The Great Campaigns: Reform and War in America, 1900–1928*, also sees continuity, even attacking Link for seeing too little. Graham claims that had it not been for the Klan, fundamentalism, and prohibition, La Follette would have caused "economic radicalism" to mass. This is doubtful. In 1924 La Follette could not have pulled the diverse elements of the progressive movement together with or without social and cultural diversions. Another exponent of the belief that the progressive reform movement continued unbroken into and through the 1920s is Clark A. Chambers, *Seedtime of Reform; American Social Service and Social Action, 1918–1933*. For a "revisionist" position see Herbert F. Margulies, "Recent Opinion on the Decline of the Progressive Movement," *Mid-America*, XLV, No. 4 (October, 1963), 250–68.

264 Lippmann comment: Walter Lippmann, "The Setting for John W. Davis," *Atlantic Monthly*, CXXXIV (October, 1924), 534.

264 Steffens observation: Joseph Lincoln Steffens, *The Autobiography of Lincoln Steffens*, 853.

264 "Throughout this period . . .": Schlesinger, *The Crisis of the Old Order, 1919–1933*, 102.

264 "Few indeed are the . . .": *ibid.*, 143–44.

264 Baruch remark: Baruch, *Baruch: The Public Years*, 203.

265 "I am buckling down . . .": McAdoo to Chadbourne, November 13, 1924, McAdoo Papers, Box 309.

Page
265   "I am having a lot . . .": *ibid.*
265   Lansing remark: Lansing to Davis, November 6, 1924, Davis Papers, Box 54; "Where Radicalism Is Really Found," *World's Work,* XLIX (November, 1924), 120.
265   For Davis's later life see Harbaugh, *Lawyer's Lawyer, passim.*
266   Lippmann prophecy: Walter Lippmann, *Men of Destiny,* 2.
266   Shaver's comment: Levine, *Defender of the Faith,* 321.
267   "its integrity and vitality . . .": Davis to Bryan, November 11, 1924, Davis Papers, Box 55.
267   Two studies are important on voting trends in 1924: Samuel J. Eldersveld, "The Influence of Metropolitan Party Pluralities in Presidential Elections Since 1920: A Study of Twelve Key Cities," *American Political Science Review,* XLIII (December, 1949), 1189–1206; and Burner, "The Democratic Party in the Election of 1924," 92–113. The twelve cities in the Eldersveld study were New York, Cleveland, St. Louis, Milwaukee, San Francisco, Los Angeles, Chicago, Baltimore, Philadelphia, Boston, Detroit, and Pittsburgh. For an analysis of the shifting voting patterns in one urban-dominated state see Huthmacher, *Massachusetts People and Politics, 1919–1933.* For the black vote see Maurice R. Davie, *Negroes in American Society,* 282.
267   Davis and Lansing attitudes: Davis to Samuel H. Holley, November 11, 1924, Davis Papers, Box 55; Lansing to Davis, November 6, 1924, *ibid.,* Box 54.
267   McAdoo's comments: McAdoo to Louis C. Humphrey, December 18, 1924, McAdoo Papers, Box 310; Levine, *Defender of the Faith,* 322.
268   Bryan's statements: news release, December 4, 1924, Bryan Papers, Box 40; Levine, *Defender of the Faith,* 322. Extreme partisanship extended not only to Bryan and McAdoo but to their major supporters. For example, Meredith of Iowa wrote to Senator Kendrick of Wyoming, even in the face of the Garden debacle, "There is no group in the country I would rather fight against than New Yorkers." This letter is dated July 17, 1924, John B. Kendrick Papers, Box 40.
269   Roosevelt's initiation of a party review: Rollins, Jr., *Roosevelt and Howe,* 206–208, and various letters December, 1924, to March, 1925, in Louis M. Howe Papers.
269   Hull statement: Hull to Hollins Randolph, December 13, 1924, Hull Papers, VIII.
269   Various replies to FDR's letter are in "General Political Correspondence, 1921–1928," Roosevelt Papers, Boxes 8–9.
270   Roosevelt's disclaimer to Shaver: FDR to Shaver, February, 28, 1925, *ibid.,* Box 6.
270   Attitude of party leaders to the proposed conference: Freidel, *Franklin D. Roosevelt: The Ordeal,* 212; Rollins, *Roosevelt and Howe,* 221; Levine, *Defender of the Faith,* 322.
271   For statistics on the 1926 congressional elections see Paul T. David, *Party Strength in the United States, 1872–1970, passim.*
271   Sample warning about an early Smith boom: FDR to Smith, May [n.d.], 1927, "General Correspondence: Alfred E. Smith, 1920–1928," Roosevelt Papers.

Page

271–272   Growing support for Smith: Rollins, *Roosevelt and Howe*, 213; Baruch, *Baruch: The Public Years*, 208; Josephson and Josephson, *Al Smith*, 350.

272   "was the longest wake . . .": Oscar Handlin, *Al Smith and His America*, 126.

273   For examples of the belief that Smith inaugurated a new political era see Lippmann, *Men of Destiny*, 7–8, and, as the title implies, Richard O'Connor, *The First Hurrah: A Biography of Alfred E. Smith*, 137.

274   On campaign contributions see Overacker, *Money in Elections*, 155, 159, 164, 169. Kenny's contribution of $282,000 for Smith was four times greater than the largest single contribution to the Republican party in 1928.

274   "permanently drive away . . .": Schlesinger, *The Crisis of the Old Order, 1919–1933*, 127.

274   Roper and Hull reactions: Roper, *Fifty Years of Public Life*, 233; Hinton, *Cordell Hull*, 185.

274–275   Sample letters written and received by McAdoo during the 1928 campaign are in McAdoo Papers, Box 339 and 340. Especially see McAdoo to J. H. O'Neil, October 10, 1928, *ibid.*, Box 340; McAdoo to F. M. Simmons, October 15, 1928, *ibid.*; McAdoo to Cummings, November 13, 1928, *ibid.*

276   For a comparison of the party platforms in 1928 see Porter and Johnson, comp., *National Party Platforms, 1840–1964*.

276   Hoover statement about Smith: Herbert Hoover, *The Memoirs of Herbert Hoover: The Cabinet and the Presidency, 1920–1933*, 198.

277   Darrow's remark about the cause of Bryan's death: Clarence Darrow, *The Story of My Life*, 270.

277   For Klan figures see Myers, *History of Bigotry in the United States*, 307, 314. For an analysis of the Klan's decline see Chalmers, *Hooded Americanism*, 291–99.

277   Heflin statement is in Myers, *History of Bigotry in the United States*, 313.

278   Jones comment: *ibid.*, 326.

278   The Democratic prohibition plank in 1928 pledged "the party and its nominees to an honest effort to enforce the eighteenth amendment and all other provisions of the federal Constitution and all laws enacted pursuant thereto." Porter and Johnson, comp., *National Party Platforms, 1840–1964*, 277. For the Republican plank see *ibid.*, 288.

278   For the AAPA movement see Fletcher Dobyns, *The Amazing Story of Repeal; An Exposé of the Power of Propaganda, passim*. See also Asbury, *The Great Illusion*, 321–22; Charles Merz, *The Dry Decade*, 212–14; Norman H. Clark, *The Dry Years; Prohibition and Social Change*, 221–22.

279   For examples of anti-Smith diatribes see Myers, *History of Bigotry in the United States*, 321, 325.

279   Election returns in 1928 are from Robinson, *The Presidential Vote, 1896–1932*, 46.

279   For the best overall, yet brief, analysis of the 1928 election see Burner, *The Politics of Provincialism*, 217–43.

280   For the connection between Smith and increased city self-consciousness see Lubell, *The Future of American Politics*, 2nd rev. ed., 39; Irving Bernstein, *The Lean Years; A History of the American Worker, 1920–1933*, 75–79; Carl N. Degler, "American Political Parties and the Rise of the City: An

Interpretation," *JAH*, LI (June, 1964), 41–59; V. O. Key, Jr., "A Theory of Critical Elections," *Journal of Politics*, XVII (February, 1955), 3–18.

280   For the black vote in 1928 see Elbert L. Tatum, *The Changed Political Thought of the Negro, 1915–1940*, 52–55, 65–66, 70, 101; E. Franklin Frazier, *The Negro in the United States*, 193, 230; Davie, *Negroes in American Society*, 282–283; W. E. B. Du Bois, "Is Al Smith Afraid of the South?," *The Nation*, CXXVII (October 17, 1928), 392–94. For the most recent analysis of the Republicans and the Negro consult Sherman, *The Republican Party and Black America*. In 1928 Hoover still received 60 percent of New York City's black vote. Manhattan Negroes would not vote Democratic until after the onset of the Depression.

281   For a brief analysis of the farm vote see Burner, *The Politics of Provincialism*, 227–28. Many westerners were of the opinion that the farm vote for the Democrats would have been much greater if *any* other candidate than Smith had run. See sample letters, Kendrick Papers, Box 48.

281   As examples of books and articles on the election of 1928 see Edmund A. Moore, *A Catholic Runs for President: The Campaign of 1928;* Ruth Silva, *Rum, Religion, and Votes: 1928 Re-Examined;* Robert M. Miller, *American Protestantism and Social Issues, 1919–1939;* Harold F. Gosnell, *Machine Politics: Chicago Model.* Gosnell claims that religion was more important. Miller says prohibition was more important. Silva claims that neither of these two issues was as decisive as the simple fact that Smith was a Democrat. Burner in *The Politics of Provincialism* generally supports Gosnell and downplays prohibition at the expense of the religious factor.

281   Moses remark: Josephson and Josephson, *Al Smith*, 145.

282   Mencken quote: O'Connor, *The First Hurrah*, 175.

EPILOGUE

283   Will Rogers comment: Will Rogers, *Autobiography of Will Rogers*, 204.

283   Roosevelt remark: Freidel, *Franklin D. Roosevelt: The Ordeal*, 183.

284   Catholicism would remain a strong politically-associative factor as well as a controversial issue with respect to the presidency throughout the ensuing three decades. As late as 1948 the composition of the Democratic convention would be 27.5 percent Catholic while the Republican would be only 6.1 percent. See Scott Grier, "Catholic Voters and the Democratic Party," *Public Opinion Quarterly*, XXV (Winter, 1961), 611–25.

284   For an analysis of the new alliances see Lubell, *The Future of American Politics*, 2nd rev. ed., *passim*.

285   Smith's remark about FDR as a suitable candidate for governor: Stiles, *The Man Behind Roosevelt*, 112.

285   Will Rogers statement: Martin, *Ballots and Bandwagons*, 255.

286–287   For the FDR-Smith feud see Warner, *The Happy Warrior*, 237–57; Farley, *Behind the Ballots*, 77–78; Josephson and Josephson, *Al Smith*, 407–409; Stiles, *The Man Behind Roosevelt*, 117–19; Proskauer, *A Segment of My Times*, 63–84; Rollins, *Roosevelt and Howe*, 227–29.

287   For Walsh's involvement with FDR see O'Keane, *Thomas J. Walsh*, 240–47.

288   Walsh's opening statement and convention reaction: Martin, *Ballots and Bandwagons*, 326.

Page

288–289 Garner statement concerning the release of his delegates: Timmons, *Garner of Texas*, 166. Freidel says that Farley first broached the subject of a Garner vice-presidency, not Rayburn. See Freidel, *Franklin D. Roosevelt: The Triumph*, 307–308.

289 For the McAdoo-Rayburn-Roper-Howe-FDR contact see McAdoo Papers, Box 369; Roper, *Fifty Years of Public Life*, 259–260. Freidel minimizes McAdoo's role somewhat. Freidel, *Franklin D. Roosevelt: The Triumph*, 310.

289 For Smith's last-minute attempts to reach McAdoo and Garner see *ibid.;* Proskauer, *A Segment of My Times*, 71–72.

289 McAdoo announcement: *Official Report of the Proceedings of the Democratic National Convention, held at Chicago, Illinois, June 27–July 2, 1932*, 325.

289–290 For reaction to and the aftermath of the McAdoo switch: Martin, *Ballots and Bandwagons*, 362; Freidel, *Franklin D. Roosevelt: The Triumph*, 311; press release, July 5, 1932, McAdoo Papers, Box 369; J. P. Fitzsimmons to McAdoo, July 2, 1932, *ibid.*

290 The vote in 1932 is from Robinson, *The Presidential Vote, 1896–1932*, 46.

290–291 The Roosevelt coalition has been the subject of much discussion. For alleged "progressive" inputs see Otis L. Graham, Jr., *An Encore for Reform: The Old Progressives and the New Deal.* For voting patterns among blacks in 1932 see Davie, *Negroes in American Society*, 283.

291 Mullen quote: Mullen, *Western Democrat*, 252.

S O U R C E S

The materials available to me in writing this book were truly voluminous. Many of these are cited in the footnotes in specific references. But some are not. This note on sources is therefore appended not only to indicate those materials which were specifically utilized but to demonstrate the magnitude of the research and writing which has already been done on the politics and related subjects of the period covered by this book.

PRIMARY SOURCES

Manuscript Collections

The manuscript collections available are numerous and multiplying rapidly. Naturally the most important are those belonging to the major participants in the Madison Square Garden drama: the Newton D. Baker Papers (Library of Congress), Charles W. Bryan Papers (Nebraska State Historical Society, Lincoln, Nebraska), William J. Bryan Papers (Library of Congress), Josephus Daniels Papers (Library of Congress), John W. Davis Papers (Sterling Memorial Library, Yale University, New Haven, Connecticut), Carter Glass Papers (Alderman Library, University of Virginia, Charlottesville, Virginia), Cordell Hull Papers (Library of Congress), Breckinridge Long Papers (Library of Congress), George Fort Milton Papers (Library of Congress), William G. McAdoo Papers (Library of Congress), Robert L. Owen Papers (Library of Congress), Frank L. Polk Papers (in Edward M. House Collection, Sterling Memorial Library, Yale University, New Haven, Connecticut), Samuel M. Ralston Papers (Lilly Library, University of Indiana, Bloomington, Indiana), Franklin D. Roosevelt Papers (Franklin D. Roosevelt Presidential Library, Hyde Park, New York), Alfred E. Smith Papers (New York State Library, Albany, New York), Claude A. Swanson Papers (Alderman Library, University of Virginia, Charlottesville, Virginia), Thomas Taggart Papers (Indiana State Library, Indianapolis, Indiana), Oscar W. Underwood Papers (Department of Archives and History, Montgomery, Alabama), and Thomas J. Walsh Papers (Library of Congress).

Of contributory, but lesser, significance are the Edward Tracy Clark Papers (Library of Congress), Calvin Coolidge Papers (Library of Congress), Irving Fisher Papers (Sterling Memorial Library, Yale University, New Haven, Connecticut), Louis M. Howe Papers (Franklin D. Roosevelt Presidential Library, Hyde Park, New York), Mercer G. Johnston Papers (Library of Congress), John B. Kendrick Papers (University of Wyoming Library, Laramie, Wyoming), Frank L. Polk Papers (Sterling Memorial Library, Yale University, New Haven, Connecticut), William H. Taft Papers (Library of Congress), and the Walsh-Erickson Papers (Library of Congress).

Of great importance for the campaign of 1924 are the Robert M. La Follette Papers (Library of Congress).

Oral History

In the Columbia Oral History Collection (Columbia University, New York), there are a number of interviews which were useful to this study: "The Reminiscences of Claude Bowers," "The Reminiscences of James F. Curtis," "The Reminiscences of John W. Davis," and "The Reminiscences of Marvin Jones." Not yet available for use when this book was being prepared were the oral interviews with Bernard Baruch, James Farley, Eugene Meyer, Frances Perkins, and Joseph Proskauer, all of which might have proved extremely valuable in assessing Smith and McAdoo.

Memoirs, Writings of Famous Men, and Autobiographies

Of the journalists leaving their impressions of the period, I found the most pertinent to be Walter Johnson, ed. *Selected Letters of William Allen White, 1899–1943* (Henry Holt and Company, New York, 1947); Charles Michelson, *The Ghost Talks* (G. P. Putnam's Sons, New York, 1944); Henry L. Stoddard, *As I Knew Them; Presidents and Politics from Grant to Coolidge* (Harper & Brothers, New York, 1927); Thomas L. Stokes, *Chip Off My Shoulder* (Princeton University Press, Princeton, New Jersey, 1940); Charles W. Thompson, *Presidents I've Known and Two Near Presidents* (Bobbs-Merrill Company, Indianapolis, 1929); William Allen White, *Forty Years on Mainstreet* (Farrar and Rinehart, New York, 1937); William Allen White, *The Autobiography of William Allen White* (Macmillan Company, New York, 1946); and William Allen White, *Masks in a Pageant* (Macmillan Company, New York, 1928).

Contemporary Republican observers who left their views are Nicholas Murray Butler, *Across the Busy Years; Recollections and Reflections*, 2 vols. (Charles Scribner's Sons, New York, 1939–40); Howard H. Quint and Robert H. Ferrell, eds., *The Talkative President: The Off-the-Record Press Conferences of Calvin Coolidge* (University of Massachusetts Press, Amherst, 1964); Calvin Coolidge, *The Autobiography of Calvin Coolidge* (Cosmopolitan Book Corporation, 1929); Herbert Hoover, *The Memoirs of Herbert Hoover: The Cabinet and the Presidency, 1920–1933* (Macmillan Company, New

York, 1952); Fiorello H. La Guardia, *The Making of an Insurgent: An Auto-
biography, 1882–1919* (J. B. Lippincott Company, Philadelphia, 1948);
George W. Norris, *Fighting Liberal; The Autobiography of George W. Norris*
(Macmillan Company, New York, 1945); C. Bascom Slemp, ed., *The Mind
of the President* (Doubleday, Page and Company, New York, 1926); James E.
Watson, *As I Knew Them* (Bobbs-Merrill Company, Indianapolis, 1936).

Foremost among the writings of the Democratic participants during this
period are Bernard M. Baruch, *Baruch: The Public Years* (Holt, Rinehart and
Winston, New York, 1960); William J. and Mary B. Bryan, *The Memoirs of
William Jennings Bryan* (John C. Winston Company, Philadelphia, 1925);
James Cannon, Jr., *Bishop Cannon's Own Story: Life as I Have Seen It* (Duke
University Press, Durham, North Carolina, 1955); James M. Cox, *Journey
Through My Years* (Simon and Schuster, New York, 1946); Josephus Daniels,
The Wilson Era: Years of War and After, 1917–1923 (University of North
Carolina Press, Chapel Hill, North Carolina, 1946); James A. Farley, *Behind
the Ballots: The Personal History of a Politician* (Harcourt, Brace and Com-
pany, New York, 1938); Cordell Hull, *The Memoirs of Cordell Hull*, 2 vols.
(Macmillan Company, New York, 1948); William G. McAdoo, *Crowded
Years: The Reminiscences of William G. McAdoo* (Houghton Mifflin Company,
Boston, 1931); Arthur F. Mullen, *Western Democrat* (Wilfred Funk, New
York, 1940); Joseph M. Proskauer, *A Segment of My Times* (Farrar, Straus
and Company, New York, 1950); Daniel C. Roper, *Fifty Years of Public Life*
(Duke University Press, Durham, North Carolina, 1941); Alfred E. Smith,
The Citizen and His Government (Harper & Brothers, New York, 1935);
Alfred E. Smith, *Up to Now: An Autobiography* (Viking Press, New York,
1929); Oscar W. Underwood, *Drifting Sands of Party Politics* (Century Com-
pany, New York, 1931); and Burton K. Wheeler, *Yankee from the West*
(Doubleday and Company, Garden City, 1962).

Providing some pithy comments and observations are Harold L. Ickes, *The
Autobiography of a Curmudgeon* (Reynal and Hitchcock, New York, 1943);
Alice R. Longworth, *Crowded Hours* (Charles Scribner's Sons, New York,
1933); Clarence Darrow, *The Story of My Life* (Grosset and Dunlap, New
York, 1932); and Lincoln Steffens, *The Autobiography of Lincoln Steffens*
(Harcourt, Brace and Company, New York, 1931).

Newspapers and Periodicals

For contemporary newspaper opinion and for eyewitness reports on the
Garden convention I consulted the Chicago *Tribune*, New York *American* (for
Bryan's articles), New York *Herald Tribune*, *New York Times*, New York
World, Philadelphia *Inquirer*, *Wall Street Journal*, and Washington *Post*.
Contemporary periodicals which proved most useful were *Atlantic Monthly*,
Century Magazine, *Christian Century*, *Current History*, *Current History Maga-
zine*, *Current Opinion*, *Forum*, *Independent*, *Literary Digest*, *Nation*, *New
Republic*, *North American Review*, *Outlook*, *Review of Reviews*, *Saturday
Evening Post*, and *World's Work*.

Convention Reports

The single most important source on the Madison Square Garden convention is Charles A. Greathouse, comp., *Official Report of the Proceedings of the Democratic National Convention, held in Madison Square Garden, New York City, June 24–July 9, 1924* (Bookwalter-Ball-Greathouse Printing Company, Indianapolis, 1924). Similar official reports are also available for the ensuing two conventions: *Official Report of the Proceedings of the Democratic National Convention, held at Houston, Texas, June 26–29, 1928* (Bookwalter-Ball-Greathouse Printing Company, Indianapolis, 1929), and *Official Report of the Proceedings of the Democratic National Convention, held at Chicago, Illinois, June 27–July 2, 1932* (Washington, D.C., 1932).

Information for the 1924 Republican convention is in George L. Hart, reporter, *Official Report of the Proceedings of the Eighteenth Republican National Convention, held in Cleveland, Ohio, June 10–12, 1924* (Tenny Press, New York, 1924).

A complete recounting of the La Follette convention can be found in the Mercer G. Johnston Papers (Library of Congress) under the title, *Proceedings, Conference for Progressive Political Action Convention, Cleveland, Ohio, July 4–5, 1924,* 2 vols.

Secondary Sources

Although the narrative of this book rests primarily on four types of primary sources (official proceedings of the conventions, the contemporary press, the memoirs and writings of the major figures, and private manuscripts), I drew upon numerous biographies, monographs, special studies, and scholarly articles to revise, reverse, supplement, or confirm the above material.

Scholarly Journals

As contributors to analysis the numerous articles I found in scholarly journals had no peer. Written by such individuals as J. Leonard Bates, Howard W. Allen, Lee N. Allen, Gilbert Fite, James H. Shideler, Stanley Shapiro, Don S. Kirschner, Paul L. Murphy, Carl N. Degler, Robert M. Miller, David B. Burner, Herbert F. Margulies, J. Joseph Huthmacher, George B. Tindall, V. O. Key, Jr., David H. Stratton, Arthur S. Link, and Paul A. Carter, these articles appeared in such diverse journals as the *American Historical Review, American Political Science Review, Alabama Review, Business History Review, Church History, Historian, Indiana Magazine of History, Journal of Abnormal and Social Psychology, Journal of American History, Journal of Politics, Journal of Southern History, Mid-America, Mississippi Valley Historical Review, New York History, Pacific Historical Review, Pacific Northwest Quarterly, Public Opinion Quarterly, South Atlantic Quarterly, Southwestern Social Science Quarterly,* and the *Wisconsin Magazine of History.* For specific citations, the footnotes should be consulted.

Biographies

There is a rich abundance of biographical works relating to politics in the twenties. Of a general character are Alfred Connable, *Tigers of Tammany: Nine Men Who Ran New York* (Holt, Rinehart and Winston, New York, 1967); John T. Salter, *Boss Rule: Portraits in City Politics* (McGraw-Hill, New York, 1935); Clinton W. Gilbert, *You Takes Your Choice* (G. P. Putnam's Sons, New York, 1924); Walter Lippmann, *Men of Destiny* (Macmillan Company, New York, 1927); Irving Stone, *They Also Ran: The Story of the Men Who Were Defeated for the Presidency* (Doubleday and Company, Garden City, 1966); Oswald G. Villard, *Prophets True and False* (Alfred A. Knopf, New York, 1928); and William Allen White, *Masks in a Pageant* (Macmillan Company, New York, 1928).

There are several biographies of Coolidge: Claude M. Fuess, *Calvin Coolidge: The Man from Vermont* (Little, Brown and Company, Boston, 1940); Donald R. McCoy, *Calvin Coolidge: The Quiet President* (Macmillan Company, New York, 1967); William Allen White, *A Puritan in Babylon: The Story of Calvin Coolidge* (Macmillan Company, New York, 1938). Of these, McCoy is the most complete but White is still the most readable. Dawes is treated in Bascom N. Timmons, *Portrait of an American: Charles G. Dawes* (Henry Holt and Company, New York, 1953); but a new biography of him needs to be written. The best on Henry Cabot Lodge is John A. Garraty, *Henry Cabot Lodge: A Biography* (Alfred A. Knopf, New York, 1953). Frank Lowden is ably treated in William T. Hutchinson, *Lowden of Illinois: The Life of Frank O. Lowden,* 2 vols. (University of Chicago Press, Chicago, 1957). Those works dealing with the political mavericks of the period are Claudius O. Johnson, *Borah of Idaho* (Longmans, Green and Company, New York, 1936); Marian C. McKenna, *Borah* (University of Michigan Press, Ann Arbor, 1961); Alfred Lief, *Democracy's Norris: The Biography of a Lonely Crusade* (Stackpole Sons, New York, 1939); Richard Lowitt, *George W. Norris; The Persistence of a Progressive, 1913–1933* (University of Illinois Press, Urbana, 1971); Homer E. Socolofsky, *Arthur Capper, Publisher, Politician, and Philanthropist* (University of Kansas Press, Lawrence, Kansas, 1962); Ray T. Tucker and Frederick R. Barkley, *Sons of the Wild Jackass* (Books for Libraries Press, Freeport, New York, 1969); Howard Zinn, *La Guardia in Congress* (Cornell University Press, Ithaca, New York, 1959); Arthur Mann, *La Guardia: A Fighter Against His Times, 1882–1933* (J. B. Lippincott Company, Philadelphia, 1959); Bella Rodman, *Fiorello La Guardia* (Hill and Wang, New York, 1962); and D. Joy Humes, *Oswald Garrison Villard, Liberal of the 1920's* (Syracuse University Press, Syracuse, New York, 1960). As yet there is no carefully researched biography of La Follette. All we have is the family effort: Fola and Belle C. La Follette, *Robert M. La Follette,* 2 vols. (Macmillan Company, New York, 1953).

Biographies of Byran or of various phases of his life are plentiful. The older ones by John O. Herrick (1925), Paxton Hibben (1929), John C. Long (1928), and Morris R. Werner (1929) have been superseded by Paolo E.

Coletta, *William Jennings Bryan*, 3 vols. (University of Nebraska Press, Lincoln, Nebraska, 1964–69). Best on Bryan's last years is Lawrence W. Levine, *Defender of the Faith: William Jennings Bryan: The Last Decade, 1915–1925* (Oxford University Press, New York, 1965). Al Smith too is well represented by biographies. Emily Smith Warner, *The Happy Warrior: A Biography of Alfred E. Smith* (Doubleday and Company, Garden City, 1956) and Frank Graham, *Al Smith, American: An Informal Biography* (G. P. Putnam's Sons, New York, 1945) are not as satisfactory as Richard O'Connor, *The First Hurrah: A Biography of Alfred E. Smith* (G. P. Putnam's Sons, New York, 1970) or Matthew and Hannah Josephson, *Al Smith: Hero of the Cities* (Houghton Mifflin, Boston, 1969). Less valuable are Oscar Handlin, *Al Smith and His America* (Little, Brown and Company, Boston, 1958) and Henry F. Pringle, *Alfred E. Smith: A Critical Study* (Macy-Masius, New York, 1927).

Works on Franklin D. Roosevelt also abound, but the four best relating to this period of history are Frank B. Freidel, *Franklin D. Roosevelt: The Ordeal* (Little, Brown and Company, Boston, 1954) and *Franklin D. Roosevelt: The Triumph* (Little, Brown and Company, Boston 1956), Kenneth S. Davis, *FDR: The Beckoning of Destiny* (G. P. Putnam's Sons, New York, 1972), and Alfred B. Rollins, *Roosevelt and Howe* (Alfred A. Knopf, New York, 1962). The only biography of John W. Davis which existed prior to 1973 was Theodore A. Huntley, *The Life of John W. Davis* (Duffield and Company, New York, 1924), mainly a campaign biography. In 1973 William H. Harbaugh published his *Lawyer's Lawyer: The Life of John W. Davis* (Oxford University Press, New York) and neatly filled the gap. Similarly, prior to 1973 the only biography of McAdoo was Mary Synon, *McAdoo: The Man and His Times* (Bobbs-Merrill, Indianapolis, 1924), again mainly a campaign biography carrying McAdoo's life only to 1919. In 1973 a new evaluation of McAdoo appeared in John J. Broesamle, *William Gibbs McAdoo: A Passion for Change, 1863–1917* (Kennikat Press, Port Washington, New York). McAdoo's later life still needs to be covered.

Biographies of other major figures of the era vary greatly in readability and scholarship. Among them are Rixley Smith and Norman Beasley, *Carter Glass: A Biography* (Longmans, Green and Company, New York, 1939); Margaret L. Coit, *Mr. Baruch* (Houghton Mifflin, Boston, 1957); Josephine O'Keane, *Thomas J. Walsh: A Senator from Montana* (Marshall Jones Company, Francestown, New Hampshire, 1955); Nancy J. Weiss, *Charles Francis Murphy, 1858–1924: Respectability and Responsibility in Tammany Politics* (Smith College, Northampton, Massachusetts, 1968); Lee Meriwether, *Jim Reed, "Senatorial Immortal"* (International Mark Twain Society, Webster Groves, Missouri, 1948); Bascom N. Timmons, *Garner of Texas: A Personal History* (Harper & Brothers, New York, 1948); Fred L. Israel, *Nevada's Key Pittman* (University of Nebraska Press, Lincoln, Nebraska, 1963); Dorothy G. Wayman, *David I. Walsh: Citizen Patriot* (Bruce Publishing Company, Milwaukee, 1952); Harold B. Hinton, *Cordell Hull: A Biography* (Doubleday, Doran and Company, Garden City, 1942); Lela Stiles, *The Man Behind Roosevelt:*

The Story of Louis McHenry Howe (World Publishing Company, Cleveland, 1954); Justin Steuart, *Wayne Wheeler, Dry Boss: An Uncensored Biography of Wayne B. Wheeler* (Fleming H. Revell Company, New York, 1928); and Virginius Dabney, *Dry Messiah: The Life of Bishop Cannon* (Alfred A. Knopf, New York, 1949).

The activities of black leaders in the 1920s remain an underdeveloped research field. The only significant biographies relating to this present study are Elliott M. Rudwick, *W. E. B. Du Bois: A Study in Minority Group Leadership* (University of Pennsylvania Press, Philadelphia, 1960); Frances L. Broderick, *W. E. B. Du Bois: Negro Leader in a Time of Crisis* (Stanford University Press, Stanford, 1959); and Edmund D. Cronon, *Black- Moses: The Story of Marcus Garvey and the Universal Negro Improvement Association* (University of Wisconsin Press, Madison, 1966).

Special Studies and Monographs

There is certainly no dearth of material on the basic cultural and social movements that affected the politics of the period. Best on nativism is John Higham, *Strangers in the Land: Patterns of American Nativism, 1860–1925* (Rutgers University Press, New Brunswick, New Jersey, 1955). Helpful in supplying statistics on the immigrant is Roy L. Garis, *Immigration Restriction: A Study of the Opposition to and Regulation of Immigration into the United States* (Macmillan Company, New York, 1927). On the KKK there are a number of good books: Kenneth T. Jackson, *The Ku Klux Klan in the City, 1915–1930* (Oxford University Press, New York, 1967); Charles C. Alexander, *The Ku Klux Klan in the Southwest* (University of Kentucky Press, Lexington, Kentucky, 1965); David M. Chalmers, *Hooded Americanism; The First Century of the Ku Klux Klan, 1865–1965* (Doubleday, Garden City, 1965); and Arnold S. Rice, *The Ku Klux Klan in American Politics* (Public Affairs Press, Washington, 1962). Older but still useful are Emerson H. Loucks, *The Ku Klux Klan in Pennsylvania: A Study in Nativism* (Telegraph Press, Harrisburg, Pennsylvania, 1936) and John M. Mecklin, *The Ku Klux Klan: A Study of the American Mind* (Harcourt, Brace, and Company, New York, 1924).

The standard work on fundamentalism is Norman F. Furniss, *The Fundamentalist Controversy, 1918–1931* (Yale University Press, New Haven, Connecticut, 1954). Other basic books dealing with religion or social action and reform are Robert D. Cross, *The Emergence of Liberal Catholicism in America* (Harvard University Press, Cambridge, Massachusetts, 1958); Robert M. Miller, *American Protestantism and Social Issues, 1919–1939* (University of North Carolina Press, Chapel Hill, 1958); and Clarke A. Chambers, *Seedtime of Reform; American Social Service and Social Action, 1918–1933* (University of Minnesota Press, Minneapolis, 1963). The Red Scare is covered in Robert K. Murray, *Red Scare: A Study in National Hysteria, 1919–1920* (University of Minnesota Press, Minneapolis, 1955). General societal bigotry is well handled in Gustavus Myers, *History of Bigotry in the United States* (Random House, New York, 1943).

Prohibition has been carefully studied from all angles. Perhaps the best general coverage is in Andrew Sinclair, *Prohibition, The Era of Excess* (Little, Brown, Boston, 1962). Others are Charles Merz, *The Dry Decade* (Doubleday, Doran and Company, Garden City, 1931); Herbert Asbury, *The Great Illusion: An Informal History of Prohibition* (Doubleday and Company, Garden City, 1950); Peter H. Odegard, *Pressure Politics: The Story of the Anti-Saloon League* (Columbia University Press, New York, 1928); Norman H. Clark, *The Dry Years; Prohibition and Social Change* (University of Washington Press, Seattle, 1965); and Fletcher Dobyns, *The Amazing Story of Repeal: An Exposé of the Power of Propaganda* (Willet, Clark and Company, Chicago, 1940).

Useful for an analysis of the Republicans and their role are Robert K. Murray, *The Harding Era: Warren G. Harding and His Administration* (University of Minnesota Press, Minneapolis, 1969), and Robert K. Murray, *The Politics of Normalcy: Governmental Theory and Practice in the Harding-Coolidge Era* (W. W. Norton and Company, New York, 1973). An excellent new introduction to Republican normalcy is Burl Noggle, *Into the Twenties: The United States from Armistice to Normalcy* (University of Illinois Press, Urbana, Illinois, 1974). Best on the oil issue is Burl Noggle, *Teapot Dome: Oil and Politics in the 1920's* (Louisiana State University Press, Baton Rouge, 1962). More sensational and far less reliable is Morris R. Werner and John Starr, *Teapot Dome* (Viking Press, New York, 1959).

Although almost thirty years old, the basic work on the La Follette movement is Kenneth C. MacKay, *The Progressive Movement of 1924* (Columbia University Press, New York, 1947). Also useful on defining and tracing progressivism are Otis L. Graham, Jr., *An Encore for Reform: The Old Progressives and the New Deal* (Oxford University Press, New York, 1967), and Otis L. Graham, Jr., *The Great Campaigns: Reform and War in America, 1920–1928* (Prentice-Hall, Englewood Cliffs, New Jersey, 1971). On labor the two standard works are Lewis L. Lorwin, *The American Federation of Labor: History, Policies, and Prospects* (Brookings Institution, Washington, D.C., 1933) and John R. Commons, *et al.*, *History of Labor in the United States*, IV (Macmillan Company, New York, 1935). However, of much more specific importance for the twenties are Philip Taft, *The AF of L in the Time of Gompers* (Harper & Brothers, New York, 1957) and Irving Bernstein, *The Lean Years: A History of the American Workers, 1920–1933* (Houghton Mifflin, Boston, 1960). Farmer discontent is handled best in the following: Nathan Fine, *Labor and Farmer Parties in the United States, 1828–1928* (Rand School of Social Science, New York, 1928); Russel B. Nye, *Midwestern Progressive Politics: A Historical Study of Its Origins and Development, 1870–1950* (Michigan State College Press, East Lansing, 1951); and Theodore Saloutos and John D. Hicks, *Agricultural Discontent in the Middle West, 1900–1939* (University of Wisconsin Press, Madison, Wisconsin, 1951).

Two works are especially good on the use of money in campaigns: Louise Overacker, *Money in Elections* (Macmillan Company, New York, 1932), and James K. Pollock, *Party Campaign Funds* (Alfred A. Knopf, New York, 1926). The standard treatment of Tammany Hall is in Morris R. Werner, *Tammany Hall* (Doubleday, Doran and Company, Garden City, 1928). On Chicago politics in the twenties one should consult Harold F. Gosnell, *Machine Politics: Chicago Model* (University of Chicago Press, Chicago, 1937).

The changing role of the Negro in American politics is receiving increasing attention. Three general works which touch on the subject are Maurice R. Davie, *Negroes in American Society* (McGraw-Hill, New York, 1949), E. Franklin Frazier, *The Negro in the United States* (Macmillan Company, New York, 1949), and John H. Franklin, *From Slavery to Freedom: A History of American Negroes* (Alfred A. Knopf, New York, 1947). Of a more specific nature are Harold F. Gosnell, *Negro Politicians: The Rise of Negro Politics in Chicago* (University of Chicago Press, Chicago, 1935); Robert L. Jack, *History of the National Association for the Advancement of Colored People* (Meador Publishing Company, Boston, 1943); Paul Lewinson, *Race, Class, Party: A History of Negro Politics and White Suffrage in the South* (Oxford University Press, New York, 1932); and Elbert L. Tatum, *The Changed Political Thought of the Negro, 1915–1940* (Exposition Press, New York, 1951). The most recent work on the Negro and the Republicans is Richard B. Sherman, *The Republican Party and Black America: From McKinley to Hoover, 1896–1973* (University of Virginia Press, Charlottesville, Virginia, 1973).

For voting behavior, social and intellectual trends, and the emerging role of regional or ethnic groups and their impact on politics, the following are important: Louis Bean, *Ballot Behavior: A Study of Presidential Elections* (American Council on Public Affairs, Washington, 1940); Wilbur J. Cash, *The Mind of the South* (Alfred A. Knopf, New York, 1941); J. Joseph Huthmacher, *Massachusetts People and Politics, 1919–1933* (Harvard University Press, Cambridge, Massachusetts, 1959); Harold D. Lasswell, *Psychopathology and Politics* (University of Chicago Press, Chicago, 1930); Seymour M. Lipset, *Political Man: The Social Bases of Politics* (Doubleday and Company, Garden City, 1960); Samuel Lubell, *The Future of American Politics*, 2nd rev. edn. (Doubleday and Company, Garden City, 1955); V. O. Key, Jr., *Politics, Parties, and Pressure Groups*, 5th edn. (Crowell, New York, 1964), and V. O. Key, Jr., *Southern Politics in State and Nation* (Alfred A. Knopf, New York, 1949).

The only book which deals at length with the political events of the year 1924 itself is William Allen White, *Politics: The Citizen's Business* (Macmillan Company, New York, 1924). This is a potpourri of daily news stories and articles written by White for such magazines as *Collier's* and *Woman's Home Companion*. The two most significant works relating to the election of 1928 are Edmund A. Moore, *A Catholic Runs for President: The Campaign of 1928* (Ronald Press, New York, 1956), and Ruth C. Silva, *Rum, Religion, and Votes:*

1928 Re-Examined (Pennsylvania State University Press, University Park, Pennsylvania, 1962). Old but still useful is Roy V. Peel and Thomas C. Donnelly, *The 1928 Campaign: An Analysis* (R. R. Smith, New York, 1931).

General Histories, Party Histories, and Statistical Studies

The best-known and most widely used general histories of the period are John D. Hicks, *Republican Ascendancy, 1921–1933* (Harper & Brothers, New York, 1960); William E. Leuchtenburg, *The Perils of Prosperity, 1914–1932* (Chicago University Press, Chicago, 1958); and Arthur M. Schlesinger, Jr., *The Crisis of the Old Order, 1919–1933* (Houghton Mifflin, Boston, 1957). Older but still useful are Preston W. Slosson, *The Great Crusade and After, 1914–1928* (Macmillan Company, New York, 1930); Mark Sullivan, *Our Times: The United States, 1900–1925*, VI (Charles Scribner's Sons, New York, 1935); and the ever-popular Frederick Lewis Allen, *Only Yesterday: An Informal History of the Nineteen-Twenties* (Harper & Brothers, New York, 1931). Although not a general history, as such, John Braeman, *et al., Change and Continuity in Twentieth Century America: The 1920's* (Ohio State University Press, Columbus, Ohio, 1968) is important because of its coverage of many aspects of the twenties in an analytical and critical fashion.

The best statistical studies which contain pertinent material on the 1920s are Paul T. David, *Party Strength in the United States, 1872–1970* (University of Virginia Press, Charlottesville, Virginia, 1972); Svend Petersen, *A Statistical History of the American Presidential Elections* (Frederick Ungar, New York, 1963); and Edgar E. Robinson, *The Presidential Vote, 1896–1932* (Stanford University Press, Stanford, California, 1934).

A general coverage of elections, together with an analysis of the major parties, can be found in Wilfred E. Binkley, *American Political Parties; Their Natural History* (Alfred A. Knopf, New York, 1962); Eugene H. Roseboom, *A History of Presidential Elections* (Macmillan, New York, 1957); Paul H. Ferguson, *The American Party Drama* (Vantage Press, New York, 1966); Ralph G. Martin, *Ballots and Bandwagons* (Rand McNally, Chicago, 1964); and Malcolm Moos and Stephen Hess, *Hats in the Ring* (Random House, New York, 1960). On political conventions, in particular, the following are satisfactory: Richard C. Bain, *Convention Decisions and Voting Records* (Brookings Institution, Washington, D.C., 1960); Paul T. David, *The Politics of National Party Conventions* (Brookings Institution, Washington, D.C., 1960); Herbert Eaton, *Presidential Timber; A History of Nominating Conventions, 1868–1960* (Free Press of Glencoe, New York, 1964); and Henry L. Stoddard, *Presidential Sweepstakes; The Story of Political Conventions and Campaigns* (G. P. Putnam's Sons, New York, 1948). Indispensable for the exact wording of platforms is Kirk H. Porter and Donald B. Johnson, comp., *National Party Platforms, 1840–1964* (University of Illinois Press, Urbana, Illinois, 1966). Works which cover the Democratic party specifically are William N. Chambers, *The Democrats, 1789–1964: A Short History of a Popular Party* (Van Nostrand, Princeton, New Jersey, 1964); David L. Cohn, *The Fabulous Democrats*

(Putnam, New York, 1956); Frank R. Kent, *The Democratic Party: A History* (Century Company, New York, 1928); and Henry Minor, *The Story of the Democratic Party* (Macmillan Company, New York, 1928).

By far the best single book covering the Democratic party during the 1920s is David Burner, *The Politics of Provincialism: The Democratic Party in Transition, 1918–1932* (Alfred A. Knopf, New York, 1968).

Theses and Dissertations

There are a host of unpublished theses and dissertations relating to all aspects of the 1920s, including politics. Among the most important are Lee Allen, "The Underwood Presidential Movement of 1924" (Ph.D. dissertation, University of Pennsylvania, 1955); J. Leonard Bates, "Senator Walsh of Montana, 1918–1924: A Liberal Under Pressure" (Ph.D. dissertation, University of North Carolina, 1952); Franklin Cook, "The Presidential Candidacy of John W. Davis" (M.A. thesis, Pennsylvania State University, 1973); Samuel J. Eldersveld, "A Study of Urban Electoral Trends in Michigan, 1920–1940" (Ph.D. dissertation, University of Michigan, 1946); Paula Eldot, "Alfred E. Smith, Reforming Governor" (Ph.D. dissertation, Yale University, 1961); Martin I. Feldman, "An Abstract of the Political Thought of Alfred E. Smith" (Ph.D. dissertation, New York University, 1963); David Gold, "The Influence of Religious Affiliation on Voting Behavior" (Ph.D. dissertation, University of Chicago, 1953); Robert E. Hauser, "Warren G. Harding and His Attempts to Reorganize the Republican Party in the South, 1920–1923" (Ph.D. dissertation, Pennsylvania State University, 1973); Don S. Kirschner, "Conflict in the Corn Belt: Rural Response to Urbanization, 1919–1929" (Ph.D. dissertation, State University of Iowa, 1964); R. Leiter, "John W. Davis and His Campaign of Futility" (Ph.D. dissertation, Harvard University, 1958); Mary A. Miller, "The Political Attitudes of the Negro, 1920–1932" (M.A. thesis, Pennsylvania State University, 1968); Larry G. Osnes, "Charles Wayland Bryan: Independent Democrat" (M.A. thesis, Wayne State College, 1965); Richard T. Ruetten, "Burton K. Wheeler of Montana" (Ph.D. dissertation, University of Oregon, 1961); James H. Shideler, "The Neo-Progressives: Reform Politics in the United States, 1920–1925" (Ph.D. dissertation, University of California, 1945); Carl S. Smith, "J. W. Davis's Campaign for the Presidency" (Senior thesis, Yale University, 1969); Warren E. Stickle, "New Jersey Democracy and the Urban Coalition, 1919–1932" (Ph.D. dissertation, Georgetown University, 1972); and Arthur W. Turner, "The Impact of Ethnic Groups on the Democratic Party in Chicago, 1920–1928" (Ph.D. dissertation, University of Chicago, 1966).

INDEX

330

ABOUT THE AUTHOR

Robert Keith Murray is Professor of American History at Pennsylvania State University and a scholar in the era of United States history that immediately followed World War I. He was born in Union City, Indiana, and studied at Ohio State University, receiving his Ph.D. in 1949. In addition to publishing articles in numerous periodicals, Dr. Murray is the author of three previous books: *Red Scare: A Study in National Hysteria, 1919–1920* (1955 and, in paper, 1964), *The Harding Era: Warren G. Harding and His Administration* (1969), and *The Politics of Normalcy: Governmental Theory and Practice in the Harding-Coolidge Era* (1973). "As many authors will admit," he says, "the idea for *The 103rd Ballot* came from the index of the previous book." His research in the Harding era provoked his interest in the state of the Democratic party in the mid-1920s and its infamous 1924 convention.

Professor Murray won the Phi Alpha Theta National Book Award for 1969 and the McKnight Distinguished Book Award for 1970. He is a member of the National Archives Commission and treasurer of the Organization of American Historians.

Professor Murray and his wife live in State College, Pennsylvania. They have three grown children, and the entire family are passionate sailors who sail their sloop in the waters around the Virgin Islands whenever time permits.